# Letters And Papers Illustrative Of The Wars Of The English In France During The Reign Of Henry The Sixth, King Of England, Volumes 1-2... - Primary Source Edition

## Joseph Stevenson

RERUM BRITANNICARUM MEDII ÆVI
SCRIPTORES,

OR

CHRONICLES AND MEMORIALS OF GREAT BRITAIN
AND IRELAND

DURING

THE MIDDLE AGES.

# THE CHRONICLES AND MEMORIALS

OF

# GREAT BRITAIN AND IRELAND

## DURING THE MIDDLE AGES.

PUBLISHED BY THE AUTHORITY OF HER MAJESTY'S TREASURY, UNDER
THE DIRECTION OF THE MASTER OF THE ROLLS.

On the 26th of January 1857, the Master of the Rolls submitted to the Treasury a proposal for the publication of materials for the History of this Country from the Invasion of the Romans to the Reign of Henry VIII.

The Master of the Rolls suggested that these materials should be selected for publication under competent editors without reference to periodical or chronological arrangement, without mutilation or abridgment, preference being given, in the first instance, to such materials as were most scarce and valuable.

He proposed that each chronicle or historical document to be edited should be treated in the same way as if the editor were engaged on an Editio Princeps; and for this purpose the most correct text should be formed from an accurate collation of the best MSS.

To render the work more generally useful, the Master of the Rolls suggested that the editor should give an account of the MSS. employed by him, of their age and their peculiarities; that he should add to the work a brief account of the life and times of the author, and any remarks necessary to explain the chronology; but no other note or comment was to be allowed, except what might be necessary to establish the correctness of the text.

a 2

The works to be published in octavo, separately, as they were finished ; the whole responsibility of the task resting upon the editors, who were to be chosen by the Master of the Rolls with the sanction of the Treasury.

The Lords of Her Majesty's Treasury, after a careful consideration of the subject, expressed their opinion in a Treasury Minute, dated February 9, 1857, that the plan recommended by the Master of the Rolls "was well calculated for the accomplishment of this important national object, in an effectual and satisfactory manner, within a reasonable time, and provided proper attention be paid to economy, in making the detailed arrangements, without unnecessary expense."

They expressed their approbation of the proposal that each chronicle and historical document should be edited in such a manner as to represent with all possible correctness the text of each writer, derived from a collation of the best MSS., and that no notes should be added, except such as were illustrative of the various readings. They suggested, however, that the preface to each work should contain, in addition to the particulars proposed by the Master of the Rolls, a biographical account of the author, so far as authentic materials existed for that purpose, and an estimate of his historical credibility and value.

*Rolls House,*
  *December* 1857.

# LETTERS AND PAPERS

## ILLUSTRATIVE OF THE WARS OF THE
## ENGLISH IN FRANCE

### DURING THE REIGN OF

# HENRY THE SIXTH,

## KING OF ENGLAND.

EDITED

BY

THE REV. JOSEPH STEVENSON, M.A.,

OF UNIVERSITY COLLEGE, DURHAM.

PUBLISHED BY THE AUTHORITY OF THE LORDS COMMISSIONERS OF HER MAJESTY'S
TREASURY, UNDER THE DIRECTION OF THE MASTER OF THE ROLLS.

VOL. II. PART I.

LONDON:
LONGMAN, GREEN, LONGMAN, ROBERTS, AND GREEN.

1864.

Printed by
Eyre and SPOTTISWOODE, Her Majesty's Printers.
For Her Majesty's Stationery Office.

# CONTENTS OF VOL. II.

# PREFACE.

# PREFACE.

§ 1. INTELLIGENCE of the death of the regent of France, and of the conclusion of the treaty of Arras, the two events with which the Preface to the former volume of this work concludes, reached England at the same time.[1] The sorrow which was felt for the loss of the duke of Bedford—and it was general and sincere—was speedily forgotten in the popular indignation excited by the union of Burgundy with France. Of these two powers the former had now become the more hateful; the success of a declared enemy is less galling than the defection of a trusted friend. Hostility modified by contempt was the prevailing feeling towards Charles; hostility intensified by fear was the prevailing feeling towards Philip. With the thoughtful this new coalition recalled the dying prophecy of Henry the Fifth, who had declared at Vincennes that the conquest of France by the English depended upon their co-operation with Burgundy. With the multitude the intelligence awoke only feelings of hatred and revenge. The duke of Gloucester, now freed from the restraint in which he had been held by his late brother, the regent, exerted himself to embitter the public mind against his old rival, and in this he was successful. It was not difficult to convince the nation that they had been cheated

---

[1] The treaty between the duke of Burgundy and the French ambassadors was concluded at Arras, 21 September 1435 (Monstrelet, ii. clxxxvii.); and the duke of Bedford died at Rouen on the 14th of the same month. See the former volume of this work, Preface, p. lxviii. note 3.

and insulted, and that throughout the negotiations at
Arras the English ambassadors had made every reasonable concession, and had acted in entire good faith and
with uniform sincerity. A despatch, written by them
with this object immediately before their abrupt departure from the Conference, was circulated by order
of the English government at Rouen among those
towns in Normandy which still owned the sovereignty
of Henry. "Certain notable clerks of good will"
were furnished with copies of the same document, and
were directed to instruct the people, by sermons and
otherwise, how the king had been guided by a sincere desire for "the reverence of God and the relief
" of the poor."[1] When the parliament met at London,
early in the month of October, the treachery of the
false duke of Burgundy formed a prominent part in
the opening homily which was delivered by the
bishop of Bath and Wells, the lord chancellor.[2] The
commons were invited to supply the means for carrying on the war which was declared to be imminent,
and they responded to the appeal with unwonted alacrity.
Besides the grant of a fifteenth, they consented to the
imposition of a tax upon land at the rate of sixpence
in the pound upon all estates of less than one hundred pounds a year, eightpence upon all above that
rent up to four hundred, and two shillings upon such
as produced a higher annual income.[3] The king and the
privy council, the lords and the commons, the clergy
and the people, for once exhibited a remarkable
degree of unanimity. Political divisions and personal
feuds were for the time forgotten, and the nation
seemed influenced by one spirit—the resolve to avenge
at all hazards the insult offered to it by the treaty

---

[1] See the Document printed in the Appendix to this Preface, p. xlv. No. 1.

[2] Rot. Parl. iv. 481, 487.
[3] Id. 486.

of Arras. The storm must break, in the first instance, over the head of the recreant duke of Burgundy. Steps were taken not only to prevent him from rendering assistance to France, but, if possible, to embroil him with his own subjects.

§ 2. Philip, upon his part, loudly proclaimed his desire to avoid a collision with his former allies, the English; and we may believe that herein he was sincere, since it obviously was his interest quietly to take possession of the enormous districts ceded to him by Charles rather than to fight for them.[1] But he was not permitted to remain neuter. His commerce was intercepted as it passed the English coast, and his vessels were captured.[2] The garrison of Calais commenced a series of aggressions, destructive as well as irritating, upon his neighbouring districts of Picardy and Flanders.[3] Henry despatched ambassadors to the emperor Sigismond, the duke of Bavaria, and the archbishop of Cologne, urging them to attack Philip's territories upon the Rhine.[4] Letters were addressed to the most important mercantile towns of

*How exhibited.*

---

[1] S. Remy, ch. clxxxvi.

[2] On 10 May 1436 a great "batellus" of Flanders is reported as having been taken. Exitus Pipæ, 14 Hen. VI. And shortly afterwards occurs the following entry to the same effect :—"Ricardo Veer, in "denariis sibi liberatis pro regardo "cujusdam navis missæ cum certis "litteris ex mandato thesaurarii "Angliæ versus Calesiam ad Jo- "hannem Radclyffe, locum tenen- "tem regis ibidem, directis, ad ipsum "informandum ac certificandum ac "marinarios ibidem de diversis na- "vibus venientibus de Britannia et "aliis partibus versus Flandriam ; "per breve generale de privato

"sigillo, inter mandata de termino "Paschæ, anno xj. regis nunc, "liij. s. iiij. d."

[3] Monstrelet, ii. ccii.

[4] See Fœd. x. 626, 627, 633, 634. Stephen Wilton, doctor in decrees, one of Henry's ambassadors, had the misfortune to fall into the hands of the duke of Burgundy, who kept him in prison from 25 April until 16 May 1436. On the twenty-fourth of the same month he appeared before the Council in London. The statement of his receipts and expenses is preserved among the Ambassador's Accounts in the custody of the Master of the Rolls.

Belgium and Holland, in which they were assured that by continuing their ancient alliance with England and separating themselves from Burgundy, they would most readily expand their commercial interests.[1] His territories were parcelled out, as if he had already ceased to be an independent prince; the duke of Gloucester obtained a grant for life of the comté of Flanders, while that of Boulogne was conveyed to John lord Beaumont.[2]

**Philip attempts to vindicate his conduct.**

§ 3. According to his usual policy, the duke of Burgundy explained, negotiated, and protested. He sent an embassy into England to vindicate the honesty of his proceedings at Arras, but his emissaries were treated with marked discourtesy. No sooner had they landed at Dover than they were told to consider themselves prisoners. Their credentials were taken from them and forwarded to London;[3] and when,

---

[1] See a copy of this letter in Monstrelet, ii. ch. cxcv. The MS. Cotton, Galba, B. i. 250, after giving the original draft, addressed "A noz " treschiers et grans amis, les burghe- " maistres, eschevyns, counsaillers " et communialte de la ville de Har- " lam," appends the following list of places to which the same letter was despatched.

Semblables Lettres,

f.   au Dordraughte. ⎤
f.   Delfe.
B.   Durgowe.
alb' Hamsterdam.
alb' Roterdam.      ⎬ HOLLANDE.
cla. Skidam.
b.   Camfor.
b.   Ermouthe. ⎦

S.   Leydene. ⎤
S.   Veer.
cla. Cericsee.      ⎬ ZEALANDE.
cla. Midelburghe. ⎦

b.   Brelle. ⎤
+l. Gerefleet.
+   Heneflete. ⎦

[2] Fœd. x. 652, Dugd. Baron ii. 53, 199. Lord Beaumont's claim appears to have originated in his descent from the old counts of Eu and Guines; Henry de Beaumont, the first of his ancestors who settled in England being the second son of Louis, son of John de Brienne, king of Jerusalem, by Agnes, heiress and vicountess of Beaumont. See Carte, ii. 177.

[3] The Issue roll of the Pell shows that on 7 May, 14 Hen. VI. [1436], a payment was made to the collector at Sandwich in consequence of an order which he had received to the effect that he should search for letters brought into England by foreigners, and that any which might be found should be forwarded to the king and council.

after some delay, they themselves were allowed to follow, they were exposed to increased indignities. They were lodged in the house of a shoemaker, the door of which they were not permitted to cross, not even to hear Mass, unless they were attended by certain officers, nominally heralds, but in reality gaolers. In vain they solicited an interview with the king or the council; before whom, however, the conduct of their master was, in the meantime, denounced with much bitterness. Henry shed tears of boyish vexation when he read the address of the letters which had been arrested at Dover; it was pointed out to him that whereas the duke had formerly styled him "his sovereign lord," he now spoke of him as "his dear lord and cousin." He was requested to observe that the title of "king of France," for which so much blood had been shed and so much money squandered, was no longer conceded to him; Philip had transferred it, by virtue of the treaty of Arras, to Charles and his heirs.[1] The members of the Privy Council were still more indignant when they saw themselves defrauded of what had been purchased by the victories of Cressi and Poictiers, Azincourt and Vernueil, and they broke out into vehement denunciations against the treason of their late ally. While they were deliberating how they might express their anger with the most marked emphasis, intelligence reached London that the duke of Burgundy had taken possession of the cities and lordships of Saint Quentin, Corbey, Amiens, Saint Riquier, Abbeville, Dourlens, and Montreuil, which until this time had been the property of the English crown.[2] This practical illustration of what might be expected from the union between France and Burgundy excited to the uttermost the fury of the Londoners, always so turbulent

---

[1] Privy Council Books, iv. 330.   |   [2] Monstrelet, ii. cxci.

and impetuous. They sacked the houses of some of
the duke's subjects who had settled in the city as
merchants, and murdered the inmates.[1] The ambassadors themselves escaped with difficulty. The treasurer
of England hurried to their obscure lodging, and succeeded in despatching them to the coast before they
were intercepted by the mob, now thirsty for more
blood. They carried with them no written reply to
their master's letters. None indeed was needed; for
when they told him how narrow had been their
own escape, and how, at every stage, they had heard
curses heaped upon his head for his ingratitude,
rebellion, and treachery, he felt that the English
nation had thoroughly fathomed his motives and
had correctly interpreted the import of the treaty of
Arras.[2]

**Prepares to besiege Calais.**

§ 4. The duke of Burgundy was cautious and politic,
but at the same time he was haughty and sensitive.
He would have outwitted the English in diplomacy
had they consented to negotiate; it would not have been
undignified for him to have acted upon the defensive
had they proclaimed war; but he could not brook the
treatment to which his ambassadors had been exposed.
His honour was wounded, and he must avenge the
insult. He made no secret of his intention; he would
strike a heavy blow at the English power in France,
and that blow should be directed against Calais. His
arrangements for the attack exhibit the skilful selfishness
of his character. He had the address to persuade the
Flemings that they, as much as he, were interested in
destroying this mart for the sale of wool, the staple
of England's commerce.[3] These great cloth-producing

---

[1] Fœd. x. 636, 637, 654.

[2] Monstrel. ii. cxci.

[3] On 19 June 1434 the duke had

issued letters, dated at Ghent, in
which he recites that the English
are making "chacun jour grant

cities of Flanders forgot that Calais was the channel through which the greater part of their enormous wealth had flowed in upon them for the last century, and that if the supply of the raw material were interrupted, the manufactured material could not be produced. They plunged into the war with that unreasoning and turbulent impetuosity at which this period of her history marks all the proceedings of Flanders.[1] Ghent alone furnished seventeen thousand men; and it was calculated that from his subjects in the Low Countries the duke received a body of no less than thirty thousand soldiers,[2] magnificently armed, and provided with all the munitions of war.[3] The districts of Langres, Autun, Châlons, and Mâcon supplied, partly by loan and partly by gift, the large sums of money required for the expedition.[4] The duke brought with him a formidable train of heavy artillery for the siege, among which were conspicuous three immense cannons, one drawn by twenty-six horses, one by thirty, and the third by fifty.[5] His preparations were completed upon such an extensive scale that, usually cautious as he was, he

---

" multitude de draps et fillez de leins, " et beaucoup plus que ancienne- " ment." He states that this is to the injury of his states of Brabant, Flanders, Holland, Zealand, Lemburg, Artois, Haynau, Namur, Marchienne, Frieze, and Malines, and the lands beyond the Meuse. Regest. xiii. 104, in the Archives at Lille.

[1] The Flemings requested that his expedition should be exclusively conducted by themselves, and the duke of Burgundy of course accepted their proposal. (Basin, i. 126.) Henry made an effort to preserve their neutrality, but in vain.

[2] An anonymous chronicle (in the Digby MS. 196, fol. 152) would

have us believe that the duke's force reached 100,000 men, while the continuation of Higden in the MS. Digby 201 (fol. 287, b.) and MS. Ashmole 796 extend it to the incredible sum of 150,000. Basin (i. 126) estimates the fighting men at more than 40,000, but I have preferred the lower computation of Monstrelet.

[3] Monstrelet, ii. cciii. and ccv.

[4] Plancher, iv. 224. See also the MS. Supplem. Franç., 292-10, p. 246, where is given a copy of the account of Mathieu Regnault, the duke's receiver-general, which ends 31 December 1436.

[5] Jean Chartier, ch. cxxix; vol. i, p. 242.

now ventured to boast that he was about to drive the English first out of Calais and then out of France. The same arrogant confidence prevailed among his troops. The Flemings loudly expressed their fear that they would find Calais without a single defender, and they took blame to themselves that they had not despatched their navy beforehand to cut off the retreat of the fugitives; "for," said they, "as soon as these English "fellows know that the gentlemen of Ghent are on their "march, they are sure to abandon their town and "escape home across the Channel.[1]

Prepara-
tions for
its defence.

§ 5. The English, however, had no such intention; Calais was a position too important to be lost without a hard-fought struggle. They knew its value as an outlet for their commerce, and the experience of a century had taught them that it was the key to France, and the basis of their military operations against that kingdom.[2] They remembered "what a precious jewel "the said town of Calais is to this realm; what profit "and refreshing groweth thereby to the king's subjects, "the which resort thither for merchandise and other "causes; what a bulwark and defence it is to this "land and the inhabitants thereof; with what pain "and labour it was subdued and brought into the "king's obeissance, as well in shedding of many a man's "blood and losing of their lives, as by outrageous costs "and charges to this land." They vowed "that if "so were that it should now perish, it should be

---

[1] Monstrelet, ii., ccv. They claimed to march in the van of the army, and to pitch their tents nearest to the besieged city. Basin i. 127.

[2] Froissart thus expresses the national sentiment of England in regard to the value of Calais:—

"Vous devez savoir et croire que "Calais est la ville au monde que "la communauté d'Angleterre aime "le mieux; car tant comme ils "seront seigneurs de Calais, ils "dient qu'ils portent les clefs du "royaume de France à leur cein-"ture." (iv. 35.)

" the greatest dishonour, rebuke, slander and shame
" that might grow to this realm." [1] The national
spirit was now thoroughly roused, "and to speak the
" truth," says Monstrelet,[2] "Henry, king of England,
" and his council, and the Three Estates of the realm,
" would rather have lost all that they had conquered
" during the previous thirty years than this single
" town." No wonder then that when "the gentlemen
" of Ghent" invested Calais, it was still garrisoned by
the English, and the Red Cross of Saint George still
floated proudly over its battlements.

§ 6. When it became known in England that Burgundy was in arms and that Calais was threatened,
the duke of Gloucester requested that he might be
appointed captain of that fortress.[3] His petition was
granted, and he busied himself in preparing for the
coming siege.[4] There was no difficulty in obtaining the
necessary supplies. The parliament, as we have seen,[5] had
contributed liberally ; and if this sum were not enough,
cardinal Beaufort had advanced nine thousand marks
specially " for the rescue of the town of Calais." [6] The
garrison was amply supplied with victuals and stores,

[1] These passages are extracted from the "Instructions issued by " the Commissioners who were sent " into different counties of England " to raise a loan for the defence of " Calais."—Privy Counc. iv. 352. b.

[2] Monstrelet, ii. ccv.

[3] Rot. Parl. iv. 483.

[4] On 17 June ships were arrested for the king's service connected with Calais, on 6 July they were actively employed in victualling that town, and on the next day 1,000l. were awarded for the stores. Shortly afterwards various payments were made to the duke of Gloucester, namely, 3,000 marks, 1,034l. 13s., and 485l. 5s. 10d. Six guns were delivered there at a cost of 26l., and again, 26l. 13s. 4d. were expended in the purchase of spades, shovels, mattocks, and "malles" of lead. All arrangements appear to have been completed by 17 July, between which date and 28 August no notices occur on the Issue Roll of the Pell, whence the previous information has been obtained.

[5] See § 1.

[6] Foed. x. 649.

and reinforced by a considerable body of troops.[1] The English nobility vied with each other in the extent and magnificence of the levies which they placed at the disposal of the government, and which they conducted in person across the Channel. The realities of the camp were intermingled with the ceremonials of the tournament ; for, in accordance with the requirements of the stately chivalry of the age, a herald presented himself before the duke of Burgundy, and requested him to await the arrival of his former antagonist, the duke of Gloucester, under the walls of Calais.[2]

Progress of the siege.

§ 7. Personal and national animosities thus stimulated to the uttermost, the siege and the defence were conducted with equal energy. Scarcely, however, had the operations commenced before it became obvious

---

William of Worcester, see the present volume (p. 761), states that the English troops were reckoned at 50,000 men, but this is probably an exaggeration. Basin (i. 130) is probably nearer the mark when he calculates the duke of Gloucester's contingent at 15,000 troops, horse and foot. The extracts from the Pell Records, printed in this volume, Appendix to the Preface, No. 11. (p. xlix.,) show that a very considerable body had crossed over before Humphrey's tardy arrival at Calais. The following is the beginning of an unfinished letter respecting these preparations, which, however inflated its diction, probably represents the popular feeling of the time. " Carissime, " ne credatur Calesiam pavescere " propter obsidionis assertionem " venturæ. Et ut amicis nostris " veritas patefiat, sciatis quod apud " Calesiam sunt homines gigantibus

" majores, leonibus ferociores, dra- " conibus terribiliores, quorum qui- " dam in equis altissimis lanceas " trahentes vibrando percussare pro_ " ponunt ; alii balistas bicornes tro- " ellis attractas in tela volucria " laxare se præparant ; alii vero ex " arcubus omne cœlum sagittarum " grandine subtexere conabuntur." MS. Ashmole, 789, fol. 172, b.

[2] In the printed editions of Monstrelet (ii. ccv.) this herald is styled " Kembrouc," but the MS. Reg. 20 D. viii. fol. 127, proves that this is an error, and that the correct title was " Pennebroc." This is confirmed by the MS. Supplem. Franç. 292-10, p. 249, at Paris, which informs us that " Le duc ecrivit a xxiv. des " plus grans seigneurs des duché " et comté de Bourgoyne, et leur " donna advis qu'estant devant " Calais, le duc de Gloucestre, par " Pennebroc, son herault, signifie " la bataille."

that the English possessed an immense advantage in commanding an uninterrupted communication with the sea. The harbour was open; vessels arrived daily from England, and troops and provisions in abundance were thrown into the garrison. The Flemings were the first to point out to the duke this defect in his arrangements, and they complained of his faulty tactics in no measured terms. Why had not his fleet arrived? Why should they besiege the town by land if he did not blockade it, according to his promise, by sea? He tried to pacify them; he assured them that the navigation of the Channel, always difficult and dangerous, was especially so during the summer; that the winds for some time past had been contrary and the weather rough; and he pledged himself that ere long his shipping would be in sight. They consented to wait for a short time, but the concession was made with an ill grace. Their martial spirit had evaporated before the rough realities of actual warfare. They suffered severely in their daily skirmishes with the English garrison, and they bethought themselves of the losses which they were sustaining by this protracted absence from their shops and warehouses. Great was their delight, therefore, when it was announced that the long-expected fleet was visible in the offing; and as it drew near, the duke and the Flemish generals rode down to the shore to welcome its arrival. At full tide four vessels detached themselves from the others and entered the harbour. They were laden with stones curiously cramped together with lead, and the duke explained to his staff that these ships were about to be sunk in the narrow channel, by which alone the town could be approached. The supplies from England would thus be cut off, and the garrison of Calais would soon be at the mercy of the besiegers. The operation was watched by many anxious eyes, but it was a failure. One of the vessels was sent to the bottom by the guns of the castle before she neared the harbour, and,

although the other three were sunk by the engineers, yet their position was so unskilfully chosen, that at ebb-tide they were left high and dry upon the beach. The English,—women as well as men—rushed down to the shore, and, undeterred by the enemy's artillery, they completed the work of destruction. The stranded vessels were broken up; portions of the timber were carried off to supply the garrison with fuel, and the remainder was burnt. Philip's army could render no assistance, nor did the fleet make any further demonstration. Next day it stood out to sea, and it was gradually lost. in the distance as it sailed northwards on its way back to Holland.[1]

**The Flemings break up the siege and retreat.** § 8. The anger of the Flemings, hitherto curbed with difficulty, now broke out into undisguised rebellion. Some of them proposed, as the simplest mode of expressing their dissatisfaction, that the duke's councillors, the lords of Croy, Noyelle, and Brimeu, should at once be beheaded; and this suggestion would probably have been adopted but for the flight of the intended victims. The English garrison, perceiving the tumult, sallied from the town, killed about one hundred and sixty of the besiegers, and carried off a number of prisoners, The duke hurried into the midst of the camp on foot and attempted to restore order. It was too late: there was an end to all subordination. A few of the officers treated him with respect, but they formed the exception; the rest declared that they were befooled and betrayed; that they had been there too long, and would continue there no longer. The common soldiers threw off all semblance of restraint; and when the duke entreated

[1] Shortly after this shameful flight, the admiral of the fleet, Jean de Hornes, accidentally falling into the hands of some of the infuriated Flemings, was murdered by them. Monstrelet, ii. ccviii.

them to preserve at least some semblance of military discipline, promising that if they would do so, he would accompany them in their march homewards, they told him to his face that they needed neither his advice nor protection. During the night the camp was one scene of uproar. The Flemings struck their tents, packed up such of their effects as they could remove, and attempted to destroy the remainder.[1] The booty which they left behind them was enormous, and as they fled they threw away their armour, for the cry was raised that the English were in hot pursuit. Their first halt was at Gravelines, where the duke attempted once more, but without effect, to restore order. Here the last shadow of discipline vanished; the army broke up into separate companies, as convenience or caprice suggested, and each man took his road homewards.[2]

§ 9. The duke of Gloucester still lingered in London; lingered even when there was no excuse for lingering. He did not cross the Channel [3] until he was roused into

*Campaign of the duke of Gloucester in French Flanders.*

---

[1] Among the stores thus left behind was " unum magnum can- " non de ære et cupro factum, " nuper ducis Burgundiæ, voca- " tum Dijion." See the Calais Accounts, 28 Nov.—10 Feb. 18 Hen. IV. upon the Foreign Roll of the Pipe. This was probably one of the large siege-pieces brought from Dijon, mentioned at § 4.

[2] Monstrelet, ii. ccv. This expedition, which continued from 11 June to 26 August cost the town of Bruges alone 34,291l., as appears by an account preserved at Lille. See Kervyn van Lettenhove, Hist. de Flandres, iv. 282.

[3] The chronology of the duke of Gloucester's expedition into Flanders has not been accurately ascertained. It appears, however, from documents printed in the Fœdera (x. 649,659) that he was at Canterbury on 27 July, and on the 30th of that month it is said of him that he was employed in active service in the parts of Calais. (Id. 653.) The Flemings broke up their encampment during the night between Saturday the 28 and Sunday 29 July, and at that time Humphrey had not arrived. He entered Flanders on 6 August, and remained in that country for nine days. (William of Worcester (p. 761). His expedition therefore, according to this chronology, may be said to have extended from the 1st to the 15th of August.

A contemporary chronicle in

activity by the intelligence that the victory which he
had promised to himself had fallen to the lot of his sub-
ordinates.    Had he left England a few days sooner
than he did, he might have had some share in the
pursuit of his retreating enemy, but even that inglorious
triumph was denied him.    Marching from Calais, he
followed the duke's track as far as Gravelines, but
again he was too late; Philip was beyond his reach.
He took an undignified revenge by pillaging the un-
protected country and murdering the unresisting pea-
santry.   The demoralised Flemings durst not meet him
in the field, and it did not suit him to lay siege to any
fortified town.    He might have marched to Lille or
Arras, and punished the duke most effectually by pro-
voking him to battle at disadvantage, or compelling
him to decline the challenge, in which latter case
Philip would have been humbled in the eyes of all
Europe; but Humphrey lacked the discretion or the
courage to adopt this measure.    The whole expedition
now degenerated into a mere marauding foray.    The
English could not carry off their plunder, and the
cattle which they attempted to drive to Calais died by
the road-side from fatigue and want of water.    The
duke of Gloucester returned home shortly afterwards;
personally he had gained little renown, and no real
advantage resulted from the campaign.    Admitting that
the duke of Burgundy had been defeated, he persuaded
the world that it was by the defection of his friends
rather than by the skill or enterprise of his enemies

the Digby MS. 169 gives a somewhat different account.  According
to this authority it was not until
2 August that the English council
commanded that Humphrey should
cross over, whereupon he embarked
at Sandwich.   His army entered
Flanders on August 9, and remained
for eleven days in that country,
seeking the duke of Burgundy.
Failing to find him, they returned by
Saint Omer's to Calais, where they
embarked on the 25th.  The Digby
MS. 201 and the Ashmole, 796, also
extend the duke's stay in Flanders
to eleven days.

The siege of Calais had proved a failure, but it had cost him little; he had played his game with borrowed men and money, and he left his allies to pay the forfeit. He still had a large disposable force in Picardy, French Flanders, Burgundy and Champagne.[1] The real sufferer was England. She had exhausted herself in an unprofitable warfare, and had given a breathing-time to Charles, of which that monarch had not neglected to avail himself.[2]

§ 10. So entirely had the attention of England become engrossed in the defence of Calais and the raid into Flanders, that in the meantime the interests of France and Normandy were forgotten. No successor to the duke of Bedford was appointed until several months after his decease, and during the interval things were allowed to run their own course. The war became a series of petty skirmishes; there was no unity of design, no consistency of action. Expeditions were extemporised according to the caprice or the zeal of each commander; if successful, the country was embittered against the invader; if they failed, they brought the English power into contempt.[3] It is unprofitable to inquire by which side the first provocation was offered or the first blow stricken. The administration which for more than ten years had endeavoured without success, yet without cessation, to soften the antipathies

*The war in France and Normandy neglected by the English.*

[1] Not more than two, or at most three thousand of the duke's own soldiers accompanied him on this expedition. Basin, i. 127.

[2] I have entered thus fully into the history of this campaign because it is the type of those which followed. They were nearly all conducted upon the same system; there was no want of zeal upon the part of the leaders, the troops fought with their usual bravery, but the balance of advantage still lay with the enemy, and no definite advantage resulted to England, although for the time she might be the victor in the field.

[3] The policy of the war, as then conducted, required that fortresses which could not be retained by an English garrison should be destroyed. See the Appendix to this Preface, No. ix.

and to blend the interests of the invader and the invaded, was now no more, and it had effected no permanent result. The passions which had been held under some appearance of control now burst into acts of undisguised violence. There was no longer any wish for a compromise; victory, vengeance, extermination were now the only ideas which found acceptance with the infuriated nationalities.[1]

§ 11. The tide of success set in steadily in favour of France. When it was known that Burgundy had withdrawn from alliance with Henry, the entire population showed itself ripe for revolt;[2] all that was needed was the guidance of a few bold leaders competent to direct the outbreak. Nor were they long wanting; men in whom the people had confidence were speedily in the field. Even before the Conference at Arras had broken up, La Hire had announced his intention of attacking our fortresses in Normandy,[3] and he kept his promise. Dieppe, so important by reason of its easy communication with England, was stormed by the marshal de Rieux, and its fall led to the surrender of Fécamp, Harfleur, Tancarville, Granville,[4] and the other

---

[1] Basin describes this state of affairs as " feralis illa odiorum et " inimicitiarum rabies," i. 95.

[2] A curious illustration of the popular feeling of the districts between Arras and Paris is afforded by a document preserved in the Archives of France. It appears by a writ of Henry VI., dated 11 October 1435, that three of his commissioners wishing to return from the Conference of Arras were compelled to adopt the following circuitous route in order to reach the capital. Setting out from Arras, they went to Calais, from Calais they went to Boulogne, where they took shipping for Treport; from Treport they went by land to Caudebec, and thence on the Seine to Rouen. The journey from Rouen to Paris, was partly by water, partly by land, in consequence of the bridge of Meulan being in the hands of the French.

[3] A muster roll, dated 2 October 1435, in the same depository at Paris, is the authority for this statement.

[4] Monstrelet, ii. cxciii. On the disturbed state of Normandy at this time, see the documents printed in the Appendix to this Preface, No. iii. and iv.

chief towns on both sides of the Seine. The mischief
did not end here; it extended into Champagne,[1] and
gradually drew nearer and nearer to Paris itself. During
the temporary absence of the bulk of the English
garrison of Pontoise, the inhabitants rose in arms, and
having without much difficulty overpowered the guard
left in charge of the town, they delivered that important
fortress to the marshal l'Isle-Adam.[2] Gradually but
surely the circle narrowed round the capital. Creil,
Saint Germain-en-Laye, Vincennes, and Saint Denis
surrendered or were carried by assault, and thus the
road was opened for a more decided measure, an attack
upon Paris itself.

§ 12. Early one morning, during the Easter week of Paris taken.
the year 1436, the English garrison left that city for
the purpose of intercepting some supplies intended for
the use of the towns which had lately fallen into the
hands of the French  Near Saint Denis they were
surprised and defeated by a large body of troops, partly
French, partly Burgundians, under l'Isle-Adam. Intelligence of their overthrow was conveyed to Paris by a
few of the English who escaped; but it speedily became known that by far the larger number had with
difficulty found refuge in a neighbouring tower, where
they were so closely blockaded that return was impossible. The garrison of Paris was thus reduced to a
mere handful of men, who, whatever might be their
courage or discipline, could not hold the city against
an assault from without or an insurrection within.
The inhabitants, who cordially hated the English,
thought it best to employ both these modes of operation. They despatched a messenger to the marshal
l'Isle-Adam, informing him that if he would appear

[1] Id. cxciv.
[2] Jehan Chartier, ch. cxiv., Monstrelet, ii. ccxiv.

before the walls, the gates would be thrown open to him. He promised the citizens that they might depend upon his co-operation, and early on the morning of the next day his troops effected an easy entrance into Paris.[1] They were immediately joined by the entire French population, who had expected their arrival, and the air rang with the shouts, " Long " live king Charles and the duke of Burgundy." It was a happy deliverance. Basin feelingly depicts the miseries to which Paris had been reduced by the English rule. The city was in a state of continual blockade by one party or the other, who endeavoured to starve out their adversaries. The neighbouring districts yielded neither cattle nor corn ; the only supplies which arrived came from Normandy by water, under the escort of a body of armed men.[2] Four hundred English soldiers, whose wages had not been paid, deserted at one time, and scattering themselves as robbers over the country, plundered and murdered the inhabitants.[3] No wonder then that the citizens of Paris hated the rule of the invaders; no wonder that they welcomed the troops who came to deliver them from such a thraldom.

§ 13. The English garrison was at this time commanded by lord Willoughby of Eresby, a brave and cool soldier, who had served under Henry the Fifth at Azincourt and the duke of Bedford at Vernueil.[4] He now proved himself equal to the difficulty of his

---

[1] The following extract from the MS. Fontanieu, 117–118, fixes the date of this event.

" Lan de grace m.cccc.xxxvj. le " Vendredy matin, trezieme jour " d'Avril, apres Pasques, les gens du " roy, notre souverain seigneur, " desquielz estoit chief et con- " ducteur haut et puissant prince,

" monseigneur Artus de Bretagne, " comte de Richemont, connestable " de France, par le moyen des bons " bourgeois et habitans de la ville " de Paris, entrerent en icelle ville " de Paris."

[2] Basin, i. 94.
[3] Journal de Paris, p. 705.
[4] Dugdale's Baronage, II. 85.

position. He had found time to concentrate his troops in the Rue St. Antoine, near the Bastille, which he had amply provided with stores and ammunitions. As it was impossible to resist the overpowering force which hemmed them in on every side, the English had no alternative but to shut themselves up within the walls of that fortress. Their position was desperate; the Bastille was tenable indeed for a time, but lord Willoughby was aware that he could not expect to be relieved, as no available force was sufficiently near at hand. He gladly surrendered, therefore, upon honourable terms, which were honourably observed; and the English troops were permitted to embark on the Seine on their way back to Rouen.

§ 14 The English were safe in Normandy, if anywhere. It was the earliest conquest of Henry the Fifth, and the troops which he brought with him had here gained their surest footing. From the time that he had landed the experiment had been made in that province to identify the interests of the conquerors with the conquered, and to blend them, if possible, into one nation.[1] The idea had also been a favourite one with the duke of Bedford, and he set himself to exercise it with uniform consistency. Although he had parcelled out the fairest lands of Normandy among his own followers, to whom he assigned the great fiefs vacated by their previous feudal lords, he encouraged the sub-tenants and humbler occupants to remain upon the soil, and he afforded them

*The English fall back upon Normandy.*

---

[1] Jean Chartier thus describes the policy of Henry the Fifth:—" Tous " les nobles et autres gens de tous " estats qui voulurent demeurer sur " leurs terres dans les pays obeissans " audit roy d'Angleterre, en lui " faisant le serment, il les recevoit; " à aucuns il rendit leurs terres, les " autres les rachetoient de ceux à " qui ce roy d'Angleterre les avoit " données, ou les prenoient à ferme; " ce qui fit que plusieurs y demeurerent, specialment les gens " d'Eglise et du commun," p. 96, ed. 1661.

all the protection that the irregular legislation of the period and the locality would admit. He familiarised them with the advantages of a representative government, he respected their peculiar customs and precedents, and he endeavoured to convince them that he desired to administer an even-handed justice. He went further: he proved that he wished to trust them, and he believed that they might be trusted. Having originated a system of local police drawn from the native population, he permitted it to be armed and disciplined so as to become an effective militia. He employed it in repressing the violence and bloodshed which was so rife throughout the land. It was a hazardous experiment, and required delicate manipulation. So long as the duke of Bedford was alive, ready to direct and if necessary to curb and control the working of his system, it was successful; but experience proved that he had created a power which might at any time turn against its author. As the English government in France grew weaker after his death, so in proportion grew the strength of the Norman population, and with its strength increased its resolution to follow the example of the inhabitants of Paris, and to shake off the yoke which galled it so heavily.[1]

*Their intended line of action.* § 15. The English yoke did press heavily, and we cannot wonder that they attempted to cast it off. With the duke of Bedford expired the theory of an union of interests ending in an union of nationalities. The idea of the conqueror and the conquered again revived. Immediately upon the death

---

[1] "Hinc cognoscere licet," (writes Polydore Vergil, in reference to the popular insurrections of the time in Normandy), "prius Æthiopem posse "mutare pellem, uti dicitur, quam "qui terram incolunt Galliam, "valde multum diligere Anglos. "Quippe Normannus diu paruit "Anglo bene acceptus, qui nunc "oblitus officii, non oblitus odii, non "dubitavit venire contra suos principes," p. 614.

of the duke was inaugurated a new system of policy, in which it was laid down as a fundamental principle "that the French having been rebels to " Henry VI., must in no wise be spared ;" and it was recommended that the leaders of the troops should " burn and ravage the country as they go, sparing " nothing." Orders were to be given "both to spoil, " waste, and subdue the countries of Anjou, Maine, " the Chartraine and Bretagne ;" in other words, the districts from Normandy to the Loire were to be devastated. In his sternest mood Henry the Fifth had always respected the asylum which the feelings of the age universally conceded to churches and other places dedicated to religion ; but it was now proposed "that " no sanctuary should serve traitors, conspirators, or " rebels," that is, that no such privilege should hereafter be extended to the French.

§ 16. Despite these disadvantages, the English flattered themselves that Normandy afforded them a stronghold which was still impregnable. The communication between it and England was still uninterrupted, easy and rapid ; and so long as it was master of the Seine, it could never suffer from the want of reinforcements, stores, and provisions. Both upper and lower Normandy were studded with castles garrisoned by a disciplined soldiery, which curbed, without difficulty, the irregular hostility of the neighbourhood. Courts of law, civil and criminal, were established over the whole province, the ramifications of which extended into the remotest parishes ; and these afforded a machinery which could be enforced or suspended at the pleasure of the dominant party. The English persuaded themselves, therefore that in falling back upon Normandy they had entrenched themselves in a stronghold all but impregnable; and that they had but to await the arrival of reinforcements from England in order to recover possession of the capital of France.

*Normandy the stronghold of the English power.*

17. Such, however, was not the case. The Norman population had, from the beginning, steadily refused to coalesce with the invaders, and many of them had preferred to leave house and home rather than hold them under the English domination. Those who remained upon the soil, although they submitted to the pressure of circumstances, evinced a determination to throw off the yoke whenever the opportunity should present itself, and that opportunity had now arrived.

§ 18. This being the position of affairs, we need not wonder that one insurrection after another broke out, and that each, though crushed for the time with a heavy hand, tended to the ultimate result by embittering yet more and more the spirit of the Normans against the invaders. Shortly before the English garrison, which had been driven from Paris, established itself at Rouen, the population of Lower Normandy, variously estimated as having consisted of from twelve to sixty thousand men, rose against their oppressors.[1] Few or many they were little better than a disorderly mob ; they were without arms, without discipline, without a leader. The earl of Arundel led them into an ambuscade as they were approaching Caen, and falling upon them with his men-at-arms, cut them down without mercy. Those who escaped took refuge in the woods, where many of them perished miserably from cold and hunger.[2]

§ 19. From Lower Normandy the spirit of resistance passed to the upper districts of the province. In the month of August 1435 Rouen was alarmed by the approach of La Hire, and in the following autumn Dieppe[3] had fallen into the hands of the insurgents. This was an

---

[1] The lower calculation is that of Monstrelet, vol. ii., f. 103 (ed. 1608) ; the higher, that of Chartier, p. 65 (ed. 1661).

[2] The details of certain executions at Caen, may be seen in the Appendix to this Preface, No. v.

[3] Chartier, p. 66 ; Monstrelet, p. 123.

important acquisition, for it afforded a safe port to the cruisers who hovered round the English coasts and intercepted the supplies which were in the course of transit to France. Rue and Crotoy, the two seaports of Picardy, situated at the mouth of the Somme,[1] passed at the same time into the hands of the enemy, and even Calais itself was threatened. Hemmed in on every side, dispirited, disorganised, defeated, and without a head, the dominion of the English in France seemed to be drawing to a close, and it became obvious, from the date of the loss of Paris, that their retention of Normandy would have a speedy and an ignominious termination.

§ 20. The arrival of the duke of York, the newly appointed governor, for a time arrested this calamity, and restored the drooping spirits of his countrymen. His high rank checked and brought into submission the various subordinate leaders, each of whom, safe for the time in his own castle, and supreme in his own district, cared little for any authority but his own. The administrative powers of the duke appear to have been considerable, and his military talents were equal to the emergency of his position. Ivry was regained, so were Pontoise and Luzarches, important steps towards the recovery of Paris itself. The navigation of the Seine was kept open by an armed vessel, which conveyed troops and stores from home ; and there is reason to believe that if the council at Rouen had been supported by the council at London, Normandy might have continued for some time longer to be an English province.

§ 21. England, however, had neither the power nor the inclination to continue the war in France, or to carry

*England unable to carry on the struggle.*

---

[1] Monstrelet p. 124.

into execution her theories of conquest or extermination. Crippled by the exertions which she had recently made to avenge herself upon the duke of Burgundy, not only was the Treasury exhausted of its ready money, but payments not yet due had been anticipated. In order in some degree to meet the applications for help which poured in from France, the king pawned the crown jewels, and entreated the assistance of his grand-uncle, the bishop of Winchester. The cardinal lent ten thousand marks, and consented to allow the king to postpone the payment of various sums in which he was indebted. Two thousand five hundred marks were raised upon the security of the fifteenths granted by the Commons, due next Whitsunday, and the staple of Calais lent twenty thousand marks. The archbishop of Canterbury contributed one thousand pounds, and loans and benevolences swelled the amount to a considerable sum. Thus provided with troops and money, the duke of York had crossed over into France as the successor to the duke of Bedford, and had set himself to the execution of the task which he had undertaken. His administration was marked by activity and prudence, and had he been adequately supported from home, it is possible that he might for a time have arrested the progress of the French; but he had speedily discovered that his difficulties were insuperable. He could have contended with the open hostilities of the French in France; but he could not neutralise the growing influence of a powerful faction in the court at home. As the king advanced towards manhood the weakness of his character became more and more conspicuous. Feeble mentally, it was obvious that he would become the tool of the boldest spirit with which he should come into contact; feeble bodily, it was doubtful how long he might survive. The house of York stood near the throne, nearer, in the opinion of many, than the house of Lancaster; but the house of

Lancaster was represented by the duke of Gloucester, the king's uncle, and it was his object to keep his rival of York at a distance. Letters accordingly were addressed to him by the Privy Council, urging him to continue at his post beyond the time specified in his indentures of military service.[1] He refused to prolong his stay, and he returned to the court. His successor was the earl of Warwick, who was appointed lieutenant-general and governor of France and Normandy on 16 July 1437.[2] He was provided with a liberal allowance of troops and money; by his commission he enjoyed powers equal to those which had been given to the duke of York, and a flattering letter was written to him expressive of the king's confidence in his administration.[3] But as he did not cross over until 6 November, the interval between the expiration of the lieutenancy of the duke of York and the arrival of the new governor was being spent by the English in a state of inactivity,[4] while the French under Charles conquered the important town of Montereau. Without having accomplished any success, he sank under the weight of the charge, and died at Rouen on the last day of April 1439.[5]

---

[1] Privy Council, v. 6, 7.

[2] Fœd. x. 647. In the Appendix to the Preface, No. vii. may be seen the arrangements entered into by the English government with the earl respecting the administration of Normandy.

[3] Hall, 187, says of the duke of York, that he returned into England neither wholly pleased, nor half content. For he secretly learnt that some men privily disdained his advancement and envied his promotion, yet (like a wise man) he kept his tongue close, whatsoever his heart thought.

[4] An interesting document showing some of the negociations which were in progress at this time, may be seen in the Appendix to this Preface, No. x.

[5] Dugdale, Baron. i. 247. So low had the English finances sunk, that when the duke of York was again solicited to act as the governor of Normandy, the government was compelled to place in his hands a large quantity of the crown jewels, which he was empowered to sell in event of his stipend remaining unpaid at the following Easter. See the Appendix to this Preface, No. viii.

§ 22. From this period the French war became more and more unpopular. Disgusted at the way in which so much treasure had been expended, the nobility refused to embark in any similar undertaking; and when the appeal was made to the nation, the answer was that the funds which were necessary could no longer be provided. England had enough to do at home, and she soon found herself in the midst of a civil war of more than ordinary duration and ferocity, which engrossed all her energies, and prevented her from looking across the Channel.

England the loser by the French wars.

§ 23. In every sense these French wars were prejudicial to the true interests of England. They drained off her treasure and her population at the period when both were essential to the development of her resources, and consequently retarded the progress which otherwise she might have made in the road of civilization. The wealth, the genius, and the energies of the nation were directed almost exclusively to warfare, while agriculture, manufactures, and commerce were neglected. And this warfare, conducted at such a costly sacrifice, gradually degenerated into a savage strife and lost all the redeeming features of a conflict waged between two generous antagonists; all humanity was gone, all courtesy, all respect for conquered valour, all gentleness in dealing with the wounded, the aged, and the helpless. Yet if England had sown the wind, she soon reaped the whirlwind. The men who had served in these wars returned debased and brutalised, familiar with the sight of bloodshed, indifferent to human suffering, regardless of the rights of property, defiant of all law save that of the stronger hand, and ripe, by the mere force of habit, for any atrocity of blood. Hence the peculiarly revolting character of the wars of the Roses; for the scenes enacted at St. Alban's and at Wakefield were but the repetition of numberless tragedies performed in France and Normandy and applauded in England.

§ 24. France, on the other hand, was emerging from France the gainer. the abyss of misery in which England was becoming engulphed, and had gradually been acquiring an immense accession of strength, morally and materially, from the trials through which she had passed. There was much to encourage her in the effort whih she was now making, and she had but to persevere in order to be ultimately successful. It united the king and the clergy, the nobles and the commonalty, by a firmer bond than they had hitherto known.[1] She had no cause to upbraid England with the result of these wars, although in themselves they were most disastrous. They strengthened the character of the people by calling into exercise those feelings of patriotism which are essential to the existence of any great nation. They nerved men to fight for their country, for their homes, for their wives and children, for all that is dearer than life itself. The Norman held a much deeper stake in the war than the Englishman did, and he played the game better and was successful. This was not done without a sacrifice, and every sacrifice ennobles and sanctifies not only the victim, but those who partake in his sufferings. Of the people some were slain in battle, some were murdered by their firesides, some were butchered on the scaffold; but the spirit thus evoked was undying. Rather than submit to the yoke of the invader they became exiles, but wherever they went they were welcomed as the apostles of liberty.

§ 25. Such is an outline of the general current of events connected with the wars of the English in France during the reign of Henry the Sixth. When Minor details. History of the art of war.

---

[1] There were many instances among the French documents, which evince the care which Charles took for the release of such prisoners as fell into the hands of the English. One of these is printed in the Appendix to this Preface, No. vi.

we examine in detail the documents which are here
printed, we find that they elucidate a variety of points
of different degrees of interest as regards not only the
general history of France and Normandy, civil and
ecclesiastical, but also their genealogy, and chiefly their
topography.  The capture and recapture of the various
towns and fortresses in these localities, which changed
hands during the struggles here described, the troops
furnished for their defence or attack, the military stores
which were required, and the precautions which were
adopted for their security, form the subject matter of
a large number of our documents.  It would neither be
easy nor expedient to specify these in detail; but an
exception may be made in favour of a few articles of
peculiar interest.  The first of these is a list of the
military stores which were found in the castle of
Rouen, upon the death of the duke of Bedford, a document which, among other reasons, is curious as illustrating the early history of artillery.  It appears from
this inventory that some of these pieces were of considerable size, carrying[1] a ball of six inches in diameter.
None of them appear to have been loaded at the
muzzle; the charge having been placed in a moveable
chamber, was inserted in the breech.  Each cannon was
provided with several of these chambers, in order to
facilitate rapidity of firing.  Hand guns, probably wall
pieces, were also in store in the same place; they were
of brass, and were mounted, some upon stands called
trivets (although they had four feet), some upon moveable frames, called wooden horses, which run upon
wheels.  Among the same stores also figures an instrument called a bricole, which had been used by the

---

[1] In the Archives at Paris is a
certificate, dated 28 October 1431,
respecting the siege of Louviers,
in which mention is made of the
preparation of cannon balls made of
stone, each of the height of 26
inches.  This size of shot is almost
incredible; there is either some
error in the numerals, or a confusion
between the diameter and the cir-
ference.

French at the siege of Louviers, and which was imperfect at the time when the inventory was taken, a portion of it having been left behind when the besiegers had hurriedly abandoned their attack upon that town.[1]

§ 26. A document of considerable interest here printed [2] furnishes us with a detailed account of the expenses incurred by the English government during the journey of Magaret of Anjou into England immediately previous to her marriage with Henry the Sixth. She was not the first princess to whom he had offered his hand, and had invited to share with him the waning glory of the throne of England. Arrived at maturity, it became important for the interests not only of the reigning family, but of the country at large, that the sovereign should become a husband and a father. In 1442 an alliance with the family of Armagnac was in contemplation. Thomas Beckington, afterwards bishop of Bath and Wells, who was instructed to visit the court of Lectoure, where the family of the count resided, to examine with great care the personal appearance of the two young princesses, and to report upon them with all speed to the king at London. The description which he transmitted was sufficiently captivating to induce Henry to proceed; and his next step was to despatch a portrait painter, named Master Hans [3] (probably a Fleming), to execute a likeness of his intended consort. The progress, however, of the arms of Charles in Guyenne effectually thwarted

*Marriage of Henry VI. with Margaret of Anjou.*

---

[1] See Th. Basin, i. 89.

[2] Vol. i. p. 443.

[3] This Master Hans had arrived at Bordeaux from England on 3 Nov. 1442. He was the bearer of a letter to De Batute, archdeacon of Rhodez, the chief councillor to the count of Armignac, in which he is described as a very competent artist, and that he was instructed to execute his commission with all possible haste, so as to return on 22 Nov. Nothing is known of the future history of this artist, nor of the portrait on which he is said to have been employed. Possibly it was never transmitted to England.

this alliance, and Henry was compelled to look elsewhere for a bride.[1]

§ 27. In the negociations which were resumed with
France in the beginning of 1444, Henry attempted to
unite diplomacy with matrimony, and to secure at once
the double advantage of a truce and a wife. An embassy
was sent, consisting of the earl of Suffolk, Adam Moleyns,
bishop of Chichester, Sir Robert Roos, the English
chancellor for France, Thomas Hoo, and others.[2] They
landed at Harfleur, and proceeding by Rouen and Le
Mans, reached Vendôme, where the conference was opened
on 8th April. It proceeded to the satisfaction of both
parties, and the most favourable results were anticipated from these amicable negociations. A week afterwards the English commissioners sailed down the Loire
from Blois (where the duke of Suffolk had visited his
former prisoner, the duke of Orleans), and joined the
royal family, at that time resident in Tours. At the
gates of the city the king of Sicily, his son, the duke
of Calabria, the dukes of Bretagne and Alençon, and
a splendid retinue of nobles welcomed the envoys of
Henry. On the following day they were presented to
Charles, who received them at his castle of Montils,
near Tours, and showed a ready anxiety to confirm
the preliminaries which had already been agreed upon
by his commissioners.

Festival
at Tours.

§ 28. Early in May the royal party was joined by the
duke of Burgundy, and on the following day the queen of
Sicily, accompanied by her daughter, Margaret of Anjou

---

[1] See " A journal by one of the
" suite of Thomas Beckington, dur-
" ing an embassy to negociate a
" marriage between Henry VI. and
" a daughter of the count of Armag-
" nac, A.D. 1442," with notes and
illustrations by N.H. Nicolas, Esq.
8vo. Lond. 1828.

[2] Fœd. xi. 53. The instructions
given by Charles to the French
Commissioners are printed in the
present work, i. 67

arrived at Tours. Shortly afterwards a treaty[1] of abstinence from war was concluded between France and England, which, although for a limited period, was intended ultimately to form the basis of a final peace. On May 24 Margaret was affianced in the church of S. Martin of Tours as the bride of the king of England, who was represented on this occasion by the marquis of Suffolk.

§ 29. A contemporaneous and unpublished account of this ceremony, drawn up by one of the English retinue, is preserved in one of the manuscripts at Oxford;[2] it contains some interesting details. Among other amusements, a trial of skill between the archers of France and England was agreed to at the suggestion of Suffolk and Pierre de Brézé, the chief minister in these negociations. Contrary to what might have been anticipated the prize, 1,000 crowns, was gained by the French, they having put forward some choice marksmen selected from the Scottish guard, who had obtained letters of naturalization, and consequently were regarded as denizens of France. On 1 May, in the afternoon, the queen and the dauphiness Margaret of Scotland, accompanied by three hundred noblemen and other knightly attendants, rode into the country to collect the May and carry it home. At the feast which succeeded the betrothal the august company was entertained by the entry of two giants, carrying each a large tree in his hands. These were followed by two camels bearing towers on their backs, in each of which was an armed man, who fought the one with the other. These festivities continued until 29 May, when the English embassy returned home-

---

[1] See Rymer, xi. 59.

[2] Bodley MS. Digby 196, f. 151. An analysis of this narrative is given by M. A. Vallet in his Histoire de Charles VII. roi de France, ii. 451 (8vo. Paris, 1863), a work which, uniting conscientious research with clearness of diction and justice of perception, is a model of an historical narrative.

wards. On Monday, June 8, the earl of Suffolk was
received by the inhabitants of Rouen with the most
rapturous rejoicing.[1] His route towards the coast was
one continued triumphal procession.

§ 30. The intelligence of this alliance and the truce by
which it was succeeded was every where received with
the greatest joy. The inhabitants of the oppressed districts of France and Normandy were so sanguine as to
believe that their calamities were now ended. The
people, so long shut up within the fortified towns, now
ventured into the country; the husbandman began to
till his long-neglected land, and the tradesman resumed his interrupted business. Intercourse between
the English and the French was now conducted upon
more equitable terms, and their commodities were in-
terchanged to their mutual advantage.[2] This kindly
feeling was further strengthened by the festivities which
attended the departure of the young queen to her husband's home. After the usual display of feasts and
tournaments at Nancy, the royal cavalcade set out
from that city, the former capital of Lorraine. It was
graced by the presence of three queens, the youthful bride
being accompanied by those of Sicily and France. Her
father escorted her as far as Bar-le-Duc, where she
was entrusted to the care of the marquis of Suffolk,
who conducted her to Paris.[3] A document which is
given in this work here takes up the narrative and
furnishes us with some interesting particulars illustra-

[1] Beaurepaire, in his États de
Normandie, p. 83, has printed an
interesting extract from the Register of the cathedral of Rouen, in
which is given an account of the
festivities which were celebrated on
this occasion. It concludes with
these expressive words : " Et ipso
" domino comite de Suffolk veniente
" per vicos et plateas, universus
" populus cum gaudio et fletu
" clamabat alta voce, *Noel, Noel.*"

[2] See Basin, i. 161, and Mathieu
d'Escouchy, i, 5, ed. G. du Fresne
de Beaucourt, 8vo. Paris, 1863.

[3] Hist. de Charles VII. par God-
frey, p. 426.

tive of her proceedings until she joined her ill-fated husband in England.

§ 31. The account which is here printed contains an *The* abstract of the expenditure incurred by the embassy sent *queen's* upon the part of the royal bridegroom, and extends *into En-* from 17 July 1444 to 16 October 1445. Two clerks of *gland.* the king's household were entrusted with the outlay, and on their return their accounts were audited by the officers of the exchequer. In addition to 4,233*l.* 12*s.* 9*d.*, which they received from the lord treasurer, they drew 995*l.* 9*s.* 2*d.* from other sources. Their expenditure commenced on 17 March, when the queen (for Margaret had been betrothed, as we have seen, though not actually married to the king) entered the English dominions at Pontoise. The outlay is arranged under heads, the first of which relates to the offerings made by her at mass in France, Normandy, and England; and these reached only the moderate sum of 4*l.* 10*s.* She was more liberal in her private almsgiving. In her journey between Mantes and Harfleur she gave 22*s.* 4*d.* to various poor people, in addition to which she distributed fourteen dresses with hoods of grey cloth, and as many pairs of shoes to fourteen women, together with a present of fourteen pence. This benefaction took place on Maundy Thursday; the number fourteen being chosen as corresponding with the queen's age. This act of liberality cost 8*l.*

§ 32. The royal party embarked on the Seine at Mantes and proceeded to Rouen. While in that city Margaret purchased certain pieces of plate which had belonged to the cardinal of Luxemburg, lately deceased; his arms were removed from it and hers were substituted. A vessel called the Cock John was specially assigned for the personal use of the young queen, while her household embarked in another called the Mary of

Hampton. They then proceeded towards England.
While on the voyage between Portsmouth and South-
ampton, two Genoese galleys passed the royal squa-
dron; and seven trumpeters who were on board having
serenaded the party, were presented by the queen with
23s. 4d.

§ 33. In addition to the retinue who accompanied
Margaret from Orleans and Lorraine, the party consisted
of the marquis of Suffolk, three barons, two baronesses,
nine knights, two ladies, six damsels, four chaplains,
fifty esquires, and 182 valets, or serving men, besides
various retainers of an inferior rank.

§ 34. When the marriage ceremonial was concluded at
Tichfield a strange gift was presented to the queen,
namely, a lion, the keep of which, along with his
travelling expenses to the Tower of London, cost the
sum of 3l. 6s. 4d. The total outlay incurred by the
embassy reaches 5,533l. 1s. 11d.

Journal of
the French
embassy to
London in
1445. § 35. It had been decided by the treaty of Tours that
there should be a temporary cessation of hostilities in
the hope that out of such an arrangement might arise
a final adjustment of the long dispute between the
two nations. A truce which might be speedily followed by a renewal of hostilities upon an extended
scale was no advantage. It gave the combatants time
to recover their breath, to recruit their exhausted
finances, to bring up new troops and stores to the
future scene of action, and to nerve themselves for a
prolonged struggle. It was clearly, then, for the interest of both parties that this state of uncertainty
should be ended, and that a peace upon fair and reasonable terms should be concluded. Such at least was
the opinion of Charles, and in furtherance of his design he sent an embassy to discuss the matter with

his nephew of England. The French ambassadors kept a journal of their proceedings, and from this document, which is fortunately extant, we gain some insight into the state of the English court as it existed in the year 1445.

§ 36. The narration commences with the arrival of the French commissioners at Calais. They were there honourably received by Garter king-at-arms and the lieutenant of the town, and on the next day the archbishop of Rheims, one of their number, carried his cross and held a confirmation of the children of the inhabitants. They crossed to Dover in safety, and reached Canterbury on Monday, July 5. Early on the following morning the archbishop received a visit from the prior, who in the name of the metropolitan and the other clergy requested him to say the office for the Translation of S. Thomas, which was to be celebrated on the following day. He complied with this request, and on Wednesday celebrated mass, and after a sumptuous dinner in the prior's hall, he again officiated at vespers. Their journey was not resumed until Friday, when they arrived at Rochester; they passed Sunday at Maidstone, and on the subsequent Wednesday they entered London. Their reception was gratifying. About a league from the city they were met by the earls of Suffolk, Dorset, Salisbury, and Shrewsbury, who were followed at a short distance by the dukes of Exeter and Warwick, four bishops, and about three hundred and fifty mounted knights and esquires, " all of whom," says the narrative, " were " dressed most richly in cloth of gold, and silk and " goldsmiths' work, and their horses had trappings of " silver gilt and goldsmiths' work, and some of cloth " of gold." Crossing the bridge they entered the city, when the different guilds and companies, each in its own picturesque costume, greeted the strangers, who

were conducted to their lodgings, favourably impressed with the welcome which they had experienced.

§ 37. On July 15 they had their first interview with the king. It took place at Westminster. They found him is a large hall ; he was seated on a chair covered with cloth of gold, and was dressed in a long robe of red and gold, trimmed with fur, which reached the ground. The drapery of the furniture was of blue diaper, embroidered with the livery of the late King Henry the Fifth ; it bore the representation of seed-pods and the motto *Jamais*. With more than questionable taste the tapestry represented a lady offering the arms of France to a lord ; the meaning of which the embassy could not fail to interpret. There was nothing objectionable, however, in the demeanour of the young king ; he came forward to meet the deputation, and uncovered his head to the count de Vendôme and the archbishop. The negociation was carried on through the English chancellor ; it extended from 15 July to the end of the month. The proceedings, which are detailed at some length, ended without any definite result ; either party being unwilling to yield to the claims of the other. The French were encouraged by the intervention of the duke of Burgundy, from whom they received more than one despatch during these proceedings. Shortly after their return the line of conduct pursued by the duke of Somerset, the governor of Normandy, gradually embittered the contending parties, until the smouldering embers burst out into an open flame, and the capture of Fougères by François de Surienne led to the results which have been detailed with so much accuracy and vigour by Blondel, an eye-witness of the strife, in the interesting volume lately published in this series of historical materials under the auspices of Sir John Romilly.

§ 38. The sources indicated in the Preface to the former volume of this work have furnished the documents contained in the present.[1]  For free access to the treasures of the Imperial Library at Paris I am under increased obligations to M. Claude and M. Léopold Delisle, who with unvarying kindness aided my researches in that rich collection of historical literature. I am indebted to the courtesy of Sir Charles Young, Garter king of arms, for the use of the Arundel manuscript of Worcester's Collections, which has furnished so many curious papers to these volumes; and' to the archbishop of Canterbury for access, through his Grace's librarian, the Rev. W. Stubbs, to a kindred volume now in the library at Lambeth.  In the arrangement and elucidation of these documents I have derived important assistance from the recently published works of M. Vallet,[2] one of the professors in the École des Chartes at Paris, of M. Charles de Beaurepaire,[3] keeper of the Archives at Rouen, and to M. G. Du Fresne de Beaucourt, editor of the Chronicle of Mathieu D'Escouchy,[4] whose labours, singly and collectively, throw much light upon the history of the wars of the English in France.

March 1864.                    JOSEPH STEVENSON.

*Sources whence these documents have been derived.*

---

[1] See Preface, p. lxxi. and seqq.

[2] Histoire de Charles VII. roi de France, et de son époque, 2 voll. 8vo. Paris, 1862, 1863 (Renouard).

[3] Les États de Normandie sous la domination Anglaise, 8vo. Paris. 1859 (Durand).

[4] Published by Société de l'Histoire de France, 2 voll. 8vo. Paris, 1863 (Renouard).

# APPENDIX TO THE PREFACE.

## No. I.

**Warrant for the payment of four pounds Tournois to Guillem Bourse, for the transcription of certain documents.**[1]

JEHAN DE MONGOMERY, chevalier, bailli de Caux, au viconte d'Arques, ou a son lieutenant, salut.

Par la deliberacion des conseulz et procureur du roy, notre seigneur, ou dit bailliage, nous avons tauxe a Guillem Bourse, clerc, pour sa paine et salaire d'avoir fait et escript les exe- cutoires de certaines lettres closes de nos seigneurs du con- seil du roy, notre seigneur, en Normendie, estans a Rouen, escriptes le v. jour de ce present moys d'Octobre; esquelles lettres sont incorporees certaines autres lettres closes, escriptes aus dits seigneurs du conseil par mes seigneurs larcevesque d'Iolk, les evesques de Lisieux, Norwilh et Saint David, les contes de Hontington et Suffolk, et monseigneur de Honguer-

A.D. 1435.
Oct. 15.

Warrant for pay- ment for copies of papers res- pecting

---

## [TRANSLATION.]

JEHAN DE MONTGOMERY, knight, bailly of Caux, to the vicomte of Arques, or to his lieutenant, greeting.

By the deliberation of the counsellors and proctor of the king, our lord, in the said bailliwick, we have made an award to Guillem Bourse, clerk, for his pains and wage in having made and written official copies of certain close letters of the council of the king, our lord, in Normandy, being at Rouen, written on the v. day of this present month of October; in which letters are incorporated certain other closed letters, written to the said lords of the council, by my lords the arch- bishop of York, the bishops of Lisieux, Norwich and Saint David's, the earls of Huntingdon and Suffolk, and my lord

---

[1] From the Additional Charter No. 124.

fford, et autres ambaxadeurs du roy, notre dit seigneur, estans
a Arras, escriptes au dit lieu d'Arras, le v. jour de Septembre,
derrain passe, esquelles lettres rescriptes par les dits ambaxadeurs estoit contenu au long les choses qui avoient este
communiquees en la convention d'Arras assemblee pour la
traitie de la paix d'entre le roy, notre souverain seigneur, et
son adversaire.  Lesquelles lettres contenoient deux fueilles de
papier.  Et par icelles lettres de nos dits seigneurs du conseil
nous estoit mande que la copie ou vidimus d'icelles lettres en-
voyssons par les bonnes villes de notre dit bailliage, et le contenu en icelles faire exposer au peuple en sermons generaulx,
et autrement, par certains notables clercs de bonne voulente,
afin que le peuple peust veoir et cognoistre clerement le devoir
en quoy le roy, notre dit seigneur, s'estoit mis, pour la reverence de Dieu, notre Createur, et le relievement du povre
peuple, de traitier la dite paix.  Le quel Guillem Bourse ait
escriptes et doublees icelles lettres par sept foiz; dont l'un
d'iceulx doubles, deuement collationne a l'original des dits
lettres, et seelle du grant seel aux causes du dit bailliage, a
este envoye aux bailli, bourgoiz, manans et habitans, de la
ville de Dieppe, le second a ceulx du Neufchastel de Lincourt,

*the pro-
ceedings
of the con-
ference at
Arras,*

---

of Hungerford, and the rest of the ambassadors of the king,
our said lord, they being at Arras, written in the said place
of Arras on the v. day of September last past; in which letters,
written by the ambassadors aforesaid, is contained at length
the matters which had been brought forward in the convention
of Arras, which had met about a treaty of peace between the
king, our sovereign lord, and his adversary.  These letters
contained two leaves of paper. And by these letters of our said
lords of the council we were commanded to send a copy, or
vidimus, of the same letters throughout the good towns of our
said baillywick, and to cause the substance of the same to be
made known to the people in public sermons, and elsewhere
by certain notable clerks of good will, to the end that the
people may see and understand clearly, how our lord, the
king, has done his duty, out of reverence to God, our Creator,
and the relief of the poor people, in treating for the said peace.
The said Guillem Bourse has written and copied these letters
seven times; one of which transcripts, duly collated with the
original of the said letters, and sealed with the great seal
used for the causes of the said bailliwick, has been sent to
the bailly, burgesses, residents and inhabitants of the town of
Dieppe, the second to the people of Neufchatel de Lincourt,

le tiers aux colliege et bourgoiz de Gournay, le quart aux
religieux et bourgoiz de Fescamp, le vme. aux bourgoiz, manans
et habitans de Monstrevillier, le vj. aux cappitaine et bourgoiz
de Harefleu, le vij. aux viconte, bourgoiz et habitans de Caudebec, esquelz executoires avoit xiiij. fueilles de papier.

Item, pour avoir semblablement doublees deux autres paires
de lettres closes de nos dits seigneurs du conseil a nous adrechans, escriptes a Rouen le x. jour de ce present moys d'Octobre,
ainsi signees,

"Par les gens du conseil du roy, notre seigneur, en Normendie,

SEBIRE,"

faisans mention de entretenir en chacun viconte de notre
dit bailliage lordonnance autresfoiz faicte, d'avoir en chacun
d'icelles vicontes un chief Angloiz lance a cheval et xx. archiers
pour la conduite des gens du dit bailliage embastonnez ;
laquelle ordonnance avoit cesse par aucun temps a excecuter
par l'ordonnance de nos dits seigneurs, et de present ont
ordonne a le remettre sus, comme les dits lettres le contiennent.
Pourquoy a convenu envoyer de nouvel les executoires d'icelles

*(marginal note: and English troops in Normandy.)*

---

the third to the college and burgesses of Gournay, the fourth
to the monks and burgesses of Fécamp, the fifth to the burgesses, residents and inhabitants of Montivilliers, the sixth to
the captain and burgesses of Harfleur, the seventh to the
vicomte, burgesses, and inhabitants of Caudebec ; which official
copies contained xiiij. leaves of paper.

Also, for having in like manner copied two other pairs of
close letters of the lords of the council addressed to us,
written at Rouen, on the x. day of this present month of
October, thus signed,

" By the members of the council of the king, our lord, in
Normandy,

SEBIRE,"

which mention that in each vicomté within our said bailliwick shall be observed the ordinance formerly made, namely,
that in each of the said vicomtés shall be an English principal
mounted lance and xx. archers, to lead the people within the
said bailliwick who are provided with arms ; which ordinance
by the direction of our said lords, had for some time past
ceased to be put in force, but now they have decreed that it
should be revived, as is contained in the said letters. In consequence whereof it has become necessary to send anew

d 2

lettres, avec mandemens et commissions pour recevoir les monstres d'icelles lances et archiers aux vicontes de Caudebec, Monstrevillier, Arques, Neufchastel et Gournay, pour une viconte, et aux centeniers, l.teniers ou paix de Caux; en quoy il a falu escrire dix fueilles de papier, et en quoy il a grans escriptures. Lesquelles escriptures veues pur nous en la presence des dits procureur et conseil, avons pour ce faite tauxe au dit Guillem Bourse la somme de quatre livres Tournois.

Si vous mandons que des deniers de votre dit viconte du terme Saint Michiel derrainement passe, vous paiez au dit Guillem Bourse la dite somme de iiij. livres Tournois. Et par rapportant ces presentes, avec quittance du dit Guillem Bourse, comme vous lui aurez paie la dicte somme, ce vous sera aloue en voz comptes, et rabatu de votre dicte recepte par ceulx a qui il appartendra. Ce faites si que deffault ny ait.

Date.        Donne a Arques, le xv. jour d'Octobre, lan mil, iiij.c. xxxv.

BOUE.

*Dorso.* Pasques, ccccxxxvj. en deniers paies par mandement. Quittance de iiij. livres Tournois pour Guillem Bourse.

---

authenticated copies of the said letters, with commands and commissions to revive the musters of the said lances and archers, to the vicomtes of Caudebec, Montivilliers, Arques Neufchâtel and Gournay, for one vicomté, and to those persons who have charge of divisions of hundreds and fifties, in the Pays de Caux; for which it has been necessary to write ten leaves of paper, containing a great quantity of matter. Wherefore we, having inspected these writings, along with the said proctor and council, have awarded to the said Guillem Bourse the sum of four pounds, Tournois.

We therefore command you to pay to the said Guillem Bourse, out of the money of your said vicomté of the term of Michaelmas last past, the said sum of iiij. pounds Tournois. And upon the production of these presents, along with the acquittance of the said Guillem Bourse, that you have paid him the said sum, it shall be allowed in your accounts and deducted from your said receipt by those persons whose duty it shall be so to do. Do this, in such manner that there be no failure herein.

Dated at Arques, the xv. day of October, in the year one thousand, iiij.c. xxxv.

BOUE.

*Dorso.* Easter, ccccxxxvj. In money paid by order. An acquittance for iiij. pounds Tournois for Guillem Bourse.

## No. II.

Expenses incurred by the English Government in the defence of Calais, when about to be attacked by the duke of Burgundy.[1]

HUMFRIDO duci Gloucestriæ, retento penes dominum nostrum regem per Indenturam inter ipsum dominum regem et præfatum ducem confectam, ad profisciscendum ad partes exteras ad ibidem dandum auxilium et rescussum villæ suæ Calesiæ per spatium unius mensis; in denariis sibi liberatis in persolutionem M$^l$ M$^l$ M$^l$ D. iiij$^{xx}$ xiiij.$l$. x.$s$. quos dictus dominus rex, de avisamento et assensu concilii sui, eidem duci liberari mandavit, tam pro vadiis suis et unius ducis, utriusque ad xiij.$s$. iiij.$d$. per diem; et duorum comitum, utriusque ad vj.$s$. viij.$d$. per diem; xj. baronum, cujuslibet ad iiij.$s$. per diem; xxiij. militum, cujuslibet ad ij.$s$. per diem; cccc.xv. hominum ad arma, cujuslibet ad xij.$d$. per diem; quam pro vadiis iiij.M. xlv. sagittariorum, cujuslibet ad vj.$d$. per diem, habendis per viam regardi ex causa prædicta; per breve generale de Privato Sigillo, inter mandata de hoc termino,

M$^l$ M$^l$ M$^l$ D. iiij$^{xx}$ xiiij.$l$. x.$s$.

Ricardo, comiti Warrwici, retento penes dominum nostrum regem per Indenturam inter ipsum dominum regem et præfatum comitem confectam, ad profisciscendum ad partes exteras ad ibidem dandum auxilium et rescussum villæ suæ Calesiæ per spatium unius mensis; in denariis sibi liberatis in persolutionem Dc.xxvj.$l$. x.$s$., quos dictus dominus rex, de avisamento et assensu concilii sui eidem comiti liberari mandavit, pro vadiis suis, unius baronis, ad iiij.$s$. per diem; trium militum, cujuslibet ad ij.$s$. per diem; lv. hominum ad arma, cujuslibet ad xij.$d$. per diem; vij.c. lxv. sagittariorum, cujuslibet ad vj.$d$. per diem, habendis per viam regardi ex causa prædicta; per breve de Privato Sigillo, inter mandata de hoc termino,

Dc.xxvj.$l$. x.$s$.

Humfrido, comiti Staffordiæ, retento per Indenturam ex causa ut supra, in denariis sibi liberatis in persolutionem cccc.lxxiiij.$l$. xvj.$s$. viij.$d$., quos dictus dominus rex, de avisamento et assensu concilii sui, eidem comiti liberari mandavit, tam pro vadiis suis ad vj.$s$. viij.$d$. per diem; iiijor militum,

---

*Marginal note:* A.D. 1436. —— Payments to the duke of Gloucester and others for services rendered in the defence of Calais.

---

[1] From the Issue Pell Roll, termino Paschæ, 14 Hen. VI., m. 12.

cujuslibet ad ij.*s.* per diem; lxiij. hominum ad arma, cujuslibet ad xij.*d.* per diem, quam pro vadiis D.xxiij. sagittariorum, cujuslibet ad vj.*d.* per diem; habendis per viam regardi ex causa prædicta; per breve generale de Privato Sigillo, inter mandata de hoc termino,

cccc.lxxiiij.l. xvj.s. viij.d.

Thomæ, comiti Devoniæ, retento per Indenturam ex causa ut supra, in denariis sibi liberatis in persolutionem ccc.iiij<sup>xx</sup>viij.<i>l.</i> xiiij.*s.* viij.*d.*, quos dictus dominus rex, de avisamento et assensu concilii sui, dicto comiti liberari mandavit, tam pro vadiis suis ad vj.*s.* viij.*d.* per diem; unius militis, ad ij.*s.* per diem; xxiiij. hominum ad arma, cujuslibet ad xij.*d.* per diem; quam pro vadiis cccc.lxx. sagittariorum, cujuslibet ad vj.*d.* per diem; habendis per viam regardi ex causa prædicta; per breve generale de Privato Sigillo, inter mandata de hoc termino,

ccc.iiij<sup>xx</sup>viij.l. xiiij.s. viij.d.

Waltero, domino Hungerforde, retento per Indenturam, ut supra, in denariis sibi liberatis in persolutionem ccc.xx.<i>l.</i> xij.*s.*, quos dominus rex, de avisamento et assensu concilii sui, dicto Waltero liberari mandavit, tam pro vadiis duorum banerettorum, utriusque ad iiij.*s.* per diem; unius militis, ad ij.*s.* per diem; xxx. hominum ad arma, cujuslibet ad xij.*d.* per diem; quam pro vadiis ccc.lxxviij. sagittariorum, cujuslibet ad vj.*d.* per diem; habendis per viam regardi; per breve de Privato Sigillo, inter mandata de hoc termino,

ccc.xx.l. xij.s.

Leoni, domino de Welles, retento per Indenturam, ut supra, in denariis sibi liberatis in persolutionem l.<i>l.</i> viij.*s.*, quos dominus rex, de avisamento et assensu concilii sui, eidem Leoni liberare mandavit, tam pro vadiis suis, ad iiij.*s.* per diem; viij. hominum ad arma, cujuslibet ad xij.*d.* per diem; quam pro vadiis xlviij. sagittariorum, cujuslibet ad vj.*d.* per diem, habendis per viam regardi; per breve generale de Privato Sigillo, inter mandata de hoc termino,

l.l. viij.s.

Johanni, domino de Beaumont, retento per Indenturam, ut supra, in denariis sibi liberatis in persolutionem iiij<sup>xx</sup>xv.<i>l.</i> iiij.*s.*, quos dominus rex, de avisamento et assensu concilii sui, eidem Johanni liberari mandavit, tam super vadiis suis, ad iiij.*s.* per diem; xx. hominum ad arma, cujuslibet ad xij.*d.* per diem; quam pro vadiis iiij<sup>xx</sup>viij. sagittariorum, cujuslibet ad vj.*d.* per diem, habendis per viam regardi; per breve de Privato Sigillo, inter mandata de hoc termino,

iiij<sup>xx</sup>xv.l. iiij.s.

Ricardo, domino Cromwelle, retento per Indenturam, ut supra, in denariis sibi liberatis in persolutionem c.xlij.*l.* iiij.*s.*, quos dominus rex, de avisamento et assensu concilii sui, dicto Radulpho liberari mandavit, tam super vadiis unius militis, ad ij.*s.* per diem; xij. hominum ad arma, cujuslibet ad xij.*d.* per diem; quam pro vadiis c.lxxv. sagittariorum, cujuslibet ad vj.*d.* per diem, habendis per viam regardi; per breve generale de Privato Sigillo, inter mandata de hoc termino,

c.xlij.l. iiij.s.

Johanni, domino Tiptot, retento per Indenturam, ut supra, ad mittendum ad partes exteras homines ad arma et sagittarios ad dandum rescussum et auxilium villæ regis Calesiæ; in denariis sibi liberatis in persolutionem lxx.*l.* xiiij.*s.*, quos dominus rex, de avisamento et assensu concilii sui, dicto Johanni liberari mandavit, tam pro vadiis xvj. hominum ad arma, cujuslibet ad xij.*d.* por diem; quam pro vadiis lxix. sagittariorum, cujuslibet ad vj.*d.* per diem; habendis per viam regardi, per breve de Privato Sigillo, inter mandata de hoc termino,

lxx.l. xiiij.s.

Philippo Curteney, militi, retento per Indenturam, ut supra, in denariis sibi liberatis in persolutionem lxxviij.*l.* viij.*s.*, quos dominus rex, de avisamento et assensu concilii sui, dicto Philippo liberari mandavit, tam pro vadiis suis, ad iiij.*s.* per diem; xij. hominum ad arma, cujuslibet ad xij.*d.*; quam pro vadiis iiij$^{xx}$[1] sagittariorum, cujuslibet ad vj.*d.* per diem; habendis per viam regardi, per breve de Privato Sigillo, inter mandata de hoc termino, lxxviij.<i>l.</i> viij.<i>s.</i>

Johanni Denham, militi, retento per Indenturam, ut supra, in denariis sibi liberatis in persolutionem lxxj.*l.* viij.*s.*, quos dominus rex, de avisamento et assensu concilii sui, dicto Johanni liberari mandavit, tam pro vadiis suis, ad iiij.*s.* per diem; xj. hominum ad arma, cujuslibet ad xij.*d.* per diem; quam pro vadiis lxxij. sagittariorum, cujuslibet ad vj.*d.* per diem; habendis per viam regardi, per breve de Privato Sigillo, inter mandata de hoc termino, lxxj.<i>l.</i> viij.<i>s.</i>

Johanni Stourtone, militi, retento per Indenturam, ut supra, in denariis sibi liberatis in persolutionem iiij$^{xx}$vij. *l.* ij.*s.*, quos dominus rex, de avisamento et assensu concilii sui, dicto Johanni liberari mandavit, tam pro vadiis suis ad ij.*s.* per diem; iiij. hominum et arma, cujuslibet ad xij.*d.* per diem; quam pro

---

[1] iiij$^{xx}$] These numerals are written on an erasure.

vadiis cxj. sagittariorum, cujuslibet ad vj.*d.* per diem, habendis per viam regardi, per breve de Privato Sigillo, inter mandata de hoc termino,      iiij$^{xx}$vj.*l.* ij.*s.*

Roberto Whityngham, armigero, retento per Indenturam, ut supra, in denariis sibi liberatis in persolutionem xxiiij.*l.* x.*s.*, quos dominus rex, de avisamento et assensu concilii sui, dicto Roberti liberari mandavit, tam pro vadiis suis et vj. hominum ad arma, cujuslibet ad xij.*d.* per diem; quam pro vadiis xxj. sagittariorum, cujuslibet ad vj.*d.* per diem; habendis per viam regardi, per breve de Privato Sigillo, inter mandata de hoc termino,      xxiiij.*l.* x.*s.*

Ricardo Wodevyle et Willelmo Hauce, armigeris, retentis per Indenturam, ut supra, in denariis eis liberatis in persolutionem xxj.*l.*, quas dominus rex, de avisamento et assensu concilii sui, eisdem Ricardo et Willelmo liberari mandavit pro vadiis xxx. sagittariorum, cujuslibet ad vj.*d.* per diem, habendis per viam regardi, per breve generale de Privato Sigillo, inter mandata de hoc termino,      xxj.*l.*

Gilberto Par, armigero, retento per Indenturam, ut supra, in denariis sibi liberatis in persolutionem xvj.*l.* quas dominus rex, de avisamento et assensu concilii sui, dicto Gilberto liberari mandavit, tam pro vadiis suis ad xij.*d.* per diem; quam pro vadiis xxj. sagittariorum, cujuslibet ad vj.*d.* per diem; habendis per viam regardi, per breve de Privato Sigillo, inter mandata de hoc termino,      xvj.*l.* ij. *s.*

Sampsoni Mombrone et Bydawe de Vyle, armigeris, retentis per Indenturam, ut supra, in denariis eis liberatis in persolutionem lvj.*s.*, quos dominus rex, de avisamento et assensu concilii sui, dictis Sampsoni et Bidawe liberari mandavit, habendis per viam regardi, per breve de Privato Sigillo, inter mandata de hoc termino,      lvj. *s.*

Johanni Watforde, armigero, retento per Indenturam, ut supra in denariis sibi liberatis in persolutionem lvj. *s.* quos dominus rex, de avisamento et assensu concilii sui, eidem Johanni liberari mandavit, tam pro vadiis suis ad xij. *d.* per diem, quam pro vadiis duorum sagittariorum, cujuslibet ad vj.*d.* per diem, habendis per viam regardi, per breve de Privato Sigillo, inter mandata de hoc termino,      lvj. *s.*

Roberto Passemer, armigero, retento per Indenturam, ut supra, in denariis sibi liberatis in persolutionem lxx.*s.*, quos dominus rex, de avisamento et assensu concilii sui, dicto Roberto liberare mandavit, tam pro vadiis suis ad xij. *d.* per

diem, quam pro vadiis trium sagittariorum, cujuslibet ad vj.*d.* per diem, habendis per viam regardi, per breve de Privato Sigillo, inter mandata de hoc termino, lxx. *s.*

Thomæ Cumberworthe, militi, retento per Indenturam, ut supra, ad mittendum ad partes exteras homines ad arma et sagittarios ad dandum auxilium et rescussum villæ regis Calesiæ; in denariis sibi liberatis in persolutionem ix.*l.* ij.*s.*, quos dominus rex, de avisamento et assensu concilii sui, dicto Thomæ liberari mandavit, tam pro vadiis duorum hominum ad arma, utriusque ad xij*d.* per diem; quam vadiis ix. sagittariorum, cujuslibet ad vj. *d.* per diem; habendis per viam regardi, per breve de Privato Sigillo, inter mandata de hoc termino, ix.*l.* ij.*s.*

Johanni Pulforde et aliis quinque sociis suis, valettis coronæ domini regis, retentis per Indenturam, ut supra, in denariis eis liberatis in persolutionem iiij.*l.* iiij. *s.*, quos dominus rex, de avisamento et assensu concilii sui, eis liberari mandavit super vadiis cujuslibet eorum ad vj. *d.* per diem, habendis per viam regardi, per breve de Privato Sigillo, inter mandata de hoc termino, iiij.*l.* iiij.*s.*

Johanni Hexham, in denariis sibi liberatis ad vices; videlicet, una vice c. marcas, et alia vice l. marcas, et alia vice ccc.*l.* de præstito super solutione vadiorum diversorum navium et vasorum arestatorum tam pro salva custodia maris quam pro passagio ducum Gloucestriæ et Norffolciæ, comitum, baronum, militum, hominum ad arma et sagittariorum, proficiscentium versus Calesiam pro rescussu ejusdem, per breve generale de Privato Sigillo, inter mandata termino Michaelis ultimo, cccc. unde respondebit.

Johanni Hexham et Radulpho Ingoldsby, in denariis eis liberatis per manus Roberti Burtone, de præstito super solutione vadiorum diversorum magistrorum et marinariorum diversorum navium et vasorum arestatorum tam pro salva custodia maris quam pro passagio ducum Gloucestriæ et Norffolciæ, necnon comitum, baronum, militum, hominum ad arma et sagittariorum, proficiscentium versus Calesiam pro recussu ejusdem, per breve generale de Privato Sigillo, inter mandata de termino Michaelis ultimo, ccc.*l.* unde respondebit.

Radulpho Ingoldesby, in denariis sibi liberatis; videlicet, per manus proprias cc.*l.*, et per manus Thomæ Gille cc.*l.* de præstito super solutione vadiorum magistrorum et marinariorum diversorum navium et vasorum, arestatorum tam pro salva custodia maris, quam pro passagio ducum Gloucestriæ et Norffolciæ, necnon comitum, baronum, militum, hominum ad arma

et sagittariorum, profisciscentium versus Calesiam pro rescussu ejusdem, per breve generale de Privato Sigillo, inter
mandata de termino Michaelis ultimo,

ccc.iiij<sup>xx</sup>viij.l. unde respondebit.

Willelmo Cantelowe, vitellario villæ Calesiæ, in denariis
sibi liberatis, recipienti denarios de Radulpho Ingoldesby, de
præstito super officio suo xiij.<i>l.</i> unde respondebit. Et respondit
inde in compoto suo, rotulo xviij. Rotulo Compotorum.[1]

Johanni Hexham, in denariis sibi liberatis per manus Ricardi Rowe, de præstito super vadiis lx. marinariorium in
quadam balingera vocata Jhesus, quam pro vitellatione ejusdem, ordinata de avisamento concilii regis per unum mensem
pro salva custodia maris, per breve generale de Privato Sigillo, inter mandata de termino Michaelis ultimo,

xxvij.l. unde respondebit.

Eidem Johanni Hexham, in denariis sibi liberatis per manus
Thomæ Pope, de Wynchelse, de præstito super solutione vadiorum magistrorum et marinariorum diversorum navium et
vasorum, ordinatorum pro salva custodia maris, per breve
generale de Privato Sigillo, inter mandata de termino Michaelis ultimo præterito,

xiij.l. vj.s. viij.d. unde respondebit.

Eidem Johanni Hexham, in denariis sibi liberatis per manus
Walteri Heymane, de præstito super cariagio diversorum ordinationum regis per mare versus Calesiam, pro salva custodia
ejusdem, per breve generale de Privato Sigillo, inter mandata
de termino Michaelis ultimo,     xx.<i>s.</i> unde respondebit.

Roberto Burtone, in denariis sibi liberatis per manus Thomæ
Gylle, de præstito super solutione vadiorum magistrorum et
marinariorum diversorum navium et vasorum super mare existentium pro salva custodia ejusdem, per breve generale de
Privato Sigillo, inter mandata de termino Michaelis ultimo,

xlv.l. xiij.s. iiij.d. unde respondebit.

Thomæ Gille et Roberto Burtone, in denariis eis liberatis
de præstito super solutione vadiorum diversorum magistrorum
et marinariorum diversorum navium et vasorum super mare
existentium pro salva custodia ejusdem, per breve generale de
Privato Sigillo, inter mandata de termino Michaelis ultimo,

viij.l. unde respondebit.

---

[1] *Willelmo . . . compotorum*] The whole of this entry is an addition made by a different hand.

Willelmo Ederiche, in denariis sibi liberatis de regardo speciali pro lodemanage ordinationum regis de Londone usque Sandewicum, per breve generale de Privato Sigillo, inter mandata de termino Paschæ, anno xj. regis nunc,

xiij.*s.* iiij.*d.*

## No. III.

Warrant for the Payment of a Messenger employed in carrying Letters respecting the state of Normandy.[1]

A TOUS ceulx qui ces lettres verront, Guillem Oldhalle, chivalier, bailly d'Alencon, salut.

Comme de nagaires nous eussions escript pluseurs lettres a noble homme, messire Jehan Fastolf, chevalier, cappitaine de Caen, faisants mention de lassemble qui avoient faite les anemis et adversaires du roy pour entrer ou pais de Normendie, comme len dit ; et auxi nous eussent escript noble et puissant seigneur, monseigneur de Scalles, grant seneschal de Normandie, et ce dit cappitaine, autres lettres que lour feissons savoir souvent lestat et puissance des dits ennemis, les lieux ou ilz soient, et les chemins quilz tendroient, affin de resister a leur entreprinses, les quelles noz lettres eussent este portees de la ville d'Essey en la ville de Caen, et celles de notre dit seigneur de Scalles, et du dit messire Jehan Fastolf

A.D. 1436.
30 April.

On the insurrections in Normandy.

## [TRANSLATION.]

To all those persons who shall see these present letters, William Oldhalle, knight, bailly of Alençon, greeting.

Whereas of late we have written many letters to the noble man, messire Jehan Fastolf, knight, captain of Caen, making mention of the gathering which had been made by the enemies and adversaries of the king, with the intention of entering upon the country of Normandy, as it is reported ; and also whereas the noble and powerful lord, my lord of Scales, grand seneschal of Normandy, and the said captain, have written to us other letters requiring us to send frequent intimation to them of the condition and force of the said enemies, the places where they are, and the roads they are taking, in order that their enterprises may be resisted, which letters of ours had to be conveyed from the town of Essai to the town of Caen, and those of our said lord of Scales, and of the said messire

[1] From the Addit. Charter, 3779.

apportees du dit lieu de Caen devers nous au dit lieu d'Essey
par Nicolas Clare, Anglois, lequel en portant icelles lettres
eust fait deux voyages du dit lieu d'Essey au dit lieu de Caen
hastivement de nuit et de jour ; et pour iceulx faire, par notre
mandement lui eussent este bailliez et delivrez, ou fait bailler
et delivrer, en la ville d'Argenthen par Richard Salins, viconte
du dit lieu, deux chevaulx, lun appertenant a Nicolas Hok,
Anglois, et lautre appertenant a Michel Cussalley ;—savoir
faisons que au jour duy, darrain jour Davril, lan mil
iiij.c. xxxvj. se presentent devant nous les dits Nicolas Hok
et Cussalley, requerans que pour les journees de leurs dits
chevaulx, qui avoient vacques en faisant les dits voyages
chacun deux jours, et empirement des dits chevaulx unt alo-
cacion diceulx voyages, leurs voulsissions faire tauxacion et
pourvoir de paiement ainsi que de raison.  Pourquoy nous
feismes venir devant nous plusieurs notables personnes, bourgois et demourans en la ville d'Argenthan, lesquelx disont
avoir veu baillir et livrer les dits chevaulx au dit Clare pour
faire les dits voyages, et auxi disont les avoir veuz alors quils
les avoir renduz et bailliez a son retour des dits voyages, les
quelx nous feismes jurer et enchargasmes de rapporter verite

---

John Fastolf, had to be conveyed from the said place of Caen
to the said place of Essai, by Nicolas Clare, Englishman,
who, in conveying the said letters, has made two journies from
the said place of Essai to the place of Caen aforesaid, hastily,
travelling by night and day ; and to do this, there were given
and delivered to him by our command, or there were caused
to be given and delivered to him, in the town of Argentan, by
Richard Salins, vicomte of the said place, two horses, the one
belonging to Nicolas Hok, Englishman, and the other belonging
to Michael Cusalley ;—we make known that upon this day, being
the last day of April, in the year one thousand iiij.c. xxxvj.,
the said Nicolas Hok and Cusalley presented themselves before
us, asking that, for the days' work of their said horses, which
have each been employed two days in making the said journies,
and also for the damage done to the said horses by occasion
of the said journies, we would be pleased to make an award
and provide reasonable payment for the same.  Wherefore we
caused to come before us several respectable persons, burgesses
and residents in the said town of Argentan, who said that they
had seen the said horses given and delivered to the said Clare
to make the journies aforesaid, and also said that they had
seen them when they were restored and given up, upon his
return from the said journies, which persons we caused to be

en leurs consciences sur savoir combien il povait bien apper-
tenir par raison aus dits Hok et Cussalley des journees do
leurs dits chevaulx et empirements ensi en iceulx a icelle
cause, lesquelx nous rapporterent en leurs consciences que il
lour povait bien appartenir par raison a chacun la somme de
vingt soulz Tournois, qui vallent pour tout la somme de quarante soulz Tournois. Veu lequel rapport ainsi fait, et auxi
atendu la necessite hastive quil estoit de porter les dits lettres,
donne sur ce en mandement au dit vicunte d'Argenthen,
que la ditte somme de xl.s. Tournois des deniers de sa recepte
il face paicment aus dits Hok et Cussalley, chacun en son
regard; en prenant quittance deulx, et de ce faisant mencion
sur ses comptes, ainsi quil est acoustume ou tel cas.

Donne au dit lieu d'Argenthan, en lan et jour dessus dits.

(*Dorso.*) Lan mil cccc. xxxvj., le premier jour de May, par
devant moy, Jehan Biart, clerc, tabellion du roy, notre seigneur,
ou siege d'Argenthen, furent presens Nicolas Clare, Anglois,
et Michiel Cussalley, denommez au blanc, lesquelx confessent

---

sworn, and charged them to speak the truth upon their consciences, that it might be known how much should fairly
and reasonably be given to the aforesaid Hok and Cussalley
for the work of their said horses, and for the injury which
they have consequently sustained; and they reported to us,
upon their consciences, that there might well and reasonably
be awarded to each of them the sum of twenty sols, Tournois,
which amounts, in all, to the sum of forty sols, Tournois.
Having regard to this report thus made, and also taking into
consideration the necessity that there was for a speedy despatch
of the said letters; we have hereupon given orders to the said
vicomte of Argentan that, out of the money which he has on
hand, he make payment of the said sum of xl.s., Tournois, to
the said Hok and Cusalley, each for his own share; taking
an acquittance from them, and making mention of the same
in his accounts, as in such case is usual.

Dated at the same place of Argentan, in the year and day
above specified.

(*Dorso.*) In the year one thousand cccc. xxxvj. the first day
of May, before me, Jehan Biart, clerk, notary of the king, our
lord, at the siege of Argentan, were present Nicolas Clare,
Englishman, and Michael Cusalley, named in the warrant, who
acknowledged that they have had and received of Richart

avoir eu et receu de Richart Saling, esquier, viconte d'Argenthen et d'Exmes, la somme de quarante soulz, Tournois, par
qui deubz leur estoient ; cest assavoir, a chacun vingt soulz,
Tournois, pour les causes contenues et desclaeres au dit blanc.
De la quelle somme de xl.s. Tournois les dits Nicolas Hok
et Cussalley quittent le roy, notre seigneur, le dit viconte, et
tous autres a qui quittance en appartient.

Tesmoing, le signe de moy, tabellion dessus dit, cy mis le
jour et an dessus dit.

J. BIART.

Saling, esquire, vicomte of Argentan and of Exmes, the sum
of forty solz, Tournois, of the person by whom they were due
to them ; that is to say, to each of them twenty sols, Tournois,
for the reasons contained and declared in the said warrant.
Of which sum of 40s. Tournois, the said Nicolas Hok and
Cusalley acquit the king, our lord, the said vicomte, and all
other persons to whom an acquittance is due.

In witness whereof, here is the signature of me, the notary
above said, placed hereto on the day and year above said.

J. BIART.

## No. IV.

Certificate for the Payment of certain Money to Jehan
Levesque and others, employed in the service of Henry
the Sixth.[1]

A.D. 1436.
8 Sept.

On the loss
of Paris
and the in-
surrection
in Nor-
mandy.

ROBERT JOSEL, lieutenant-general de noble homme Hue
Spencier, escuier, bailli de Costentin, au viconte de Valongnes,
ou a son lieutenant, salut.

### [TRANSLATION.]

ROBERT JOSEL, lieutenant-general of the noble man, Hue
Spencier, esquire, bailly of the Côtentin, to the vicomte of
Valognes, or to his lieutenant, greeting.

---

[1] From the Addit. Charter, 3787. Another copy, omitting the indorse-
ment, is contained in the MS. Fontanieu, 117–118.

Nous, par ladvis, deliberacion, et conseil de noble et puissant
seigneur, messire Raoul le Sage, chevalier, seigneur de Saint
Pierre, conseilleur du roy, notre seigneur, et de pluseurs
autres officers dicellui seigneur en dit bailliage, avons tauxe
a venerable et discrepte personne, maistre Jehan Levesque,
maistre en theologie, pour sa paine et salaire de dun voyage
par lui nagueres fait de Valongnes en royaume d'Engleterre,
ung religieux et ung clerc en sa compaignie, par devers le
roy, notre dit seigneur, messeigneurs les cardinal d'Engleterre,
monseigneur le duc de Glocestre, et aultres notablez seigneurs
du grant conseil du roy, notre dit seigneur, porter certaines
lettres closes depar mon dit seigneur de Saint Pierre et depar
messeigneurs de Scalles et de Fastol, touchantes le fait du roy,
notre dit seigneur, la rebellion de la ville de Paris, et la venue
des enemis assembles a Granville,[1] et exposer a mes dits

---

We, by the advice, deliberation, and counsel of the noble and
powerful lord, messire Raoul le Sage, knight, lord of Saint
Pierre, councillor of the king, our lord, and of many other
officers of the same lord in the same bailliwick, have allowed
to the discreet and venerable person, master Jehan Levesque,
master in theology, for his trouble and wage in a journey by
him lately made from Valognes into the kingdom of England,
with a monk and a clerk in his company, to the king, our
said lord, and to my lords the cardinal of England, my lord
the duke of Gloucester, and other noble lords of the great
council of the king, our said lord, to carry closed letters from
my said lords of Saint Pierre and from my lords Scales and
Fastol, touching the affairs of the king, my said lord, the
rebellion of the city of Paris, and the arrival of the enemies
assembled at Granvelle, and to state to my said lords of

---

[1] *Granville*] This passage is
illustrated by the following extract
from a letter of Hugh Spencer,
dated 26 May, 1436, preserved in
the Archives of France :— "To
" Martin Donblet, who set out from
" Coutances on the 12 of May to
" go to the town of Caen, to messire
" Jehan Fastolf, to carry closed
" letters written by messire Richard
" Harynton, knight, bailly of Caen,
" and lieutenant of the said town of
" Coutances, to the effect that news
" had reached them from lieutenant
" and vicomte of Avranches that
" the person who styles himself the
" duke of Alençon, Charles of
" Anjou, and the count of Perdriac,
" the enemies of the king our lord,
" were coming to join themselves
" with the sires of Loheac, La Roche,
" Lebueil, and other adversaries,
" who had arrived at Granville.
" There were also other news, to the
" effect that the said enemies were
" at Granville aforesaid, and were
" making fortifications round their
" quarters."

seigneurs d'Engleterre certaines choses de bouche qui en-
chargies envoient este au dit mestre Jehan. Et le tout pour
le fait du roy, notre dit seigneur, et de sa seignourie de
France et de Normendie.

En quel voyage faesant le dit mestre Jehan a vacque, tant en
allant, sejournant au dit lieu d'Engleterre, en atendant ses
expeditions, que en rettournant au dit lieu de Valongnes, et
auxi du dit lieu de Valongnes allant pardevers les habitans
des villes de Carenten et Saint Lo, aux quelz le roy, notre
dit seigneur, rescripvoit ses lettres closes, le dit mestre Jehan
vacqua, le dit religieux et clerc en sa compaignie, espasse de
chinquante et ung jour, commenchant le xx. jour d'Avril,
desrain passe, ainsi que le tous nous a este certiffie par mon
dit seigneur de Saint Pierre; par ladvis et deliberacion duquel
nous avons tauxe au dit mestre Jehan, pour chacun jour quil
a vacque en dit voyage, pour lui et sa dicte compaignie, la
somme de vingt soulz, Tournois, avecques la somme de dix
neuf salus dor pour ses passages daller et retourner; qui
vallent en somme toute la somme de soixante dix sept livres,
xviij.*s.* iiij.*d.*, Tournois.

Sy vous mandons que, des deniers de votre recepte, vous

---

England certain matters verbally, with which the said master
Jehan has been entrusted; the whole being on the business of
the king, our said lord, and his lordship in France and Normandy.

In accomplishing which journey the said master Jehan has
been employed, as well in going, tarrying in the said place of
England, waiting for his despatches, as in returning to the
said place of Valognes; and also going from the said place
of Valognes to the lieutenants of the towns of Carentan and
Saint Lo, to whom the king, our said lord, has written his
closed letters, the said master Jehan has been engaged, in
the company of the said monk and the clerk, for the space of
fifty-one days, beginning on the xx. day of April last past,
as the whole has been certified to us by my said lord of Saint
Pierre; by whose advice and deliberation we have awarded to
the said master Jehan, for each day that he has been employed
in the said journey, for himself and his said company, the
sum of twenty sols Tournois, with the sum of nineteen salus
of gold for their passage in going and returning; which
amount, in the whole, to seventy-seven livres, eighteen *s.*,
four *d.* Tournois.

Wherefore we command you to pay and deliver the said

paicz et delivres au dit mestre Jehan la dicte somme. Et par rendant ces presentes en vos comptes, avecques quittance du dit mestre Jehan, icelle somme vous sera deduite et rabatue sur votre dicte recepte par messeigneurs de la chambre des comptes.

En tesmoing de ce nous avons seellees ces presentes du seel donc nous usons ou dit office, le viij. jour de Septembre, lan mil, quatre cens, xxxvj.

JOSEL.

(*Dorso.*) Lan mil iiij.c. xxxvj., le x. jour de Septembre, devant Pierres Moreau, tabellion a Vallounges, fut present maistre Jehan Levesque, maistre en theologie, qui confessa avoir eu et receu de Guillem Osber, viconte de Vallounges, la somme de soixante dix sept livres xviij.*s.* iiij.*d.* pour les causes contenues au blanc; dont il se tint content, et en quitta le roy, notre seigneur, le dit viconte, et tous autres.

MOREAU.

---

sum out of the money which you have received, to the said master Jehan; and upon the production of these presents, together with the discharge of the said master Jehan, this sum shall be deducted and allowed from your receipts, in your accounts, by the lords of the chamber of accounts.

In witness hereof, we have sealed these presents with the seal which we use in the said office, the viij. day of September, in the year one thousand, four hundred, thirty and six.

JOSEL.

(*Dorso.*) In the year one thousand iiij.c. xxxvj., the x. day of September, before Pierres Moreau, notary of Vallognes, was present master Jehan Levesque, master in theology, who acknowledged that he had had, and received of Guillem Osber, vicomte of Vallognes, the sum of seventy-seven livres, xviij. *s.*, iiij. *d.* for the causes contained in the certificate; whereof he holds himself satisfied, and thereof he acquits the king, our lord, the said vicomte, and all others.

MOREAU.

---

## No. V.

WARRANT for the payment of xiiij.*l.* iiij.*s.* vj.*d.* for the execution of certain criminals at Caen.[1]

A.D. 1436.
27 Sept.
———
Warrant
for pay-
ment of
certain
executions
at Caen.

EUSTACE QUEMNET, lieutenant general de noble homme, messire Richart Haryngton, chevalier, bailli de Caen, au viconte du dit lieu, ou a son lieutenant, salut.

Pour ce que par sentence et condempnation de justice, Girot Tricquet, meistre et executeur de la haulte justice du roy, notre seigneur, es vicontes de Caen et Baieux, a executes et mis a mort les personnes denommes, et par la fourme desclairee cy apres; cest assavoir, Gueriot Lorier de Tillie, Guillem le Petit de Breville, traistres, larrons et ennemis du roy, notre dit seigneur, decappites, et leurs corps pendus au gibet; Jehan du Bois, natif de Perche, Jehan Radigues, natif Danjou, larrons et desrobeurs en chemins publiques, pendus au gibet; et Guillem le Maistre, dit Lescherie, traistre, larron, murdrier, ennemi et adverssaire du dit seigneur, trayne, le poing couppe, decapite, et le corps pendu au gibet; et que le dit Tricquet nous a sur ce requis tauxacon et ordonnance

---

### [TRANSLATION.]

EUSTACE QUEMNET, the lieutenant general of the noble man, messire Richard Haryngton, knight, bailly of Caen, to the vicomte of the said place or to his lieutenant, greeting.

Since, by the sentence and judgment of the law, Girot Tricquet, master-executioner of the capital jurisdiction of the king, our lord, in the vicomtés of Caen and Baieux, has executed and put to death the persons designated, and by the form specified as under; that is to say, Gueriot Lorier of Tillé, Guillem le Petit of Bréville, traitors, robbers, and the enemies of the king, our said lord, beheaded, and their bodies hanged on a gibbet; Jehan du Bois, a native of Perche, Jehan Radigues, a native of Anjou, thieves and robbers on the public highways, hanged upon a gibbet; and Guillem le Maistre, surnamed Lescherie, traitor, thief, murderer, enemy and adversary of the said lord, who was drawn, had his hand cut off, and his body hanged upon the gibbet; whereupon the said Tricquet has requested of

---

[1] From the Addit. Charter, 3789.

de paiement, et mesmes pour une clace prinse pour faire la trayn et execution du dit Lescherie; nous a icellui Tricquet, pour son droit et salarie dicelles execucions, avons tauxe par ces presentes, cest assavoir, pour le dit trayn dix soulz, Tournois, pour le poing couppe dix solz, pour chacun decapitacion xx. solz, pour chacun pendre xl. solz, et pour la dite clae iiij.*s.* vj.*d.*, Tournois. Valent toutes icelles paiemens la somme de quatorze livres, quatre solz, six deniers, Tournois.

Si vous mandons et commandons que des deniers de votre recepte vous paiez, bailliez, et delivres au dit Tricquet le dit somme de xiiij.*l.* iiij.*s.* vj.*d.*, laquelle, par rapportant ces presentes avecques quittance suffissant du dit Tricquet, vous sera alouee en voz comptes et rabatue de votre recepte par tout ou il appartient, sans aucun contredit ou difficulte.

Donnee a Caen, le vingt septiesme jour de Septembre, lan Date. mil, iiij.c. xxxvj.

N. HUET.

(*Dorso.*) Lan mil, iiij.c. xxxvj., le xxvij. jour de Septembre, fut present Girot Tricquet, maistre de la haulte justice du roy, notre seigneur, ou baillaige de Caen, qui confessa avoir

---

us that he might have his allowance and order for payment, as also for a hurdle required in drawing and executing the said Lescherie; we by these presents have awarded to the said Tricquet as his due and payment for the said executions, that is to say, for the drawing aforesaid ten sols Tournois, for cutting off the hand ten solz, for each beheading xx. sols, for each hanging xl. sols, and for the said hurdle iiij.*s.* vj.*d.*, Tournois. All these payments aforesaid amount to the sum of fourteen livres, four sols, six deniers, Tournois.

Wherefore we order and command you that, out of the money which you have on hand, you pay, give, and deliver to the said Tricquet, the said sum of xiiij.*l.* iiij.*s.* vj.*d.*, which (upon the production of these presents, along with a sufficient acquittance of the said Tricquet,) shall be allowed to you in your accounts, and be deducted from your receipt wherever shall be fitting, without any contradiction or difficulty.

Dated at Caen, the twenty-seventh day of September, in the year one thousand, iiij.c. xxxvj.

N. HUET.

(*Dorso.*) In the year one thousand, iiij.c. xxxvj., on the xxvij. day of September, was present Girot Tricquet, chief executioner in the capital jurisdiction of the king, our lord, in the bailliwick of Caen, who acknowledged that he had had

e 2

eu et receu de honnourable homme et sage, Jehan Randulf, viconte de Caen, la somme de quatorze livres, quatre solz, six deniers, Tournois, qui tauxes lui avoient este pour les causes contenues au blanc fait comme dessus.

N. HUET.

---

and received from the honorable and discreet man, Jehan Randulf, vicomte of Caen, the sum of fourteen livres, four sols and four deniers, Tournois, which had been awarded to him for the reasons contained in the paper given as above.

N. HUET.

---

## No. VI.

MANDATE, by Charles the Seventh, for the payment of 4,200l. Tournois, to Poton de Santrailles.[1]

A.D. 1437.
May 1.

Grant to Poton de Santrailles towards the payment of his ransom.

CHARLES, par la grace de Dieu, roy de France, a notre ame et feal president de noz comptes, levesque de Laon, general conseillier sur le fait et gouvernement de toutes noz finances ou pais de Languedoc, salut.

Nous voulons et vous mandons expressement que, par notre ame et feal conseillier, maistre Mace Heron, receveur general de nos dits finances ou dit pays de Languedoc, vous, des deniers de ta recepte, faictes paier, baillir et delivrer a notre bien ame Poton, seigneur de Santrailles, premier escuier de corps et maistre de notre escuierie, la somme de quatre mil deux cens livres, Tournois, pour partie de la somme de six

---

[TRANSLATION.]

CHARLES, by the grace of God, king of France, to our beloved and faithful president of our accounts, the bishop of Laon, counsellor-general on the business and management of all our finances in the country of Languedoc, greeting.

We will and command you expressly that, by our beloved and faithful counsellor, master Mace Heron, receiver-general of our said finances in the said country of Languedoc, you, out of the money which you have on hand, cause to be paid, given, and delivered to our well-beloved Poton, lord of Santrailles, chief esquire of the body and master of our horse, the sum of four thousand two hundred livres, Tournois, as

---

[1] From the Addit. Charter, 3804.

mil reaulx que ia pieca nous lui avons donnee et octroyee, tant pour la recompensation des pertes et dommaiges quil avoit eues a cause de la detention et emprisonnement faite par noz enciens ennemis et adversaires, les Anglois, de sa personne, comme pour lui aidier a paier la grant finance et raencon a quoy ilz lont mis. Et par rapportant ces presentes, avec quittance souffisant sur ce du dit Poton, nous voulons la dicte somme de iiij.M. ij c. livres, Tournois, estre allouee es comptes et rabatuee de la recepte du dit receveur par noz amez et feaulx gens de noz comptes, ausquelz nous mandons que ainsi le facent sans aucun reffuz ou contredit, non obstant quelzconques ordonnances, mandemens, ou deffences a ce contraires.

Donne a Pezenas, le premier jour de May, lan de grace Date. mil, cccc. trente et sept, et de notre regne le quinziesme, souz notre seel ordonne en labsence du grant.[1]

Par le roy, en son conseil.

---

part of the sum of six thousand reals which we have formerly given and granted him, as well in recompense for the losses and damages which he has sustained in consequence of the personal detention and imprisonment which he has undergone from our ancient enemies and adversaries, the English, as also to assist him in paying the heavy charge and ransom which they have fixed upon him. And upon the production of these presents, along with a sufficient acquittance hereupon made by the said Poton, it is our pleasure that the said sum of iiij.M. ij.c. livres, Tournois, shall be allowed in the accounts and deducted from the receipt of the said receiver by our beloved and faithful officers of our accounts, whom we command that they do this without any refusal or gainsaying, notwithstanding any ordinances, commands, or injunctions to the contrary whatsoever.

Dated at Pezenas, the first day of May, in the year of grace one thousand cccc. thirty and seven, and the fifteenth of our reign, under our seal used in the absence of the great.

By the king, in his council.

---

[1] It appears from the Additional Charter 3805, that upon the same day the king made a grant of 1,000l. Tournois to Jehan de Vendosme, vidame de Chartres, "pour lui aidier "a soy acquitter de la finance et "raencon a la quelle il a este mis "par nos anciens ennemis, les "Anglois, de les quelles il a este par "long temps prisonnier, pour la "quelle prison il a encoref de ses "hostages et des seellez es mains de "nos diz ennemis."

## No. VII.

Questions submitted to Henry the Sixth by Richard, earl of Warwick, respecting the government of France and Normandy ; with the king's answers thereto.[1]

A.D. 1437.
11 May.

Agreement as to the government of France and Normandy by the earl of Warwick.

HENRICUS, Dei gratia rex Angliæ et Franciæ et dominus Hiberniæ, omnibus ad quos præsentes litteræ pervenerint, salutem.

Inspeximus quosdam articulos nobis per carissimum et fidelem consanguineum nostrum, Ricardum comitem Warwici, administratos, ac responsiones eorumdem articulorum per nos datas, in hæc verba.

First, sithen it hath liked your highness to wille and desire me to doe you service in youre realme of France and duchee of Normandie, as your lieutenant there, like it unto your grace that I may be answered in my demands off certain articles following, as well longing for the weel and conservation of your lordships and lands on that side, as to have your good and gracious answer in other articles following, longeyng to my self; the which I trust to God shall not be thought unto your highness unreasonable, considering that it may wele be conceived of reason in youre good lordship that my said going over at this time is full farre from the case of my years and from the continuall laboure off my person att seiges and daily occupation in the warre, seeing the lenght off tyme that I have belaboured in the service off nobull kings off good memory, your grandsire and fadere, and about youre self, as well in youre warrs as about your noble person.

*Item.* What power and auctoritie it liko your highness that I should have in exercising the said service?

*Responsio.* The king will that you have as large and ample power as the duke off Yorke had; useing hit after the forme of an instruction that shall be given thereupon unto him.

*Item.* To wete what puisance off men of armes and archers, and what paiement, shall be sent overe at this present armie?

*Responsio.* He shall have paiement for iiij. c. speers and the bows theretoo, that shall goo with him, and the viij. c. speers and the bowes theretoo that beth beyond the sea shall be paid and contented in monoye and merchandise there.

---

[1] From the MS. Harl. 6986, fol. 1.

*Item.* To know what estate it like you of youre grace that I shall have for my person?

*Responsio.* The king will that he have yearly, for his estate, during such his absence, xx. M. frankes, and to be about his person xxx. speers and the bowes theretoo.

*Item.* To weite in what wise, and for how long, it shall like your seid highness to purvey for your lande there at this time?

*Responsio.* The king hath appointed at this time provision for the keeping of the land for a yere and an half; and before the end thereoff to purvey therefore for the time to come as the necessity shall require, in the manner and fourme conteigned more at large in an acte by the kings commandment maade on the same, remaignyng in the king's counsail.

*Item.* That the lords that be sent after, that is to say, Beaumont, Willoughby, and Bourgchier, mowe be entretede to doe youre highnesse service in this present armie, or at least ij. of hem.

*Responsio.* Willoughby is agreed to goe, and another shall be entreted to goe also.

*Item.* If it like your highness, I desire to have certain stuff of artillerie; that is to say, for iiij. M. bowes and x. M. sheafe of arrowes, iiij. c. groce of strings, and a M. spere shafts; and that it like youre seid highness to purvey stuff off gonnes, gonne powdere, stones and othere artillerie and habilliments for the warre, such as shall think unto youre lordship necessarie and sufficient for the defence and safeguarde off youre townes and castles in your said reaume and duchee.

*Responsio.* The king sent over bot late agoe by Glocestere grete stuff of such necessaries and habiliments for the werre, the which he supposeth beth not as yet spended; and over that, my said lord off Warwicke shall have with him xv. c. bowes and iij. M. shefs of arrows, a c. groce off strings, iiij. c. spere shafs; and moo spere shafs may be purveyed in Normandie, whereof the prices be better there than here. And as towards gonnes, the king is not advised to spare any from hence. Matter for powder he shall have xl. c. with him, and stones he may have in Normandy; and he shall have more off the abovesaid things from tyme to tyme as the cas shall require.

*Item.* That all manner off process made, or to be made, ageinst me, your seid humble liege man, in your Exchequier,

for apprestes, whatever they be, waiges of warre, receit, relief, commissions made to me and to othere not returned, nor thestretes thereof brought into Exchequier, . . . . . al other processes made, or to be made, against me in the foresaid Exchequier, except the sommons of the Pipe for yerely fermes which I owe to pay to you, be put in respite for the time of my seid abiding in your service; and thereupon warrantes under your prive or grete seal, as the case shall require, be maad sufficient from tyme to tyme, direct to the tresorore and barons for the time being, to respite the seid processes and to surcese in making of hem during the seid time.

*Responsio.* Hit is granted.

*Item.* That if any lordships, manoures, lands or tenements holden of you in chief discend, remaigne, revert, or in any wise falle unto [me] afore my coming home into this reaume, that after the inquisition thereoff returned in the chancellarie in the fourme accustomed, I may have lyverie off hem at suyt off one off my generall atournes, afore myne homage done unto you, if any be due therefore; and that the seid homage, and all process to be maad therefore, be respited unto my coming agen into this land, without fyne making for the same respite.

*Responsio.* Hit is granted.

*Item.* If I die in youre seid service, or be soo letted by sickness, or other cause ageynst my will, soo that I may noght performe fully your content touching the seid service duryng the terme that I shall be witholden fore, that nether I, nor myne heres, ne executors, be not compelled to restore the moneye the which I shal receive of you for my self and my retinue bycause of your seid service, nor noon account to make thereoff in any wise.

*Responsio.* Hit is granted as it is desired; provided alway that if the caas so happen that he die, (that God forbede!) before the end of the terme of his witholding, and that after his death any off his retinue within the seid terme withdraw him, that in that caas his executors shall make, att the kings cost, the suyts to the kings behove ageynst him that so with-drawed him.

*Item.* That it like your highness to grant to me, or to other persons by me hereafter to be named, your letters pattentes off lycence in due forme under your grete seal, without fyn, to give and grant to the dane and chapitres off the church collegiatt off Our Lady off Warwick, lands, tenements, or other possessions, to the yerely value off xl.*l.* over all charges and

reprises, and the same dean and chapiter to receive the same lands and tenements, or other possessions, to have and to hold to hem and to her successors for evermore, to fynd, sustain and augment divine service in the same churche, and to praye for the good estate of you and other that they be bound to pray for, after the ordinance of me, or of other persons of me to be named.

*Responsio.* The king hath graunted this as it is desired.

*Item.* Forasmuch as there is due unto me certain sommes of moneye, as for monie lente and service doon unto you, ye being in your reaume of Fraunce; that is to say, for moneye that I borowed for the safeguarde of Meaulx, xj.c. vj.*l.* xiij.*s.* iiij.*d.*, also for the wages of xx. speres and lx. bowes for two moneths, the time of your coronation in France, an c. iiij$^{xx}$ xix.*l.*, and by a bill of debenture of Hotoftes, that time tresorer of the warres, as it appeereth by the seid debenture, an c. iiij$^{xx}$ xviij.*l.* vij.*s.* iij.*d.* ob., I beseech you that I may have paiment in hand off the seid sommes, the which amounteth in all the some of xv. c. iiij.*l.* vij.*d.* ob., to the end to make me ready to doe your highnesses service within this present viage, and considering that it is trewe duete unto me that I ask.

*Responsio.* The king wole that off the sommes aboveseid my seid lord of Warrwicke have a $\mathtt{M}^l$ marc in hand, and that for remenent off the seid sommes over the seid $\mathtt{M}^l$ marc that he have sufficient assignment; or else for the same sommes there be laid and delivered unto him, for his suretee thereof, certain of the kings joiaulx to wedde for the space of iij. yere from the feste off S. Michell next, and that thereupon there be maade a warrant to the tresorere and chamberlains to paie and assigne, or else to leye to wedde as above.

*Item.* That there is as due unto me and my souldeours a grete and notable somme off moneye for the safeguard off your town of Challeys, the tyme that I was capitain there, I beseech you that be any off your counsail it like your highness to purvey some way how I shall mowe rathest neghe payment, or agreement, of the said somme.

*Responsio.* The king considereth well by the report of my said lord that, as he saith, there is and shall be founde due unto him for the foresaid cause the summ off v.$\mathtt{M}^l$. c.lxxv.*l.* ix.*s.* xj.*d.* ob., and for the same cause to his said souldiors the summ off vij.$\mathtt{M}^l$. cccc.iiij.$^{xx}$*l.* xviij.*s.* iij.*d.* is also and shall be found due by the king, the names off the which souldiours, and also the sommes off moneye that beth due unto everich of hyem, my said lord wol doo the king to

be certified be credible writing, to the intent that he shall
mowe entret hem for theire duty in that party as that him
shall seem most best and prouftable for his availe; and also
the king considereth that my said lord hath graunted to release unto him, off the abovesaid some of v.ᴹˡ c.lxxv.*l.* ix.*s.* xj.*d.*
the some of ᴹˡ. *l.* on the condicion that off the remenant off
his seid duetee he may have payment, or sufficient assignement, for somoche the king will and commandeth that there
be made a warrant sufficient under his privie seal, directed to
the tresorer and chamberleins of his Exchequer, commanding
him that my said lord, releasing a ᴹˡ. *l.* unto the king of such
somes off moneye as beth and shall be found due unto him for
the cause byforsaid, that off the remanent off the same sommes,
that soo beth and shall be founde due unto him over the seid
ᴹˡ. *l.*, they doe make unto him paiement, or sufficient assignement, off such good as shall growe and come unto the kings use.

*Item.* That if any off the appointments maad here by you, our
soveraigne lord, be any off your counsaile be broken, and ye
certified and notified thereoff, that I may in such caas then be
free to return agene into this reaume with your good lordship, without any charge or blame to be laid upon me therefore, in any wise; beseeching furthermore your said highness
theese said matters aforesaid longing to the wele and conservation of your lands and lordships to have for your oune wele
and tenement so recommanded that they be likeliod off mannes
reason stand and abide in your obeisance; for elles it should
cause you a grete dispence off good at this time and not the
conclusion that ye desire, which God defende! Wherefore I
beseech youre good lordship in my most humble wise to ab-
bridge myne answers in the demands abovesaid; and elles
accepting my trew devoir and acquitable hold me fully for
excused that I dare not aventure so grete a losse as might
fall to you, and to me also, off my poor worship.

*Responsio.* If there be lack off any off the covenants unto
my said lord of Warwick, he may send unto the king and
certifie thereoff for to purvey therefore, and after such certificate, if that the king purvey not in that partie within vj.
wekes after that he is so certified, if that wynde and weder
lete it not, that then it may be lewfull for him to returne,
without charge or blame to be laid upon him in any wise;
and if the caas happen, the king holdeth him fore discharged,
and so dischargeth him.

Nos autem tenorem articulorum et responsionum prædictorum, ad requisitiouem præfati comitis, duximus exemplifi-
candum per præsentes.

In cujus rei testimonium has litteras nostras fieri fecimus patentes.

Teste meipso, apud manerium nostrum de Kennington, xj. die Maii, anno regni nostri quinto decimo.

Per breve de Privato Sigillo.

Examinatum per RICARDUM WYMBYSSHE, et } Clericos.
　　　THOMAM SMYTHE,

---

## No. VIII.

Memorandum of proceedings in Council respecting the payment of certain sums due to the duke of York.[1]

THE x. day of Feverer, the xvj. yere etc., in the Sterr Chambre at Westminster, my lord, the duc of York, desired by mouthe of my lordes of the kynges counseil that thereas to the kynges behove he delivered late to therle of Suffolk in Fraunce xj.c. l. marcs, the whiche was besett on the kynges werres there, of the whiche somme, by promesse made by the seid erle and other of the kynges counseil there, paiement shuld have been made to the same duc in the feste of Seint Martin in wynter, the xv. yere of the kynges regne, and the whiche as yit is unpaied, that he myght have thereof prest paiement, as reson wol.

To the whiche his desire it was answered by my seid lordes that, as touchying prest paiement at this tyme of the seid sommes, as it is above desired, it myght not godely be doon, consideryng the grete charges that the kyng most at this tyme of necessitee bere. But theire advis was, yf it liked the kyng, that certain of the kynges joialx were leide in plegge to the seid duc for the saide somme of xj.c. l. marcs, by the kynges lettres patentes, unto the terme of Seint Michel next comyng and the feste of Pasque thenne next folowyng, by the whiche lettres patentes, the seid duc shuld have poair, that yf it soo happened that he were not paied of the seide somme at the seide feste of Pasque, that thenne it shulde be leveful unto hym to kepe the seide joialx as his owen propre good, with sufficeant power in the same lettres patentes to aliene the seid

*[marginal notes:]* A.D. 1438. 10 Feb. Jewels to be assigned to the duke of York in security for payment of his services in France and Normandy.

---

[1] From Rymer's Collections contained in the MS. Sloane, 4607, fol. 284.

joialx, yf that hym shulde like, withoute distourbance or empeschement of the kyng, or of his heirs or exeeutours for ever-
more.    Purveid alwey that suche joialx as he shold so take
sholde mowe be preised by joust and indifferent men, that is
to say, oon chosen for the kynges and another for the partie
of my seid lord of York; and that hereupon the keper of the
kynges prive seal have poair to make sufficeant warantz under
Prive Seal to the tresorer and chamberleins of the kynges Eschequier, to leye unto the seid duc, for the seide cause, certain
of the kynges joialx to wedde, suche as theim shal seeme good,
by the commaundement of the kyng, as other sufficeant warrant to the chanceller of Englande to make upon theffect of
thaboveseide matiere unto the seid duc sufficcantes lettres patentes, as mencion is made of above.

The xxiij. day of Feverer above writen, the kyng, oure
souverain lord, in his secree chambre withynne his castelle of
Wyndesore, commanded that thaboveseid acte sholde be executed, after theffect, purport and contenue of hit.

Presente, my lordes the chanceller and therle of Suffolk.[1]

---

### By the Kyng.

Ryght trusty and right welbeloved cosin.  We sende to yow
at this tyme oure lettres of poiar and commissione, as for your
lieutenancie and governaille in oure behalve in oure reume of
France and duchie of Normandie, and with hem we sende to
yow oure answeres yeven to certein articles late ministred by
yow to us and oure conseil, with other articles of instruction
avised by us and oure seid conseil, the whiche we wole that
ye observe in the office committed unto you.  Prayeng yow
that, (considering the greet jupardie that the said cuntrees
standen in, and thenterprise that dayly fallen there by oure
ennemyes, and also the grete hurt and losse that daylye ren-
neth upone us, as wele for youre longe abode as for the costes
of shyppes which, as it [is] noht unknowen to you, standen us
to grete charge,) withouten lenger delaye ye with youre retenue take your passage into oure said reume and duchie, to
the consolation and comfort of oure trewe subgettes there.

And, right trusty and right welbeloved cosin; for asmuche
as oure welbeloved secretarie, maister Laurence Calot, dis-
poseth hym at this tyme for to passe with yow into oure said
duchie, there for to abide and for to do` to us and to yow
such service as he can in his best wyse, as he oweth to do,

---

[1] Sewed to the above is the document which follows.

we praye yow that ye have hym specially recommended, as
well to som lyflode as to his wages parteignyng to his office,
after theffect of a cedule whiche we sende to yow closed withynne these. And God have yow in His kepyng.

Yeven under oure Prive Seel, at Westminster, tho xij. day of
May.

> To oure right trusty and right welbeloved cosin, Richard,
> duc of York, oure lieutenant of oure reume of France
> and duchie of Normandie.

---

## No. IX.

### Mandate from Henry VI. for the Destruction of the Fortresses of Longchamp and Neufmarché.[1]

HENRY, par la grace de Dieu, roy de France et d'Angleterre,
a noz amez et feaulx le tresoriers et generaulx gouverneurs
de toutes noz finances, tant de France comme de Normendie,
salut et dilection.

Comme, par le plaisir et voulente de Dieu, notre Createur,
et la grant diligence que y ont mise noz beaulx cousins, les
seigneurs de Talbot et de Faucomberge, et autres plusieurs
noz vassaulx et subgiez, les fortresses de Longchamp et
Neufmarchie soient mises en notre obeissance; les quelles
places ne sont pas necessaires a tenir; voulans obvier aux
inconveniens qui par le moyen des dessus dites places pour.

*A.D. 1438. 19 March.*

*Certain fortresses to be dismantled.*

---

### [TRANSLATION.]

HENRY, by the grace of God, king of France and England,
to our beloved and faithful the treasurers and governors-general
of all our finances, as well in France as in Normandy, greeting
and love.

Since, by the pleasure and will of God, our Creator, and by
the great diligence employed herein by our good cousins, the
lords of Talbot and Fauconberg, and many others, our vassals
and subjects, the fortresses of Longchamp and Neufmarché
are reduced under our power; the occupation of which places
is not necessary; we, wishing to prevent the dangers which
might arise by means of the said places, if it should happen

---

[1] From the Addit. Charter, 133.

roient advenir, se daventure lune dicelles places estoit prise
par les dits ennemiz, confiens a plain en voz sens, vaillance,
loyaulte, et bonne diligence, nous, par ladviz et deliberacion
de notre tres chier et tres ame cousin Richart, conte de
Warrewyk, notre lieutenant general et gouverneur de nos dits
royaume de France, paiz et duchie de Normendie, vous avons
commis et ordonnez, commettons et ordonnons par ces presentes, que les places dessus dictes faictes, ou faictes faire par
autres, telz que vouldrez a ce commettre et ordonner, tantost
et incontinent demolir, abatre et arraser par le pic au prez de
terre entierement, et telement que aucun dores en avant ny
puisse trouver refuge, logeiz, ne retrait. Et de pour ce faire
assembler, employer, et en besongnier, gens de guerre, pyon-
niers, manouvriers et autres a ce necessaires et requiz, et a
eulx ordonner et faire payer salaires telz que verrez et trouverez appartenir pour le dit abatement et demolition faire et
parfaire, soit par assiettes de deniers sur le pays, ou autrement de noz dits finances de Normandie, comme adviserez
estre affaire pour le plus convenable et moins dommagable;
voulans que les dits assiettes et payements, qui par vostre
ordonnance auront este faiz en ceste partie, soient dautel

that either of them should be taken by the said enemies,
trusting fully in your discretion, courage, loyalty, and good
diligence, by the advice and deliberation of our very dear
and well beloved cousin Richard, earl of Warwick, our lieutenant-general and governor of our said kingdom of France
and country and duchy of Normandy, have commissioned and
appointed you, and do commission and appoint you by these
presents, by yourselves or such others as you may please to
commission and appoint hereto, immediately and without delay
entirely to demolish, overthrow, and level them with the earth
by the pickaxe, and in such wise that no one henceforth may
find refuge, lodging, nor retreat therein. And for this end,
to cause to be assembled, employed, and engaged soldiers,
pioneers, labourers, and other persons necessary and requisite
for the same, and to appoint for them and cause to be paid
to them such wages as you shall see and find to be fitting
for the doing and accomplishing of the said overthrow and demolition, whether it be by assessments of money upon the country
or otherwise out of our said finances of Normandy, as you
shall decide shall be done for the greatest convenience and the
least damage; it being our pleasure that the said assessments
and payments, which shall have been made by your direction
in this behalf, shall be of the same effect and weight in all

effect et valeur en toutes choses en employement et allouement
de comptes et autrement, en quelque maniere, comme se faiz
estoient par vertu et auctorite de noz lettres et mandemens
propres. De ce faire vous donnons plain pouvoir, auctorite, et
mandement especial par ces presentes. Mandons et commandons a tous noz justiciers, officiers, et subgiez, que a vous
et voz commis et deputez en ce faisant, obeissent et entendent
diligemment; car ainsi nous plaist il estre fait.

Donne en notre ville de Rouen, le xix. jour de Mars, lan de
grace mil cccc. trente sept, et de notre regne le seiziesme.

Par le roy, a la relation de monseigneur le conte de
Warrewyk, lieutenant general et gouverneur de France
et Normandie.

CALOT.

---

respects in the employment and allowance of accounts, and
otherwise, in any way whatsoever, as if they had been done
by virtue and authority of our letters and direct commands.
To do this we give you full power and authority, and an
especial command by these presents. We order and command all our justices, officers, and subjects to obey and
diligently to assist you and your commissioners in so doing;
for it is our pleasure that thus it should be done.

Dated in our city of Rouen the xix. day of March, in the
year of grace one thousand cccc. thirty-seven, and of our reign
the sixteenth.

By the king, at the relation of my lord, the earl of Warwick, lieutenant-general and governor of France and
Normandy.

CALOT.

## No. X.
### Account of the Expenses of Sir John Popham, in an Embassy into Bretagne.[1]

Auditores { Robertus Frampton, baro.
{ Rogerus Appeltone, clericus.

A.D. 1438.
19 March.

COMPOTUS Johannis Popham, militis, thesaurarii hospitii domini regis Henrici sexti, tam de denariis per ipsum receptis,
quam de vadiis et custibus suis, missi in ambassiata ipsius

Expenses
of sir John

---

[1] Of the two documents which follow, the former is taken from the Foreign Roll of the Pipe, 13-16 | Hen. VI., an. xvj., membrane E; collated with another copy in the bundle "Nuncii, 637," in the custody

**Popham in regis** ad prædilectum consanguineum suum, comitem Warre-
**Bretagne.** wici, locum tenentem regis prædicti et gubernatorem regni
sui Franciæ et ducatus sui Normanniæ, et ad alios in eodem
ducatu, et etiam ad alia loca in nunciis ipsius domini regis,
per breve regis Henrici sexti de Privato Sigillo suo, datum
iiij°. die Februarii anno regni sui xvij.[1] thesaurario, baronibus et camerariis hujus scaccarii directum, et irrotulatum
in memorandis de anno xvij. inter brevia directa baronibus de
termino Sancti Hillarii eodem anno, rotulo xxj. ex parte Re-
memoratoris regis. In quo quidem brevi, inter cætera, continetur, quod monstravit regi et concilio suo præfatus Johannes
Popham, chivalier, thesaurarius hospitii regis, qualiter eidem
domino regi nuper placuit ipsum Johannem transmittere ad
prædilectum consanguineum regis, comitem Warrwici, locumtenentem suum et gubernatorem regni sui Franciæ et ducatus
sui Normanniæ, et ad alios infra eundem ducatum, et etiam
ad alia loca in diversis nunciis ipsius regis; qua de causa
præfatus Johannes recepit certam summam pecuniæ ad Receptam Scaccarii regis de præstito.

Quapropter rex, considerans præmissa, de avisamento et
assensu dicti concilii sui, mandavit præfatis thesaurario et
baronibus quod debite computent cum præfato Johanne Popham, aut cum una alia idonea persona nomine ipsius Johannis,
per sacramentum alterius eorum, de omnibus denariis sic per
ipsum ex causa prædicta receptis; faciendo eidem Johanne
debitam allocationem per sacramentum prædictum de xl.s. per
diem, juxta statum unius baneretii; videlicet, a die quo idem
Johannes ex causa prædicta recessit extra civitatem suam
Londoniæ versus partes transmarinas, usque ad diem redditus
sui ad eandem civitatem; una cum custibus rationabilibus pro
passagio et repassagio suis maris. Et de eo, quod per dictum
compotum præfato Johanni invenietur fore debitum, præfati
thesaurarius et camerarii eidem Johanni faciant habere solutionem, aut sufficientem assignationem prout ratio exigit et
requirit; videlicet, de hujusmodi receptis, vadiis, et custibus
suis, ut infra.

RECEPTA DENARIORUM.

Idem reddit compotum de c.l. per ipsum receptis, xxij. die
Januarii, termino sancti Michaelis, anno xvj.[2] de thesaurario

of the Master of the Rolls. The
second is from the bundle "Nuncii,
"637," the original statement by Sir
John Popham; it is written upon
paper, of which the water-mark is
couple of crossed keys.

[1] *xvij.*] Namely, 4 Feb. A.D.
1439.
[2] *xvj.*] His embassy extended from
19 March, A.D. 1438, to 23 June,
and again from that day until
October 20, in the same year.

et camerariis ad Receptam Scaccarii regis prædicti, de præstito, super vadiis et expensis suis per ipsum regem missi in
nunciis suis usque Roane, versus comitem Warrwici, locumtenentem et gubernatorem regni Franciæ et ducatus Normanniæ, et ad alios in ducatu prædicto, et etiam ad alia loca in
nunciis ipsius domini regis, quas dictus dominus rex, de avisamento et assensu concilii sui, præfato Johanni Popham ex
causa prædicta præfatis thesaurario et cameriis de præstito
per breve suum liberare mandavit, sicut continetur in Pelle
Memorandorum ad eandem Receptam Scaccarii regis de
eisdem termino et anno, et etiam in quodam rotulo ipsius
Johannis Popham de particulis, inde hic in thesauro liberato.

Summa receptæ, c.l.

### VADIA ET EXPENSÆ.

Quas idem computat in vadiis suis, ad xl.s. per diem, per
ipsum regem de avisamento et assensu concilii sui missus in
nunciis prædicti domini regis usque Roane, in partibus Normanniæ, ad præfatum comitem Warrwici, locumtenentem et
gubernatorem regni Franciæ et ducatus sui Normanniæ, et
ibidem morando cum concilio domini regis regni sui Franciæ,
et deinde equitando in Britanniam ad dominum ducem Britan-
niæ pro certo tractatu pacis ibidem cum bastardo de Orl-
eaunce, et cum aliis ambassiatoribus domini ducis Orliancnsis
ibidem ex parte regis Angliæ cum ambassiatoribus de partibus
Franciæ ibidem habendo et tento, juxta tenorem cujusdam in-
structionis tam magno quam privato sigillis et signeto regis
consignatæ, præfato comiti Warrwici, archiepiscopo de Roane,
cancellario Franciæ, ac Johanni Popham et aliis de concilio
regis tunc ibidem existentibus directæ, et penes ipsum Johannem remanentis ; videlicet, a xix. die Martii dicto anno xvi.,[1]
quo die idem Johannes Popham recessit de civitate regis
Londone versus partes prædictas, usque xxiij. diem Junii tunc
proximo sequentem, quo die rediit usque Cherborghe ad re-
diendum in Angliam, ad faciendum domini regi relationem
de materiis prædictis, sic per præfatos comitem et alios de
concilio domini regis in partibus transmarinis ac per præfatum
Johannem Popham finitis et conclusis ; scilicet, eundo, morando,
et redeundo per iiij$^{xx}$xvj. dies, prout idem Johannes dicit
super sacramentum suum, ultimo die et non primo computato,
c.iiij$^{xx}$xij. l. per breve regis prædictum, supra in titulo hujus
compoti annotatum, et prout hujusmodi vadia allocantur Johanni

[1] *xvj.*] His embassy extended from 19 March, A.D. 1438, to 23 June, and again from that day until October 20, in the same year.

f

Tiptoft, baneretto, nuper misso in ambassiata regis versus partes exteras, rotulo quinto regis Henrici quinti, rotulo compotorum, et Johanni Cobham, baneretto, nuper misso iu ambassiata regis usque partes Franciæ, rotulis secundo et tertio regis Richardi secundi, rotulo compotorum, sicut continetur in dicto rotulo de particulis.

Et in consimilibus vadiis ejusdem Johannis Popham, ad xl. *s.* per diem, existentis apud Cherborghe prædictum prædicto xxiij. die Junii, quo die recepit quoddam breve regis de privato sigillo suo ad expectandum alios de concilio domini regis supervenientes de Anglia ad tractandum alias diversas materias cum concilio adversarii domini regis in partibus Franciæ, quo tempore magister Johannes Raynyllc superveniebat ex mandato domini regis, præfatum Johannem Popham informando per aliud breve ejusdem regis de privato sigillo suo, et secum deferendo quandam novam commissionem ex parte domini regis abbati de Fiscampo et eidem Johanni Popham ac aliis infra commissionem prædictam specificatis directam, ad tractandam novam pacem cum concilio Dolfyny Franciæ pro pace habenda inter ipsum dominum regem et præfatum Dolfynum, adversarium suum; et sic redcundo de Cherborghe prædicta usque Roanc, ad consulendum cum cancellario Franciæ et comito Warrewici, et aliis de concilio domini regis tunc ibidem existentibus; quo quidem concilio ibidem finito et responso per concilium Franciæ, et sic deinde redeundo usque Houndefleto pro reskippagio suo, hominum equorum et hernesiæ suorum ibidem habendo, et ab inde redeundo usque civitatem regis Londoniæ supradictam; videlicet, de hujusmodi vadiis suis a prædicto xxiij. dio Junii, dicto anno xvj., usque xx. diem Octobris tunc proximo sequentem, quo die idem Johannes rediit ad civitatem regis Londoniæ supradictam, virtute novæ commissionis prædictæ; scilicet, eundo, morando, et redeundo, per cxix. dies, ut dicit super sacramentum suum, ultimo dic et non primo computato, cc.xxxviij. *l.* per breve regis supradictum, in titulo hujus compoti annotatum, et prout consimilia vadia allocantur præfatis Johanni Tiptoft et Johanni Cobham, supra in proxima particula præcedenti annotata, sicut continetur ibidem.

Et repassagio maris sui ipsius Johannis Popham, xiiij. hominum, servientium suorum, et xvj. equorum et hernesiæ suorum, secum venientium ultra mare, et eskippatorum apud Houndefleto in Normannia in quadam navi vocata le Swanne de Sandewyche, conducta pro xvj. *l.* in grosso, pro reskippamento ipsius Johannis, hominum et equorum prædictorum, cum hernesiis suis, cum summa festinatione, propter festinam

informationem domino regi et concilio suo de toto facto suo in hac parte faciendam et liberandam; .prout idem Johannes dicit super sacramentum suum, xvj. *l.*, virtute brevis regis prædicti, supra in titulo hujus compoti annotati, sicut continetur ibidem.

Summa vadiorum prædictorum, una cum repassagio maris, cccc.xlvj. *l.*

Et habet superplus ccc.xlvj. *l.*

De[1] quibus habiturus est solutionem vel satisfactionem aliunde, prætextu brevis domini regis de privato sigillo suo annotati supra in titulo hujus compoti. Quod quidem breve liberatur thesaurario et camerariis ad Receptam Scaccarii, xxvij. die Aprilis, anno. xvij. regis prædicti.

---

Memorandum, that sire Johne Popham, tresorere of the kyngges hous, departed fro Londone the xix. day of Marche, the ӡere of the kynge the xvjth, to goe into Normandy to my lorde of Warwyke, and also into Brethayne to the duke of Brethayne, for certane trete to be made with the Bastarde of Orlyance, and othir of the duke of Orlyance councelle, and also with othiere ymbassetors of the Frenche parte, like as it shewithe playnely by the instruccions ӡevine of oure soverein lorde the kynge unto the saide sir Johne Popham. In the wheche bysenees and labors aforesaid sir Johne Popham was occupite unto the xxiij. day of Juin next folowying, that he come to Churboro for to have comme home to Engelonde to have made relacione to the kynge how he had done in that matere that he was sende fore, whereas he recevede the same day ij. Pryve Seles fro the kyng, by the wheche the kyng commaundet hym to abyde stylle in that contre tho comynge over of certane of hys councelle, tho whiche he wolde sende over, that the foresaide Johne Popham and thay sholde labor in grete and chargeable maters for the kynge in that contre, like as is shewede more playnly by the saide letters of the Pryve Ceille. And so he aboode there and at Roone for the comynge of thayme that the kynge sholde sende thedere, like as he was commaundet by the Pryve Ceilles, unto the xxviij. day of August next folowyng, the whiche thyme maister Johne Raynylle come thedere out of Engelonde fro the kynge, and told hymme that there sholde comme no manne out of Engelonde, like as the kynge hadde wrytyn by the Pryve Ceilles; but broӡte

---

[1] This passage does not occur in the separate copy on the roll among the accounts of the " Nuncii."

a new comicione fro tho kynge unto the foresaide Sir John Popham, by the wheche the kyng ordeynte hym and othur for to
bygynne a new trete withe the Dolfynes parte for a trew to
by takyn bytwyxe tho kynge and the saide Dolfyne, like as the
kyng wrote more playnely to my lorde of Warwyke and to the
Chaunceler of Fraunce, and as shewethe playnle by the dowble
comicione. Whereopon my saide lorde of Warwyke and the
Chaunceller wretene in alle hast to the bastarde of Orlyance
and othur of the Dolfynes councelle, praying thame to send
theme word of the disposicione of the Dolfyne in that mater,
and where and whene the ymbassitors mighte asymble for to
trete opone the foresaide trew, like as the duke of Orlyance
hadde byhyȝte the kyng. Whereopone the Bastarde wrote unto
my lorde of Warwyke aȝane and let hym wette that he hadde
spokyne with the saide Dolfyne of thys mater, and that the
saide Dolfyn wolde geve non answere without avice of councelle, and that he wolde in alle hest take avice of hys councelle, and thereopone the foresaide Bastarde wold send to my
lorde of Warwyke a playne answhere in the mater; the whiche
answhere come not to my lorde of Warwyke nor to the foresaide
Sir Johne Popham unto the last day of Septembre, the wheche
day there comme letters fro the saide bastarde of Orlyance,
the wheche were wrytyn tho xx. day of Septembre at Bloysz,
like as it ys shewede playnly by the dowbles of the letters
that the Dolfyn, the wheche that he callethe ys kynge, hadde
takyn avice of thys mater by hys councelle, and wolde not in
noo wyse trete of trew neither of peisse unto the thyme he
hadde sende hys ymbassators into Engelonde to the duke of
Orlyance, and that he hadde answere agane fro hym. Wherefore my lorde of Warwyke and the Cháunsseller of France
and othure of the kyngges councille at Roone thoȝtone that
the tarryynge there of the saide sir Johne Popham was ned-
fulle no longure; wherefore as sone as [he] mighte by dely-
vered of thame there and at Roone, he shope hymme into
Engelondewarde in the goodliest hast that he might, and spede
hymme in seche wyse that, blest by God, he comme to Londone agene the xx. day of October last past, the whiche
amownthe that the foresaide sir Johne Popham hath byne out
in that viage in the kyngges serves for to accompte fro the
xix. day of Marche that last was, that he departede fro Londone, unto the xx. day of October that last was, that he comme
agane to Londone, cc. dayes and xvij.

# LETTERS AND PAPERS

ILLUSTRATIVE OF THE

# REIGN OF KING HENRY THE SIXTH.

VOL. II.

g

# LETTERS AND PAPERS

ILLUSTRATIVE OF THE

# REIGN OF KING HENRY THE SIXTH.

---

## 1423.

SECURITY granted by the duke of Bedford to the duke of Bretagne, about to come to Paris.[1]

JEHAN, regeant le royaulme de France, duc de Bethfort; scavoir faisons a tous a qui il appartient, comme tres haut et tres excellent prince feu de bonne memoire, le roy de France derrainement trepasse (que Dieu absolve !), et nous ayons envoye nos ambassadeurs par devers hault et puissant prince, nostre tres chier et tres ame frere, le duc de Bretagne, pour icelluy prier et requerir que, pour le bien public du

*A.D. 1423. Feb. 12.*

*A previous meeting had been arranged, but interrupted by the death of the late king.*

---

### [TRANSLATION.]

WE, JOHN, regent of the kingdom of France, duke of Bedford, make known to all whom it concerns that the late most high and most excellent prince, of good memory, the king of France lately deceased (whom God pardon !) and we have sent our ambassadors to the high and powerful prince, our very dear and well-beloved brother, the duke of Bretagne, to pray and require him that, for the

---

[1] From the Portef. Fontanieu, 113–114, where it is given as having been obtained from the

"Titres du chasteau de Nantes, armoire Q, cassette E. cotte xxiii." A pendent seal in red wax remains.

royaulme de France, et pour entendre a besogner au
bien et conservation de la seigneurie dicelluy, il voulsist venir pardevers monseigneur le roy et nous ;
et depuis la partie des dits embassadeurs, mon dit
seigneur le roy soit alle de vie a trepassement, par
quoy soit plus grand besoin de pourveoir au gouvernement dicelluy quonques mais, auquel gouvernement la
presence de notre dit beau frere de Bretaigne est tres
profitable.   Pourquoy desirons auttant, et plus que
paravant, que notre dit beau frere veigne en la bonne
ville de Paris ; ou se nous, nostre beau frere le duc
de Bretagne, ou lun [1] de nous, ne puisse etre ou aller
au dit lieu de Paris par exoine de maladie, ou autrement, en autre ville de ca Paris, aussi pres ou plus
pres que nest Paris, ou nous et luy aviserons etre
convenable, afin que par son moyen et avisement

---

public good of the realm of France, and with a view to
employ himself in the good and preservation of the lordship of the same, he would be pleased to come to my lord
the king and us ; and since the departure of the said ambassadors, my said lord the king has departed from this life,
in consequence of which there is still greater necessity
than ever to provide for the government of the same, for
which government the presence of our said good brother
of Bretagne is very advantageous.   Wherefore we desire as
much, and more than hitherto, that our said good brother
should come to the good city of Paris ; or if we, or
our good brother the duke of Bretagne, or either of us,
cannot be in, or go to, the said place of Paris, by reason
of sickness or otherwise, in some other city on this side
Paris, as near, or nearer, than Paris is, where we and he
shall agree upon as fitting ; in order that by his means and

---

[1] *Lun*] Lou. MS.

nous puissions dun meme vouloir proceder et besoigner au gouvernement du dit royaulme.

Et pour ce que nous avons entendu que aucuns Dangers now anti- cipated,
de son pays, non bien informez des amities et bien
veiullances dentre nous et lui, ont fait aucuns doubtes
quil peust encourir aucun peril ou danger, ou ses gens
et biens estans au dit voyage, quon les voulsist contraindre a faire aucuns promesses ou octroys outre
leurs grez et volontez ; et aussi quaucuns autres de
son pays, quil pouvoit amener avec lui, se pourroient
estre armez de party contraire et faict aucuns exploits,
par quoy ils doubteroient davoir empeschement en corps
ou en biens ; combien que nous tenons que de toutes
ces choses nostre dit beau frere ne fait aucun doubte,
neantmoins pour satisfaire aux doubtes dessusdits, et
autres opinions et imaginations soupconneuses quon
pouvoit penser en ceste matiere, et pour monstrer
notre bonne intencion aux doubtes et imaginans, pour

deliberation we may proceed by one will and attend to the
government of the said kingdom.

And since we have heard that there are some persons
in his country who, not being well informed respecting
the friendship and goodwill which exist between us and
him, have been somewhat apprehensive that he might
incur some peril or danger, or his people and goods, which
should be in the said journey, that they might be compelled to make some promises or grants contrary to their
inclination and will ; and also that some others of his
country, whom he might bring with him, might arm
themselves against the opposite side, and some exploits
be done by which they are apprehensive that they might
be injured in body or goods ; although we are persuaded
that on all those points our said good brother has no
apprehension, nevertheless to satisfy the fears above-mentioned, and other suspicious opinions and imaginations,
which people might surmise in this matter, and to show
our good intention in regard to these fears and conjectures,

and obvia-
ted by the
present safe
conduct. ce que voulons que nostre dit frere et ses gens aillent
le dit voyage et retournent seurement et sauvement
avec leurs biens, avons donne et octroye par ces presentes, donnons et octroyons, pour et au nom de mon
dit seigneur le roy de France et Dangleterre, et de
nous, de ses subjects, de nous et de tous autres tenans
le party de mon dit seigneur le roy et le nostre,
bonne et loyalle seurete et ferme asseurance a nostre
dit beau frere le duc de Bretagne, et a tous ses gens
quil voudra amener avec lui, tant de son sang que
autres, soient prelatz, barons, et autres, de quelconque etat ou condition quilz soient, venans ou dit
voyage, armez ou desarmez, avec leurs chevaux, har-
nois, joyaulx, et autres biens quelconques, en venant,
sejournant et retournant du dit voyage, tant de jour
que de nuit, a pied ou a cheval, par mer, eau douce
et par terre, sans ce quil leur soit mesfaict en corps
ny en biens, ny autrement, ny donne empeschement,

------

because we wish that our said brother and his people should
go upon the said journey and return surely and safely with
their goods, we have given and granted, and by these
presents do give and grant, for and in the name of my
said lord the king of France and England, and of us, of
his subjects, of us and of all others who belong to the
party of my said lord the king and ours, good and faithful
security and firm assurance to our said good brother the
duke of Bretagne, and to all his people whom he may please
to bring with him, as well those of his own blood as others,
whether they be prelates, barons, and others, of what
estate or condition soever they be, who shall come in the
said journey, armed or unarmed, with their horses, harness,
jewels, and other goods whatsoever, coming, remaining and
returning from the said journey, as well by day as by night,
on foot and on horseback, by sea, fresh water, and land,
that they be not misused either in body or goods, nor otherwise, nor that they experience any hinderance or incon-

ny destourbier en aucune maniere ; ny que nostre dit
beau frere, ou ses dits gens, ny aucuns deulx, soient
aucunement contraincts a faire aucuns octroiz ou promesses outre leur liberalle voulonte ; ains que lui et
ses dits gens avec leurs biens, ensemble ou par partie,
toutes voyes quil plaira a notre dit beau frere, sen
puissent retourner franchement et liberallement en son
pays. Et ce promettons et jurons tenir loyaulment, en
bonne foy et parolle de prince, sans jamais aller en-
contre. Et si aucune chose estoit attentee, ou innovee
par aucun des subjets de mon dit seigneur le roy, ses
alliez et les nostres, a lencontre de ceste presente
asseurance (ce que Dieu ne veuille !), promettons in-
continant et sans delay le faire reparer[1] bien et
deubment.

Pourquoy nous mandons et commendons a tous et
chacuns les dits subjets de mon dit seigneur le roy et
les nostres, soient capitaines de villes, chasteaux,

---

venience in any manner ; nor that our said good brother,
or his said people, nor any of them, should be in any wise
compelled to make any grants or promises against their free
will ; but that he and his said people, together with their
goods, may return freely and unrestrainedly to their own
country, together or severally, provided always that this
shall please our said good brother. And this we promise
and swear to keep truly, in the good faith and upon the
word of a prince, without ever violating it. And if anything be attempted or altered by any of the subjects of my
said lord the king, his allies and ours, in opposition to
this present security (which may God forbid !), we promise
that immediately and without delay we will cause it to
be amended well and duly.

Wherefore we order and command all and each of the
said subjects of my said lord the king and ours, whether they
be captains of towns, castles, fortresses, ports or passages,

---

[1] *Faire reparer*] Faire et reparer, MS.

fortresses, ports, passaiges, gens darmes et de traict, et autres quelconques, nostre presente seurete et assurance tenir fermement, sans lenfraindre en aucune maniere ; et faire franche entree et issue ez villes, chasteaux, forteresses, ports et passaiges soubz lobeissance de mon dit seigneur le roy et le nostre, a nostre dit frere de Bretaigne, ses gens et leurs biens ; et leur donner conseil, confort, ayde et assistance, si mestier est, et sils en sont requis.

Date.

Donne devant Meulent, en nostre siege, le douziesme jour de Fevrier, lan de grace mil, quatre cens vint deux.

Ainsi signe,

Par monseigneur le regent le royaulme de France, duc de Bethfort.[1]

MILET.

men-at-arms and archers, and all others whomsoever, to observe firmly our present security and assurance, without violating it in any manner ; and to give free entrance to, and issue from, the towns, castles, fortresses, ports and passages which are in obedience to my said lord the king and us, to our said brother of Bretaigne, his people, and their goods ; and to give them counsel, comfort, aid, and assistance, if need be, and they be thereto requested.

Given before Meulent, in our siege, the twelfth day of February, in the year of grace, One thousand, four hundred and twenty-two.

Thus signed,

By monseigneur the regent of the realm of France, duke of Bedford.

MILET.

[1] Philip, duke of Burgundy, issued a document exactly similar to that given above, with the exception only of the necessary alterations of style at the beginning. It concludes thus : " Donne en nostre ville de Lille, le vint cinquieme jour de Fevrier, lan de grace, mil quatre cens, vingt et deux, soubs notre seel secret, en labsence du grand." " Ainsi signe. Par monseigneur, le duc, en son conseil." A copy of this document occurs in the Portef. Fontanieu, 113–114.

## 1423.

RECEIPT by Robert Jolivet, abbot of Mont Saint Michel, for various sums received by him while in the service of the duke of Bedford.[1]

SAICHENT tuit que nous, Robert, par la permission divine, humble abbe du Mont Saint Michiel, chancellier et garde du seel prive de monseigneur le regent le royaume de France, duc de Bedford, confessons avoir eu et receu de Pierre Surreau, receveur-general de Normandie, la somme de deux cens deux livres, dix solz, Tournois, par trois voiages par nouz faiz en la compaignie de mon dit seigneur le regent.

Le premier, de Rouen a Amiens,[2] en lassemblee illec faite de mon dit seigneur, et de messeigneurs les ducs

A.D. 1423.
July 3.

Receipt for money allowed

for these several journeys.

---

[TRANSLATION.]

KNOW all men that we, Robert, by the divine permission, the humble abbot of Mont Saint Michiel, chancellor and keeper of the privy seal of my lord the regent of the realm of France, duke of Bedford, acknowledge that we have had and received of Pierre Surreau, receiver-general of Normandy, the sum of two hundred and two pounds, ten solz, Tournois, for three journeys by us made in the company of my said lord the regent.

The first, from Rouen to Amiens, in the meeting there made by my said lord, and my lords the dukes of Burgundy

---

[1] From the original in the MS. Gaignières, 266, fol. 93.

[2] This entry is further illustrated by the following extract from the Account of the Receiver-General of Normandy, contained in the Supplement Français, 9436-4, p. 350.

"A . . . . monseigneur Raoul le Saige, chevalier, conseillier du

roy, notre seigneur, au quel ont este paiez, par le dit receveur-general des deniers de la dite recepte, la somme de ij. cens, lxiiij. livres Tournois, pour xliiij. jours quil a afferme avoir vacquez ou voyage par lui fait, par lordonnance de mon dit seigneur le regent, avecques les autres conseilliers du roy et de mon dit seigneur, de la

## LETTERS AND PAPERS:

et de Bretaigne; ou nous avons vacque
dix sept jours, commencans le vj. jour
ement passe.

de Rouen a Paris, ou nous avons vacque
trois jours, commencans le xxviij. jour
avril.

------

where we were employed for the space of
beginning on the vj. day of April last past.
from Rouen to Paris, in which we were em-
space of three days, beginning on the xxviij.
month of April.

------

Amiens, et dilec
otoy et ailleurs,
pour estre et assister [a] certaine
journee tenue au dit lieu Damiens
par monseigneur le regent et monseigneur le duc de Bourgongne,
pour plusieurs grosses besongnes
touchans lonneur, bien, et prouffit
du roy et de son royaume, iceulx
jours commencans le derrenier jour
de Janvier, mil, cccc., xxiij. et
finans le xiij. jour de Mars ensuivant, tous inclus, au pris de vj.
livres Tournois, a lui tauxes pour
chacun jour qui chevauche pour
les besongnes et affaires du roy,
comme dit est cy dessus.

"Pour ce icy, par deux quittances de lui faites, la premiere le
xxiiij. jour de Janvier, cccc. xxiij.,
et lautre le xviij. jour de Mars
ensuivant, cy rendus.

"ij. c. lxiiij. livres Tournois."

To .... monseigneur Raoul
le Saige, knight, councillor of the
king our lord, to whom have been
paid, by the said receiver-general
of the finances of the said receipt,
the sum of ij. c. lxiiij. livres Tournois, for xliiij. days which he states
that he has employed in a journey
by him made, by the direction of
my said lord the regent, along with
the other councillors of the king
and of my said lord, from the city
of Rouen to Amiens, and thence
into Pontieu, to Crotoy and elsewhere, to be present and assist at
a certain meeting held in the said
place of Amiens by my lord the
regent, and monseigneur the duke
of Burgundy, for various great
matters touching the honor, the
good, and the profit of the king
and of his realm; the said days
commencing on the last day of
January, one thousand cccc.xxiij.,
and ending on the xiij. day of
March following, both included, at
the rate of vj. livres Tournois, to
him allowed for each day that he
shall be on his journey, for the
business and affairs of the king,
as is said above.

"Wherefore here, by two acquittances by him made, the first
on the xxiiij. day of January,
cccc. xxiij., and the other the xviij.
day of March following, here given
up.

"ij. c. lxiiij. pounds Tournois."

Et le tiers, de Paris a Troyes, pour le mariage de mon dit seigneur, ou nous avons vacque par lespace de xxv. jours entiers, commencans le iiij. jour de May ensuivant.

Lesquelz font xlv. jours entiers, au pris de deux nobles par jour, a nous tauxes par mon dit seigneur le regent, qui est le double de noz gaiges ordinaires; le noble compte pour xlv. s. Tournois. De la quelle somme de ij. c. ij. li. x. s. Tournois nous nous tenons pour content, et en quittons le roy, mon dit seigneur, le regent, le dit receveur-general et tous autres.

En tesmoing de ce, nous avons seelle ces presentes de Date. notre seel et signe de notre main, le iij^me. jour de Juillet, lan mil, cccc., vint et trois.[1]

Ita est,

R. ABBAS MONTIS.

---

And the third, from Paris to Troyes, for the marriage of my said lord, on which we were employed for the space of xxv. whole days, beginning on the iiij. day of May following.

The which make xlv. entire days, at the rate of two nobles by the day, to us allowed by my said lord the regent, which is double our ordinary wages, the noble computed at xlv. s. Tournois. Of the which sum of ij. c. ij. li. x. s. Tournois we hold ourselves content, and thereof we acquit the king, my said lord, the regent, the said receiver-general, and all others.

In testimony whereof, we have sealed these presents with our seal and signed them with our hand, the iiij. day of July, in the year one thousand, cccc. twenty and three.

So it is,

R. ABBAS MONTIS.

---

[1] The remainder of the receipt from this point is in the autograph of the abbot.

Lesquelx xlv. jours nous affermons avoir vacquez es dits trois voyaiges.

R. ABBAS.

---

The said xlv. days we affirm that we were employed in the said three journeys.

R. ABBAS.

---

## 1423.

WRIT from Henry the Sixth, ordering the collection of 80,000l. Tournois, being a portion of 200,000l. granted by the Three Estates of Normandy.[1]

A.D. 1423.
Dec. 19.

The Three Estates having granted 200,000l. Tournois,

HENRY, par la grace de Dieu, roy de France et Dangleterre, a noz amez et feaulx, Hemon de Belcnap, escuier, tresorier general, gouverneur de noz finances de France et commis au pays de Normandie, et Pierre Surreau, receveur general ou dit pays, salut et dilection.

---

[TRANSLATION.]

HENRY, by the grace of God, king of France and England, to our beloved and faithful Hemon de Belcnap, esquire, treasurer-general, governor of our finances of France, and commissioner for the country of Normandy, and to Pierre Surreau, receiver-general of the said country, greeting and love.

---

[1] From the MS. Fonds Franç., 9436-4.

Comme pour pourveoir a la garde, sceurte et deffence de notre duchie de Normandie et pays de la conqueste faicte par feu notre tres chier seigneur et pere (cui Dieux pardoint!), au recouvrement des places du Mont Saint Michel, Ivry, et autres, voisines de notre ditte duchie, que occupent noz adversaires, a entretenir et soustenir justice, et extirper les brigans, qui en divers lieux de notre ditte duchie ont fait ou temps passe, et font, plusieurs maulx, pilleries et roberies, notre tres chier et tres ame oncle Jehan, regent notre royaume de France, duc de Bedford, se soit transporte en notre ville de Caen, et en icelle ait fait assambler les gens des Trois Estas de noz diz duchie et pays de conqueste, lesquels gens des Trois Estas nous aient liberaument octroye et accorde la somme de deux cens mille livres Tournois, pour convertir et employer es choses dessus dictes; de la quelle somme nous, par ladviz de notre dit oncle, avons ordonne presentement

———— —— —— —— ———

Since, in order to provide for the keeping, safety, and defence of our duchy of Normandy and the country which was conquered by our late very dear lord and father (whom God pardon!), for the recovery of the places of Mont-Saint-Michel, Ivry, and others, contiguous to our said duchy, which are occupied by our said adversaries, for the preservation and support of justice, and the extirpation of the brigands who, in divers places of our said duchy, have committed in time past, and do commit, many evil deeds, thefts, and robberies, our very dear and well-beloved uncle, John, regent of our realm of France, duke of Bedford, has betaken himself to our town of Caen, and therein caused to be assembled the members of the Three Estates of our said duchy and conquered country, and these members of the Three Estates have liberally granted and accorded to us the sum of two hundred thousand pounds Tournois, to spend and employ on the matters above-said. And of this sum, we, by the advice of our said uncle, have at

et hastivement estre cueillie et levee la somme de quatre vins mille livres Tournois pour tourner, convertir et employer ou paiement des gens darmes ordonnez pour la garde, sceurte et deffence dicelle notre duchie et autres choses dessus dictes.

Si vous mandons, commandons et expressement enjoingnons, en commettant, se mestier est, et a chacun de vous, que, appellez des gens nottables, noz officiers et autres, acoustumez estre appelez en tel cas et en ce congnoissans, vous assez et imposez la dicte somme de iiij$^{xx}$ mil livres Tournois en et sur les villes, vicontez et receptes de nos diz duchie de Normandie et pays conquis ; en commettant de par nous en chascune ville et viconte et recepte personnes souffisans pour asseoir et imposer particulierement sur les habitans du diz lieux a ce contribuables, le fort portant le foible, sans en ce comprendre les gens deglise, qui autrement y contribueront ; les nobles frequentans les armes, ou

80,000l. of that sum is hereby required now to be raised.

---

this time appointed that there should be speedily collected and levied the sum of fourscore thousand pounds Tournois, to use, spend, and employ in the payment of the men-at-arms appointed for the keeping, safety, and defence of our said duchy, and the other things above-said.

Wherefore we order, command, and expressly enjoin you, appointing you, if it be necessary, and each of you, that, after you have summoned people of respectability, our officers and others, whom it is usual to summon in such a case, and who have cognisance thereof, you assess and impose the said sum of iiij$^{xx}$ thousand pounds Tournois on and upon the towns, vicomtés, and divisions of our said duchy of Normandy and conquered country ; appointing, on our part, in each town, vicomté, and division, persons qualified to assess and impose it in detail upon the inhabitants of the said places who ought to pay thereto, the rich helping the poor, without comprehending therein churchmen, who contribute thereto in another way ; nobles who follow arms, or persons who from bodily infirmity are

qui par impotence de corps sont excusez, selon la
coustume du pays, et les miserables personnes, en
maniere telle que icelle somme de iiij$^{xx}$ mil livres
Tournois puist venir ens et estre levee franchement,
entierement, et sans aucune diminucion, a notre prouffit,
pour estre convertie et employee a la garde, sceurte et
deffence de nos dits duchie et pays conquis, au recouvrement et delivrance des dits places, entretenir et
soustenir justice, et extirper les diz brigans, et non
ailleurs ; et en ce que dit est procedez et faictes proceder tellement et si diligemment que dedens le xv.
jour du moys de Janvier prochainement venant la
dicte somme de iiij$^{xx}$ mil livres Tournois puist estre
cueillie, levee, et apportee par devers vous, receveur, a
la quelle recevoir nous vous avons commis, et par ces
presentes commettons ; en contraingnant et faisant
contraindre tous ceulx qui pour ce seront imposez, a
paier leur impost ; et ceulx qui particulierement seront

---

excused, according to the custom of the country, and the
people who are in distress, in such wise that this sum of
iiij$^{xx}$ thousand pounds Tournois may accrue and be levied
honestly, entirely, and without any diminution, for our
profit, to be spent and employed upon the keeping, safety,
and defence of our said duchy and conquered country,
for the recovery and deliverance of the said places, to keep
and maintain justice, and extirpate the said brigands, and not
otherwise. And in this matter afore-said you shall proceed, and cause to be proceeded, in such wise and so
diligently, that before the xv. day of the month of
January next coming, the said sum of iiij$^{xx}$ thousand
pounds Tournois shall be collected, levied, and conveyed
to you, the receiver, to receive which we have commissioned you, and by these presents we do commission you ;
compelling and causing to be compelled all those persons
who shall be taxed for the same to pay their impost ;
and those persons who are severally commissioned and

commiz et ordonnez a la recepte a rendre compte de
ce quilz auront receu, par toutes voyes et manieres
deues et raisonnables, et comme il est acoustume pour
nos propres debtes.   De ce faire vous donnons povoir,
auctorite, et mandement especial, mandons et commandons a tous nos justiciers, officiers et subgiez que a
vous, et a chascun de vous, en ce faisant, obeissent et
entendent diligemment.

Date.       Donne en notre dicte ville de Caen, le xix. jour de
Decembre, lan de grace mil, cccc. xxiij. et de notre
regne le second.

Ainsi signe, Par le roy, a la relation de monseigneur
le regent le royaume de France.

R. VERET.

---

appointed for the receipt thereof, to render an account of
what they shall have received by all ways and manners
due and reasonable, and as it is usual to do in regard
to our own debts.   To do this, we give you power,
authority, and special command ; and we order and command all our justices, officers, and subjects diligently to
obey and give heed to you, and each of you, in so
doing.

Dated in our said town of Caen, the xix. day of December, in the year of grace one thousand cccc. xxiij.,
and of our reign the second.

Thus signed, By the king, at the relation of my lord
the regent of the realm of France.

R. VERET.

## 1424.

ARRANGEMENTS made by Charles the Seventh for the payment of the ships which conveyed troops from Scotland into France.[1]

CHARLES, par la grace de Dieu roy de France, a tous ceulx qui ces presentes lettres verront, salut.

Comme des lannee derrenierement passe, nous eussions envoye ou pais et royaume Descosse notre tres chier et tres ame cousin le conte de Bouchan,[2] connes-

A.D. 1424.
April 28.

Charles VII. recites the issue of his efforts to procure troops from Scotland,

[TRANSLATION.]

CHARLES, by the grace of God king of France, to all those who shall see these present letters, greeting.

Since, during the year last past, we sent into the country and realm of Scotland our very dear and well-beloved cousin, the earl of Buchan, constable of France, and in his com-

---

[1] From the MS. Fontanieu, 113–114.

[2] An account preserved in the Gaignières MS. 772–1, p. 541 (being the thirteenth and last account of master Hemon Raguier, the treasurer of the wars of Charles VII.) extending from 1 March 1424 to the last of September 1433, contains a few particulars about these Scottish auxiliaries which are worth notice, as giving authentic information of the troops which Charles had at his disposal at this time.

" DESPENSE.

" Premierement, le fait dune armee mise sus par le roy alencontre de son dit adversaire Dang-

leterre, et aucuns a luy rebelles et desobeissans, estans en son royaume ;

" Premierement ;

" Gens darmes et de trait sous messeigneurs les contes Douglas et de Bouchan, connestable de France, du pays et royaume Descosse ;

" Cest assavoir, que le roy, par lettres donnees a Bourges, le 24 Avril, 1424, apres Pasques, retint mes dits seigneurs Douglas et Bouchan ensemble au nombre et charge de 2,500 hommes darmes et de 4,000 archers du dit pais Descosse.

" Le roy, par lettres donnees a Chinon, le 9 Mars, 1424, retint monseigneur le conte de Richemont, connestable de France, an

table de France, et en sa compaignie nos amez et feaulz maistre Jehan de Crammach, esleu conferme de Cathenes, Francois seigneur de Grignaulx, chevalier, et maistre Guillaume de Quiesdeville, noz conseillers, Guillaume le Boucher, nostre escuyer descuierie, et Nicolas de Voisines, nostre secretaire, avec grant nombre de navires, pour charger et amener pardeca notre treschier et tresame cousin le conte de Douglas, et les gens darmes et de trait du dit pais Descosse,

---

pany our beloved and faithful master John de Crammach, [bishop] elect and confirmed of Caithness, Francis lord of Grignaulx, knight, and master William de Quiesdeville, our councillors, William le Boucher, our esquire of the horse, and Nicolas de Voisines, our secretary, with a great number of ships to carry and convey hither our very dear and well-beloved cousin the earl of Douglas, and the men-at-arms and archers of the said country of Scotland, who at this

---

nombre et charge de 200 hommes darmes et mil hommes de trait.

"Monseigneur Jehan Stewart, chevalier banneret, connestable de larmee Descoce, un chevalier bachelier, 150 hommes darmes, du pays Descoce de sa charge de la compaignie du dit conte."

---

EXPENSE.

"In the first place : in the matter of an army raised by the king against his said adversary of England and others in rebellion and disobedience to him, being within his realm ;

"In the first place :

"Men-at-arms and archers under my lords the earls of Douglas and Buchan, constable of France, of the country and realm of Scotland ;

"That is to say, that the king, by letters dated at Bourges, the 24 April 1424, after Easter, retained my said lords Douglas and Buchan, together with the number and charge of 2,500 men-at-arms and 4,000 archers of the said country of Scotland.

"The king, by his letters dated at Chinon, the 9 of March 1424, retained monseigneur the count of Richemont, constable of France, with the number and charge of 200 men-at-arms and one thousand archers.

"My lord John Stewart, knight banneret, constable of the army of Scotland, one knight bachelor, 150 men-at-arms, of the country of Scotland of his charge in the company of the said earl."

qui sont de present venuz en ce royaume soubz la charge et conduitte de noz dis cousins de Douglas et de Bouquen, lesquelz navirez estoient fretez jusques a certain terme, comme il appert par les lettres daffretement sur ce faictes ; et pour les doubtes et adventures de la mer qui tous les jours peuent avenir, nous, doubtans que plus longuement que le dit terme prins avecques les maistres du dit navire, noz dis cousin de Bouquen et ambaxadeurs, et aussi les dits navires ne demourassent par vent contraire ou autrement ; et affin que par faulte de paiement, ou bonne seurte dicellui, les maistres ne sen retournassent par deca, se il advenoit que il faulsit que ilz demourassent plus que le dit terme, eussions donne pouvoir a noz dits cousin and ar-et ambaxadeurs de traitter de nouvel avec les dits ranges for the pay-maistres sur le fretement des diz navires, et de nous ment of the obliger a iceulx de leur paiement, se le cas advenoit ships in which they quilz demourassent plus que le dit terme, lequel cas were con-est advenu. Et pour ce nous aient nos dis cousins et veyed.

---

time have come into this realm, under the charge and leading of our said cousins of Douglas and of Buchan, the which ships were hired for a certain time, as appears by the letters of hire hereupon made ; and in consequence of the dangers and accidents of the sea, which may occur at any time, we, being apprehensive that not only our said cousin of Buchan and the ambassadors, but also the said ships, might be detained by contrary winds, or otherwise, longer than the said term agreed upon with the masters of the said fleet ; and lest by default of payment, or good security for the same, the masters would not return hither should it happen that they were compelled to remain longer than the said term, have given power to our said cousin and the ambassadors to treat afresh with the said masters respecting the hire of the said ships, and to bind us to them for their payment, if it should so happen that they should remain longer than the said term, which event has happened. And in consequence of this our said cousins and

ambaxadeurs obligie en grans sommes de deniers a les
paier yceulx maistres xxxij. jours apres ce quilz seroient
arrivez en ce royaume es pays a nous obeissans, lequel
terme est desja passe, et neantmoins pour les grans
affaires que nous avons a present, navons pu paier ce
qui du estoit aus diz maistres, mais leur avons fait
requerir que ilz voulsissent attendre leur dit paiement
jusques a la feste Saint Michiel prouchain venant, et
que les peines contenues es dits lettres obligatoires
neussent aucun cours jusques au dit terme de Saint
Michiel, ce quilz ont accorde bien et voulentiers, parmi
ce que nous leur avons promis de confermer, ratiffier,
et approuver toutes et chacunes les obligations a eulx
faites par nos diz cousin et ambaxadeurs, et nous
obligier de leur faire baillier bonnes et seures assignations jusques a la somme a eulx due pour leur paiement, et de ycelles faire cueillir et lever a noz propres
coustz et despens ; et en outre que ou cas que faulte

ambassadors have bound us in great sums of money to be
paid to these masters xxxij. days after they shall have
arrived in this realm in the districts which are obedient to
us, which term is already passed, and nevertheless, in consequence of the great business that we have at present,
we have not been able to pay what was due to the said
masters, but we have caused a request to be made to
them that they would be pleased to wait for their said payment until the feast of Michaelmas next coming, and that
the penalties contained in the said letters obligatory should
have no force until the said term of Michaelmas, which
they have granted well and willingly, provided that we
would promise them to confirm, ratify, and approve all and
each the bonds to them made by our said cousin and
the ambassadors, and oblige ourselves to cause good and
sure assignations to be given to them to the extent of the
sum to them due for their payment, and to cause them to
be collected and levied at our own proper costs and expenses ; and moreover, that in case there were any default

y auroit au dit terme de Saint Michiel, en toute ou
en parte, nous serions daccord que les peines contenues
es dits obligacions faictes par nos dits cousin et ambaxadeurs eussent adonques cours pour la part et
portion qui leur en seroit deu ; savoir faisons que, considere les grans services qui nous ont ainsi fait les diz
maistres et ceulx du dit navire, nous, par ladvis et
deliberation de notre conseil, leur avons accorde et
ratiffie, accordons et ratiffions, toutes les choses dessus
dites.

Et premierement, louons, ratiffions et accordons toutes
et chascunes les obligacions ainsi faictes aus dits maitres
par noz diz cousin et ambaxadeurs, lesquelles nous
voulons tenir de point en point, le dit terme de Saint
Michiel venu, tant au regard du principle que des
peines en cas de faute de paiement total.  Et se faulte
y avoit en aucune partie seulement, nous voulons les
dits peines avoir cours *pro rata*, selon le portion qui
seroit deue.

---

at the said term of Michaelmas, in the whole or in part,
we should agree that the penalties contained in the said
obligations made by our said cousin and ambassadors should
then have effect as regards that part and portion which
thereupon should be due to them :—we made known that,
considering the great services which the said masters and
those of the said fleet have thus rendered us, we, by the
advice and deliberation of our council, have granted and
ratified to them, and do grant and ratify, all the things
which follow.

And in the first place, we approve, ratify, and grant all
and each of the bonds thus made to the said masters by
our said cousin and ambassadors, which we are willing to
observe from point to point upon the arrival of the said
term of Michaelmas, as well as regards the principal as the
penalties, in the event of the failure of the entire payment.
And if there be a failure in some part only, we are willing
that the said penalties should have effect *pro rata*, according
to the portion which should be due.

Et aussi leur avons promis et accorde, promettons et accordons, faire baillier bonnes et seures assignations pour le recouvrement de ce qui leur est deu, et les faire cueillir et lever a noz propres coustz et despens, et porter a La Rochelle au dit terme de Saint Michiel, pour destribuer a chacun de sa part et portion ; cest a scavoir,—

A Cosmes Aires de Ribdieu,[1] pour reste de ij M. xvj. c. escuz dor du coing de France, seize cens soixante quatre escus et demy.

A Lobbes Cheppy, pour reste de xix. c. xliiij. escus, seize cens quinze escus.

A Pierre Yvaignes, de reste de xj. c. lxiiij. escus, neuf cens quarente trois escus dor.

A Peruche de Lassau, du reste de M. lij. escus, quatre cens trente trois escus dor.

---

And also we have promised and granted them, and do promise and grant, that we will cause to be made and delivered to them good and sure assignations for the recovery of what is due to them, and to cause the same to be collected and levied at our proper costs and expenses, and to be conveyed to La Rochelle at the said term of Michaelmas, in order to distribute to each his own part and portion, that is to say :

To Cosmes Aires of Ribdieu, for the balance of ij. M. xvj. c. crowns of gold, of the currency of France, sixteen hundred and sixty-four crowns and a half.

To Lobbes Cheppy, for the balance of xix. c. xliiij. crowns, sixteen hundred and fifteen crowns.

To Pierre Yvaignes, for the balance of xj. c. lxiiij. crowns, nine hundred and forty-three crowns of gold.

To Peruche de Lassau, for the balance of M. lij. crowns, four hundred and thirty-three crowns of gold.

---

[1] *Ribdieu*] Or, Kibdieu.

A Parrotis de Boulmar, de reste de ij. M. c. liij. escus, dix huit cent vingt huit escus, trois quarts dor.

A Jehan Landede, de reste de xviij. c. lxiiij. escus, quinze cens quarente neuf escus dor, un quart.

A Othona de Lance, de reste de xvj. c. xliiij. escus, treze cens cinquante quatre escus dor.

A Jehan Fanches, de reste de xiij. c. iiij$^{xx}$xviij. escus, onze cens cinquante deux escus et demi dor.

A Perrot Loppes, pour Sanches Martines, de reste de xvj. c. xxiiij. escus, neuf cens dix sept escus dor, trois quarts.

A Jehan de Lassau, de reste de xj. c. xxiiij. escus, neuf cens trente neuf escus dor, trois quarts.

A Othona Loppes de Saciolle, de reste de xj. c. xxiiij. escus, huit cens soixante trois escus et demi dor.

---

To Parrotis de Boulmar, for the balance of ij. M. c. liij. crowns, one thousand eight hundred crowns and three-quarters of gold.

To Jehan Landede, for the balance of xviij. c. lxiiij. crowns, one thousand five hundred and forty-nine crowns of gold and a quarter.

To Othona de Lance, for the balance of xvj. c. xliij. crowns, one thousand three hundred and fifty four crowns of gold.

To Jehan Fanches, for the balance of xiij. c. iiij$^{xx}$xviij. crowns, one thousand one hundred and fifty-two crowns and a half of gold.

To Perrot Loppes, for Sanches Martines, for the balance of xvj. c. xxiiij. crowns, nine hundred and seventeen crowns of gold and three-quarters.

To Jehan de Lassau, for the balance of xj. c. xxiiij. crowns, nine hundred and thirty-nine crowns of gold and three-quarters.

To Othona Loppes de Saciolle, for the balance of xj. c. xxiiij. crowns, eight hundred and sixty-three crowns and a half of gold.

A Othona Dariolle, pour Jehan Gacie de la Cosne, de reste de xij. c. xlviij. escus, mil soixante escus et demi dor.

A Berthelemy de Saint Vincent, pour reste de iij. M. vj. c. liij. escus Tournois, trois mille quatre vings quatre escus dor.

A Jehan Go, pour reste de vij. c. iiij$^{xx}$xv. escus, six cens onze escus trois quars, et demi dor.

Au dit Jehan Go, pour autre reste xj. c. escus, huit cens cinquante huit escus dor.

Et a Tassin Pestel, pour reste de xvij. c. escus, seze cent vingt huit escus dor, deux tiers.

Et montent ensemble les dits restes a la somme de vingt mille cinq cens quatre escus dor.

Toutes lesquelles choses, et chacunes dicelles, nous avons promis et accorde, promettons et accordons par ces presentes, en bonne foy et parolle de roy, tener

───────────────

To Othona Dariolle, for Jehan Gacie of La Cosne, for the balance of xij. c. xlviij. crowns, one thousand and sixty crowns and a half of gold.

To Berthelemey de Saint Vincent, for the balance of iij. M. vj. c. liij. crowns Tournois, three thousand four score and four crowns of gold.

To Jehan Go, for the balance of vij. c. iiij$^{xx}$xv. crowns, six hundred and eleven crowns, three-quarters and a half of gold.

To the said Jehan Go, for another balance of xj. c. crowns. eight hundred and fifty-eight crowns of gold.

And to Tassin Pestel, for the balance of xvij. c. crowns, one thousand six hundred and twenty-eight crowns of gold and two-thirds.

And the said balances amount together to the sum of twenty thousand five hundred and four crowns of gold.

All which things, and each of them, we have promised and agreed, and do promise and agree by these presents, ¹n good faith, and upon the word of a king, to hold firm

fermes et estables, et ycelles entretener et accomplir tout par la forme et maniere que dessus, et mesmement paier au dit terme de Saint Michiel ce que reste a paier des dittes sommes, sans aller ne venir au contraire de ce ne des autres choses devant dittes en quelque maniere que ce soit. Et quant a nous, avons obligie et obligons par ces dits presentes au dit maitres, et a chacun deux pour sa part et portion, tous nos biens, meubles et immeubles, presens et a venir. Et oultre, pour ce que chacun des dits maitres pourroit avoir a faire de ces presentes pour la seurete de son paiement, nous voulons que par vertu du Vidimus de ces presentes fait soubz seel royal, avec la lettre daffretement et obligacion sur se faicte par noz diz cousin et ambaxadeurs, soit paie a chacun des dits maitres ce qui lui sera deue, comme sil avoit ce present original. Auquel Vidimus ainsi fait, voulons pleine foy estre adjoustee. En tesmoing de ce nous avons fait mettre notre seel a ces presentes.

---

and secure, and wholly to observe and fulfil the same in the form and manner above-said, and especially to pay at the said term of Michaelmas what remains to be paid of the said sums, without opposing or contravening this or the other matters before-said in any way whatsoever. And as for ourselves, we have bound, and do bind ourselves by these said presents, to the said masters and to each of them for his part and portion, in all our goods, moveable and immoveable, present and to come. And moreover, in order that each of the said masters may have an interest in these presents for the security of his payment, we will that by virtue of the Vidimus of these presents made under our royal seal, with the letters of freight and the obligation thereupon made by our said cousin and the ambassadors, there be paid to each of the said masters what shall be due to him, the same as if he had this present original, to which Vidimus, thus made, we wish that full faith should be given. In testimony whereof we have caused our seal to be put to these presents.

Date.

Donne a Bourges, le xxviij. jour de Avril, apres Pasques, lan de grace mil, cccc. vint et quatre, et le second de notre regne.

Par le roy en son conseil,

*Signe,* Le Picart, *avec paraphe.*

---

Dated at Bourges, the xxviij. day of April, after Easter, in the year of grace one thousand, cccc. twenty and four, and the second of our reign.

By the king, in his council.

*Signed,* Le Picard, *with a flourish.*

---

## 1424.

Mandate for the muster of troops to meet at Vernon on 3d of July, to proceed to raise the siege of Ivry.

A.D. 1424.
June 26.

John
Salvain,

Jehan Salvain, escuyer, bailly de Rouen, au viconte du Pont del Arche, ou a son lieutenant, salut.

Comme nagaires nous ayons receu certaines lettres du roy, notre sire, par les quelles il nous estoit mande que nous feissions crier et publier que tous contes, barons, chevaliers, escuiers, nobles et non nobles, tenans

---

### [Translation.]

John Salvain, esquire, bailey of Rouen, to the sheriff of Pont del Arche, or to his lieutenant, greeting.

Forasmuch as we have of late received certain letters of the king, our lord, by the which we were commanded to cause it to be proclaimed and published that all counts, barons, knights, esquires, nobles, and non-nobles, holding

¹ From the MS. Fontanieu, 113-114.

fiefz et ariere fiefz, et autres qui ont accoustume a poursuir armes, fussent pretz, montez et armez bien et souffisamment, pour servir le roy, notre dit seigneur, ou il leur seroit ordonne par tres hault et tres excellent prince, monseigneur le regent le royaume de France, duc de Bedford, lesquelles lettres nous ayons fait proclamer par tout le dit bailliage ou len accoustume a faire cris, et quilz fussent au xxviij. jour de May derrenierement passe, montez et armez souffisamment, selon les dictes lettres, devant nous a Rouen; et il soit ainsi que de nouvel nous ayons receu autres lettres du roy, notre dit seigneur, des quelles la teneur ensuit.

HENRY, par la grace de Dieu, roy de France et Dangleterre, au bailli de Rouen, ou a son lieutenant, salut.

*by virtue of letters of Henry VI.,*

Pour aucunes nouvelles survenues a notre tres cher et tres ame oncle, Jehan, regent notre royaume de

---

fiefs and arrear-fiefs, and others who have been wont to follow arms, should be ready, mounted and armed well and sufficiently, to serve the king, our said lord, where it shall be appointed them by the most high and most excellent prince, my lord the regent of the realm of France, duke of Bedford, the which letters we have caused to be proclaimed throughout the whole of the said bailliwick where it is customary to make proclamations, and that they should be, on the xxviij. day of May last past, mounted and armed sufficiently, according to the said letters, before us at Rouen; and so it is that we have lately received other letters of the king, our said lord, the copy of which follows.

HENRY, by the grace of God, king of France and of England, to the bailly of Rouen, or to his lieutenant, greeting.

In consequence of certain news which have come to our well-beloved and very dear uncle, John, regent of our king-

France, duc de Bedford, de la partie de noz ennemis et adversaires, eulx vantans voulloir venir briefment lever le siege mis devant la ville et forteresse Divry, et pour resister a leur puissance, et autres causes a ce nous mouvans, nous, par ladvis de notre dit oncle, vous mandons et expressement enjoignons par ces presentes que, incontinent ces lettres vues, vous faictes faire commandement a tous les nobles suyans et frequentans les armes, de quelque nacion quilz soient, en votre bailliage, sur paine dencourir notre indignation et de perdre et forfaire leurs fiefz, quilz soient montez, armez et arrayez souffisamment, tant hommes darmes comme archers, pardevers notre dit oncle en notre ville de Vernon, dedans le iij. jour de Juillet prouchain venant. Et ce faictes, et faictes faire et accomplir par tout votre dit bailliage, si diligamment et par telle maniere que en ce nait aucun delay ou deffaut; en nous certiffiant suffisamment sur ce.

———————

dom of France, duke of Bedford, from the party of our enemies and adversaries, who boast that they will speedily come to raise the siege which we have laid before the town and fortress of Ivry, and to resist their power, and for other causes us moving thereto, we, by the advice of our said uncle, command and expressly enjoin you by these presents that, immediately upon the sight of these letters, you cause orders to be given to all the nobles who follow and frequent arms, of what nation soever they be, within your bailliwick, under the penalty of incurring our anger and of losing and forfeiting their fiefs, that they be mounted, armed and equipped sufficiently, as well men at arms as archers, with our said uncle in our town of Vernon, by the iij. day of July next coming. And this you shall do, and cause to be done and performed throughout the whole of your said bailliwick, with such diligence and in such wise that herein there be no delay nor shortcoming; certifying us sufficiently thereof.

Donne a Pontoise, soub notre seel ordonne en lab- Dated
sence du grant, le xxiiij. jour de Juing, lan de grace, 24th June
M. cccc. xxiiij., et de notre regne le second.

Et estoient ainsi signees, Par le roy, a la relation
de monsieur le regent de France, duc de Bedford.

J. MILET.

Par vertu desquelles nous vous mandons que vous orders the
faictes commandement a tous les nobles suyants et muster of
frequentans les armes, de quelque nacion quilz soient, Rouen.
estant en votre viconte, que, sur la peine contenue es
dites lettres, ilz soient montez, armez et arrayez souffisamment, tant hommes darmes comme archers, par
devers nous, a Rouen, dedans le premier jour de Juillet
prouchainement venant, afin de aller en notre compaignie devers mon dit seigneur le regent dedans · le
iij. jour du dit mois de Juillet a Vernon. Et ce faictes
et faictes faire jouxte les dits lettres si diligamment
que deffaut ny ait ; en nous certiffiant au vray de tout

---

Dated at Pontoise, under our seal appointed in the absence of the great, the xxiiij. day of June, in the year of
grace M. cccc. xxiiij., and of our reign the second.

And they were signed thus : By the king, at the relation
of my lord, the regent of France, duke of Bedford.

J. MILET.

By virtue of which we command you that you give
orders to all the nobles following and frequenting arms, of
what nation soever they be, who are within your vicomté,
that, under the penalty contained in the said letters, they
be mounted, armed and equipped sufficiently, as well men-
at-arms as archers, with us, at Rouen, by the first day of
July next coming, in order to proceed in our company to
my said lord the regent by the iij. day of the said month
of July to Vernon. And this do and cause to be done
according to the said letters, with such diligence that there
be no failure therein ; certifying us truly of all that you

ce que fait en aurez, pour en certiffier souffisamment mon dit sieur le regent, ainsi que mande nous est par les dites lettres.

*Date.*        Donne a Rouen, le xxvj. jour de Juing, lan de grace mil, cccc. vingt et quatre.

COLLATION FAICTE.

*Signe,* DUBUST, *avec paraphe.*

---

shall have done therein, in order that my said lord the regent may be sufficiently informed thereof, as we have been commanded to do by the said letters.

Dated at Rouen, the xxvj. day of June, in the year of grace, one thousand cccc. twenty and four.

COLLATED.

*Signed,* DUBUST, *with a flourish.*

---

## 1424.

RECITAL of a writ from the duke of Bedford relating to the musters of troops to be employed in the siege of Guise.[1]

A.D. 1424.    JEHAN DE LUXEMBOURG, seigneur de Beaurevoir, Aug. 3.    commis par monseigneur le regent a recepvoir les Recital of    monstres et revues de la charge messire Thomas de

---

[TRANSLATION.]

JEHAN DE LUXEMBOURG, lord of Beaurevoir, commissioned by my lord the regent to take the musters and reviews under the charge of messire Thomas de Rempston,

---

[1] From the MS. Fontanieu, 113–114.

Rempston, chevalier, a tous ceulx qui ces presentes verront, salut.

Savoir faissons que a jourdhuy avons acertene des biens sens, loyaulte et bonne diligence de notre tres chier et bien ame chevalier messire Jaques de Leuyn, gouverneur Doisi, par vertu et povoir a nous donne et commis par mon dit seigneur le regent, dont la teneur est telle ;

JEHAN, regent le royaume de France, duc de Bedford, a notre tres chier et tres ame cousin, Jehan de Luxembourg, seigneur de Beaurevoir, salut et dilection.

Nous vous mandons et commettons par ces presentes, de par monseigneur le roy et de par nous, que les monstres, vues et revues des gens darmes et archiers

*a writ by the duke of Bedford for musters for the siege of Guise.*

---

knight, to all those persons who shall see these presents, greeting.

We let you know that to-day we have been informed of the good discretion, loyalty and good diligence of our very dear and well-beloved knight, messire Jaques de Leuyn, governor of Oisi, by the authority and power to us given and committed by my said lord the regent, of which this is the copy :

JOHN, regent of the realm of France, duke of Bedford, to our very dear and well-beloved cousin, Jehan de Luxembourg, lord de Beaurevoir, greeting and love.

We command you, and we commit to you by these presents, on the part of my lord the king, and on our part, that you make and receive, or cause to be made and received by your commissioners and deputies, from month to month, during the time that they shall be along with you in the service of my said lord the king, and of us, the musters, inspections and reviews of the men-at-arms and

du pays Dangleterre estant en la charge de notre
ame et feal conseiller et chambellan, messire Thomas
Rempston, chevalier, ordonne avec vous pour le siege
de Guise et autres places a lenviron, pour mettre en
lobeissance de mon dit seigneur le roy, vous faictes et
recevez, ou faictes faire ou recevoir, par vous commis
et depputez, de mois en mois, durant le tems quilz
seront ou service de mon dit seigneur le roy et de
nous, par devers vous ; en recevant et passant es
monstres, gens darmes et archiers souffisans, bien
montez, habilliez et arriez, selon quil appartient, et
cassant les autres qui ne seroient souffisans ; et les
noms de ceulx qui seront passes et receus a monstres
certiffiez, ou faictes certiffier, soubz votre seel ou de
vous commis, pour valoir et servir au paiement de notre
dit chambellan et diceulx gens darmes et de trait, comme
il est accoustume, et pour valoir avecques ces presentes,
ou Vidimus dicelles, en descharge dicellui qui faira le
dit paiement, comme il appartiendra pour raison.  De

archers of the country of England, which are in the charge
of our beloved and faithful councillor and chamberlain,
messire Thomas Rempston, knight, appointed along with
you for the siege of Guise and the other places round
about it, to reduce them into the obedience of my said
lord the king ; receiving and passing at these musters
sufficient men-at-arms and archers, well mounted, accoutered and arrayed, according to what is fitting, and
rejecting such others as are not sufficient ; and certifying,
or causing to be certified, under your seal, or the seal of
your deputy, the names of those persons who shall be
passed and received at musters, that they may be effective and serve for the payment of our said chamberlain
and of those men-at-arms and archers, as it is usual,
and to be sufficient, along with these presents or the Vidimus of the same, for the discharge of the person who
shall make the said payment, as it shall be fitting, by

ce faire nous vous donnons[1] a tous que a vous et a vous commis et depputez en ceste partie obeissent et intendent diligement.

Donne a Paris, soubz notre seel, le vj. jour de Juing, lan mil iiij. c. vingt et quatre.

Avons commis, et commettons par ces presentes, le dit messire Jaques a voir et recevoir lesquelles monstres et revues, et aussi pouvoir de les passer et casser, et generalement de y autant faire en toutes choses que faire pouvons par vertu du dit pouvoir dessus transcriptz.

Donne, en tesmoing de ce, au siege devant Guise, le *Date.* iij. jour Daoust, lan mil iiij. c. vingt et quatre.

---

reason. And to do this we command all persons to obey and give heed diligently to you and your commissioners and deputies in this behalf.

Dated at Paris, under our seal, the vj. day of June, in the year one thousand, iiij. c. twenty and four.

We have commissioned, and do commission by these presents, the said master Jaques to inspect and receive these musters and reviews, and also to have authority to pass and to reject them, and generally to do as much therein in all matters as we ourselves can do by virtue of the said power above transcribed.

Dated, in testimony thereof, at the siege before Guise, the iij. day of August, in the year one thousand, iiij. c. twenty and four.

---

[1] *Vous donnons*] We should probably read, "commandons."

1424.

WRIT of Henry the Sixth, ordering the collection of
an aid of 60,000*l.* Tournois granted by the Three
Estates of Normandy for the payment of arrears
due to the army at Michaelmas, 1424.[1]

A.D. 1424,
Oct. 12.

The king

after re-
citing how
unforeseen
expenses
had arisen,

HENRY, par la grace de Dieu, roy de France et
Dangleterre, a notre ame et feal escuier, Hamon de
Belknap, tresorier et gouverneur general de noz finances
en France et Normandie, salut et dilection.

Comme en lannee finie a la Saint Michiel derrenierement passe, notre tres chier et tres ame oncle
Jehan, regent notre royaume de France, duc de Bedforde, eust retenu, pour la sœurte et deffense de notre
dit pais de Normandie, et pour resister a noz ennemiz,
certain nombre de cappitaines, gens darmes et de trait,
et depuis, pour subjuguer et mettre en notre obeissance
les places occupees par nos diz ennemiz par sieges et

[TRANSLATION.]

HENRY, by the grace of God, king of France and of
England, to our beloved and trusty esquire, Hamon de
Belknap, treasurer and governor-general of our finances of
France and Normandy, greeting and love.

Since, in the year which ended at Michaelmas last past,
our very dear and well-beloved uncle, John, the regent
of our kingdom of France, duke of Bedford, engaged, for
the safety and defence of our said country of Normandy
and to resist our enemies, a certain number of captains,
men-at-arms, and archers, and after that, in order to
reduce and bring under our obedience, by sieges and otherwise, the places occupied by our said enemies, as well

[1] From the MS. Fonds Franç. 9436–4.

autrement, tant Gaillon, Yvry, le Mont-Saint-Michiel, Nogent le Rotrou, Senonces, Beaumont en Allencon, comme autres, que durant le dit an il ait fait assieger, (et par ce moyen ont este et sont plusieurs en notre obeissance,) comme aussi pour notablement et puissamment la compaigner pour estre et tenir la journee prinse a lencontre de nos dits annemis devant Yvry, et apres devant Verneuil ou Parche, ou mois Daoust derrenierement passe, laquelle, par la grace de Notre Seigneur, tres hault vaillance et diligence de notre dit oncle et de noz bons subgiez, qui la ont este en tres grant nombre, a este et est encores de tel honneur, bien et prouffit, comme nottoire peut estre a chacun, considere la puissance de nos diz ennemiz, ait convenu a notre dit oncle faire plusieurs retenues dautres gens darmes et de trait oultre le nombre avise au commencement du dit an, pour la garde du dit pais, pour les gaiges desquels et pour yceulx entretenir, lui

---

Gaillon, Ivry, the Mont-Saint-Michiel, Nogent le Rotrou, Senonces, and Beaumont in Alençon, as others, which during the said year he has caused to be besieged (and by this means many of them have been, and are, in obedience to us), as also in order that he might be notably accompanied when he went in force to be present at and take part in the battle given to our said enemies before Ivry, and afterwards before Verneuil in Perche, in the month of August last past, which, by the grace of our Lord, the most illustrious valour and diligence of our said uncle and of our good subjects, who were there in very great number, has been,, and is yet, in such honour, good, and profit, as is notorious to every one, considering the power of our said enemies, it has been necessary for our said uncle to make many retenues of other men-at-arms and archers, besides the number decided upon at the beginning of the said year, for the keeping of the said country, for the wages and support of whom he has been

LETTERS AND PAPERS :

34 LETTERS AND PAPERS:

a convenu prandre les deniers qui octroiez avoient este par les gens des Trois Estas de notre dit pais pour paier les souldoiers et gaiges des cappitaines, gens darmes et de trait primierement retenus pour la deffence du dit pais, tellement que nous et notre dit oncle sommes demoures en tres grans restes et debtes envers les diz cappitaines ordonnez pour la garde du dit pais.

(to meet which the Three Estates had granted an aid),

Pour les quelles choses rcmonstrer aux gens des diz Trois Estas, tant de France comme de Normandie, et aussi pour avoir conseil, advis et aide sur les besongnes et affaires de notre dit royaume de France pour ceste presente annee, commencant a la dicte Saint Michiel, notre dit oncle, par meure deliberacion du conseil, a fait, au premier jour de ce present mois Doctobre, assembler en notre dicte ville de Paris la plus grant partie des gens des diz Trois Estas de notre dit royaume et pais de Normandie; lesquelz de Normandie, oye la requeste sur ce a eulx faicte, nous ont

compelled to take the sums which have been granted by the members of the Three Estates of our said country, to pay the soldiers, the wages of the captains, the men-at-arms and archers who were at first engaged for the defence of the said country, in such wise that we and our said uncle are bound by very great balances and debts to the said captains appointed for the keeping of the said country.

To state which things to the members of the said Three Estates, as well of France as of Normandy, and also to have counsel, advice, and aid upon the business and affairs of our said realm of France for this present year, beginning on the said Michaelmas, our said uncle, after mature deliberation of his council, has, upon the first day of this present month of October, caused to be assembled in our said city of Paris the greater part of the members of the said Three Estates of our said kingdom and country of Normandy, and they of Normandy, having heard the re-

accorde ung pareil aide que a este celluy de soixante
mil livres Tournois, nagueres leve sur eulx ou mois de
Juillet derrenierement passe, pour le derrain paiement
de la somme de ii. c. M. livres Tournois a noz par eulx
octroiee a Caen ou mois de Decembre derrain passe,
. pour icelle somme estre convertie, cest assavoir, l. M.
livres Tournois, avecques la revenue de notre dit pais
de Normandie et conqueste des termes de Saint Michiel
et Saint Remy, derrain passe, et autres arrerages deuz
es dits pais et duchie, ou paiement des restes par nous
deues a cause des gages et regars des diz cappitaines
et souldoiers du dit pais de Normandie du dit an;
trois M. livres Tournois pour certaines necessaires besongnes advisees estre affaire a Harfleur et Honnefleur,
et le demourant ou paiement des soudoiers estans a
siege tant per mer comme par terre devant la place
du Mont Saint Michiel.

---

quest hereupon made to them, have granted us an aid
similar to that of sixty thousand livres Tournois, formerly
levied upon them in the month of July last past, for the
last payment of the sum of ij. c. thousand livres Tournois,
granted to us by them at Caen in the month of December
last past, in order that this sum should be spent, that is
to say, l. M. pounds Tournois, with the revenue of our said
country of Normandy and conquered country of the terms
of Saint Michael and Saint Remy last past, and other
arrears due in the said country and duchy, for the payment
of the balances by us due for the wages and rewards of
the said captains and soldiers of the said country of Normandy of the said year; three thousand pounds Tournois
for certain necessary matters which it was decided should
be done at Harfleur and Honfleur; and the remainder for
the payment of the soldiers who are at the siege, as well
by sea as by land, before the fortress of Mont-Saint-
Michiel.

6d7lí

**orders the levy of 60,000*l.* Tournois for the expenses of the war, &c.**

Si vous mandons, commandons et expressement enjoingnons que, ces lettres veues, vous mettez, assees et imposez sur les bourgois, manans et habitans du dit duchie de Normandie et pais de conqueste, le pareil et semblable aide que a este le dit autre aide de lx *M.* livres Tournois, pour le dit derrain paiement, par bailliages, vicontez et eslections et villes, comme en tel cas est accoustume de faire; non comprins en ce les gens deglise, nobles vivans noblement, frequentans les armes, ou qui par viellesse ou impotance de corps en sont excusez, et miserables personnes qui par pourete, selon la coustume, en sont exemptes; et icelle assiette envoiez par egalle portion pardevers les esluz, vicontes et officiers des lieux, pour les asseoir par paroisses, comme en tel cas est accoustume de faire, et les faittes cueillir et lever tellement et si diligemment que dedens le jour de la Toussaint prochain venant icelle somme soit apportee franchement, quittement et sans aucune diminucion devers notre bien ame Pierre

---

Wherefore we order, command, and expressly enjoin you that, when you have seen these letters, you affix, assess, and impose upon the burgesses, residents, and inhabitants of the said duchy of Normandy and conquered country, an aid like and similar to that other said aid of lx. thousand pounds Tournois, for the said last payment, by bailliwicks, vicomtés, divisions, and towns, as in such case it is usual to do; not including herein churchmen, nobles living as nobles, those who exercise arms, or who by age or bodily infirmity are excused therein, and distressed persons, who in consequence of their poverty are excused, according to custom. And this assessment you shall send by equal portions to the assessors, sheriffs, and officers of the places, that they may be assessed by parishes, as in such cases it is usual to do; and cause them to be collected and levied in such manner and with such diligence that before the day of All Saints next coming, that sum may be faithfully, entirely, and without any diminution

Surreau, receveur general des dittes finances de Normandie, lequel nous avons commis par ces presentes a icelle recevoir, pour la convertir et emploier es choses dessus dittes, et non ailleurs ; en contraingnans a ce tous ceulx qui seront a contraindre par toutes voies deues et raisonnables, comme acoustume est pour nos propres debtes. De ce faire vous donnons povoir et mandement especial ; mandons et commandons a tous nous justiciers, officiers, et subgiez que a vous et a voz commis et deputez es choses dessus dittes, leurs circonstances et dependances, obeissent et entendent diligemment, et vous y donnent et prestent confort et aide, se mestier leur est, et requis en sont.

Donne a Paris, le xij. jour Doctobre, lan mil, cccc. Date. xxiiij. et de notre regne le second.

Ainsi signe ; Par le roy, a la relation de monseigneur le regent, duc de Bedford.

*Signe*, DE RINEL.

conveyed to our well-beloved Pierre Surreau, receiver-general of the said finances of Normandy, whom we have commissioned by these presents to receive the same, that it may be expended and employed in the matters above-said, and not otherwise; compelling all those persons who are to be compelled by all due and reasonable ways, as is usual in regard to our own debts. To do this, we give you power and special command; and we order and enjoin all our justices, officers, and subjects to be obedient and give diligent heed to you, your commissioners and deputies in the matters above-said, their circumstances and dependences, and therein give and afford assistance and aid, if need be, and they be required thereto.

Dated at Paris, the xij. day of October, in the year one thousand cccc. xxiiij., and of our reign the second.

Thus signed, By the king, at the relation of my lord the regent, the duke of Bedford.

*Signed*, DE RINEL.

## 1424.

RECITAL of letters of Henry the Sixth, respecting
troops to be raised for the siege of Montfort.[1]

A.D. 1424.
Oct. 20.
———
Recital of
letters of
Henry VI.
respecting
the siege of
Montford.

JEHAN SALVAIN, chevalier, bailli de Rouen, au vicomte du Pont del Arche, ou a son lieutenant,
salut.

Nous avons a jourdhuy receu les lettres patentes
[de] notre souverain seigneur, seellees du seel de
leschequier, dont la teneur sensuit :—

HENRY, par la grace de Dieu roy de France et
Dangleterre, aux [baillies] de Rouen, de Caux, Dalencon, et Devreux, et aux viscontes des dits lieux, ou a
leurs lieutenantz, salut.

Comme puis naguieres que notre ame et feal conseiller, Jehan Fasto, chevalier, maitre dostel de notre

---

### [TRANSLATION.]

JOHN SALVAIN, knight, bailly of Rouen, to the viscount
of Pont de l'Arche, or to his lieutenant, greeting.

We have to-day received letters patent from our sovereign lord, sealed with the seal of the exchequer, the contents of which are as follows :—

HENRY, by the grace of God, king of France and England, to the bailiffs of Rouen, of Caux, of Alençon, and of
Evreux, and to the viscounts of the said places, or to their
lieutenants, greeting.

Since, not long ago, our beloved and faithful counsellor,
John Fasto, knight, master of the household of our very

---

[1] From the MS. Fontanieu, 113-114.

treschier et tresame oncle, Jehan, regent notre dit royaume de France, duc de Bedford, sest parti des parties
de devers Le Mans, dont il a le gouvernement, en entencion de aller devers notre dit oncle, noz ennemiz et
adversaires ont mis siege devant la fortresse de Montford, ou pais du Maine, en notre tres grant displai-
sance, et ou grief et prejudice de noz bons et loyaulz
subgiez du pais denviron, et plus pouroit estre se par
nous ny estoit brief pourveu de remede convenable.
Pour ce est il que nous, voullans a ce remedier par
toutes voyes et manieres a nous possibles, vous mandons, commandons et expressement enjoignons, que incontinent, ces lettres vues, vous, et chascun de vous,
comme a luy appartendra, faciez crier et publier de
par nous, que tous ceux qui ont accoustumez eulx
armer et suyvir les guerres, tantost et sans delay
apres la publication de ces dictes presentes, se traient
souffisamment montez et armez en notre ville Dalen-

---

dear and well beloved uncle, John, regent of our said kingdom of France, duke of Bedford, having set out from the parts
near Le Mans, of which he has the government, with the
intention of going to our said uncle, our enemies and adversaries have laid siege to the fortress of Montford, in the
county of Maine, to our very great displeasure, and to the
hurt and prejudice of our good and loyal subjects of the
neighbouring places, and might do more if by us there
were not made a speedy provision for a fitting remedy.
Therefore it is that we, wishing to remedy this by all ways
and means possible to us, order, command and expressly
enjoin you, that immediately after these letters have been
seen, you and each of you, as shall belong to him, shall
cause to be proclaimed and published on our part, that all
those who are accustomed to arm themselves and to follow
the wars, directly and without delay after the publication of
these said present letters, shall proceed, sufficiently mounted
and armed, to our town of Alençon, before our said coun-

con par devers notre dit conseiller et autres qui par
nous ou notre dit oncle sont, ou seront, commis a
lexpulsion de nos diz ennemis tenant le siege devant
icelle notre forteresse; en les contraignant, par la prinse
de leur corps et de leurs biens, et autrement comme
vous verriez estre expediant pour le bien et advancement de la besoigne.   Pourveu que les villes, chas-
teaulx, et forteresses dont ilz partiront, demeurent suffisamment garnies; non obstans quelxconques oppositions
ou appellacions que se pouroient faire au contraire.
De ce faire vous donnons pouvoir, auctorite, et mandement especial; mandons et commandons a tous nos
justicierz, officiers, et subgiez que a vous et a vos
commis et deputez en ceste partie, entendent et obeissent diligamment, et vous prestent et donnent conseil,
confort, aide, et prisons, si mestier en avez et requis
en soient.

Donne a Rouen, soubz le seel de notre eschequier,
le xvij. jour Doctobre, lan de grace, mil, iiij. c. xxiiij. et

---

sellor and others, who, by us or our said uncle, are, or
shall be commissioned for the expulsion of our said enemies
who hold the siege before that our fortress; compelling
them by taking their bodies and their goods, and otherwise
as you shall see to be expedient for the good and advancement of the business.   Provided that the towns, castles, and
fortresses from which they shall set out, shall remain sufficiently garrisoned, notwithstanding any obstacles or appeals
which might be made to the contrary.   To do this, we give
you power, authority, and a special mandate; we order and
command all our justices, officers, and subjects, that to you
and to your commissioners and deputies in this part, they
give heed and obey diligently, and give and afford you
counsel, comfort, help, and prisons, if there be need for it,
and they be required thereto.

Given at Rouen, under the seal of our exchequer, the
xvij[th] day of October, in the year of grace, one thousand,

de notre regne le second. Ainsy signe, Par le roy, a
la relacion des gens tenant leschequier.

GRESLE.

Sy vous mandons que les dits lettres dessus transcriptes vous fassiez cryer et publier bien et deuement,
ou lon a acoustume a faire . crys et publicacions en
votre ditte vicomte; en les accomplissant au surplus
selon leur forme et teneur, sy et par telle maniere que
deffault ny ait.

Donne a Rouen, le xx. jour Doctobre, lan de grace <sub>Date.</sub>
mil iiij. c. xxiiij.

Collation faicte,<br>
*Signe,* DUBUST, *avec grille.*[1]

---

iiij. c. xxiiij. and the second of our reign. Thus signed by
the king, at the relation of the keepers of the exchequer.

GRESLE.

Wherefore, we command you that the said letters above
written you shall cause to be proclaimed and published rightly
and duly, where it is the custom to make proclamations
and publications in your said vicomté, discharging them,
moreover, according to their form and purport, so and by
such a manner as that no default shall therein happen.

Given at Rouen, the xx[th] day of October, the year of
grace, one thousand, iiij. c., xxiiij.

Collated.

*Signed,*      DUBUST, *with a flourish.*

---

[1] In the same collection is another document addressed by Thomas Maistresson, esquire, bailly of Caux, to the vicomte of Monstervillers, which, after reciting the king's writ, as incorporated in the mandate printed above, proceeds thus :—

" Par vertu desquelz lettres, et pour les adcomplir, nous vous mandons et comettons, se mestier est, que diligeamment vous faciez cryer et publier par tous les lieux de votre dit vicomte et ressort acoustumez a faire crys, que tous

1424.

RECEIPT for money expended upon the English artillery employed by the earl of Salisbury at Meulan and Crotoy.[1]

A.D. 1424.
Nov. 4.

ROBERT COTES, escuier, nagaires maistre des ordonnances faittes pour treshault, puissant, et excellant prince,

---

[TRANSLATION.]

ROBERT COTES, esquire, formerly master of the ordinance made for the very high, puissant, and excellent prince,

---

Engloiz et autres estans ou dit bailliage, qui ont accoustume de prendre gaiges et soudoies du roy, notre dit seigneur, se traient diligemment montez et armez suffisamment, en la ville Dallencon devers monseigneur Jehan Fastol, chevalier, nomme es dits lettres dessus transcriptes, ou devers autres qui par le roy, notre dit seigneur, ou par monsr. le regent seront a ce ordonne, pour et a la fin disclaree es dits lettres royaulx; en les contraignant a ce par la forme et maniere qui est contenu es dits lettres, sy que diffault ny ait.

"Donne a Rouen, le xviij. jour Doctobre, lan mil, iiij. c. xxiiij.

"Collation faite,

"_Signe_,    DESQUETOT,

"_avec paraphe._"

---

"By virtue of which letters, and to accomplish them, we order and commission you, if need be, that diligently you shall cause them to be cried and published in all places of your said vicomté and jurisdiction,

in which it is accustomed to make proclamations; that all Englishmen and others being in the said baillywick, who are accustomed to take wages and pay from the king our said lord, shall diligently proceed, mounted and armed sufficiently, to the town of Alençon, before my lord John Fastol, knight, named in the said letters, transcribed above, or before others who, by the king our said lord, or by our lord the regent, shall be for this purpose ordained, for and to the end declared in the said royal letters, compelling them thereto, according to the form and manner which is contained in these said letters, that there may be no short-coming.

"Dated at Rouen, the xviij. day of October, in the year one thousand iiij. c. xxiiij.

"Collated,

"_Signed_,    DESQUETOT,

"_with a flourish._"

---

[1] From the MS. Fontanieu, 113–114.

monseigneur le regent le royaume de France, duc de Bethfort, certiffie lui avoir eu et receu de noble et puissant prince monseigneur le comte de Salisbury et du Perche la somme de six vingts escus dor dune part, et la somme de deux cents vingt livres Tournois dautre part, mises, converties, et employees es ordonnances de mon dit seigneur le regent, tant au siege qui fut devant le pont de Meulant, comme pour le siege de Crotay, et lesquelles sommes sont a rendre a mon dit seigneur le conte, comme le dit Robert dist et affirme.

*Receipt for money expended on the English artillery.*

Mil, cccc. **xxiiij.** le Samedi, iiij. jour de Novembre. *Date.*

*Signe,* TESSON et PREUDOMME, *avec paraphe.*

---

my lord the regent of the kingdom of France, duke of Bedford, certifies that he has had and received from the noble and puissant prince my lord the earl of Salisbury and Perche the sum of six score crowns of gold on one part, and the sum of two hundred and twenty pounds Tournois on the other part, disbursed, expended, and employed for the ordnance of my said lord the regent, as well for the siege which was before the bridge of Meulan as for the siege of Crotoy, which sums are to be repaid to my said lord the earl, as the said Robert says and affirms.

One thousand four hundred and twenty-four, Saturday, the fourth day of November.

*Signed,* TESSON and PREUDOMME, *with a flourish.*

1424.

Recital of an Indenture by which the duke of Bedford retains Sir John Fastolf for military service in the conquest of the comté of Maine.[1]

A.D. 1424. Nov. 27.

Recital of an indenture between the duke of Bedford and Sir John Fastolf, respecting military service in Maine.

A TOUS ceulx qui ces lettres verront ou oiront, Pierres Dubust, garde du seel des obligacions de la viconte de Rouen, salut.

Savoir faisons que lan de grace mil, quatre cent vingt quatre, le xxix. jour de Janvier, par Robert le Vigneron, clerc, tabellion jure en la dite viconte, nous fu tesmongne avoir veu une lettre, scelle du scel de monseigneur le regent, en fourme de denture, saines et entieres, desquelles la teneur ensuit :—

Ceste Endenture faicte par entre tres hault, tres excellent, et tres puissant prince, monseigneur le re-

[TRANSLATION.]

To all those who shall see or hear these letters, Pierres Dubust, keeper of the seal of obligations of the vicomté of Rouen, greeting.

We make known that in the year of grace one thousand four hundred and twenty-four, the twenty-ninth day of January, Robert le Vigneron, clerk, and sworn notary in the said vicomté, witnessed to us that he had seen a letter sealed with the seal of my lord the regent, in form of an indenture, whole and entire, of which the copy is as follows :—

This Indenture made between the very high, very excellent and most puissant prince, my lord the regent

[1] From the MS. Fontanieu, 113–114.

gent le royaume de France, duc de Bedford, dune part, et monsieur Jehan Fastolf, conseiller et grant maistre dhostel et lieutenant ou Maine et es marches denviron du dit monseigneur le regent, et gouverneur Dalencon, dautre part, tesmongne que le dit monseigneur le grant maistre est demoure devers mon dit seigneur le regent capitaine de quatre vins hommes darmes a cheval, sa personne en ce comprinse, et de deux cens quarante archiers, pour ung an entier, commenchant a la feste Saint Michiel derrainerement passee, et finissant a la dite Saint Michiel prouchainement venant, qui sera lan mil, cccc. vingt et cinq, pour emploier a la conqueste du dit pais et conte du Maine et des marches denviron, occupez par les ennemis et adversaires du roy, notre souverain seigneur, et du dit monseigneur le regent, et partout aillieurs en ceste royaume de France ou le dit monseigneur le regent le vouldra ordonner, pour lesquels ils aura et

---

of the kingdom of France, duke of Bedford, on the one part, and my lord Johan Fastolf, counsellor and grand master of the household and lieutenant of Maine and the neighbouring marches for my said lord the regent, and governor of Alençon, on the other part, witnesses that the said monsieur the grand master is retained towards my said lord the regent as captain of fourscore men-at-arms on horse, his own person therein included, and of two hundred and forty archers, for a whole year, beginning at the feast of St. Michael last past, and terminating at the said Saint Michael next coming, which will be the year one thousand four hundred and twenty-five, to be employed in the conquest of the said country and comté of Maine and the neighbouring districts, occupied by the enemies and adversaries of the king, our sovereign lord, and of the said lord the regent, and in any other place within this kingdom of France which the said lord the regent shall choose to appoint; for which he shall have and receive

prendra gaiges ; cest assavoir, pour chevalier banneret, capitaine de gens darmes, quatre solz desterlinz le jour, monnoie Dangleterre. Pour chevalier bachilier, auxi capitaine, deux solz desterlins. Pour homme darmes a cheval, douze deniers desterlinz le jour ; avecquez regars accoustumez. Et pour chacun archier, six deniers le jour, de la dicte monnoye, le noble Dangleterre compte pour six sols huit deniers desterlins, ou monnoye Franchoise coursable a la valleur ; a commencier iceulx gaiges du jour des premieres monstres que le dit monseigneur le grant maistre fera des dictes gens darmes et archiers par devant les gens de commis du roy, notre dit seigneur, ou dit monseigneur le regent ; et lui en sera fait prest et paiement, ses monstres faictes, avant la main, des deniers et finances tant de France, comme de Normandie, par lordonnance de messcigneurs les tresoriers et generaulx gouverneurs les dits finances, et par la main du changeur du tresor du tresorier des guerres du roy,

---

wages ; that is to say, for a knight banneret, captain of men-at-arms, four solz sterling a day of English money. For a knight bachelor, also being a captain, two solz sterling. For a man-at-arms on horse twelve pence sterling a day, with the customary rewards. And for each archer, sixpence a day, of the said money, the noble of England counted at six sols eightpence sterling, or French current money at this valuation ; these wages to begin from the day of the first musters that my said lord the grand master shall make of the said men-at-arms and archers before the commissioners of the king, our said lord, or my said lord the regent ; and ready payment hereof shall be made to him in advance when these musters have been made, from the money and revenues, as well of France as of Normandy, by the command of my lords the treasurers and governors-general of the said revenues, and by the hands of the banker of the treasurer of the treasures of war of the king our said lord, in Paris, or

notre dit seigneur, a Paris, ou du receveur-general des
dictes finances en Normandie, ou par lun deulx, pour
six sepmaines entieres, et a la fin du premier quartier
pour autres six sepmaines entieres, et dillecques en
avant de quartier en quartier, selon ses monstres ou
reveuez quil sera tenuz de faire devant les diz gens
et commis du roy, notre dit seigneur, et du dit
monseigneur le regent, de quartier en quartier, et toutes
les fois qui en sera requis devant les dits commis.

Et aura le dit monseigneur le regent auxi bien la
tierche partie des gaignes de guerre du dit monsieur le
grant maistre, comme la tierce partie des tierces dont
les gens de sa retenue seront a lui respondans de
leurs gaignes de guerre, soient ils prisonniers, proyes,
ou autres choses prinses, et tous autres droits accoustumez ; desquelz tierces et droitz ainsi deuz au dit
monseigneur le regent le dit monsieur le grant maistre
sera tenu de certiffier de quartier en quartier les diz
tresoriers et generaulx gouverneurs, le dit changeur,

---

of the receiver-general of the said finances in Normandy, or
by one of them, for six whole weeks, and at the end of the
first quarter for other six whole weeks, and thenceforth
beforehand from quarter to quarter, according to the musters or
reviews which he shall be obliged to make before the said
officers and commissioners of the king, our said lord, and
of my said lord the regent, from quarter to quarter, and
at each time at which he may be required thereto before the
said commissioners.

And the said lord the regent shall also have the third
of the spoils of war of the said monsieur the grand master,
as also the third part of the thirds for which the men of his
retinue shall answer to him from their spoils of war, be
they prisoners, spoil, or other prizes, and all other customary
rights ; of which thirds and rights due to the said lord the
regent, the said monsieur the grand master shall be bound
to certify from quarter to quarter the said treasurers and
governors-general, the said banker, or other person, to

ou autre quil appartiendra, quant il demandera ses gaiges, et den rendre compte en la chambre des comptes par le fermier du dit monseigneur le grant maistre, ou de lexecuteur ou executeurs de son testament. Et aurra icelui monseigneur le grant maistre tous les prisonniers, se aucuns durant le dit temps par lui ou aucuns de ses dits compaignons prins ; forspris et exceptez roys et princes, dont quilz soient, et filz de roys, et en especial Charles qui sappelle dauphin de Viennoys, et autres grans cappitainnes ou gens du sanc royal, et auxi cheftains[1] et lieutenants ayans povoir des diz roys et princes, et forspris aussi ceulx qui tuerent et murdrirent feu Jehan, naguerres duc de Bourgogne, et en furent sachans et consentans, ou ad ce conseillans et aydans ; ensembles les consentans, particippans, ou adherens de la traison faicte au duc de Bretaigne par Olivier de Blois et ses complisses ; lesquelz tous et chascun demourront au dit monseigneur

whom it may belong, when he shall ask his wages, and thereof to render an account in the chamber of accounts by the farmer of the said lord the grand master, or of the executor or executors of his will. And my said lord the grand master shall have all the prisoners, if there be any taken during the said time by him, or any of his said companions; save and except kings and princes, whoever they may be, and kings' sons, and especially Charles who calls himself dauphin of Viennoys, and other great captains, or those of the blood royal, and also chiefs and lieutenants having power from the said kings and princes, and excepting also those who killed and murdered the late John, formerly duke of Burgundy, and thereto were knowing and consenting, or were thereto counselling and aiding ; together with the consenters, participants, or adherents to the treason done to the duke of Bretaigne by Oliver de Blois and his accomplices ; all and each of whom shall belong to my

[1] *Cheftains*] Chrestains, MS.

le regent, et pour lesquelz il fera raisonnable agreement a cellui, ou ceulx, qui les auront prins. Moiennant lesquelles choses, le dit monseigneur le grant
maistre a promis et promet de servir le roy, notre dit
souverain seigneur, et le dit monseigneur le regent,
par lui ou ses commis souffisans, pour quy il voudra
respondre, et de employer les dictes gens darmes et
de trait a la conqueste du dit pais et conte du Maine
et des marches denviron, ou ailleurs en ceste dit royaume de France, ainsy et par les meilleurs voyes et
manieres quil advisera, et que mon dit seigneur le
regent lui vouldra ordonner. [Et] gardera, et fera
tenir et garder, a son pouvoir les peuple et subgiez
obeissans au roy, notre dit seigneur, de toutes forces,
violence, pilleries, roberies, prinses de vivres, chevaulx,
et autres bestaulx, et de toutes autres exactions quelzconques.

En tesmoing desquelles choses, a la partie de ceste
presente endenture demouree devers le dit monseig-

---

said lord the regent, and for whom he shall make reasonable agreement with him or them who shall have taken
them. These things provided, my said lord the grand
master has promised, and promises, to serve the king,
our said sovereign lord, and my said lord the regent, by
himself or his sufficient deputies, for whom he will answer,
and to employ the said men-at-arms and archers in the
conquest of the said country and comté of Maine and the
neighbouring districts, or elsewhere in this said kingdom
of France, in such wise and by the best way and manner
which he shall know, and which my said lord the regent
shall appoint to him. [And] he will hold and cause to
hold and keep, to the best of his power, the people and
subjects obedient to the king, our said lord, from all force,
violence, pillages, robberies, seizure of food, horses, and
other cattle, and from all other exactions whatsoever.

In witness of which things, to the part of this present
indenture which remains with my said lord the grand

neur le grant [maistre] icellui monseigneur le regent
a fait mettre son sceel.

Date.          Donne a Paris, le xxvij. jour de Novembre, lan de
grace mil, iiij. c. vingt et quatre.

Ainsi signe,

Par monseigneur le regent le royaulme de France,
duc de Bedfort,

R. VERET.

En tesmoing de ce, nous, a la relacion du dit tabellion, avons mis a cest present Vidimus le seel des
dits obligacions. Ce fut fait lan et jour premiers dessus
diz.

*Signe*, VIGNERON, *avec paraphe.*

--------------------

[master], my said lord the regent has caused his seal to
be put.

Dated at Paris, the xxvij. day of November, the year
of grace one thousand, iiij. c. and twenty-four.

Thus signed,

By my lord the regent of the kingdom of France, the
duke of Bedford,

R. VERET.

In witness of this, at the relation of the said notary,
we have put to the present Vidimus the seal of the said
obligations. This was done the year and day above-
mentioned.

*Signed*, VIGNERON, *with a flourish.*

## 1424.

ACQUITTANCE by Robert Jolivet, abbot of Mont Saint Michel, for money paid to him for attending the deliberations of the Three Estates at Paris.[1]

NOUS, Robert, abbe de Mont Saint Michel, conseiller du roy, notre seigneur, et de monseigneur le regent le royaume de France, duc de Bedford, confessons avoir eu et receu de Pierre Surreau, receveur-general de mon dit seigneur, la somme de trois cens cinquante quatre livres Tournois, pour le paiement de lix. jours entiers, que nous afermons avoir vacquiez ou voiage par nous fait par lordonnance et commandement de mon dit seigneur le regent, de la ville de Rouen en la ville de Paris, devers mon dit seigneur [le] regent, pour estre et assister aux conseaulx avec les gens de Trois Estaz des pais de France et Normendie, mandes par mon dit seigneur le regent et monseigneur le duc de Bourgongne estre en la dicte ville de Paris. Les diz

A.D. 1424. Dec. 21.

Acquittance for money paid for attending the Estates Paris.

---

[TRANSLATION.]

WE, Robert, abbot of Mont Saint Michel, councillor of the king, our lord, and of our lord the regent of the realm of France, duke of Bedford, acknowledge that we have had and received of Pierre Surreau, receiver-general of my said lord, the sum of three hundred and fifty-four pounds Tournois, for the payment of lix. whole days, which we affirm we have employed in a journey by us made, by the direction and command of my said lord the regent, from the city of Rouen to the city of Paris, to my said lord the regent, in order to be present and assist at the conferences with the members of the Three Estates of the countries of France and Normandy, which were summoned by my said lord the regent and my lord the duke of Burgundy, to be in the said city of Paris. The said days beginning

---

[1] From the original in the MS. Gaignières, 266, fol. 99.

D 2

jours commencans le xiij. jour de Septembre derrain
passe, et finans le dixieme jour de Novembre ensuivant, tous inclus, cccc. xxiiij., au pris de vj. livres
Tournois pour chacun jour, a nous tauxes et ordonnez
par lettres de garand de mon dit seigneur le regent,
donnees le xx. jour du mois de May, cccc. xxiiij., ex-
pedites par le tresorier, oultre et par dessus noz gaiges
ordinaires, qui sont au feu de mil livres Tournois par
an.  De la quelle somme de iij. c. liiij. livres Tournois,
nous nous tenons pour contens et bien paiez, et en
quittons le roy, notre dit seigneur, mon dit seigneur le
regent, le dit receveur·general, et tous autres.

Date.      En tesmoing de ce, nous avons seelles ceste presente
quittance de notre seel, le xxj. jour de Decembre, lan
mil, cccc., vint et quatre.

R. ABBE DU MONT.[1]

---

on the xiij. day of September last past, and finishing on
the tenth day of November following, all included, cccc.
xxiiij., at the rate of vj. pounds Tournois for each day, to
us allowed and ordained by letters of warrant of my said
lord the regent, dated the xx. day of the·month of May,
cccc. xxiiij., expedited by the treasurer, over and above our
usual wages, which are at the rate of a thousand pounds
Tournois by the year.  Of the which sum of iij. c. and
liiij. pounds Tournois we held ourselves content and well
paid, and thereof we acquit the king, our said lord, my
said lord the regent, the said receiver-general, and all
others.

In witness whereof we have sealed this present acquittance with our seal, the xxj. day of December, in the year
one thousand, cccc., twenty and four.

R. ABBOT OF THE MOUNT.

---

[1] This signature is autograph.

## 1425.

MANDATE from the Council of Normandy, addressed to the Governor of Verneuil, respecting the fortifications of that castle and town.[1]

TRESCHIER ET GRANT AMI,

NOUS avons sceu que, combien que plusieurs et diverses fois notre tres redoubte seigneur, monseigneur le duc de Bedford, regent le royaume de France, vous ait par plusieurs fois mande et rescript par ses lettres faire faire certains bolevers, avisez a estre faiz es chastel, tour, et yssue dehors de Verneuil; neantmoins vous avez este de ce faire delaiant, qui vous vient a grant charge. Et attendu la prouchainete des ennemis, et les maineres subtilz et deceptis moiens quilz tiennent par traison et autrement, est vraysemblable que tresgrant inconvenient en peult advenir, se en tres grant dilligence ny est pourveu. Et pour ce que

A.D. 1425.
April 24.

The fortifications of Verneuil to be augmented, the order for which had hitherto been neglected.

---

[TRANSLATION.]

VERY DEAR AND GREAT FRIEND,

WE have known that, although many and divers times our very dread lord, my lord the duke of Bedford, regent of the realm of France, has at many times sent and written to you by his letters, that you would cause certain bulwarks to be made, which it has been decided should be made, in the castle, tower, and gate of Verneuil; nevertheless you have delayed so to do, which has become to you a great imputation. And, considering the nearness of the enemies, and the subtle dealings and deceptive means which they employ, by treason and otherwise, it is probable that very great damage may therefrom arise, unless provision be made with very great diligence. And because at present there

---

[1] From the original in the MS. Gaignières, 557.

de present est aussi grant mestier que onques maiz de faire faire les diz bollevers, considere les nouvelles venues freschement a mon dit seigneur le regent, que le dit lieu de Verneuil est vendu, nous vous prions, et neantmoins chargons tres expressement depar le roy, notre seigneur, et mon dit seigneur le regent, sur tant que en vouldres respondre, et toutes excusacions cessans, que vous communiques avec le lieutenant et autres officers du dit lieu, et acomplisses de point en point es dits lettres de mon dit seigneur le regent, autrefois a vous envoies pour raison des dits bolevers, en faisant faire iceulx boulevers jour et nuit a la plus tres grant celerite que faire se pourra ; et a y besongner y contraingnes tous manouvriers de la dicte ville et viconte et autres convenables et necessaires pour le dit ouvrage, tellement que en toute haste ilz soient faiz, et que en doiez estre recommande, et que inconvenient nen advengne. Sachans que se diffaulte y a nous en deschargerons sur vous.

---

is greater need than was ever before to cause the said bulwarks to be made, if we consider the news which have freshly reached my said lord the regent, that the said place of Verneuil is sold, we pray you, and nevertheless charge you very expressly, on the part of the king, our lord, and my said lord the regent, as far as you can answer therein, and all excuses set aside, that you communicate with the lieutenant and the other officers of the said place, and accomplish from point to point the said letters of my said lord the regent, formerly sent to you respecting the said bulwarks, by causing the said bulwarks to be made day and night, with the greatest possible expedition ; and to effect this you shall there compel all the workmen of the said town and vicomté, and other persons fitting and necessary for the said work, in such wise that in all haste it be finished, and that therein you may be praised, and that no damage may arise therefrom. Knowing that if there is any shortcoming, we are discharged therein as regards you.

Treschier et grant ami, notre Seigneur soit garde de vous.

Escript a Rouen, le xxiiij. jour Davril, apres Pasques. Date.

Nous avons ordonne et commande a Montfort, lieutenant du maistre des eaues et forestz (que la acorde), vous bailler et delivrer bois pour les dits bollevers faire, tant et si avant que mestier sera. Si pourvoyes a la batement et charroy sans delay.

Les gens du conseil du roy, notre seigneur, in Normandie.

SEBIRE.

(*Dorso.*) A notre treschier et grant ami, le viconte de Verneuil, ou son lieutenant.

---

Very dear and great friend, our Lord be your keeper.

Written at Rouen, the xxiiij. day of April, after Easter.

WE have directed and commanded Montfort, the lieutenant of the master of the waters and forests (who agrees thereto), to give and deliver wood to you for the making of the said bulwarks, so much and so speedily as need shall be. Therefore see about the boats and carriage without delay.

The members of the council of the king our lord, in Normandy.

SEBIRE.

(*Dorso.*) To our very dear and great friend, the vicomte of Verneuil, or his lieutenant.

1425.

ACCOUNTS of Jehan Milet and Jehan de Pressy, respecting the siege and surrender of Moynier in Champagne.[1]

A.D. 1425.
June 24.
———
Accounts
respecting
the siege of
Moynier.

COMPTE particulier de maistre Jehan Milet, notaire, et secretaire du roy, notre sire, dun voyage par luy faict ou pais de Champagne avec M. Pierre de Fontenoy, seigneur de Rance, conseilleur et gouverneur des finances du roy, pour cause de la journee prise au jour de Saint Jehan Baptiste, 1425, pour la reddition de Moynier, que tient et occupe messire Eustache de Conflans.

iiij. livres Tournois par jour.

COMPTE particulier de sire Jehan de Pressy, conseilleur du grant conseil du roy, notre sire, dun voyage par luy fait en Champagne pour le siege de Moynier.

[TRANSLATION.]

THE private account of master Jehan Milet, notary, and the secretary of the king our lord, of a voyage by him made into the country of Champagne with M. Pierre de Fontenoy, lord de Rance, counsellor, and the governor of the finances of the king, in consequence of the journey undertaken upon the day of St. John the Baptist, 1425, for the surrender of Moynier, which messire Eustache de Conflans holds and occupies.

iiij. pounds Tournois by the day.

THE private account of sire John de Pressy, councillor of the great council of the king, our lord, of a journey by him made into Champagne for the siege of Moynier.

[1] From the MS. Fontanieu, 113–114.

vj. livres Tournois par jour.

Asseruit per juramentum ad burellum, et habuit cedulam cameræ.

Auditus ad burellum, die 19 Martii, 1425.

---

vj. pounds Tournois by the day.

===

## 1425.

### THE account of Philip de Morvillier, of his expenses in the service of Henry the Sixth.[1]

COMPTE particulier de monseigneur Philippe de Mor- A.D. 1425. July 31.
villier, conseilleur du roy, notre sire, et premier president en parlement, de certain voyage par lui nagaires Personal
faict pour le roy, notre sire, de cette ville de Paris en account of Philip de
la ville de Rouen, par devers monseigneur le regent le Morvillier.
royaume de France, duc de Bethford, pour aucunes
choses touchant le bien et prouffit du roy, notre

---

### [TRANSLATION.]

THE private account of my lord Philippe de Morvillier, counsellor of the king, our lord, and first president
in the parliament, of a certain journey of late made by him
for the king, our lord, from this city of Paris to the city
of Rouen, to my lord the regent of the kingdom of France,
the duke of Bedford, for certain matters touching the good
and profit of the king, our lord, or of his kingdom of

---

[1] From the MS. Fontanieu, 113-114.

seigneur, ou de son royaume de France, comme par les lettres du roy notre seigneur, donnees le dernier jour de Juillet, lan 1425, lesquelles sont transcrites au dos de ce present compte, peut plus a plain apparoir.

Et premierement,

### RECEPTE.

Receipt.     De Guillaume le Muet, changeur du tresor du roy, notre sire, par quittance de mon dit seigneur le premier president, donne le dernier' jour de Juillet, dernier passe, xl. viij. livres Tournois.

*In the margin.*  Corrigatur in Thesauro.

### DESPENCE.

Expendi-     Le premier president parti de cette ville de Paris
ture.        le Mercredi, premier jour Daoust, 1425, pour aller au
             dit lieu de Rouen, ou il a vacque, tant en allant au

---

France, as by the letters of the king, our lord, dated on the last day of July, in the year 1425, which are written at the back of this present account, may more plainly appear.

And firstly—

### RECEIPT.

From Guillaume le Muet, changer of the treasure of the king, our lord, by an acquittance of my said lord the first president, dated on the last day of July, last past, xl. viij. pounds Tournois.

*In the margin.*  Corrigatur in Thesauro.

### EXPENDITURE.

The first president set out from this city of Paris on Wednesday, the first day of August, 1425, to go to the said place of Rouen, when he was employed, as well in going to

dit lieu, sejournant illec, comme en retournant a Paris, jusquau Mardi, vij. du dit mois inclus, ou quel temps sont sept jours entiers, que, au prix de viij. livres Tournois a luy tauxes et ordonnez par le roy, notre dit seigneur, par jour, valent lvj. livres Tournois.

Summa expensæ per se, lvj. l. T. Sic debentur ei, viij. l. T.

Et debet per finem cujusdam compoti sui particularis soluti ad Omnium Sanctorum, 1424, de quodam viagio per ipsum facto sic de Paris apud Hesdinum, in comitiva domini regentis regnum Franciæ, ducis Bedfordiæ, xvj. l. T. Restat quod debet viij. l. T.

Redduntur regi istæ viij. l. T. in recepta communi compotus thesauri a termino Nativitatis, 1425, et ibi corrigitur, et sic quietus hic.

*In the margin.* Asseruit per juramentum ad burellum die auditionis hujus compoti vacasse in dicto viagio per tempus in serie designatum.

Auditus ad burellum, die ultima Augusti, M. cccc. xxv.


## *On the back.*

HENRY, par la grace de Dieu, roy de France et Dangleterre, a nos amez et feaux conseillers, les tresoriers generaux, gouverneurs de nos finances de France, salut et dilection.

––––– –– –––––– ––––

the said place and staying there, as in returning to Paris, until Tuesday the vij. of the said month, included, in which time are seven whole days, which, at the rate of viij. pounds Tournois, allowed and appointed to him by the king, our said lord, for each day, amounts to lvj. pounds Tournois.

HENRY, by the grace of God, king of France and England, to our beloved and faithful counsellors, the treasurers-general, the governors of our finances of France, greeting and love.

Nous, par lavis de notre grant conseil, vous mandons, commandons et expressement enjoignons, que par notre ame Guillaume le Muet, changeur de notre tresor a Paris, vous faites paier, bailler et delivrer, des deniers de nos dits finances, a notre ame et feal conseiller, monseigneur Philippe de Morvillier, premier president en notre parlement a Paris, ou a son certain commandement, pour tant de jours quil vacquera, tant en allant de notre dite ville de Paris en notre ville de Rouen, auquel lieu iceluy notre conseiller est ordonne aller avec notre ame et feal cousin le chancelier de France par devers notre tres cher et ame oncle Jehan, regent notre royaume de France, duc de Bedfort, pour aucunes nos affaires, comme en retournant en notre dite ville de Paris, cest assavoir, pour chacun jour quil vacquera au dit voyage, allant, sejournant, et retournant, viij. livres Tournois, que nous luy avons tauxee et tauxons par ces presentes, prendre et avoir des deniers de nos dits finances, outre et par dessus ses

---

We, by the advice of our great council, order, command, and expressly enjoin you that you cause to be paid, given, and delivered by our beloved Guillaume le Muet, changer of our treasure in Paris, to our beloved and faithful counsellor my lord Philippe de Morvillier, first president in our parliament in Paris, or at his certain commandment, out of the money of our said finances, for as many days as he shall spend, as well in going from our said city of Paris to our city of Rouen, to which place this our counsellor is ordered to go, along with our beloved and faithful cousin the chancellor of France, to our very dear and beloved uncle, John, the regent of our kingdom of France, duke of Bedford, for certain of our affairs, as in returning to our said city of Paris, that is to say, for each day that he shall spend on the said journey, going, staying, and returning, viij. pounds Tournois, which we have allowed and do allow to him by these presents, to take and have from the money of our said finances, over and above his ordinary

gages ordinaires; voulant que prest et payement luy
soit fait presentement au dit prix pour six jours, a
compter du jour de son partement de notre dit ville
de Paris; et apres son retour, entier payement pour
tant de jours quil affirmera avoir vacque au dit
voyage, comme dit est.   Et par rapportant ces presentes, avec quittance de notre dit conseilleur contenant affirmacion des jours quil affirmera avoir vacque
ou dit voyage, tout ce qui paie lui aura este a cest
cause, et au dit pris de viij. livres Tournois par chacun
jour, sera alloue ez comptes et rabatu de la recepte
du dit changeur par nos amez et feaux gens de nos
comptes de Paris, aus quels nous mandons que ainsy
le facent sans aucun contredit ou difficulte.

Donne a Paris, le dernier jour de Juillet, lan de Date.
grace, 1425.

wages; it being our wish that prest and payment be made
to him at this time at the said rate for six days, to count
from the day of his departure from our said city of Paris;
and after his return entire payment for as many days as
he shall affirm that he has spent on the said journey, as is
said; and upon the production of these presents, along with
the acquittance of our said counsellor containing his statement as to the days that he shall affirm he has spent on
the said journey.   And upon the production of these presents, along with the acquittance of our said councillor,
which contains a statement of the days which he shall
affirm he was absent in this journey, all that shall
have been paid to him on this account and at the said
rate of viij. pounds Tournois for each day, shall be allowed
in the accounts, and deducted from the receipt of the said
changer by our beloved and faithful keepers of our accounts
of Paris, whom we command that they do thus without
any contradiction or difficulty.

Dated at Paris, the last day of July, the year of grace
1425.

Par le roy, a la relation de son grant conseil.
JEAN MILET.

By the king, at the relation of his grand council.
JEAN MILET.

## 1425.

ACCOUNT of costs incurred in levying an aid for the expenses of the siege of Moynier.[1]

A.D. 1425.
Aug. 29.

Expenses of Jacques Braulart and Jehan, de Pressy.

COMPTE particulier de monsieur Jacques Braulart, conseilleur du roy notre sire, et president en la chambre des enquestes de son parlement a Paris, dun voyage par lui faict par lordonnance de monseigneur le duc de Bedford, regent le royaume de France, et messeigneurs du conseil, de Paris a Rheims, a Chaalons, a Epernay et au siege devant Moinyer[2], pour procurer

[TRANSLATION.]

THE private account of monsieur Jacques Braulart, councillor of the king our lord, and president in the chamber of inquests of his parliament at Paris, of a journey made by him, by the command of my lord the duke of Bedford, regent of the realm of France, and my lords of the council, from Paris to Rheims, to Chaalons, to Epernay, and to the

---

[1] From the MS. Fontanieu, 113–114.

[2] In the same collection is a document, of which the following is the title :—

"Compte particulier de Pierre evesque et comte de Beauvais, conseilleur du roy, notre seigneur, dun voyage par luy fait au pays de Champagne, en la compagnie de monseigneur le comte de Salisbury et du Perche, de monseigneur de Rance, et autres, envoyez au dit pays depar le roy, notre dit seigneur, tant

et lever, avec Jehan de Pressy, conseilleur du roy, notre
sire, certaine ayde imposee par le roy, notre dit
seigneur, ez dioceses de Rheims, de Chaalons, de
Troyes, et de Langres, et icelle convertir au payement des gens darmes pour le siege de Moynier, et
dicelles gens darmes recevoir les monstres. Pour le
quel voyage luy a ete tauxee la somme de iiij. livres
Tournois par chacun jour, outre et par dessus ses gages
ordinaires, comme par lettres du roy, notre dit seigneur,
donnees le 29 jour Daoust, 1425, dont la copie[1] est
ecrite au dos de ce present compte, puet plainement
apparoir.

---

siege before Moinyer, in order to procure and levy, along
with Jehan de Pressy, the councillor of the king, our lord,
a certain aid imposed by the king, our said lord, in the
dioceses of Rheims, of Chaalons, of Troyes, and of Langres,
and to employ it in the payment of the men-at-arms for
the siege of Moynier, and to receive the musters of the
said men-at-arms. For which journey there has been
allowed him the sum of iiij. pounds Tournois for each day,
over and above his usual wages, as may plainly appear by
the letters of the king, our said lord, dated the 29th day of
August, 1425, of which the copy is written at the back of
this present account.

---

pour le fait du siege de Moynier comme pour autres affaires."

"The personal account of Pierre bishop and count of Beauvais, councillor of the king, our lord, of a journey by him made into the country of Champagne, in the company of my lord the earl of Salisbury and Perche, of my lord de Rance, and others, sent into the said country by the king, our said lord, as well upon the business of the siege of Moynier, as for other affairs."

The accountant states that his expedition occupied forty-five days, that is to say, from 19 December, 1425, to 1 February next following.

[1] *La copie*] This transcript does not occur upon the present document.

## RECEPTE.

De Guillaume le Muet, changeur du tresor, par la lettre du dit monsieur Jacques Braulart, donnee le 3$^e$ jour de Septembre, 1425,     iiij$^{xx}$ iiij. livres Tournois.

## DESPENCE.

Le dit monsieur Jacques Braulart se party de Paris le 3$^e$ jour de Septembre, lan 1425, pour faire le dit voyage ; au quel il a vacque, tant en allant et venant par plusieurs fois ez lieux dessus dit, demourant illec pour besongner au fait de la dite commission, comme en retournant, depuis le dit 3$^e$ jour de Septembre jusquau 15$^e$ jour Doctobre au dit an, lun et lautre jour inclus, ou quel temps sont compris xliij. jours ; qui, ou pris de iiij. livres Tournois par jour a luy tauxez, comme dit est, valent viij$^{xx}$ xij. livres Tournois.

---

## RECEIPT.

From Guillaume le Muet, money changer, by the letter of the said monsieur Jacques Braulart, dated the 3rd day of September, 1425,     iiij$^{xx}$ iiij. pounds Tournois.

## EXPENSE.

The said monsieur Jacques Braulart left Paris on the 3rd day of September in the year 1425, to make the said journey ; in which he was employed, as well in going and coming at many times in the places abovesaid, remaining there to give attention to the execution of the said commission, as in returning, from the said 3rd day of September till the 15th day of October in the said year, both days included, within which time are comprised xliij. days, which, at the rate of iiij. pounds by the day to him allowed, as is stated, amount to     viij$^{xx}$ xij. pounds Tournois.

*In the margin.*

Asseruit per juramentum ad burellum die auditionis hujus compoti vacasse in dicto viagio per tempus in serie designatum.

Auditus ad burellum, die 22 Octobris, 1425.

---

1426.

### Account of the expenses incurred by the First President of the Parliament of Paris during his journey into England along with the duke of Bedford.[1]

COMPTE particulier de monseigneur, monseigneur Philippe de Morvilliers, conseiller du roy, notre seigneur, et premier president en parlement, dun voyage par lui fait pour le roy, notre dit seigneur, de cette ville de Paris au royaume Dangleterre, en la compagnie de monseigneur le regent le royaulme de France, duc de Bedford, pour aucunes causes qui grandement touchent le bien du roy, notre dit seigneur, et de son royaume.

A.D. 1426.
April 6.

Account of Philippe de Morvilliers.

---

[TRANSLATION.]

THE private account of my lord Philippe de Morvilliers, councillor of the king, our lord, and first president in the parliament, of a journey by him made for the king, our said lord, from this city of Paris to the realm of England, in the company of my lord the regent of the realm of France, the duke of Bedford, for certain causes which greatly affect the good of the king, our said lord, and of his kingdom.

---

[1] From the MS. Fontanieu, 113–114.

Et premierement,

### RECETTE.

De Guillaume le Muet, changeur du tresor du roy, notre seigneur, a Paris, par quittance du dit conseiller, donnee le 24 jour de Novembre, 1425,

vij.<sup>c</sup> xx. livres Tournois.

### DESPENCE.

Le dit monseigneur le premier president a vaque ou dit voyage, tant en allant, sejournant et retournant, lespace de vj<sup>xx</sup> ij. jours entiers, commences le 3 jour de Novembre, dernier passe, que il parti de cette ville de Paris pour aller au dit voyage, et finissant le 3 jour Davril, lan 1426, apres Pasques, que il retourna au dit lieu de Paris, au retour du dit voyage, lun et lautre inclus, qui, a lestimation de viij. livres Tournois par

---

And in the first place—

### THE RECEIPT.

Of Guillaume le Muet, money changer of the king, our lord, at Paris, by the acquittance of the said councillor, dated the 24th day of November 1425,

vii. c. xx. pounds Tournois.

### OUTLAY.

The said lord, the first president, has been employed in the said journey, as well in going, tarrying, and returning, for the space of vj<sup>xx</sup> ij. whole days, beginning on the 3rd day of November, last past, on which he set out from this city of Paris to go on the said journey, and finishing on the 3rd day of April in the year 1426, after Easter, when he returned to the said place of Paris, on his return from the said journey, both days included, which, at the rate of

jour a luy tauxes par chacun jour quil vacqueroit au
dit voyage, comme par les lettres du roy, notre dit
seigneur, transcriptes [1] au dos de ce present compte,
puet apparoir, montent ix$^c$ lxxvj. livres Tournois. Pour
ce ix$^c$ lxxvj. livres Tournois.

    Summa expensæ per se, ix$^c$ lxxvj. livres
    Tournois.
    Sic debentur ei ij$^c$ lxvj. livres Tournois.
Habuit cedulam cameræ vj° Aprilis, 1426, post, Pascha.

### In the margin.

Dominus primus præsidens præsens ad burellum asseruit per juramentum, die auditionis compoti, vacasse
in dicto viagio per tempus in serie designatum.
 Solutus est per Thesaurarium ad Sanctum Joannem,
1426. Auditus ad burellum, 5° die Aprilis, 1426, post
Pascha.

---

viij. pounds Tournois by the day to him allowed for each
day on which he should be employed in the said journey,
as by the letters of the king, our said lord, copied on the
back of this present account, may appear, amount to
     ix. c. lxxvj. pounds Tournois.
   Consequently ix. c. lxxvj. pounds Tournois.

---

[1] *Transcriptes*] This transcript is not extant in the MS. whence the
present document is derived.

## 1427.

LETTER from Richard de Beauchamp, earl of Warwick,
to John Salvain, bailly of Rouen, requesting immediate reinforcements.[1]

A.D. 1427.    *(Coppie.)* LE conte de Warrewyk et Daubemalle,
March 19.  cappitaine et lieutenant general du roy, et de mon-
_____   seigneur le regent, etc.
Immediate
reinforce-
ments       Tres chier et bien ame.  Pour ce que presentement
urgently
demanded. nous sont venues certaines nouvelles que devons estre
          combatus Samedi prouchain venant, ou Dimence au
          plus tart, par les ennemis et adversaries du roy, entre
          les queulx seront et doivent estre pour tout certain
          cellui qui se dit dalphin, le duc de Bretaigne, Artus
          de Bretaigne, et autres, tous ensemble et comme chiefz,

---

## [TRANSLATION.]

*Copy.*  THE earl of Warwick and Albemarle, captain
and lieutenant-general of the king and of my lord the
regent, etc.

Very dear and well beloved.  Forasmuch as at this present
time certain news have come to us that we shall be attacked
on Saturday next ensuing, or on Sunday at the very latest,
by the enemies and adversaries of the king, among whom
there will be most certainly the person who styles himself
the dauphin, the duke of Bretaigne, Arthur of Bretaigne, and

---

[1] From the contemporaneous copy in MS. Gaignières, 557.

nous vous mandons, chargons, et tres expressement
enjoingnons depar le roy, mon dit seigneur, le regent
et nous, que venez hastivement par deca nuit et jour,
acompaignie de plus grant nombre de gens que re-
truvrer purrez et facez, et faictes faire. Cependant
commandons tres expres a tous les Anglois et autres
demourans en votre bailliage, tant hommes darmes que
gens de trait, que incontinent, a toute haste et dilligence a eulx possible, tant de jour que de nuyt, ilz
viennent devers nous les mieulx habilles que pourront,
et y soient dedens le dit jour de Samedi, ou le Dymence,
tres parfaictement matin, sur paine destre repputez
rebelles et desobbessans au roy, et sur tout le service
que ilz lui doibvent faire, et en ce ne faire faulte sur
tout ce que desirez et amez le bien du roy, et de sa
seigneurie, et votre honneur; en faisant crier ban en
icellui votre baille. Tres chier et bien ame, notre
Seigneur soit garde de vous.

---

others all together, and as leaders, we command, charge, and
most straightly enjoin you on the part of the king, my
said lord, the regent, and ourselves, that you come hastily
hither, night and day, accompanied by the greatest number
of people you can find and cause to come. Nevertheless
we expressly command all the English and other inhabitants of your bailiwick, as well men-of-arms as archers,
that forthwith, with all the haste and diligence to them
possible, as well by day as by night, they come to us,
arrayed to their best ability, and be there by the said Saturday, or on Sunday very early in the morning, under pain
of being accounted rebels and disobedient to the king, and
by all the service which they are bound to do him; and
herein do not fail, as you desire and love the welfare of the
king and his sovereignty, and your own honor; causing
proclamation hereof to be made in this your bailliwick. Very
dear and well-beloved, our Lord be your protector.

Escripte tres en haste, en notre host devant Pontorsson,[1] le xix. jour de Mars, heure de midi.

> *Ainsi signe,* J. VOULLANT, etc.

En subscripcion des dits lettres est escript ce que
ensuit : A notre chier et bien ame messire Jehan
Salvain, bailli de Rouen, ou a son lieutenant.

> COLLACION FAITE.

---

Written in great haste, in our army before Pontorson,
the xix. day of March, at the hour of noon.

> *Signed thus,* J. VULLANT, etc.

As the address of this said letter was written what follows :
To our dear and wellbeloved messire Jehan Salvain, bailly
of Rouen, or to his lieutenant.

> COLLATED.

---

[1] An original receipt given by John Harebotel, master of the ordnance and artillery of the regent of France, to the receiver-general of Normandy, Pierre Surreau, states that the former had received from the latter 200*l.* Tournois, "pour " tourner et convertir au paiement " des gaiges des cannoniers, macons " et charpentiers, et autres choses " necessaires de mon dit office, pour " le siege de Pontorson." Dated 17 February, 1426–27.

To this document (which is preserved in the Cabinet des Titres at Paris) is appended a seal in red wax, on which is a shield with the bearing of three hounds, two and one; with the crest, a dog's head. The legend is, " S. Jehan Hare- " botel."

## 1427.

RECITAL of a Mandate by Richard de Beauchamp, earl
of Warwick, summoning troops to meet lord Scales
at Avranches.[1]

JEHAN SALVAIN, chevalier, bailli de Rouen et de
Gisors, au viconte de Pontaudemer, ou a son lieutenant,
salut.

Nous avons au jour duy receu les letters de tres
hault et puissant seigneur, monseigneur le conte de
Warrewyk et Daubmalle, cappitaine et lieutenant
general du roy, notre seigneur, et de monseigneur le
regent, desquelles la teneur ensuit.

RICHARD de Beauchamp, conte le Warrewik et Daubemalle, seigneur le Despensier et de Lisle, cappitaine et
lieutenant general du roy, notre seigneur, et de mon-

A.D. 1427.
March 22.
___
Recital of a
mandate
for the
levying of
troops to
meet lord
Scales at
Avranches.

[TRANSLATION.]

JEHAN SALVAIN, knight, bailly of Rouen and Gisors, to
the vicomte of Pontaudemer, or his lieutenant, greeting.

We have to-day received letters from the very high and
puissant lord, my lord the earl of Warwick and Albemarle,
captain and lieutenant-general of the king, our lord, and
of my lord the regent, of which the contents follow.

RICHARD de Beauchamp, earl of Warwick and Albemarle,
lord le Despensier, and de Lisle, captain and lieutenant-
general of the king, our lord, and of my lord the regent,

---

[1] From the contemporaneous official copy in MS. Gaignières, 557.
A small fragment of a seal in
brown wax remains. This document is written upon paper,
of which the water-mark is an
angel with expanded wings.

seigneur le regent, sur le fait de la guerre en Normendie, Anjou, Le Mans, et les marches de Bretaigne, au bailli de Rouen, ou a son lieutenant, salut.

Pour ce que est venu a notre vraye congnoissance que les ennemis et adversairez du roy sont assemblez en grant nombre prouchaine de nos marches, en entencion de nous venir combatre, ou dardoir, courir et guerper le pays du roy, comme len dit ; nous, desirans obvier aux inconveniens que atant de ce pourroient ensuir et remedier sur ce, vous mandons, chargons, et tres expressement enjoignons de par le roy, mon dit seigneur, le regent, et nous, que tantost et incontinent, ces presentes par vous receues, vous faces assembler par crye et autrement, tous Anglois vivans sur le pais et non estans en garnison, et autres suyvans les armes ; et iceulx admener hastivement et sans delay, a ce quilz soient dedens xxiiij. jour de ce present moys au plus tart a Avranches, devers notre tres chier et ame cousin

---

in the matter of the war in Normandy, Anjou, Le Mans, and the marches of Bretaigne, to the bailly of Rouen, or his lieutenant, greeting.

Since we have been fully informed that the enemies and adversaries of the king are assembled in great numbers near our marches, with the intention of coming to fight us, or to burn, to overrun, and to occupy the country of the king, as it is said ; we, wishing as well to obviate the damages which might follow from this, and to provide a remedy for the same, command, charge and most expressly enjoin you, on the part of the king, my said lord, the regent and ourselves, that immediately and forthwith that these presents shall be received by you, you cause to be assembled, by proclamation and otherwise, all the English living in the country and not being in garrison, and others following arms ; and lead them hastily and without delay, so that they may be on the xxiiij. day of this present month at the latest, at Avranches, with our very dear and

le sire de Scalles, pour tenir les champs en son compaignie, et resister aux dampnables propos et malles
enterprinses des diz ennemis, a la conservation de la
seigneurie du roy, ses pays et subgiez. En contraignant
ad ce faire iceulx Anglois et nobles venir par la prinse
de leurs corps et expliccation de leurs biens, et sur
paine de la confiscation diceulx, dont faire vous donnons povoir, commission, et mandement especial par
ces presentes. Mandons et commandons a tous les
vrays hommes, liges et subgez du roy et mon dit
seigneur le regent, que a vous, voz commis et depputez
en ce faisant, obeissent bien et deuement, vous prestent
et donnent conseil, confort, aide, et prisons, se mester
est, et par vous en soit requis.

Donne en notre host devant Pontorsson, le xvij. jour
de Mars, lan mil iiij. c. et xxvj.

Ainsi signe, Par monsieur le conte, cappitaine et
lieutenant general.

J. VOULLENT.

---

beloved cousin, the lord of Scales, to keep the field in his
company, and resist the damnable purposes and wicked
enterprises of the said enemies, to the preservation of the
lordship of the king, his country and subjects. Constraining
those English and nobles to come and do this, by taking
their persons and the seizure of their goods, and under pain
of the confiscation of the same, to do which we give you
power, commission, and special command by these presents.
We order and command all the true liegemen and subjects of
the king and my said lord the regent, that they obey well
and duly you, your commissioners and deputies in so
doing; lending and giving you counsel, comfort, aid, and
prisons, if need be, and they thereto be by you required.

Given in our army, before Pontorson, the xvij. day of
March, the year one thousand iiij. c. and xxvj.

Thus signed, By my lord the earl, captain and lieutenant-
general.

J. VOULLENT.

Sy vous mandons et commandons tres expressement que tantost et incontinent, ces presentes par vous receues, vous faces assembler par cry et autrement tous les Anglois vivans sur le pays et non estans en garnison, et autres suyvans les armes, et iceulx envoyes hastivement et sans delay a ce quilz soient dedens le xxiiij. jour de ce present moys au plus tart a Avranches devers monseigneur Descalles, pour tenir les champs en sa compaignie et resister aux dampnables proopos et malles enterprinses des dits ennemis, a la conservacion de la seigneurie du roy, notre seigneur, ses pais et subges. En contraignant a ce iceulx Angles et nobles venir, par la prinse de leur corps et expleccacion de leurs biens, et sur paine de la confiscacion diceulx, en acomplissement ou surplus des dictes lettres, jouxte leur fourme et teneur. Mandons et chargons en oultre, de par le roy, notre seigneur, a tous les cappitaines, souldoyers et gens de garnison de votre dit viconte, et autres qa ce par vous seront requis, que ilz soient

-----

Whereupon we order and command you very expressly that forthwith and immediately that these presents are by you received, you will cause to be assembled by proclamation and otherwise all the English living in the country and not being in garrison, and others following arms, and send them hastily and without delay, so that they may be by the xxiiij. day of this present month at the latest at Avranches, with my lord Scales, to hold the field in his company and resist the damnable purposes and wicked enterprises of the said enemies, to the preservation of the sovereignty of the king our lord, his country and subjects. Constraining those English and nobles to come, by the seizure of their persons and the arrest of their goods, and under penalty of confiscation of the same, in accomplishing what follows in the said letters, according to their form and import. We moreover order and charge, on the part of the king, our lord, all captains, soldiers and men of the garrison of your said vicomté and others who shall be required by you

en votre confort et aide a ces choses acomplir, mettre a execucion le contenu es dictes lettres, ce faisans sy ce par telle maniere que deffault ny ayt. Et nous certiffiant de la reception des presentes, et de tout cc que fait en avez, se mestier est, affin de ne . . . .[1]

Donne a Rouen, le xxj. jour de Mars, lan mil Date. iiij. c. xxvj. Collation faict.

DUBUST.

Et depuis lexecutore du dit mandement fait, nous avons aujourduy, xxij. jour de Mars, mil, iiij. c. xxvj. receu certaines lettres closes a mon dit seigneur le conte de Warrewyk, desquelles nous vous envoyons la coppie cy atachee, affin que hastivement vous les faces leir et proclamer par toute votre dicte viconte, avecques le mandement dessus desclaire.

---

thereto, that they will comfort and aid you in accomplishing these things, so as to put into execution the contents of these said letters, doing this in such a manner that there be no failure herein. Certifying us of the receipt of these pretents and of all that you have done therein, if need be, in order that no . . . . .

Dated at Rouen, the xxj. day of March, the year one thousand iiij. c. xxvj. Collation has been made.

DUBUST:

And since the execution of the said commandment has been made, we have to-day, the xxij. day of March, one thousand iiij. c. xxvj. received certain closed letters for my said lord, the earl of Warwick, of which we send you the copy hereto attached, in order that you may cause them to be read and proclaimed hastily in the whole of your said viscomté, along with the command above declared.

---

[1] *De ne* . . . . . ] The sentence ends thus imperfectly in the MS.

Escript comme dessus.

(*Dorso.*) Parties de messages et de voyages.

Ces lettres [1] furent receuez le Dymenche, xxiij. jour de Mars, cccc. xxvj., environ heure de dix heures, presens, T. Cuysac, escuier, Robert de Scalles, Jehan Cardonel, Pierre Bailleterie, et autres.[2]

---

Written as above.

(*Dorso.*) The particulars of the messages and journeys.

These letters were received on Sunday, xxiij. day of March, cccc. xxvj., about the hour of ten o'clock ; present, T. Cuysac, esquire, Robert de Scalles, Jehan Cardonel, Pierre Bailleterie, and others.

---

## 1428.

RECEIPT for money awarded to Robert Jolivet, abbot of Mont Saint Michel, for attending the Great Council at Paris.[3]

A.D. 1428.
June 21.

Nous, Robert, abbe du Mont Saint Michiel, conseillier du roy, notre seigneur, confessons avoir eu et

---

[TRANSLATION.]

WE, Robert, abbot of Mont Saint Michiel, counsellor of the king, our lord, acknowledge that we have had and received

---

[1] *Ces lettres*] This paragraph is written by a different hand.

[2] A memorandum follows which states that the import of the above document was publicly read and proclaimed at the assizes of Pon-taudemer, held by Robert de Scalles, the lieutenant of my lord the bailly of Rouen, upon Tuesday the first day of April, before Easter.

[3] From the original in the MS. Gaignières, 266.

receu de Pierre Surreau, receveur general de Nor- *Receipt by* mandie, la somme de trois cens six livres Tournois, *the abbot of Mount* pour le paiement de cinquante ung jour que nous *S. Michael* affirmons avoir vacquez ou voiage par nous fait en la *for money received in* compaignie de monseigneur de Saint Pierre, par lor- *the service* donnance et mandement de monsieur le regent le roy- *of Henry* aume de France, duc de Bedford, de ceste ville de *VI.* Rouen en la ville de Paris, par devers mon dit seigneur le regent et messeigneurs du grant conseil du roy, pour pluseurs grosses besongnes et affaires touchans grandement le bien et proutfit du roy, la venue de monseigneur le conte de Salisbury, et larmee qui doit venir presentement du pais Dengleterre, aviser et conclurre ou ilz seroient envoiez ; et aussi pour la venue faite en la dicte ville de Paris de monseigneur le duc de Bourguongne ; pour lesquelz affaires nous avons este mandez par mon dit seigneur le regent. Les diz jours commencans le xxviij. jour Davril, que nous partismes de la dicte ville de Rouen, et finans le xvij. jour de

---

of Pierre Surreau, receiver-general of Normandy, the sum of three hundred and six pounds Tournois, for the payment of fifty-one days, which we affirm we have spent on the journey made by us in the company of my lord of Saint Pierre, by the command and order of monsieur the regent of the kingdom of France, duke of Bedford, from this city of Rouen to the city of Paris, to my said lord the regent and my lords of the grand council of the king, for several important matters and affairs touching greatly the welfare and profit of the king, the arrival of my lord the earl of Salisbury, and the army which should come presently from the country of England, to deliberate and conclude where they should be sent ; and also for the arrival in the said city of Paris of my lord the duke of Burgundy ; for which affairs we have been summoned by my said lord the regent. These ten days commencing on the xxviij. day of April, on which we set out from the said city of Rouen, and ending on the xvij. day of this present month

ce present mois de Juing, que nous retournasmes en la dicte ville, tous inclus,[1] au pris de vj. livres Tournois pieca a nous ordonnez et tauxes par le roy, pour chacun jour que nous chevauchons et sommes hors de ceste dicte ville de Rouen pour les affaires du roy, notre dit seigneur, oultre et par dessus noz gaiges ordinaires. Montent les diz jours a la dicte somme de iij. c. vj. livres Tournois dessus dicte. Dont nous noz tenons pour contens et bien paie, et en quittons le roy, le dit receveur general, et tous autres.

Date.

En tesmoing de ce, nous avons seelle ces presentes lettres de quittance de notre seel, le xxj. jour de Juing, lan mil cccc. et vint huit.

R. ABBAS MONTIS.[2]

of June, when we returned to the said town, all included, at the rate of vj. pounds Tournois, formerly to us ordained and awarded by the king for each day that we shall be on horseback and are absent from this said city of Rouen for the affairs of the king, our said lord, over and above our ordinary wages. The ten days amount to the afore-said sum of iij. c. vj. pounds Tournois. Of this we hold ourselves satisfied and well paid, and thereof we acquit the king, the said receiver-general, and all others.

In witness of this we have sealed these present letters of acquittance, with our seal, the xxj. day of June, in the year one thousand cccc. and twenty-eight.

R. ABBAS MONTIS.

[1] *Tous inclus*] These two words are erroneously repeated.

[2] The signature is autograph. No seal remains.

## 1428.

MANDATE of Henry the Sixth for levying the first payment of the aid of nine score thousand pounds Tournois, granted by the country of Normandy at the meeting of the Three Estates at Rouen.[1]

HENRY, par la grace de Dieu, roy de France et Dangleterre, a nos tres chiers et bien amez Hamon de Belknap, escuier, tresorier et general gouverneur de noz finances en France et en Normandie, et Pierre Surreau, receveur general de nos dittes finances en Normandie, salut et dilection.

Comme, par ladviz et deliberacion de notre tres chier et tres ame oncle, Jehan, regent notre royaume de France, duc de Bedford, nous ayons fait assembler, au viij. jour de ce present mois de Septembre, en notre ville de Rouen, les gens des Trois Etats de notre duchie de Normandie et pais de conqueste faitte par feu notre tres chier seigneur et pere (dont Dieu

*A.D. 1428. Sept. 14.*

*A grant of 200,000l. Tournois, having been made by the Three Estates of Normandy,*

------

### [TRANSLATION.]

HENRY, by the grace of God, king of France and England, to our very dear and well-beloved Hamon de Belknap, esquire, treasurer and governor-general of our finances in France and Normandy, and to Pierre Surreau, receiver-general of our said finances in Normandy, greeting and love.

Since, by the advice and deliberation of our very dear and well-beloved uncle, John, the regent of our realm of France, duke of Bedford, we have caused the members of the Three Estates of our duchy of Normandy and the country conquered by our late very dear lord and father

------

[1] From the contemporaneous copy in the MS. Franç, 9436–5.

ait lame!), et a iceulx, en la presence de notre dit oncle, ayons fait remonstrer, exposer et dire les grans desir et affeccion que nous et notre dit oncle avons de songneusement et diligemment, par la grace de notre Seigneur, entendre a entretenir larmee presentement estant mise sus pour le reboutement de noz ennemis et recouvrement de pluseurs noz pais, villes et forteresses, soubz le gouvernement de notre dit oncle par notre tres chier et ame cousin, le conte de Salisbury, et en especial pour le recouvement de la cite Dangiers et de la place du Mont Saint Michiel, estant en notre dit pais et duchie de Normandie; mettre et entretenir bonne justice en nos diz pais et duchie, les villes, places et forteresses diceulx estre seurement gardees; les brigans et noz ennemis extirper et repulser; tellement que noz bons, vrais et loyaux subgiez, demourans et estans en nos dits pais et duchie, puissent faire seurement leurs marchandises

---

(of whom God have the soul!), to be assembled in our said city of Rouen on the viij. day of this present month of September, and have declared, exposed, and told them, in the presence of our said uncle, the great desire and affection which we and our said uncle have, by the grace of God, carefully and diligently to give heed to and maintain the army at this time raised for the repulse of our enemies and the recovery of many of our countries, towns, and fortresses under the government of our said uncle, by our very dear and beloved cousin, the earl of Salisbury; and in especial for the recovery of the city of Angers and the fortress of Mont Saint Michel, which is in our said country and duchy of Normandy; to introduce and preserve good justice in our said country and duchy; that the cities, places, and fortresses of the same should be safely kept; that the brigands and our enemies should be extirpated and repulsed, in such wise as that our good, true, and loyal subjects, who reside and dwell within our said country and

et labeurs, et soubz nous vivre en bonne paix et tranquilite. Les quelles choses ne povons faire ne soustenir, attendu les petites revenues de nos diz pais, sans avoir aide de nos diz bons, vrais et loyaulx subgiez, en leur requerant que pour ce faire nous voulsissent aidier de la somme de deux cens mil livres Tournois, a cueillir et lever a trois termes durant lannee commencant le jour Saint Michiel prouchain venant ; les quelles noz bons, vrays et loyaux subgiez nous ont liberalment ottroye la somme de ix. m.[1] livres Tournois pour ce faire ; en nous requerant et notre dit oncle que, se faire se povoit bonnement, a tant nous en voulsissions passer, et se passer nous ne povoyons, ilz se rapportoient du surplus au bon plaisir de nous et de notre dit oncle pour emploier les vij$^{xx}$. m. livres Tournois au paiement des gens darmes et de trait, des forteresses

---

duchy, may safely trade and labour and live under us in good peace and tranquillity ; things which we cannot do nor carry on, in consequence of the scanty revenues of our said country, without having the aid of our said good, true, and loyal subjects ; requiring of them that for this cause they would be pleased to aid us in the sum of two hundred thousand pounds Tournois, to be collected and levied at three terms during the year commencing on Michaelmas day next coming, and our said good, true, and loyal subjects have liberally granted us the sum of nine [score] thousand pounds Tournois to do this, requesting us and our said uncle that, if it were at all possible, then we would be so good as do without it, and if we could not do without it, they would, moreover, refer themselves to the good pleasure of ourselves and our said uncle to employ the vij$^{xx}$. m. pounds Tournois for the payment of the men-at-arms and archers, of the fortresses and towns of our said

---

[1] *ix. m.*] Such is the reading of the MS., but we should doubtless read lx$^{xx}$ m.

et villes de nos diz duchie et pais de conqueste et
garde des chemins, par la forme et maniere quilz ont
este gardez in ceste presente annee finissant a ceste
prouchaine Saint Michiel, et sur le surplus . . . . le
paiement de ij. c. lances et les archiers pour quatre
mois pour le recouvrement du dit Angiers, et tout
loutreplus del octroy dessus dit ou recouvrement du
dit Mont Saint Michiel, et non aillieurs.

the king
orders the
collection
of the first
portion
thereof.

Les quelz octroy et requeste nous avons receuz
agreablement ; et en iceulx entretenant vous mandons,
commandons et expressement enjoingnons, que vous
mettez, asseez et imposez sur les bourgois, manans
et habitans de nos diz duchie et pais de conqueste la
somme de iiij$^{xx}$. M. livres Tournois pour le premier
paiement du dit octroy, par bailliages, vicontez, eslections et villes, comme en tel cas est acoustume de
faire, le plus egalment que faire le pourrez ; non
comprins en ce les gens desglise, (qui par autre
maniere pourront contribuer et aidier aux choses

---

duchy and conquered country, and for the keeping of the
roads, according to the form and manner in which they
have been kept during this present year ending at Michaelmas next coming ; and with the remainder [they would
provide for] the payment of ij. c. lances and the archers
for four months for the recovery of Angers aforesaid, and
all the balance of the tax above-said for the recovery of
the said Mont Saint Michel, and not otherwise.

And this grant and request we have received with satisfaction ; and in accepting the same, we order, command,
and expressly enjoin you to affix, assess, and impose upon
the burgesses, residents, and inhabitants of our said duchy
and conquered country, the sum of iiij$^{xx}$. M. pounds Tournois, for the first payment of the said tax, by bailliwicks,
vicomtés, divisions, and towns, as in such cases is usually
done, as equally as is possible ; not comprehending herein
churchmen (who can contribute to and assist the matters

dessus dittes,) nobles vivans noblement, frequentans les armes, ou qui par viellesse ou impotence de corps en sont excusez, et miserables personnes qui par pouvrete, selon la coustume du pais, en sont exemps. Et icelle assiette envoyez pardevers les esleuz, vicontes et officiers des diz lieux pour les asseoir par paroisses, comme en tel cas est acoustume de faire; et avec la ditte somme de iiij$^{xx}$. M. livres Tournois asseez et imposez sur les habitans des bailliages de Coustantin et Caen et ressort ancien diceulx, la somme de x. M. livres Tournois pour partie de la somme par eulx accordee et envoyee ou mois Daoust derrenierement passe sur eulx estre levee pour le recouvrement du dit Mont Saint Michiel, oultre le dit octroy general; et icelles sommes faittez cueillir et lever tellement et si diligemment que dedans le xv. jour du mois de Decembre prouchainement venant elles soient apportees franchement, quittement et sans aucune dimi-

---

before-said in another way), nobles who live like nobles, those who follow arms, or who by old age or infirmity of body are herein excused, and persons in distress, who by their poverty, according to the custom of the country, are exempt from the same. And send this assessment to the assessors, vicomtes, and officers of the said places, in order that they may assess them by parishes, as in such case it is usual to do. And along with the said sum of iiij$^{xx}$. M. pounds Tournois, assess and impose upon the inhabitants of the bailliwicks of Coutantin and Caen, and the ancient jurisdiction of the same, the sum of x. M. pounds Tournois, as part of the sum by them granted and sent, in the month of August last past, to be levied for the recovery of the said Mont Saint Michel, beyond the said general tax. And these sums you shall cause to be collected and levied in such wise and so diligently that, by the xv. day of the month of December next coming, they shall be carried freely, fully, and without any diminution to you,

nucion, pardevers vous, Pierre Surreau, receveur general
de nos dittes finances en Normandie, lequel nous avons
commis et commettons par ces presentes a icelles
sommes recevoir pour les convertir et emploier es
choses dessus dittes, et non ailleurs.  En contraignant
a ce tous ceulx qui pour ce seront a contraindre par
toutes voies deuez et raisonnables, et comme acoustume
est de faire pour nos propres debtes.   De ce faire
vous donnons povoir et mandement especial ; mandons et commandons a tous noz justiciers, officiers et
subgiez, que a vous, voz commis et deputez en ce
faisant, obeissent et entendent diligemment.

Date.     Donné a Rouen, le xiiij. jour de Septembre, lan de
grace mil cccc. vingt huit, et de notre regne le vj.

Ainsi signe, Par le roy, a la relation de monseigneur
le regent, le duc de Bedford.

*Signe,* J. DE RINEL.

---

Pierre Surreau, receiver-general of our said finances in
Normandy, whom we have commissioned, and do commission
by these presents, to receive these sums, to spend and
employ them in the matters above-said, and not otherwise.
Compelling thereto all those persons who are herein to
be compelled, by all due and reasonable means, and as
it is usual to do for our own debts.   To do this, we
give you power and special command ; and we order and
command all our justices, officers, and subjects that they
diligently obey and give heed to you, your commissioners
and deputies, in so doing.

Dated at Rouen, the xiiij. day of September, in the year
of grace one thousand cccc. twenty-eight, and of our reign
the sixth.

Thus signed ; By the king, at the relation of my lord
the regent, the duke of Bedford.

*Signed,* J. DE RINEL.

## 1428.

LETTER from the Council of Normandy to the lieutenant of Argentan, informing him of an intended
attempt to betray that place.[1]

TRECHIER ami. Nous avons presentement sceu que
par le moien daucuns estans eu chastel et ville Dargentem,[2] le duc qui fu Dalencone doit avoir entree
dedens brief jours. Pour laquelle cause nous avons
rescript et prie messire Guillem Oldalle, chivalier,
soy traire par la dit[3] lieu Dargentem[3] per vous[4] advertir, aider et conforter de son povoir jusques a ce que
par monseigneur le regent y soit autrement pourveu,
auquel nous escripvons. Et avons prye et charge le
dit Oldalle, et vous mesmes chargons, que tous

A.D. 1428.
Oct. 6.

The castle
and town of
Argentan
about to be
betrayed
to the duke
d'Alençon.

---

[TRANSLATION.]

VERY dear friend. We have just now learned that, by
means of certain persons who are in the town and castle
of Argentan, he who of late was the duke d'Alençon
shall have an entrance therein within a few days. For which
cause we have written and entreated messire William Oldalle,
knight, to proceed to the said place of Argentan to inform,
aid and comfort you according to his power, until other provision be made therein by my lord the regent, to whom
we have written. And we have prayed and charged the
said Oldalle, and we charge you also, that all those persons,

---

[1] From the original, upon paper,
in the MS. Gaignières, 557.

[2] *Dargentem*] Written on an
erasure.

[3] *Par le dit*] Above the line, in-
stead of *audit*, which is cancelled.

[4] *Vous*] Originally *pour advertre
vous*.

ceulx, et celles,[1] que seront suspectz, soient sans delay boutes hors du dit chastel et ville Dargentem,[2] et vous y gouvernes tellement et si dilligamment et seurement comme la matiere le requiert, et sur le painne qui y appartient. Toutesfois se mon dit seigneur le regent ne vous a pourveu et mande creue, ou que le bailli ne vous en ait pourveu, et vous navez xx. lances et les archiers, les prenez et tenez en votre place, et facez voz monstres devant juge. Et vous faictes pourveoir de vivres par le bailli sur le pais, et il leur sera deduit sur laide procheinement a levir, que on espoire en Decembre.

Treschier ami, le Saint Espirit vous ait in Sa garde.

Date.
Escript a Rouen, le vj. jour Doctobre.

----

male and female, who shall be suspected, be without delay expelled from out of the said castle and town of Argentan, and that you govern yourself in such wise and so diligently and securely as the matter requires, and upon the penalty which thereunto appertains. Moreover, if my said lord the regent has not provided and sent you a reinforcement, or if the bailly has not provided you therewith, and you have not xx. lances and the archers, take them and keep them in your place, and make your musters before a judge. And cause provision of victuals to be made for you by the bailly for the country, and a deduction for the same shall be made him from the aid which is about to be levied, as is expected, in December.

Very dear friend, the Holy Ghost have you in His keeping.

Written at Rouen, the vj. of October.

----

[1] *Et celles*] An interlineation.
[2] *Dargentem*] The scribe had begun to write Dale — when he cancelled these letters.

Les gens du conseil du roy, notre seigneur, en Normandie.

SEBIRE.

(*Dorso*.) A notre treschier ami, le lieutenant du
cappitaine Dargentem.

---

The members of the council of the king, our lord, in
Normandy.

SEBIRE.

(*Dorso*.) To our very dear friend, the lieutenant of the
captain of Argentan.

===

## 1428.

RECEIPT for the expenses of Robert Jolivet, abbot
of Mont Saint Michel, when deliberating, along
with the Council, upon the siege of Orleans.[1]

Nous, Robert, par la permission divine, abbe de
Mont Saint Michiel, conseilleur du roy, notre seigneur,
confessons avoir eu et receu de Pierre Surreau, re-

A.D. 1428.<br>Dec. 6.<br>───<br>Receipt by<br>the abbot

### [TRANSLATION.]

WE, Robert, by divine permission, abbot of Mont Saint
Michel, counsellor of the king, our lord, acknowledge that
we have had and received of Peter Surreau, receiver-general

---

[1] From the original in the MS. Gaignières, 266. There, however, is no signature, and the seal has been torn off.

of Mont St. Michel for money received in the service of the English.

ceveur general de Normandie, la somme de soixante livres Tournois, qui deuz nous estoient pour le paiement de dix jours, commencans le xij. jour de Novembre derrenerement passe, et finans le xxj. jour du dit mois, inclus, que nous affermons avoir vacquez ou voiage par nous fait, par lordonnance de monseigneur le regent le royaume de France, duc de Bedford, de ceste ville de Rouen en la ville de Mante par devers mon dit seigneur le regent, en la compaignie du premier president de parlement et du seigneur de Saint Pierre, conseillers du roy, mon dit seigneur, pour le fait du siege Dorleans et autres grans affaires touchans le bien du roy, notre dit seigneur, et mon dit seigneur le regent, apres le mort de monseigneur le conte de Salisbury, au pris de vj. livres Tournois pour jour, a nous pieca tauxes et ordonnez par lettres du roy, notre dit seigneur, oultre et pardessus noz gaiges ordinaires, pour chacun jour que nous chevauchons hors de la dicte ville de Rouen pour les besongnes et affaires du dit seigneur. Montent les

---

of Normandy, the sum of sixty pounds Tournois, which were due to us for the payment of ten days, commencing on the xij. day of November last past, and finishing on the xxj. day of the said month, included, which we affirm that we have spent on the journey by us made by the command of my lord the regent of the kingdom of France, duke of Bedford, from this city of Rouen, to the town of Mante, to my said lord the regent, in the company of the first president of the parliament and of the lord of Saint Pierre, counsellors of the king, my said lord, upon the business of the siege of Orleans, and other important affairs touching the good of the king, our said lord, and my said lord the regent, after the death of my lord the earl of Salisbury, at the rate of vj. pounds Tournois by the day, to us formerly awarded and ordained by the letters of the king, our said lord, over and above our ordinary wages, for each day that we are on a journey from the said city of Rouen for the business and affairs of the said lord. The ten days

diz jours a la dicte somme de lx. livres Tournois. De laquelle nous nous tenons pour contens et bien paiez; et en quittons le roy, notre seigneur, le dit receveur general, et tous autres.

En tesmoing de ce nous avons scelle ceste presente Date. quittance de notre seel, le sixieme jour de Decembre, lan mil, cccc. et vint huit.

---

amount to the said sum of lx. pounds Tournois. For which we hold ourselves satisfied and well paid, and thereof we acquit the king, our said lord, the said receiver-general and all others.

In witness whereof we have sealed this present acquittance with our seal, the sixth day of December, the year one thousand, cccc. and twenty-eight.

---

### 1429.

WRIT of Henry the Sixth authorizing the collection of two-tenths imposed upon the clergy of Normandy by the pope.[1]

A.D. 1429.
April 8.

Henry VI. directs the collection of a tax upon the clergy of Normandy.

HENRY, par la grace de Dieu, roy de France et Dangleterre, a notre ame Pierre Surreau, receveur general de Normandie, salut.

---

[TRANSLATION.]

HENRY, by the grace of God, king of France and England, to our well-beloved Pierre Surreau, receiver-general of Normandy, greeting.

---

[1] From the contemporaneous copy in the MS. Fonds Franç., 9436–5.

Comme par bulles de notre saint pere le pappe, octroyees a nous et a notre tres chier et tres ame oncle, Jehan, regent notre royaume de France, duc de Bedford, les gens desglise de notre pais de Normandie par octroiz fais par eulx, soient tenus envers nous en deux dismes, ou equivalentes sommes, pour convertir et emploier a la deffense dicellui pais, et par especial pour lexpulsion de noz adversaires estans en la place du Mont Saint Michiel ; et sur ce le proces ait este deuement fait par notre ame et feal conseillier levesque de Beauvais, juge apostolique en ceste partie, lequel ait ordene en chacun diocese commissaires et receveurs pour imposer et asseoir, lever, cueillir, et recevoir les dits dismes, nous vous mandons et commettons par ces presentes que vous prenez et recevez des ditz receveurs ou commis particuliers les deniers des dismes dessus diz, en faisant en aide de droit contraindre a ce tous ceulx qui pour ceste cause seront imposez a paier leur impost par prinse, arrest et detention de leurs

---

Since, by bulls of our holy father the pope, granted to us and to our very dear and wellbeloved uncle, John, the regent of our kingdom of France, duke of Bedford, the churchmen of our country of Normandy, by taxes by them made, are bound to us in two-tenths, or equivalent sums, to be spent and employed for the defence of that country, and in especial, for the expulsion of our adversaries who are in the stronghold of Mont Saint Michel ; and the process hereupon has been duly made by our beloved and faithful counsellor, the bishop of Beauvais, judge apostolic in this matter, who has appointed commissioners and receivers in each diocese to impose and assess, levy, collect and receive the said tenths ; we command you and commission you by these presents to take and receive of the said receivers or private commissioners the money of the tenths above-said, aiding justice by compelling hereto all those persons who for this cause shall be taxed, to pay their impost, by seizure, arrest and detention of their goods

biens et temporel, reservez les biens sacrez de leglise, qui sont exceptez par les dictes bulles ; nonobstans oppositions ou appellations a ce contraires, et tout selon la forme des proces sur ce fais. Et les deniers qui en vendront, emploiez et convertissez ou paiement des gens darmes et de trait, et aultres choses necessaires pour les faiz et affaires dessus diz, selon les monstres et reveues qui seront deuement faittes des dittes gens darmes et de trait par les commissaires qui a ce sont, ou seront, ordonez et commis. Et par rapportant ces presentes monstres et reveues, avec quittances souffisant, tout ce que paie aurez pour la cause dessus ditte sera aloue en voz comptes et rabatu de votre recepte par noz amez et feaulx les gens de noz comptez a Paris, ausquels nous mandons que ainsi le facent, sans aucun contredit ou difficulte.

Donne a Paris, le viij. jour Davril, lan de grace, Date. mil, cccc. xxix. apres Pasques, et de notre regne le vij.

---

and temporalities, excepting the consecrated goods of the church, which are excepted by the said bulls, notwithstanding oppositions or appeals contrary thereto, according to the form of the process hereupon made. And the money which shall arise for the same you shall employ and expend in the payment of the men-at-arms and archers, and in other necessary matters for the business and affairs above-said, according to the musters and reviews of the said men-at-arms and archers, which shall be duly made by the commissioners who are, or shall be, appointed and commissioned hereto. And upon the production of these present musters and reviews, along with a sufficient acquittance, all that you shall have paid for the cause aforesaid shall be allowed in your accounts and deducted from your receipt by our beloved and faithful keepers of our accounts at Paris ; whom we command to do so, without any gainsaying or difficulty.

Dated at Paris, the viij. day of April, the year of grace, one thousand cccc. xxix. after Easter, and of our reign the vij.

Ainsi signe, Par le roy, a la relation du conseil tenu par monseigneur le regent, duc de Bedfort.

*Signe,* MILET.

---

Thus signed ; By the king, at the relation of the council held by my lord the regent, duke of Bedford.

*Signed,* MILET.

---

## 1429.

RECEIPT by Robert Jolivet, abbot of Mont Saint Michel, for money received in the service of the English.[1]

A.D. 1429.
April 27.

Receipt by the abbot of Mont S. Michel.

NOUS, Robert, par la permission divine, abbe de Mont Saint Michiel, conseilleur du roy, notre seigneur, confessons avoir eu et receu de Pierre Surreau, receveur general de Normendie, la somme de quatre cens cinquante livres Tournois, que deue nous estoient par le roy, notre dit seigneur, pour le paiement de soixante quinze jours que nous affermons par ces

---

[TRANSLATION.]

WE, Robert, by divine permission, abbot of Mont Saint Michel, counsellor of the king, our lord, acknowledge that we have had and received from Pierre Surreau, receiver-general of Normandy, the sum of four hundred and fifty pounds Tournois, which were due to us from the king, our said lord, for the payment of seventy-five days which we

---

[1] From the original in the MS. Gaignières, 266.

presentes avoir vacque ou voyage par nous fait en la
compaignie de messire Raoul le Saige, chevalier,
seigneur de Saint Pierre, conseilleur dicellui seigneur,
de ceste ville de Rouen en la ville de Paris, par lordonnance et mandement de monseigneur le regent le
royaume de France, duc de Bedford, pardevers luy et
le conseil du roy, notre dit seigneur, pour les affaires
et besongnes dicelui seigneur, touchans le siege
Dorleans, la venue de monseigneur de Bourgongne a
Paris, estre et assister aux conseulx, et illec traictier
de pluseurs autres grandes et haultes matieres touchans
lonneur et prouffit du roy et sa coronne de France.
Iceulx jours commences le dixieme jour de Fevrier
derrienierement passe, que nous partismes de ceste
dicte ville pour aler ou dit voyage, et finans le vint
cinquesme jour de ce present moys Davril, que sommes
retournez et arrivez en ycelle; au pris de vj. livres
Tournois par jour, a nous pieca ordonnez et tauxes,
oultre et pardessus noz gaiges ordonnaires, quant nous

---

affirm by these present letters that we have spent in a
journey by us made in the company of messire Raoul le
Saige, knight, lord of Saint Pierre, counseller of the said lord,
from this city of Rouen to the city of Paris, by the direction and command of my lord the regent of the kingdom
of France, duke of Bedford, before him and the council of
the king, our said lord, for the affairs and business of our said
lord touching the siege of Orleans, the arrival of my lord
of Burgundy at Paris, to be present and assist at the
councils, and there to treat of many other great and important matters touching the honour and profit of the
king, and of his crown of France.  These days commencing
on the tenth day of February last past, when we set out
from this said city to go on the said journey, and ending
on the five and twentieth day of this present month of
April, when we returned and arrived here ; at the rate of
vj. pounds Tournois daily, to us formerly appointed and
awarded, over and above our ordinary wages, when we are

vacquons hors ceste dicte ville pour les besongnes et affaires du dit seigneur. Montent les dites jours a la dicte somme de quatre cens cinquante livres Tournois; de la quelle somme de iiij. c. l. livres Tournois nous nous tenons pour contens et bien paiez, et en quittons le roy, notre dit seigneur, le dit receveur general et tous autres.

Date.    En tesmoing de ce, nous avons signe ceste presente quittance de notre saing manuel et seelle de notre seel, a Rouen, le vint septiesme jour Davril, lan mil, cccc. et vint neuf.

R. ABBAS MONTIS.[1]

---

employed out of this said town, upon the business and affairs of the said lord. The said days amount to the said sum of four hundred and fifty pounds Tournois, of which sum of iiij. c. l. pounds Tournois we hold ourselves satisfied and well paid, and hereof we acquit the king, our said lord, the said receiver-general, and all others.

In witness of this, we have signed this present acquittance with our sign manual, and sealed it with our seal, at Rouen, the twenty-seventh day of April, in the year one thousand, cccc. and twenty-nine.

R. ABBAS MONTIS.

---

[1] This signature is autograph. The seal no longer exists.

1429.

RECITAL of letters of Henry the Sixth for the levying
of troops to join the regent of France.[1]

GUILLAUME BRETON, chevalier, bailly de Caen, et
commissaire du roy notre sire en ceste partie, au
viconte du dit lieu de Caen, ou a son lieutenant,
salut.

Aujourdhuy avons receu les lettres patentes du dit
seigneur, saines et entieres en scel et escripture, desquelles la teneur ensuit:

HENRY, par la grace de Dieu, roy de France et
Dangleterre, au bailly de Caen, ou a son lieutenant,
salut.

Pour les nouvelles certaines survenues a notre tres
chier et tres ame oncle Jehan, regent notre royaume
de France, duc de Bedfort, que le daulphin, notre
adversaire, en sa personne, avecques sa puissance de

A.D. 1429.<br>May 30.<br>———<br>Recital of

Letters of<br>Henry VI.<br>summoning<br>troops to<br>meet the<br>regent of<br>France.

[TRANSLATION.]

GUILLAUME BRETON, knight, bailly of Caen, and lieutenant of the king, our lord, in this matter, to the vicomte
of the said place of Caen, or to his lieutenant, greeting.

To-day we have received the letters patent of the said
lord, whole and entire in the seal and writing, of which
the copy is as follows.

HENRY, by the grace of God, king of France and England, to the bailly of Caen, or to his lieutenant, greeting.

In consequence of the certain intelligence which has come
to our very dear and well-beloved uncle, John, regent of
our kingdom of France, duke of Bedford, to the effect that
the dauphin of France, our adversary, in person, along with

[1] From the MS. Fontanieu, 115–116.

gens et de habillemens de guerre, se met sur les
champs, en voulente et entencion de pranre assegier
les villes et places de notre royaume et seigneurie de
France estans en notre obeissance, ou de faire aucune
autre entreprinse alencontre de nous et de noz pays
et subgez, se sur ce ne lui estoit donne resistance,
ainsi que il appartient. Pour laquelle cause notre dit
oncle est disposez soy mettre sus et en personne a
toute puissance tele quil plaira a Dieu lui ordonner,
sur quoy il a fait, et fait, sa diligence de jour en jour
demander gens ses feables, tant de la nacion de France
comme Dangleterre, pour approchier notre dit adversaire et le rebouter de ses entreprises et par battaille,
se mestier est, et il attent en lieu ou notre dit oncle
avecquez son armee le puist appruchier.    Et pour ce
que la chose est grande, et desirons que notre dit
oncle soit accompagniez ainsi que a son estat appartient, et que besoing est, attendu la puissance de

———— ·——— —— ——— ·— ——

his army and military equipage, has taken the field, with
the will and intention of undertaking the siege of those
towns and places of our kingdom and lordship of France
which are in obedience to us, or to make some other
attempt against us and our country and subjects, unless
such resistance as is fitting be made to him herein.  For
which cause our said uncle intends to take the field in
person with all such power as it shall please God to
afford him ; wherein he has done, and is doing, his diligence from day to day by asking his faithful people, as
well of the nation of France as of England, in order to
draw near to our said adversary, and to drive him back
from his intentions, and this by battle, if it be necessary,
and he await in such a place as our said uncle, with his
army, can approach him.    And because the matter is a
weighty one, and we desire that our said uncle should be
accompanied in such wise as is fitting his rank, and is
necessary, when we take into account the power of our

notre dit adversaire, par ladvis de notre dit oncle
vous mandons et expressement enjoignons que incon-
tienent, ces lettres vues, vous assemblez toutes gens
darmes et de trait, et autres qui ont accoustumez suir
les armes, de votre baillage, de quelque estat quilz
soient, (les places dicelui votre bailliage necessaires a
garder demourans fournies et en seurete,) avecquez tele
compagnie que pourrez finer promptement, vous traiez
montez, armez et habillez souffisamment, par devers
notre dit oncle au lieu de Pontoise ou de Mante, le
plus hastivement que vous pourrez, et faisant venir
apres vous ceulx qui au jour de votre partement ne
seront prestz, et au plus tard dedans le iiij$^e$ jour de
Juing prouchain venant; au quel lieu de Pontoise ou
de Mante (ou cas que notre dit oncle seroit passe
outre) vous trouverez gens pour vous recevoir avecquez
votre dite compagnie, veoir les monstres de ceulx qui
seront venus, et ordonner et appointier pour leur paie-

---

said adversary, we, by the advice of our said uncle, command and expressly enjoin you that, as soon as you have
seen these letters, you assemble all the men-at-arms and
archers, and such others as are accustomed to follow arms,
within your bailliwick, of what condition soever they may
be (provided that the places within your said bailliwick
which ought to be guarded continue garrisoned and in safety)
and that with such a company as you can quickly collect,
you proceed, sufficiently mounted, armed, and accoutered,
to our said uncle at the place of Pontoise or of Mante,
as speedily as you can, causing those persons to come
after you who at the day of your departure shall not be
ready, and at the latest by the iiij. day of June next
coming ; at which place of Pontoise or of Mante (should
it happen that our said uncle shall have passed forwards)
you will find people to receive you with your said company, to inspect the musters of those who shall have
arrived, and to arrange and settle for their payment, as

ment, ainsy quil appartiendra. Et gardez, sur paine
de privacion de votre office et dautre grieve pugnicion,
que en ce nait aucune faulte ; en contraignant a ce
tous ceulx de votre dit bailliage, soient en bonnes
villes ou sur les champs, se ilz nont juste excusation
pour la garde des places, villes, ou autres charges
necessaires a eux commises, et telement que notre dit
oncle soit content ; en certiffiant dedans le dit jour de
votre bonne diligence, et telement que hastivement il
ait de vous nouvelles sur ce, pour cognoistre quelle
compaignie lui vendra de votre bailliage.

Donne a Paris, le xxvᵉ jour de May, lan de grace
mil cccc. vint et neuf, et de notre regne le septiesme.

Ainsi signe, Par le roy, a la relacion de monseigneur
le regent de France, duc de Bedfort.

J. MILET.

---

shall be fitting. And take care, under pain of the de-
prival of your office, and of other grave penalty, that
herein there be no default ; thereto compelling all those
persons of your said bailliwick, whether they be in the
good towns or in the country, unless they have a just
excuse in consequence of the custody of the places, towns,
or other necessary charges committed to them, and in such
wise that our said uncle shall be satisfied ; certifying us,
within the said day, of your good diligence, and in such
manner that speedily he shall have news from you hereupon, so that he may know what force shall come to him
from your bailiwick.

Dated at Paris, the xxv. day of May, in the year of
grace, one thousand cccc. and twenty-nine, and of our reign
the seventh.

Thus signed, By the king, at the relation of my lord the
regent of France, the duke of Bedford.

J. MILET.

Par vertu des quelles lettres royaulx dessus transcriptes, et pour le contenu dicelles accomplir, nous
vous mandons et tres expressement enjoignons, en
commetant, se mestier est, que incontinent, ces lettres
vues, vous assemblez toutes gens darmes et de trait,
et autres qui ont accoustume suir les armes, estans
en votre dite vicomte, de quelque estat quilz soient,
(les places dicelle viconte necessaires a garder demou-
rantes fournies et en seurete) tant par cry publique
que autrement, deuement, en leur faisant, ou faisant
faire, commandement de par le roy, notre dit seigneurr
que promptement ilz se traient montez, armez et habillez suffisamment, devers nous a Caen, pour en notre
compagnie aler a Pontoise ou a Mante devers monseigneur le regent le plus hastivement que faire se
porra, en faisant venir apres vous ceulx qui ne seront
prestz pour partir avecques vous au dit lieu de Pontoise ou Mante, en telle haste quilz y soient au plus

—————————— — —  —— ————

By virtue of which royal letters above transcribed, and
in order to accomplish the contents of the same, we command and most expressly enjoin you, commissioning you,
if need be, that immediately upon the sight of these letters
you assemble all those men-at-arms and archers, and others,
who have been in the habit of following arms, who are in
your said vicomté, of what estate soever they be (the
places within the said vicomté, which ought to be guarded,
being garrisoned and in safety), as well by public proclamation as otherwise, in due manner, making them, or causing
to be made for them, commandment upon the part of the
king, our said lord, that without delay they betake themselves, mounted, armed, and accoutered sufficiently, to us
at Caen, in order to go from thence in our company to
Pontoise or to Mante to my lord the regent, as hastily
as possibly may be, causing those persons to follow you
who shall not be ready to set out with you to the said
place of Pontoise or Mante, in such haste that they be
there at the latest upon the iiij. day of June next coming,

tard le iiij^e jour de Juing prochain venant, et illec sera ordonne de leur paiement, ainsi quil appartiendra. Et a ce contraignez tous ceulx de votre dite viconte, soient en bonnes villes ou sur les champs, silz nont juste excusation pour la garde de places, villes, ou autres charges necessaires a eulx commises, et tout jouxte le contenu es dites lettres transcriptes ; en nous certiffiant deuement de ce que fait en aurez, affin que en ce faictes que deffault ny ait.

Date.     Donne a Baieux, le penultieme jour de May, lan mil, cccc. vingt et neuf.

Collation faite.

Signe,   N. HUET.

and there such arrangements shall be made concerning their payment as shall be fitting. And to do this you shall compel all those of your said vicomté, whether they be in the good towns or in the country, unless they have a just excuse in consequence of the custody of the places, towns, or other necessary charges committed to them ; and all according to the contents of the said letters which are transcribed ; certifying us duly of what you have done, in order that you do not act herein that there be any failure.

Dated at Baieux, the penultimate day of May, in the year one thousand cccc. and twenty-nine.

Collated.

Signed,   N. HUET.

## 1429.

STATEMENT respecting the outlay of 20,000 francs for the payment of troops raised by the duke of Burgundy for the service of Henry the Sixth.[1]

*A.D. 1429. July.*

*20,000 francs awarded to the duke of Burgundy for the pay*

DENIERS[2] baillez a monseigneur le duc de Bourgongne, conte de Flandres, Dartois et de Bourgongne, par lordonnance de monseigneur le regent le royaume

[TRANSLATION.]

MONEY delivered to my lord the duke of Burgundy, count of Flanders, of Artois and of Burgundy by the command of my lord the regent of the kingdom of France,

---

[1] From the original Register of Accounts, Fonds Franç., 9436-5 (Franç. 4488, or MS. Bigot, 114) p. 537.

[2] Appended is a marginal note, in Latin, relative to further transactions in the same matter. From this it appears that, notwithstanding the statements contained in this document, the auditors still objected. The king, the duke of Burgundy, and John Abonnel executed the letters required of them, but the difficulties were not removed, the entry was not allowed, and was cancelled. Ultimately, however, it was sanctioned " ad " onus dictorum domini ducis Bur- " gundiæ et Johannis Abonnel, de " quibus respondeant loco et tem- " pore, ut prius."

The same volume of Accounts contains the following extracts :—

" A Pierre Surreau, receveur general du dit pays et duchie de

Normendie, . . . . . . pour x jours, commencans le xxij. jour du dit moys de Juillet et finant le dernier jour du dit moys ensuivant, tous incloix, quil afferme, comme dessus, avoir vacque ou voyage par luy fait, par lordonnance et commandement de mon dit seigneur le regent, de la ville de Rouen a Arras, pardevers monseigneur de Bourgongne porter hastivement la somme de xx. M. livres Tournois, et la delivrer a son tresorier pour la converter ou paiement des gens darmes et de trait de son armee quil faissoit mettre sus au dit temps pour venir servir le roy, notre dit seigneur, alencontre de ses ennemis estans ou pays de France et Brye, et retournant au dit lieu de Rouen, au pris de iiij. livres Tournois par jour, montans

"xl. livres Tournois."

" To Peter Surreau, receiver-general of the said country and duchy

*of troops raised by him.*

de France, duc de Bedford, et par appointement fait entre eulx et messeigneurs du grant conseil du roy, nostre seigneur, estans a Paris ou mois de Juillet, M. cccc. xxix., pour convertir et emploier ou paiement des gens darmes et de trait que mon dit seigneur de Bourgongne avoit entencion de amener es parties de France de ses pays ou service du roy alencontre des ennemis qui lors se trayoient a puissance es dits

---

duke of Bedford, and by agreement made between them and my lords of the great council of the king, our lord, being at Paris in the month of July M. cccc. xxix. to spend and employ it in the payment of the men-at-arms and archers whom my said lord of Burgundy had the intention to bring into the parts of France from his country for the service of the king against the enemies who at that time

---

of Normandy . . . . . for x. days, commencing on the xxij. day of the said month of July, and ending on the last day of the said month following, all included, which he affirms, as above, that he has spent in the journey made by him, by the order and command of my said lord the regent, from the city of Rouen to Arras, to my lord of Burgundy, to carry hastily the sum of xx. M. pounds Tournois, and to deliver it to his treasurer to employ it in the payment of the men-at-arms and archers of his army which he caused to be raised at the same time to come and serve the king, our said lord, against his enemies being in the country of France and Brie, and returning to the said place of Rouen, at the rate of iiij. pounds Tournois by day, amounting to xl. pounds Tournois."

This document is further illus-trated by the Additional Charter 369, which contains letters of Henry VL, king of France and England, to Sir Tho. Blount, knight, treasurer of the finances of Normandy, ordering him to cause Pierre Surreau to pay to Jehan Abonnel, called Le Gros, governor of the extraordinary expenses of the duke of Burgundy, 19,500 pounds Tournois, as the pay of eight hundred men-at-arms, and one thousand archers, retained by the duke of Burgundy, for the king's service before Compiègne, for one month, commencing 10th August, at the rate of fifteen francs for a man-at-arms, and seven and a half francs for an archer. Dated Rouen, 11th Aug. 1430.

Attached is the warrant of Sir Tho. Blount to Pierre Surreau to pay the above sum.

parties de France, et dont es deux chapitres subsequens est plus a plaine faicte mencion. Lesquelles deniers, montent xx. M. livres Tournois, avoient este par le dit receveur general mis et emploiez cy devant en la Despence de ce compte, ou chaptre de "Deniers baillez " a officiers et autres," dont il est accomptez. Mais pour les causes escriptes sur la partie, icelle avoit este royee. Et pour ce par vertu des lettres royaulx depuis par le dicte receveur general impetrees est cy reprinse la dicte partie par la maniere qui sensuit.

A monseigneur le duc de Bourgongne, conte de Flandres, Dartois et de Bourgongne, auquel, par appointement fait en la ville de Paris ou mois de Juillet, mil, cccc. xxix. [au] temps de ce present compte, pour et ou nom du roy, notre seigneur, entre monseigneur le duc de Bedford, gouvernans et regent le royaume de France, et les gens du grant conseil du

---

wcre advancing in force in the said parts of France, and of which more clear mention is made in the two subsequent chapters. Which money, amounting to xx. M. pounds Tournois, has been previously placed and employed by the said receiver-general in the Expense of this account, in the chapter of " Money given to officers and others," for which he is accountable. But on account of the reasons written on that entry it has been cancelled. And therefore, by virtue of the letters royal obtained by the said receiver-general since that time, the said entry has here been resumed in the following manner.

To my lord the duke of Burgundy, count of Flanders, of Artois, and of Burgundy, to whom, by agreement made in the city of Paris in the month of July, one thousand, cccc. xxix. at the time of this present account, for, and in the name of the king, our lord, between my lord the duke of Bedford, governor and regent of the kingdom of

roy, notre dit seigneur, estans au dit lieu de Paris,
dune part, et le dit monseigneur le duc de Bourgongne
dautre part, touchant le paiement de gens darmes et
de trait, qui adonc le dit monseigneur le duc de Bourgongne avoit fait, ou faisoit, mander et mettre sus en
plusieurs et diverses contrees de ses pays pour servir
le roy, notre dit seigneur, a la defence de son dit
royaume de France, le dit monseigneur, le gouvernans, et les dictes gens du conseil du roy, notre dit
seigneur, dedens certain brief jour apres le partement du dit monseigneur de Bourgongne de la dicte
ville de Paris, lui devoient envoier la somme de xL M.
livres Tournois, monnoye courant ou dit royaume de
France, cest assavoir xx. M. frans comptans, et des
joyaulx certaine quantite, pour emprunter et faire
finance par le dit monseigneur de Bourgongne aux
fraiz et dispens du roy, notre dit seigneur, dautres
xx. M. frans, pour tout convertir et emploier ou paie-

------

France, and the members of the great council of the king,
our said lord, being in the said town of Paris, on one part,
and the said lord the duke of Burgundy on the other part,
touching the payment of the men-at-arms and the bowmen
whom the said lord the duke of Burgundy had then caused to
be summoned, or was now summoning and raising in many and
several districts of his country, to serve the king, our said
lord, for the defence of his said realm of France, the said
lord, the governors and the said members of the council
of the king, our said lord, within a certain brief time after
the departure of the said lord of Burgundy from the said
city of Paris, should send to him the sum of xl. M. pounds
Tournois in current money of the said kingdom of France;
that is to say, xx. thousand francs paid down, and a certain
quantity of jewels on which to borrow and raise, by my
said lord of Burgundy, at the expense and cost of the
king, our said lord, other xx. M. francs, to employ and spend
the whole upon the payment of the said men-at-arms and

ment des dits gens darmes et de trait, et dautres affaires necessaires pour le fait et avancement de larmee du dit monseigneur de Bourgongne. Pour lâccomplissement et entertenement du quel appointement le dit monseigneur le gouvernant et regent de France ait tantost apres envoye pardevers icelui monseigneur le duc de Bourgongne, estant en sa ville Darras, par Pierre Surreau, receveur general de Normandie dessus nomme, des deniers de sa recepte, la somme de xx. M. frans en blans de x. ď. Tournois piece, pour convertir et emploier ou paiement dessus dicte.

Et pour ce que chose impossible estoit au dit receveur general de Normandie de avoir et reconnier les monstres, faire les paiemens, et prendre ses acquitz des dits gens darmes et de trait, qui se assembloient en plusieurs et diverses contrees des pays du dit monseigneur le duc de Bourgongne, tant de Picardie, Flandres, comme de Bourgongne et dautres marches, ainsi que on avoit acoustume faire en tel cas, et que

---

bowmen and other things necessary for the business and advancement of the army of the said lord of Burgundy. For the accomplishment and furthering of which agreement, my said lord the governor and regent of France has directly afterwards sent to the said lord of Burgundy, being in his town of Arras, by Pierre Surreau, receiver-general of Normandy above mentioned, from the money of his receipt, the sum of xx. M. francs in blancs of x. deniers Tournois a-piece, to spend and employ them in the above mentioned payment.

And because it was a thing impossible for the said receiver-general of Normandy to take and inspect the musters, to make the payments and take his acquittances from the said men-at-arms and bowmen who were assembled in many and different parts of the lands of the said lord the duke of Burgundy, as well in Picardy and Flanders, as in Burgundy and the other borders, as they were accus-

le dit receveur general avoit entencion et propos de
faire, se il eust peu bonnement par lordonnance du
dit· monseigneur le duc de Bourgongne, et pour pourveoir a ce que default ny eust ou paiement des dits
gens darmes et de trait, et pour lavancement de larmee
dessus dicte, le dit receveur general bailla et delivra
la dicte somme de xx. M. frans a Jehan Abonnel, dit
Le Gras, conseiller et gouverneur de la despense ex-
traordinaire de mon dit seigneur de Bourgongne, pour
tourner et convertir, par ceulx que le dit seigneur
ordonneroit, ou paiement des dits gens darmes et de
trait, comme par lettres de mon dit seigneur de Bourgongne et lettre de recepte du dit Jehan Abonnel
sur ce faites le xxviij. jour du dit mois de Juillet,
faisans plus a plain de ce qui dit est mencion, par
lesquelles mon dit seigneur de Bourgongne et le dit
[Jehan Abonnel] ont promis et sont tenus faire avoir
et baillir au dit Pierre Surreau bons et souffisans acquitz

---

tomed to do in such a case, and as the said receiver-general intended and purposed to do, if he could rightly by the
order of the said lord the duke of Burgundy, and to provide
that there shall be no default in the payment of the said men-
at-arms and bowmen, and for the advancement of the above
mentioned army, the said receiver-general gave and delivered
the said sum of xx. M. francs to Jehan Abonnel, called Le
Gras, counsellor and governor of the extraordinary expenses
of my said lord of Burgundy to spend and employ it, by
those persons whom the said lord shall ordain, for the
payment of the said men-at-arms and bowmen, as may
appear by letters of my said lord of Burgundy, and
by a letter of receipt from the said Jehan Abonnel hereupon made on the xxviij. day of the said month of July,
making mention more fully of what is said, by which
my said lord of Burgundy and the said [Jehan Abonnel]
have promised and are bound to give to the said Pierre
Surreau good and sufficient acquittances adequate to be

valables pour emploier en la despense de ses comptes, et len faire tenir quitte envers le roy, notre dit seigneur, ces choses peuent apparoir. Le quel Pierre Surreau, receveur general de Normandie, apres la delivrance des dictes xx. M. francs par lui faicte au dit Jehan Abonnel, comme dit est, ait obtenu lettres du roy, notre dit seigneur, donnees le vj. jour Daoust ensuivant ou dit an M. cccc. xxix., adrecans aux gens de ses comptes, tresoriers et gouverneurs de ses finances de France et de Normandie, par les quelles, narration faicte des choses dessus dicte, estoit mande et expressement enjoinge que par raportant les dictes lettres, les lettres de mon dit seigneur de Bourgongne sur lordonnance de delivrer les dits xx. M. francs au dit Abonnel, et celles du dit Abonnel sur la reception dicelle some, allouer en sa despense des comptes du dit receveur general la dicte somme de xx. M. frans, sans aucune contredit ou difficulte. Par vertu desquelles lettres royaulx, dicelles

---

employed in the Expense of his accounts, and to cause him to be held acquitted therein towards the king, our said lord. The said Pierre Surreau, receiver-general of Normandy, after the deliverance of the said xx. M. francs by him made to the said Jehan Abonnel, as has been said, has obtained letters from the king, our said lord, dated the vj. day of August following in the said year M. cccc. xxix. addressed to the keepers of his accounts, treasurers and governors of his finances of France and of Normandy, by which letters, after a statement of the things above mentioned has been made, it was commanded and expressly enjoined that, upon the production of the said letters, the letters of my said lord of Burgundy respecting the command as to the deliverance of the said xx. M. francs to the said Abonnel, and these of the said Abonnel for the receipt of this sum, there be allowed in his Expenditure of the accounts of the said receiver-general the said sum of xx. M. francs, without any contradiction or difficulty. By virtue of which royal letters,

de mon dit seigneur de Bourgongne et Abonnel, le dit Pierre Surreau, receveur general, ait mis et voulu mettre et emploier cy devant en la despense de ce present compte, cest assavoir, ou chapitre de "Deniers baillez a officiers qui en sont tenus de compter," la dicte somme de xx. M. frans. Mais pour ce que aux commissieres ordonnez par le roy, notre dit seigneur, a oir en la ville de Rouen le dit compte, le precedent et les deux autres comptes ensuivants du dit receveur general, nestoit souffisants apparu de lordonnance du roy, ou de mon dit seigneur le gouvernant et regent de France fait au dit receveur general de baillir les dits xx. M. frans au dit Jehan Abonnel, ainsi que dit est dessus, et quil ne leur estoit aucunement apparu de la diligence ou poursuite faite par le dit receveur general pardevers le dit monseigneur de Bourgongne et Abonnel, pour avoir et reconnier deulx acquitz souffisans des dits xx. M. frans, comme promis lavoient, et

---

of those of my said lord of Burgundy and Abonnel, the said Pierre Surreau, the receiver-general, has placed and wished to place and employ heretofore, in the Expenditure of this present account, that is to say, in the chapter of " Monies given to officers who are bound to give account " for it," the said sum of xx. M. francs. But because the commissioners appointed by the king, our said lord, to audit in the city of Rouen the said account, the former and the two other following accounts of the said receiver-general, did not consider as sufficient the mandate of the king, or of my said lord the governor and regent of France, made to the said receiver-general, to give the said xx. M. francs to the said Jehan Abonnel, as it is above mentioned, and because they were by no means certified of diligence or pursuit having been made by the said receiver-general in regard to my said lord of Burgundy and Abonnel for having and obtaining from them sufficient acquittal of the said xx. M. francs, as they had promised, and as they were

que par leurs dictes lettres tenus y estoient, par
quoy il sembloit aus dits commissaires que le roy,
notre dit seigneur, nestoit pas souffisamment acquittez
envers les dits gens darmes et de trait, et aussi que
les dits lettres royaulx nestoient pas verifiees des dits
gens des comptes et tresoriers, ausquelles elles adre-
coient, comme dit est, le dits commissaires aurient
refuse a passer et allouer en la despense de ce dit present compte les dits xx. m. francs dessus dits, et iceulx
sur icelui compte avoient roye de tous poins. Pour
quoy le dit Pierre Surreau, receveur general, avant
la cloisture dicelui, ait depuis du roy notre dit seigneur obtenu ses autres lettres de relievement, donnees
a Paris le xiiij. jour de Januer, m. cccc. xxix., adrecans
aux commissaires dessusdits et aux commissaires ordonnez a la closture des dits comptes oyr au dit
lieu de Rouen passes a la relation de mon dit seigneur
le regent et gouvernant le royaume, par lesquelles,
narracion faite, et pour les causes contenues en icelles,

---

bound thereto by their said letters, in consequence of this
it seemed to the said commissioners that the king, our said
lord, was not sufficiently acquitted as regards the said men-
at-arms and bowmen, and also that the said royal letters
were not verified by the said accountants and treasurers,
to whom they were addressed, as has been said, the said
commissioners refuse to pass and allow in the Expense of
this said present account the said xx. m. francs above mentioned, and cancelled them entirely in this account. Wherefore the said Pierre Surreau, receiver-general, before the
closing hereof, has since obtained from the king, our said
lord, other letters of relief, dated at Paris, the xiiij. day
of January, m. cccc. xxix. addressed to the above mentioned commissioners and to the commissioners ordained
for the closing of the audit of the said accounts at the
said place of Rouen which are past at the relation of
my said lord the regent and governor of the kingdom,
by which a recital having been made, and on account

leur est mande expressement que en reportant les
autres lettres, les lettres de mon dit seigneur de
Bourgongne, et celles du dit Abonnel, dont dessus est
faite mencion, avecques les dits lettres de relievement,
ilz allouent en la Despense des comptes du dit receveur general la somme de xx. M. francs devant dicte,
sans aucun contredit ou difficulte. Parmi ce que les
dits monseigneur le duc de Bourgongne et Jehan
Abonnel demouront tenus envers le roy, notre dit
seigneur, de la dicte somme de xx. M. frans, et dont
le roy, notre dit seigneur, par ses dits lettres de
relievement veult que par les dits commissaires ilz
soient chargiez comme il appartendra, a fin de les
recouvrer en temps et en lieu. Laquelle chose le
roy, notre dit seigneur, veult par ses dits lettres
ainsi estre faicte, non obstant les refuz mis et faiz
par les dits commissaires, et la cause de la radiacion
dicelle somme, dont par les dits lettres le dit rece-

---

of the causes contained therein, it is expressly commanded,
that on the production of the second letters, the letters
of my said lord of Burgundy, and those of the said
Abonnel, of which mention is made above, with the said
letters of relief, they should allow in the Expenditure of the
accounts of the said receiver-general the sum of xx. M.
francs already mentioned, without any contradiction or
difficulty. Provided that the said persons, my lord the duke
of Burgundy and Jehan Abonnel shall remain holden to
the king, our said lord, in the said sum of xx. M. francs,
and with which the king, our said lord, by his said letters
of relief, wills that they should be changed by the said
commissioners as shall be fitting, in order that they may
be recovered in due time and place. Which thing the
king, our said lord, wishes to be so done by his said letters,
notwithstanding the refusals put and made by the said
commissioners, and the cause of the cancelling of the said
sum, of which the said receiver-general has been and is

veur general a este et est releve, et quelconques ordonnances et lettres subreptices a ce contraires. Pour
ce, et par vertu de toutes les lettres dessusdictes ci
rendues, la dicte somme de xx. M. francs, valent
xx. M. livres Tournois.

---

relieved by the said letters, and of whatever fraudulent
ordinances and letters contrary to these. For this cause,
and by virtue of all the letters above mentioned here produced, the said sum of xx. M. francs; which are worth
xx. M. pounds Tournois.

---

### 1429.

MANDATE for the levying of troops to join the duke
of Bedford at Paris, to proceed against Charles the
Seventh about to attack that city.[1]

A TOUS ceulx qui ces presentes lettres verront ou A.D. 1429.
orront, Michiel Durant, viconte de Rouen, salut. Aug. 27.

Savoir faisons que, lan de grace mil, cccc. xxix., le Recital of
viij. jour de Septembre, nous veismes les lettres patentes Letters of
du roy, notre seigneur, desquelles la teneur ensuit, Henry VI.
for the

---

[TRANSLATION.]

To all those who shall see or hear these present letters,
Michiel Durant, vicomte of Rouen, sends greeting.

We make known that in the year of grace one thousand
cccc. xxix., the viij. day of September, we have seen the
letters patent of the king our lord, the contents of which
are as follows.

---

[1] From the MS. Fontanieu, 115–116.

levying of
troops to
oppose
Charles
VII.

HENRY, par la grace de Dieu, roy de France et
Dangleterre, au bailly de Rouen, ou son lieutenant,
salut.

Pour ce que notre ennemy et adversaire tient derechief les champs en sa personne, et sest logie environ
notre bonne ville de Paris, dispose, comme len dit, de
donner bataille a notre tres cher et bien ame oncle,
Jehan, regent notre royaume de France, duc de Bet-
ford, nous, qui desirons pour notre honneur et conservation de notre bonne ville de Paris, estre resiste
par bataille et autrement a notre dit ennemi et adversaire, vous mandons et commettons par ces presentes que faciez faire commandement depar nous, sur
peine de confiscacion de terres et biens meubles, les
corps demourans a notre volente, a tous chevaliers,
escuiers, et autres hommes darmes et de trait, nobles
et non nobles, tenans fiefs et arrierefiefs, et toutes
autres personnes qui ont accoustume de poursuir les
armes, tant Anglois comme Normans, que dedans deux
jours apres la publication de ces presentes faite au

---

HENRY, by the grace of God king of France and England,
to the bailly of Rouen, or his lieutenant, greeting.

As our enemy and adversary again has taken the field in
person, and is quartered near our good city of Paris, disposed, as they say, to give battle to our very dear and
well beloved uncle, John, the regent of our kingdom of
France, duke of Bedford, we, desiring for our honour and
the preservation of our good city of Paris that our said
enemy and adversary be resisted by battle and otherwise,
order and commission you by these presents to cause commandment to be made from us, under pain of confiscation
of their lands and moveable goods, while their bodies remain at our disposal, to all knights, squires, and other men-
at-arms and bowmen, nobles and those not nobles, holding
fiefs and arrierefiefs, and all other persons who are accustomed
to follow arms, as well English as Normans, that within
two days after the publication of these presents made at

lieu de la viconte ou ils sont demourans, ils viennent a cheval, ou a pie, habillez et armez soufissament, chacun selon son estat, au dit lieu de Rouen par devers vous, pour prendre deniers, gaiges et souldees deuz et raisonnables pour aller a Paris devers notre dit oncle au x. jour de Septembre prochain venant, auquel temps notre dit oncle espere avoir bataille contre notre dit ennemi et adversaire. En procedant contre les delaians et deffaillans par les pienes dessus dites, sans dissimulation quelconques.

Et afin que acun ne puisse de ce pretendre ygnorance, nous voullons ces presentes estre publiees solemnellement a haulte voix et son de trompe par tous les lieus de votre bailliage, ou len a acoustume de faire cris et publications. De ce faire, et de recevoir les monstres des dessus dis, ou de les casser, se le cas le requiert, et aussi de les certiffier ou il appartiendra, donnons a vous et aux vicontes de votre bailliage, ou a lun deulx avecques vous, pouvoir, auctorite et mande-

---

the place of the vicomté where they are living, they come on horse, or on foot, sufficiently accoutred and armed, each one according to his condition, to the said place of Rouen to you, that they may receive due and reasonable money, wages and pay, to go to Paris to our said uncle on the x. day of September next coming, at which time our said uncle hopes to have battle with our said enemy and adversary. Proceeding against the delayers and defaulters by the penalties above-mentioned, without any dissimulation whatsoever.

And in order that no one may feign ignorance of this, we will that these presents be solemnly published aloud and by the sound of the trumpet, in all the places of your bailliwick where it is usual to make proclamations and publications. To do this and to receive the musters of the persons above-mentioned, or to reject them if need require it, and also to certify them where it shall be fitting, we give to you and the vicomtes of your bailliwick, or to one of them along with you, power, authority, and special

ment especial. Mandons et commandons a tous justiciers, officiers et subgez que a vous, vos commis et
depputez en ce faisant, obeissent et éntendent diligemment.

Donne a Vernon, le xxvij. jour Daoust, lan de grace
mil cccc. xxix., et de nostre regne le septiesme.

Ainsy signe, Par le roy, a la relacion de monseigneur
le regent, duc [de] Bedford.

J. DE RAINEL.

Date.      En tesmoing de ce, nous avons mis a ce present
Vidimus, ou Transcript, le grant seel aux causes de la
dicte viconte, lan et jour precedemment dessus diz.

PETIT.

Collation faite.

---

command. We order and command all justices, officers,
and subjects, that they diligently obey and give attention
to you, your commissioners and deputies in doing this.

Dated at Vernon, the xxvij. day of August, in the year
of grace one thousand cccc. xxix., and the seventh of our
reign.

Thus signed, By the king, at the relation of my lord the
regent, the duke of Bedford.

J. DE RAINEL.

In witness of this, we have affixed to this present Vidimus,
or Transcript, the great seal for the causes of the said
vicomté, the year and day already above-mentioned.

PETIT.

Collation has been made.

## 1429.

SUMMONS for troops to meet the duke of Bedford to oppose the French, who are about to attack Paris.[1]

JEHAN, regent le royaume de France, duc de Bedford, a nos tres chiers et bien amez maistre Richart Cordon, nostre counseiller, maistre Raoul Partrer, secretaire de monseigneur le roi et de nous, et Pierre Baille, notre tresorier, salut et dillection.

Savoir vous faisons que, pour resister aux dampnables entreprises des ennemiz de mon dit seigneur le roi et de nous, qui sefforcent de conquerir pais en ses terres et seigneuries et es notres, et mesmement de subjuguer la bonne ville de Paris, nous ayons nagaires fait crier et publier ou duchie de Normandie et pays de conqueste faite par feu notre tres chier seigneur et frere, (dont Dieu ait lame!) que tout homme suivant

A.D. 1429.
Aug. 27.

Troops required to repulse the French who are about to attack Paris.

---

### [TRANSLATION.]

JOHN, regent of the kingdom of France, duke of Bedford, to our very dear and well beloved master Richard Cordon, our councillor, master Raoul Partrer, secretary of my lord the king and of ourselves, and Pierre Baille, our treasurer, greeting and love.

We give you to understand that, in order to resist the damnable enterprises of the enemies of my said lord the king and of ourselves, who are attempting to conquer districts within his lands and lordships, and in ours, and especially to reduce the good city of Paris, we have of late caused to be proclaimed and published in the duchy of Normandy and the country conquered by our late very dear lord and brother, (whose soul may God have!) that

---

[1] From the MS. Fontanieu, 115–116.

H 2

et qui a accoustume de suir les armes, tant Anglois
comme Normands, se tirent devers les baillis des lieux
prestz pour venir servir mon dit seigneur le roy et
nous aux gaiges accoustumez. En comettant les dits
baillis, et chacun deulx, a recevoir les monstres dicelles
gens darmes et de trait, chacun es mettes de notre
bailliage.

Et pour ce que iceulx baillis, pour loccupation quilz
ont fait de notre dite armee, ne peuvent, ne pourroient,
du tout entendre a recevoir toutes les monstres quil
conviendra faire a ceste cause, tant a Caen, Rouen,
Mante, Paris, ou ailleurs, ou nous serons, nous vous
avons commis, et par ces presentes commettons, ou
les deux de vous, a icelles monstres ou reveues recevoir
et veoir de toutes les gens darmes et de trait, comprins
chevaliers, bannerets, et bacheliers, tant Anglois comme
Normands et autres, qui nous vendront servir en la
dicte armee, et vous donnons pouvoir, auctorite et

---

every person who follows and who has been accustomed to
follow arms, as well English as Normans, should betake
themselves to the baillies of the districts, ready to serve
my said lord the king and us at the accustomed wages.
Commissioning the said baillies, and each of them, to receive
the musters of these men-at-arms and archers, each within
the limits of our bailliwick.

And because these baillies, in consequence of the business
which they have had about our said army, are not and will
not be able duly to attend to the taking of all the musters
which ought to be made on this account, as well at Caen,
Rouen, Mante, Paris, as elsewhere, where we shall be, we have
commissioned you, and by these presents we do commission
you, or two of you, to receive and inspect all these musters
or reviews of all men-at-arms and archers, comprising knights,
bannerets and bachelors, as well English as Normans and
others, who shall come to serve us in the said army, and
we give you especial power, authority, and commandment

mandement especial de icelles monstres prendre et recevoir ; en passant ceux qui seront a passer et cassant
ceux qui seront a casser, comme en tel cas est accoustume de faire ; et en certifiant, soubz vos sainge ou
signetz, ou des deux de vous, des noms et surnoms
de ceulz que passez aures le receveur general de Normandie, ou autre ordonne a paier leurs diz gaiges par
la forme et maniere accoustume.   De ce faire vous
donnons povoir et mandement especial ; mandons a
tous cappitaines, gens darmes et de trait, que a vous,
es choses touchans ceste present, connoissent, obeissent,
et entendent diligemment.

Donne a Vernon, le xxvij. jour Daoust, lan de grace Date.
mil, cccc. vingt neuf.

Par monsieur le regent, duc de Bedford.

Signe, DE RINEL.

---

to take and receive these musters : passing those which ought
to be passed and rejecting those which ought to be rejected,
as in such case is wont to be done ; and certifying under
your signature or seals, or those of two of you, the names
and surnames of those persons whom you shall have passed,
to the receiver-general of Normandy, or some other person
appointed to pay their said wages, in the form and manner
accustomed.   To do this we give you power and especial
commandment; ordering all captains, men-at-arms and archers,
that they acknowledge, obey, and diligently give heed to
you in the matters touching this present.

Dated at Vernon, the xxvij. day of August, in the year
of grace one thousand cccc. and twenty-nine.

By my lord the regent, the duke of Bedford.

Signed, DE RINEL.

1429.

MANDATE from the duke of Bedford ordering the despatch of troops, the French being about to attack Paris.[1]

BY THE REGENT OF FRANCE, DUKE OF BEDFORD.

A.D. 1429.
Sept. 1.
——
The French being about to assault Paris, troops are required.

RIGHT trusty and welbeloved. For as much as my lordes ennemis and oures ben assembled in great puissance at Saint Denis in France, and other places aboutez, for to laye the siege unto Paris, and there to abide til thai have the town or elles the bataille, as we ben credibly informed, and fully purpose us, with our Lordes mercy, for to merch for to gif thaim there saide bataille by the viij. or ix. day of this moneth of Septembre; we pray yow hertly, and alsoo charge and commande yow straitly, uppon pain of alle that ye may forfaite anenst my lord and us, that ye comme unto us in al haste possible, so that ye be with us at the last by the saide ix. day, with al the fela-shipe that ye may raise or gete in any wise, on horse-bac and in fote, your place seurely ordeinde fore and kept. And the bailli of Caen[2] shall bothe receve the monstres and telle yow where ye shal have redy paiement of your wages. And failleth not her of, as ye love the conservacion of this londe, and as ye wol answere to my lordes and us therefore in tyme com-yng. And weteth wele for certain that hit lay never in oure power sith we had the regency of France so wele as it doth now, bothe of lordes, landes and other, to rewarde men. The whiche thing we promette yow

---

[1] From the original, upon paper, in the MS. Gaignières, 557.

[2] *Caen*] Written upon a blank.

faithfully for to do largely unto al tho that come to us at this tyme. And owre Lord have you in His keping.

Yevene under oure signet, at Vernon, the first day Date. of Septembre.

Moreover [1] we pray yow hertilye that ye sende unto us Henrye Montone, with al the retinue and felashipe that ye hade last, or moo, yif ye may moo gete. And that ye sende us of the best marchers and the best horsed men that ye can or may gete in al the cuntree. And at Caen we have ordenned your saide retinue to have a hoole monneth waages in hand. And we wol that your self abide stille upon the sauvegarde of Faloize, and that ye take good heed thereunto, boothe day and nighte, and that ye bee wel wer of traisons.

Yevene as above.

(*Dorso.*) To oure righte trusty and welbeloved squier, Thomas Gower, lieutenant of Faloise.

*In another hand.*

Receu ces lettres le vij. jour de Septembre.

---

[1] *Moreover*] The whole of this postscript is written in a different ink.

1429.

NOTICE of money paid for a messenger to hasten the arrival of the army coming from England into France.[1]

A.D. 1429.
Sept. 3.

A mes-
senger
sent into
England to
hasten the
despatch of
troops into
France.

A JEHAN CORBUISSIER, escuier . . . . a lui paye par le dit receveur general, iiij^xx vj. li. vij. s. vj. d. Tournois, pour le paiement de xxvij. jours entiers, commencans le xxj. jour de Juillet, mil, cccc. xxix. et finans le xxvj. jour Daoust, ensuivant, tous inclus, quil a affermez avoir vacquez en ung voyage par lui fait, par lordinance de mes dis seigneurs du conseil, ou dit pais Dangleterre porter lettres closes au roy, notre dit seigneur, a monseigneur le duc de Glocestre, monseigneur le chancelier Dangleterre, et autres seigneurs du conseil du roy, notre dit seigneur, ou dit pays, tant pour le fait de larmee ordonnee pour le siege du dit

[TRANSLATION.]

To JEHAN CORBUISSIER, esquire, . . . . . payed to him by the said receiver-general, iiij^xx vj. li. vij. s. vj. d. Tournois, for the payment of xxvij. whole days, beginning the xxj. day of July, one thousand, cccc. xxix., and finishing on the xxvj. day of August following, all included, which he has affirmed to have spent in a journey made by him, by command of my said lords of the council, to the said country of England to carry closed letters to the king, our said lord, to my lord the duke of Gloucester, my lord the chancellor of England, and others, lords of the council of the king, our said lord, in the said country, as well in the matter of the army provided for the siege of the said

[1] From the contemporaneous copy in the MS. Franç., Fonds, 9436–5, p. 645.

Mont Saint Michiel, comme pour soliciter et avancer les grans seigneurs, capitaines et armee ordonnez par le roy, notre dit seigneur, venir en France, oultre larmee qui desja y estoit venue. Pour chacun des quelx jours lui a este tauxee par notre dit seigneur, et par leurs lettres donnees a Rouen, le derniere jour Daoust ou dit an mil, cccc. xxix., la somme xl. s̃. Tournois, qui montent lxxiiij. ƚi. Tournois, et aussi pour son passage de la mer ix. salues dor, valant a xxvij. s̃. vj. đ. Tournois piece, xij. ƚ. vij. s̃. vj. đ., comme par les dits lettres cy rendues appert.

Pour ce ycy paye, par vertu des dictes lettres, pour Date. les causes et parties dessus dictes, par quittance de lui faicte le iij. jour de Septembre, mil, cccc. xxix. cy rendue, iiij<sup>xx</sup> vj. ƚi. vij. s̃. vj. đ. Tournois.

---

Mont Saint Michel, as to solicit and hurry on the grand lords, captains, and army appointed by the king, our said lord, to come into France, over and above the army which has already come hither. For each of which days an allowance has been made to him by our said lord, and by their letters dated at Rouen, the last day of August of the said year one thousand, cccc. xxix., of the sum of xl. s. Tournois, which amount to lxxiiij. li. Tournois, and also for his passage on the sea, ix. salues of gold, of the value of xxvij. s. vj. d. Tournois the piece, xij. li. vij. s. vj. d., as appears by the said letters here surrendered.

Paid therefore here, by virtue of the said letters, for the causes and particulars above mentioned, by acquittal made by him the iij. day of September, one thousand cccc. xxix., here rendered, iiij<sup>xx</sup> vj. li. vij. s. vj. d. Tournois.

## 1429.

LETTER from the council of Normandy to the lieutenant of the bailly of Caux, respecting certain
payments to the garrisons in Normandy.[1]

A.D. 1429.
October 5.

Arrange-
ments for
the pay-
ment of
certain
garrisons in
Normandy.

TRESCHIER et grant amis.

Il a este ordonne par monseigneur le regent que les
forteresces Deu, Gamaches, Monceaulx, Neufchastel et
autres forteresses des frontieres, seroient gardes sur
les revenues de chacun des diz lieux, en tant que ilz
pourront porter ; et se ilz ne suffisent, les souldoiers
des lieux seront parpaiez par argent ou provisions,
ainsy quil est mande au bailli. Et en ensuivant la
dicte ordonnance, le recepveur general a commis le
viconte Darques a faire recete, ou faire faire, des choses
dessus dictes. Et aussy a este faite limitacion des
paroisses du pais, que chacun cappitaine aura pour

---

[TRANSLATION.]

VERY dear and great friend.

It has been ordered by my lord the regent that the
fortresses of Eu, Gamaches, Monceaux, Neufchatel and
other fortresses of the frontiers, should be kept out of
the revenues of each of the said places, [in so far as they
shall be able to bear it ; and if they are not sufficient, the
soldiers of the places shall be fully paid by money or provisions, as has been commanded to the bailly. And in
following up the said ordinance, the receiver-general has
commissioned the vicomte of Arques to grant, or cause to
be granted, a receipt for the things above mentioned. Also
there has been made a limitation of the parishes of the
country which each captain shall have, that he may have

---

[1] From the contemporaneous copy, upon paper, contained in the MS.
Gaignières, 557.

avoir provision ou argent pour le paiement, anchois du peuple, en la presence des cappitaines. Et semble estre la dicte limitacion bien, la quelle vous envoions enclos[1] en ces presentes; affin que, sélon les dites lettres royaulx adrechans a maistre Jehan Dorelle et au bailli, ou son lieutenant, y soit procede par la meilleur maniere et plus au soullagement du peupple que faire se pourra, pour votre honneur et recommendacion.

Treschier et grant ami, le Saint Espirit vous ait en Sa garde.

Escript a Rouen, le v. jour Doctobre.    Date.

Et estoit escript en la marge de bas des dites lettres; Les gens du conseil du roy, notre seigneur, en Normendie.

Aussy signe,

SEBIRE.

---

provision or money for the payment, in the first place, of the people, in the presence of the captains. And the said limitation seems to be good, which we send enclosed to you in these presents; in order that according to these said letters royal addressed to master Jehan Dorelle and to the bailly, or his lieutenant, it may be procceded therein by the best manner possible for the consolation of the people, for your honour and recommendation.

Very dear and great friend, may the Holy Spirit have you in His keeping.

Written at Rouen, the v. day of October.

And on the margin at the bottom of the said letters, was written; The members of the council of the king, our lord, in Normandy.

Thus signed,

SEBIRE.

---

[1] *Enclos*] This enclosure has not been preserved.

Et en la superscription des dites lettres ; A notre
treschier et grant ami, le lieutenant du bailli de Caux,
a Arques.

> Collation faite par moy, Guillem Bauchen, tabel-
> lion Darques, le x⁰ jour de May, lan mil, iiij. c.
> et xxx.
>
> BAUCHEN.

And in the superscription of the said letters ;—To our
very dear and great friend, the lieutenant of the bailly of
Caux, at Arques.

> Collation was made by me, Guillem Bauchen, notary of
> Arques, the x. day of May, in the year one thousand,
> cccc. xxx.
>
> BAUCHEN.

## 1429.

LETTER from the council of Normandy, apparently to
Richard Norbury, respecting the defence of Pontoise.[1]

A.D. 1429.
Nov. 4.

Caution recom-
mended as to the
safety of Pontoise.

TRES chier seigneur et grant ami. Notre tres redoubte seigneur, monseigneur le regent, vous a naguaires escript tres expressement, et encores de present
par son ordonnance escripvons et prions de nous tres
effectueusement, que vos xl. lanches et les archiers
vous mettes et tenez, et faictes mettre et tenir con-

[TRANSLATION.]

DEARLY beloved lord and great friend. Our very redoubted
lord, my lord the regent, has of late written to you very
expressly, and again at this time by his command we write
and pray you upon our part most affectionately, that you
keep up and maintain your xl. lances and the archers, and
cause them to be kept up and maintained continually for

---

[1] From the original in the MS. Gaignières, 649–5. It is upon paper, but being pasted down, the water mark is not visible.

tinuelement, a la sauve garde de Pontoise, sans deffaulte. En faisant tres bonne dilligence de faire faire
guet et garde tellement que ne soiez surspris par
malle garde. Et quant au regard du paiement, faictes
monstres par devant le provost et guernetier de Pontoise, a ce commis. Et icelles faictes, vous serez paies
dargent comptant par le recepveur general de tant de
temps que vous vous y tendres ; vers lequel vous envoiez
vos monstres pour votre dit paiement. Et ne veuillez
faire deffault que nayes vos gens a la dicte ville.
Tres chier seigneur et grant ami, le Saint Esperit vous
ait en Sa garde.

Escript a Rouen, le iiij. jour de Novembre.     Date.

> Les gens du conseil du roy, notre seigneur,
> en Normandie.
>
> SEBIRE.

(*Dorso.*) A notre tres chier et grant ami, messire
Richard (?) Norbury (?) . . . . . .

---

the safeguard of Pontoise, without fail. Making the best
diligence to cause such a watch and guard to be kept so
as that you be not surprised for want of good vigilance.
And as regards the payment, make your musters before the
provost and overseer of the salt-garner of Pontoise, who
are commissioned thereto. And these things being done,
you shall be paid ready money by the said receiver-general
for so much time as you remain there, to whom you shall
send your musters for your said payment. And be pleased
not to fail by not having your men at the said town.
Very dear lord and great friend, the Holy Spirit have you
in His keeping.

Written at Rouen, the iiij. day of November.

> The members of the council of the king our
> lord in Normandy.
>
> SEBIRE.

(*Dorso.*) To our very dear and great friend, Richard (?)
Norbury (?) . . . . . .

1429.

RECEIPT by Robert Jolivet, abbot of Mont Saint Michel, for money received from the English in consequence of services rendered to them.[1]

A.D. 1429.
Nov. 8.

Receipt for money from the English for services rendered.

NOUS, Robert, par la permission divine abbe du Mont Saint Michiel, conseiller du roy, notre seigneur, confessons avoir eu et receu de Pierre Surreau, receveur general de Normendie, la somme de quatre vins seize livres Tournois, pour le paiement de seize jours entiers, commencans le iiij. jour Doctobre, mil, cccc. xxix., et finant le xxix. jour du dit moys ensuivant, tous inclus, que nous affermons par ces presentes avoir vacque ou voyage par nous fait en la compaignie de monseigneur le cardinal Dangleterre et monseigneur de Bourgoigne, pour adviser au gouvernement du pays

[TRANSLATION.]

WE, Robert, by divine permission abbot of Mont Saint Michel, counsellor of the king our lord, acknowledge to have had and received of Pierre Surreau, receiver-general of Normandy, the sum of ninety-six pounds Tournois, as payment of sixteen whole days, commencing the iiij. day of October, one thousand cccc. xxix., and ending on the xxix. of the said month following, all included, which we affirm by these present letters that we have spent in the journey made by us, in company with my lord the cardinal of England and my lord of Burgundy, to deliberate concerning the government of the country of France, and treat of a

[1] From the original in the MS. Gaignières, 266. The seal has been torn off.

de France, et traictier de treues avec les ennemis du roy, notre seigneur, les quelles estoient meues par mon dit seigneur de Bourgogne, et pour pluseurs autres grandes matieres touchants le bien de ce royaume; au pris de vj. livres Tournois par chacun jour, a nous pieca ordonne, quant nous chevaucherons pour les affaires dicelui seigneur hors ceste dicte ville, oultre et pardessus noz gaiges ordinaires de notre dit office de conseilleur.　Montent les dites jours a la dite somme de iiij<sup>xx</sup> xvj. livres Tournois.　De la quelle somme nous nous tenons pour contens et bien paiez, et en quittons le roy, notre seigneur, le dit receveur general, et tous autres.

En tesmoing de ce, nous avons signe ceste presente Date. quittance de notre saing manuel, et seelle de notre seel, au dit lieu de Rouen, le huitieme jour de Novembre, mil cccc. et vint neuf.

R. ABBE DU MONT.[1]

truce with the enemies of the king, our lord, which was moved by my said lord of Burgundy, and for many other important matters touching the good of this realm; at the rate of vj. pounds Tournois for every day, formerly allowed us, when we shall be on a journey on the affairs of the said lord and absent from this said city, over and above our ordinary wages of our said office of counsellor.　The said days amount to the said sum of iiij<sup>xx</sup> xvj. pounds Tournois.　For which sum we hold ourselves satisfied and well paid, and thereof acquit the king, our master, the said receiver-general, and all others.

In witness of this, we have signed this present acquittance with our sign manual, and sealed it with our seal, at the said city of Rouen, the eighth day of November, one thousand cccc. and twenty-nine.

R. ABBE DU MONT.

[1] This signature is in the abbot's autograph.

1430.

MANDATE for the payment of pioneers and labourers
employed in the siege of Torcy.[1]

A.D. 1430.
Jan. 23.
———
Pioneers
and la-
bourers,
required
for the
siege of
Torcy, to
be paid
their
wages. HENRY, par la grace de Dieu, roy de France et
Dangleterre, au vicomte Darques, ou a son lieutenant,
salut.

Pour ce que sommes suffisamment informez que, pour
le bien et avancement du siege presentement mis de
par nous devant le chastel et place forte de Torchy,
est, entre autres choses, besoing avoir grande quantite
de pionniers et manouvriers, tant de ta viconte que
dautres ou pais de Caux, nous, par ladvis de notre
tres cher et tres ame oncle, Jehan, regent notre
royaume de France, duc de Bedford, te mandons et
commandons expressement que tous les pionniers et

———

[TRANSLATION.]

HENRY, by the grace of God, king of France and of
England, to the vicomte of Arques, or to his lieutenant,
greeting.

Since we are sufficiently informed that, for the good and
advancement of the siege at this time laid for us to the
castle and stronghold of Torchy, there is need, among
other things, to have a great number of pioneers and
labourers, as well from your vicomté as from others in the
Pais de Caux, we, by the advice of our very dear and
well-beloved uncle, John, regent of our kingdom of
France, duke of Bedford, command and enjoin you expressly that out of the money of your receipt you pay

———

[1] From the MS. Fontanieu, 115–116.

manouvriers que en ta viconte ont ete, ou seront mis en besongne au dit siege par ordonnance de notre bailli de Caux, tu, des deniers de ta recepte, paies et contentes de leurs peines et labours en raisonnable et compettent pris, telement quilz puissent etre illec entretenuz, et ce par maniere de prest; lequel prest voulons et entendons estre recouvre sur les subgiez de la viconte par ordonnance et assiette du dit bailli, que voulons estre faicte loyaument et sans exceder ce qui au cas appartient, et appartiendra.

Donne a Rouen, le xxiij. jour de Janvier, lan de grace mil, cccc. vint neuf, et de notre regne le huictieme. Date.

Par le roy, a la relation de monseigneur le regent, duc de Bedford.

*Signe*, DROSAY, *avec paraphe.*

---

and satisfy for their trouble and labours all the pioneers and labourers who have been, or shall be, sent into your vicomté to labour at the said siege by the command of our said bailly of Caux, at a reasonable and fitting rate, in such manner that they be retained there, and this by prompt payment; and this advance we will and intend should be recovered from the subjects of the vicomté by the ordinance and assessment of the said bailly, which we will should be done fairly and without exceeding what is, and shall be, fitting in this case.

Dated at Rouen, the xxiij. day of January, in the year of grace one thousand, cccc. and twenty-nine, and of our reign the eighth.

By the king, at the relation of my lord the regent, the duke of Bedford.

*Signed*, DROSAY, *with a flourish.*

### 1430.

MANDATE and proceedings upon the levying of an assessment for the prosecution of the war in Normandy.[1]

A.D. 1430. April.

Assessment made for prosecution of the war in Normandy,

ASSIETTE faicte par nous, Edouard a Paouel, esleu sur le fait des aides ordonnez pour la guerre es vicontez Dargenten, Dexmes, Danffront et St. Silvin, sur la dite viconte de Danffront, de la somme de neuf cens soixante quinze livres Tournois, lan mil cccc. et xxx., le . . . . . jour Davril apres Pasques ; presens ad ce et appelez Nicolas Normant, viconte du dit lieu de Danffront, le conseil et procureur de tres haut et puissant prince, monseigneur le regent le royaulme de France, duc de Bedford et Dalencon, les sergens de la dite vicomte, et plusieurs autres notables personnes ; icelle[2] assiette faicte par vertu du mandement de messieurs les tresorier et receveur generaulx des

---

### [TRANSLATION.]

THE assessment made by us, Edward a Paouell, elected to carry out the aids ordained for the war in the vicomtés of Argentan, Exmes, Domfront and St. Silvain, for the said vicomté of Domfront, of the sum of nine hundred and seventy-five pounds Tournois, in the year one thousand cccc. and xxx., the . . . . day of April, after Easter ; there being for this purpose present and summoned Nicolas Normant, the vicomte of the said place of Domfront, councillor and proctor of the most high and powerful prince, my lord the regent of the realm of France, duke of Bedford and of Alençon, the serjeants of the said vicomté and many other persons of note; this assessment being made by virtue of the commandment of my lords the treasurer and receiver-general

---

[1] From the MS. Fontanieu, 115–116. [ [2] *Icelle*] The MS. reads "icelles."

finances du roy, notre sire, en Normandie ; duquel la teneur ensuit.

THOMAS BLOUNT, chevalier, tresorier et general gouverneur des finances du roy, notre sire, en Normandie, et Pierre Sureau, recepveur general des dits finances, commissaires du roy, notre sire, en cette partie, aux esleuz sur le fait des aides a Dampfront et au vicomte du dit lieu, ou a leur lieutenant, salut.

Recevez par nous les lettres du roy, notre dit seigneur, donnees a Rouen, le xxvᵉ jour de Fevrier darrenier passe, par lesquelles nous est mande et commis asseoir, faire, cueillir, lever et recepver, dedans le viij. jour Dapvril prouchainement venant, la somme de lxᴹ. livres Tournois pour le second et derrenier paiement de laide de vijˣˣ.ᴍ. livres Tournois ottroyez au roy, notre dit seigneur, par les gens des Trois Estatz du duchie de Normandie et pays de conqueste, faitte par feu de bonne memoire son feu seigneur et pere (dont

---

by virtue of the following mandate.

---

of the finances of the king, our lord, in Normandy, of which the copy is as follows.

THOMAS BLOUNT, knight, treasurer and governor-general of the finances of the king, our lord, in Normandy, and Pierre Sureau, receiver-general of the said finances, the commissioners of the king, our lord, in this part, to these persons who are elected in the matter of the aids of Domfront, and to the vicomte of the said place, or his lieutenant, greeting.

There have been received by us the letters of the king, our said lord, dated at Rouen, the xxv. day of February last past, by the which we are commanded and appointed to tax, make, collect, levy and receive, within the viijth day of April, next coming, the sum of lx.ᴍ. pounds Tournois, for the second and last payment of the aid of vijˣˣ.ᴍ. pounds Tournois, granted to the king, our said lord, by the members of the Three Estates of the duchy of Normandy and the country conquered by his late lord and father, of

Dieu ait lame!) en lassemblee faicte a Rouen, au moys de Novembre derrenier passe, pour tourner et convertir ou paiement des gens darmes et de trait estans en garnison es villes et forteresses du dit duchie de Normandie et pays de conqueste, et ou recouvrement et delivrance de Torcy, Aumalle, Conchez, et autres forteresses denviron, nuisans, et non ailleurs.

Et oultre la dite somme, nous est mande asseoir sur les habitants du bailliage de Costetin, ressort et enclaveure diceluy, la somme de ij. M. livres Tournois pour icelle somme convertir ou paiement de iiij$^{xx}$v. lancez et les archiers a cheval, de nouvel a la requeste diceulx habitans mis sus et ordonnez pour deux moys, pour la garde dicelui bailliage, et demolicion des places que ont emparees et emparent les ennemis pres Davranchin et de Vires.

Et aussi par icelles nous est mande asseoir sur le demourant des dits habitants du dit duche et pays de

---

noble memory, deceased, (whose soul may God keep!) in the assembly made at Rouen in the month of November last past, to spend and employ it in the payment of the men-at-arms and archers who are garrisoned in the towns and fortresses of the said duchy of Normandy and the conquered country, and for the recovery and deliverance of Torcy, Aumale, Conches, and other fortresses round about, which are hurtful, and not otherwise.

And besides the said sum, we are commanded to assess upon the inhabitants of the bailiwick of the Cotentin, the jurisdiction and district comprehended within the same, the sum of two thousand pounds Tournois, to employ this sum in the payment of iiij$^{xx}$v. lances and the archers on horseback lately raised and appointed, at the request of the said inhabitants, for two months, for the protection of the said bailiwick, and for the demolition of the places which the enemy have taken, and are taking, near the district of Avranches and Vire.

And also we have been commanded by the same to levy upon the residue of the said inhabitants of the said duchy

conqueste, la somme de huit mille livres Tournois, pour convertir en paiement des gens darmes et de trait ordonnez pour les bastilles qui se feront devant Torcy, et pour le recouvrement de Gaillart, Louviers, Conches, et autres places occupees par les dits ennemis.

Noꭟs, eu sur ce advis et deliberacion de plusieurs des conseillers et officiers du roy, notre dit seigneur, avons ordonne, et ordonnons par ces presentes, estre assis, cueilly et leve sur les habitans de la dite ville et viconte de Danffront, pour leur cotte, part, et porcion des dits deux sommes de lx. M. livres Tournois, et de viij. M. livres Tournois, la somme de neuf cens soixante et quinze livres Tournois, par assiettes deuement par vous faictes sur chacune des villes et paroisses dicelle viconte, non comprins en ce les gens deglise, nobles vivans noblement, frequentans les armes, ou qui par impotence de corps en sont excusez, et miserables personnes, lesquielx le roy, notre dit seigneur, en exempte par ses dits lettres.

---

and the conquered country, the sum of eight thousand pounds Tournois, to employ in the payment of the men-at-arms and archers ordained for the bastilles which are being made before Torcy, and for the recovery of Gaillard, Louviers, Conches, and other places occupied by the said enemies.

We, having thereupon had the advice and deliberation of many of the councillors and officers of the king, our said lord, have ordained, and do ordain by these presents, that there shall be assessed, collected, and levied upon the inhabitants of the said town and vicomté of Domfront, for their quota, part and portion of the said two sums of lx. M. pounds Tournois, and of viij. M. pounds Tournois, the sum of nine hundred and seventy-five pounds Tournois, by assessments duly made by you upon each of the towns and parishes of the said vicomté, without including churchmen, nobles who live as such, persons following arms, or those who by bodily weakness are excused therefrom, and persons in distress, whom the king, our said lord, exempts therefrom by his said letters.

Si vous mandons, et par vertu du pouvoir a nous donne, commettons, que tantost et sans delay, appelles avec vous le conseil et procureur du roy au dit lieu de Danffront, les sergens dicelle viconte, et autres personnes notables en nombre suffisant, vous faictes assiette bonne et loyalle de la dite somme de ix°lxxv. livres Tournois, par sergenteries sur chacune des villes et paroisses dicelle viconte, selon la puissance des habitans dicelle, au mielx et plus loyaument et esgallement que faire se pourra; et icelle assiette faicte, la baillies, ou faictes baillier, aux habitans dicelles villes et paroisses pour leur porcion asseoir sur eulx, la cueillir, lever et apporter par devers nous, Nicolas Normant, viconte du dit lieu de Danffront, lequel nous avons commis, et commettons, par ces presentes, a icelle somme recepver hastivement, tellement que dedans le dit viij° jour Dapvril prouchainement venant elle puise etre paye, delivree et apportee franchement, entierement, et sans aucune dimi-

---

Wherefore we command you, and by virtue of the power to us given we commission you, speedily and without delay to call to you the councillor and the proctor of the king for the said place of Domfront, the sergents of the same vicomté, and other persons of note in sufficient number, and to make a good and true assessment of the said sum of ix. c. lxxv. pounds Tournois by sergentries upon each of the towns and parishes of the said vicomté, in proportion to the ability of the inhabitants of the same, according to the best, the fairest and the most equal manner possible; and when this assessment has been made, that you deliver it, or cause it to be delivered, to the inhabitants of the same towns and parishes, so that they may assess their portion upon themselves, may collect it, levy it and convey it to master Nicolas Normant, the vicomte of the said place of Domfront, whom we have appointed, and do appoint by these presents, to receive this sum with haste, in such wise that within the viijth day of April next coming it may be paid, delivered, and conveyed freely, entirely and without

nution par devers nous, Pierre Surreau, recepveur general de Normandie, pour la convertir et employer es choses dessus dites ; pourveu que, au devant de quelconques contraintes, la publicacion de ces presentes precede de quinze jours en icelle viconte. Et toutes icelles choses, leurs circonstances et deppendances, faire et accomplir, donnons povoer a vous, au dit viconte, et a chacun de vous, si comme a lui appartendra. Mandons a tous les officiers du dit seigneur que a vous et vos commis et deputez obeissent et entendent diligemment.

Donne a Rouen, le premier jour de Mars, lan mil <small>Date.</small> iiij. c. et vingt neuf.

*Ainsi signe,* V. FARRY.

Et icelle assiette faicte par sergenteries sur chacune des villes et paroisses dicelle viconte, et baillee et cueillie et recepvee, a honnourable homme et saige, Nicolas Normant, escuier, viconte du dit lieu, et com-

---

any diminution, to us, Pierre Surreau, receiver-general of Normandy, to expend and employ it on the matters abovesaid ; provided that the publication of these presents shall precede by fifteen days any distresses whatever within the said vicomté. And we give power to you, to the said vicomte, and to either of you, as far as to him shall appertain, to do and accomplish all these things, and the matters connected with and dependent upon the same. We command all the officers of the said lord to obey and give diligent aid to you and your commissioners and deputies.

Dated at Rouen, the first day of March, in the year one thousand iiij. c. and twenty-nine.

*Signed thus,* V. FARRY.

And this assessment made by sergenties upon each of the towns and parishes of this vicomté, and given and collected and received, to the honorable and discreet man, Nicolas Normant, esquire, vicomte of the said place, and appointed

mis a icelle somme recepvrer, pour en faire recepte et
en rendre compte comme il appartiendra soubz notre
signet et saing manuel de Jehan de Dompierre, clerc
de la dite election.

Et avecques ce, y a ete assis pour les coustages et
paine de clers, la somme de xxxj. livres Tournois.

———————

to receive the same sum, to make a receipt for the same
and to render an account thereof, as to him shall appertain,
under our signet and the sign manual of Jehan de Dompierre,
clerk of the said circuit.

And moreover, there has been assigned for the costs and
trouble of the clerks, the sum of xxxj. pounds Tournois.

———————

## 1430.

LETTER of Thomas Ruras to the council at Rouen,
  requesting that payment be made to the carpenters, masons, etc., employed at the siege of
  Gaillard.[1]

A.D. 1430.   MES treschiers et tres honnoures seigneurs.
April 13.     Tout humblement comme je puis a vous me recom-
The pay-   mande.   Et vous plaise savoir que jay receu les
ment of the

———————

### [TRANSLATION.]

My very dear and much honoured lords.

As humbly as I can I recommend myself to you.   And
may it please you to know that I have received the gra-

———————

[1] From the original in the MS. Gaignières, 557.   It is written upon
paper, but no watermark is visible.

gracieuses lettres de mon tres redoubte seigneur, artisans at the siege of Gaillard is urgently requested.
monseigneur le regent, cy enclus. Combien que, par
vertu de la commission que jay du roy, notre seigneur, je feisse et donnasse a Jehan Lunberi, es-
cuire, soubz-mareschal de lost et seige estant devant
Gaillard, commission pour tenir devers lui des charpentiers, macons et manouvriers, iceux emploier et
faire besongnier es choses necessaires estre faictes
pour lemparement et fortifficacion du dit seige, laquelle commission messire Thomas de Beaumont et
moy avons fait faire au dit Lunbery, et a icellui
Lunbery en excersant icelle tres bien, grandement et
honnourablement fait besongner et faire de jour en
jour entour icellui siege ; et avec les laboureurs
qui lon a peu recouvrer, a fait tenir et besongner ou
dit siege les personnes, charpentiers et macons, declaires
en notre escroe de parchemin cy enclose, par lespasse de temps en icelle contenuz.

Et pour ce que sans iceux avoir, len ne peut

---

cious letters of my very redoubted lord, my lord the regent,
here enclosed. Since, by virtue of the commission which
I have from the king, our lord, that I might make and give
to Jehan Lunberi, esquire, under-marshal of the army and
siege which is before Gaillard, commission to keep with him
carpenters, masons and workmen, to employ them, and to take
care that all things necessary for the strengthening and
fortification of the said siege, messire Thomas de Beaumont
and I have caused this commission to be given to the said
Lunbery, and the said Lunbery has exercised it very well,
and efficiently and honourably has given heed and employed
himself from day to day, in the matter of this siege ; and
along with the labourers whom it has been possible to
obtain, has caused the persons, carpenters and masons,
mentioned in our scroll of parchment here enclosed, to be
kept and employed at the said siege during the space
of time mentioned therein.

And because, unless these persons be had, the things

bonnement faire ou dit siege les choses necessaires
que faire y fault, et que sans paiement a ceulx, et
chacun deulx faire, de tant de temps que ilz ont
servi et serviront, ilz ne pourroient eulx y tenir,
maiz sen veullerent partir, et desia sen fussent
alez, ne fust ce que par le dit Lumberi leur[1] . . . .
este preste argent pour avoir leurs vies et substractions ; le partement des quelx seroit . . . . dommaige des habitans ou dit siege et retardement des
choses qui de necessite y convient . . . . faitez ;—
vous supplie tant que je puis, que il vous plaise
faire paiement au porteur de ces lettres pour iceux
charpentiers et macons de tout de temps comme ilz
ont servi, jouxte la declaration cy enclose, et les
pouvoir de paiement pour le temps advenir; ou autrement convendroit quilz se departissent.

---

which necessarily ought to be done at the said siege
cannot be performed, and because unless payment be made
to them, and to each of them, for as much time as they
have served, and shall serve, they cannot continue there,
but will depart thence, and would have taken themselves
off already, had it not been that money had been advanced to them by the said Lumberi that they might
have the necessaries of life and " substractions ; " the
departure of whom would be . . . . . . . . a damage
to those who continue at the said siege and a delay in the
matters which of necessity ought there to be done ;—I
entreat you as much as I can, that it would please you
to cause payment to be made to the bearer of these letters
for the said carpenters and masons for all the time which
they have served, according to the declaration here enclosed ;
and to make provision for their payment for the future ;
or otherwise it is certain that they will depart.

---

[1] *Leur* . . . . . ] Here the document is slightly damaged by a hole
at the fold of the paper.

Mes treschiers et tres honnurez seigneurs, se chose vous plaise moy commandre, je suy prest de accomplir de tout mon cueur vos[1] bons plaisirs et commandemens au plaisir de Dieu, notre Createur, qui vous doint joye parfite.

Escript au siege devant Gaillard, le xiij. jour Date. Davril.

Votre humble servant en tout,
THOMAS RURAS.[1]

(*Dorso.*) A mes treschiers et treshonnoures seigneurs, messires du conseil du roy, notre seigneur, a Rou[en].

---

My very dear and most honoured lords, if it please you to command me to do anything, I am ready to do it with all my heart, to accomplish your wishes and commands, with the permission of God, our Creator, Whom I pray to give you perfect joy.

Written in the siege before Gaillard, the xxiij. day of April.

Your humble servant entirely,
THOMAS RURAS.

(*Dorso.*) To my very dear and most honoured lords, the lords of the council of the king, at Rouen.

---

[1] *Cueur vos*] Cueur accomplir vos, MS.
[1] The surname, which is rather obscure, is autograph, and is sur- mounted by a device, executed by the pen, which (apparently) represents a swan.

## 1430.

LETTER from Henry the Sixth to the officers of his Accounts at Paris, announcing his arrival at Calais.[1]

### DEPAR LE ROY.

A.D. 1430.
April 23.

Henry has arrived in safety, and his army will speedily follow.

A NOS amez et feauz gens de nos comptes a Paris.

Nos amez et feaux; nous tenons certainement que desirez savoir nouvelles de notre etat. Pourquoy vous signiffions que aujourdhuy sommes arrivez en ceste notre ville de Calais, en tres bonne prosperite de notre personne, la mercy notre Seigneur; et ordonnons venir apres nous notre armee en bonne dilligence; laquelle passee, aurez plus avant et de pres de nos nouvelles.

---

### [TRANSLATION.]

#### FROM THE KING.

To our beloved and faithful the officers of our accounts at Paris.

Beloved and faithful; we are fully persuaded that you desire to know news of our condition. Wherefore we let you know that to-day we have arrived in this our town of Calais with our person in a prosperous state of health, by the mercy of our Lord; and we have arranged that our army shall come after us as speedily as possible; and when it has crossed over, you shall ere long have further news of us.

---

[1] From the MS. Fontanieu, 115–116, where it is stated that it was obtained from the Chambre des Comptes, memor. J. fol. 65.

Donne au dit Calais, sous notre signet, le jour de Date.
Saint Georges, xxiij. jour Davril.

RINEL.

Recus de iiij. jour de May, lan M. CCCC. XXX.

———————

Given at tho said Calais, under our seal, the day of Saint
George, the xxiij. day of April.

RINEL.

Received on the iiij. day of May, the year M. CCCC. XXX.

═══════════

## 1430.

LETTERS of John, duke of Bedford, acknowledging the
receipt of 5,000l. Tournois, from Pierre Surreau,
expended in the pay of troops employed in the
protection of Paris.[1]

JEHAN, regent le royaume de France, duc de Bed- A.D. 1430.
fordt, a tous ceulx qui ces presentes lettres verront, May 25.
salut.
Comme ou mois de Septembre darrenement passe, Henry VI.
having
nous eussions fait emprunter de notre tres cher et borrowed
9,388l. 10s.

———————

[TRANSLATION.]

JOHN, regent of the realm of France, duke of Bedford,
to all those who shall see these present letters, greeting.
Since, in the month of September last past, we caused
to be borrowed of our very dear and well-beloved uncle,

---

[1] From the contemporaneous copy in the MS. Fonds Franç., 9436–5.

Tournois
from
cardinal
Beaufort,
the duke
of Bed-
ford gives
orders as
to the
application
thereof.

tres ame oncle, le cardinal Dangleterre, la somme de
ix. M. iij. c. lxxxviij. *l.* x. *s.* Tournois, et pour icelle
somme lui rendre et restituer dedans le jour de la
Saint Jehan Baptiste prouchainement venant, lui avons
baille nos lettres obligatoires et engaige plusieurs de
nos joyaulx et vesselle dor et dargent, laquelle somme
nous mandasmes a Pierre Surreau, receveur general de
Normandie, quil receust pour lemploier ou paiement
des gens darmes, que lors avions mandez venir devers
nous pour secourir la bonne ville de Paris, et rebouter
le dauphin et les ennemis, qui lors estoient devant la
ditte ville de Paris ; la quelle somme il receust, et
dicelle emploia partie ou dit paiement des gens darmes,
par notre ditte ordonnance.

Savoir faisons que ajourduy nous avons eu et receu
du dit Pierre Surreau, receveur general de Normandie,
sur et en deduction de la ditte somme par lui receue,
comme dit est, la somme de v. M. livres Tournois ; de

---

the cardinal of England, the sum of ix. M. iij. c. lxxxviij. *l.*
x. *s.* Tournois, and, in order that this sum might be repaid and restored to him by the day of Saint John the
Baptist next coming, we have given him our letters of
bond and put in pawn many of our jewels and plate
of gold and silver, which sum we commanded Pierre Surreau, receiver-general of Normandy, to receive, in order
that he might employ it in the payment of the men-at-
arms whom we had then ordered to come to us for the
succour of the good city of Paris, and to drive back the
dauphin and the enemies who at that time were before
the said city of Paris.   This sum he has received, and
he has employed part of it in the said payment of the
men-at-arms, by our said appointment.

We make known that this day we have had and received of the said Pierre Surreau, receiver-general of
Normandy, for and in deduction of the said sum by him
received, as is said, the sum of v. M. pounds Tournois ;

la quelle somme nous nous tenons pour contens et bien
paiez, et en quittons le dit Pierre Surreau et tous
autres ; et voulons et consentons par ces presentes que
le dit Pierre Surreau face recepte en ses comptes du
demourant dicelle somme montant iiij. M. ccc. lxxxviij. *l.*
x. *s.* Tournois, affin que, en temps et en lieu, la puissions recouvrer sur monseigneur le roy, comme par
raison appartiendra, et que en faisant la ditte recepte
en ses comptes dicelle somme de iiij. M. ccc. lxxxviij. *l.*
x. *s.* Tournois, icellui Pierre Surreau demeure a tousjours quitte envers nous de toute la dessus ditte somme
de ix. M. iij. c. iiij$^{xx}$. viij. *l.* x. *s.* Tournois, et dicelle
somme le quittons par ces presentes.

Donne a Rouen, soubz notre scel, le xxv. jour de Date.
May, lan de grace M. iiij. c. xxx.

Ainsi signe, Par monseigneur le regent le royaume
de France, duc de Bedford.

*Signe*, BRADSCHAWE.

---

of which sum we hold ourselves satisfied and well paid,
and thereof we acquit the said Pierre Surreau and all
other persons ; and we will and consent by these presents
that the said Pierre Surreau may enter the receipt in his
accounts of the balance of this sum, which amounts to
iiij. M. ccc. lxxxviij. *l.* x. *s.* Tournois ; in order that, at
[due] time and place, we may recover it from my lord
the king, as by reason is fitting ; and that, when he
makes the said receipt in his accounts of the said sum
of iiij. M. ccc. lxxxviij. *l.* x. *s.* Tournois, the said Pierre
Surreau may continue for ever acquitted as regards us of
the whole of the above said sum of ix. M. iij. c. iiij$^{xx}$. viij. *l.*
x. *s.* Tournois, and of this sum we acquit him by these
presents.

Dated at Rouen, under our seal, the xxv. day of May
in the year of grace M. iiij. c. xxx.

Thus signed ; By my lord the regent of the realm of
France, duke of Bedford.

*Signed*, BRADSCHAWE.

## 1430.

MANDATE for the re-payment of sixteen pounds Tournois, expended in the fees of certain messengers employed in the service of the English.[1]

A.D. 1430.
June 29.

Money
expended
upon
various
messengers
and others,
to be
repaid to
Richard
Golduit.

HUE SPENCIER, bailli de Caux, au viconte Darques, ou a son lieutenant, salut.

Richart Golduit a baille et paie, par notre commandement et ordonnance, a plusieurs personnes, plusieurs sommes de deniers, lesquelz personnes, pour le bien du roy notre sire et par deliberacion de conseil, nous avons ordonne faire plusieurs voiaiges, tant de jours comme de nuys, en plusieurs lieux et places; des quelz voiaiges et sommes diceulx deniers la declaracion ensuit.

Cest assavoir; le ij. jour Davril avant Pasques derrenierement passe, a Jehan Boursier, pour avoir porte, de la ville de Lislebonne devers les cappitaines de Hare-

- - - - - - - - - -

### [TRANSLATION.]

HUE SPENCIER, bailly of Caux, to the vicomte of Arques, or to his lieutenant, greeting.

Richard Golduit has given and paid, by our command and direction, to several persons, several sums of money, which persons, for the good of the king, our lord, and by the deliberation of the council, we have commanded to make several journeys, as well by day as by night, to several places and towns; of which journeys and sums of money the specification follows.

That is to say; on the ij. day of April, before Easter last past, to Jehan Boursier, for having carried closed letters from the town of Lillebonne to the captains of

---

[1] From the MS. Fontanieu, 115–116.

fleu, Neeville, Valmont, et autres cappitaines du dit
bailliage, lettres closes de nous, pour leur faire savoir
quilz se teinssent prestz pour aller au service du roy,
notre sire, comme mande nous avoit este par monsieur
le regent, touttefois que len leur feroit assavoir, xx.
sols Tournois. ,

Item, le xij. jour du dit moys, a Raoulin Fillaistre,
pour avoir porte du siege de Torcy, lettres et mandemens de nous aux vicontes de Caudebec et Moustrier-
villier, pour faire venir certains deniers qui avoient este
assiz sur les villes et paroisses de leurs vicontez, pour
paier les manouvriers du dit siege de Torcy, xx. sols
Tournois.

Item a Eliot, poursuivant, pour avoir porte lettres
de monsieur de Brinkeley, lun des cappitaines du dit
siege, et de nous, devers nos seigneurs du conseil du
roy, notre seigneur, a Calaiz, pour le bien dicellui
seigneur et du dit siege, iiij. sols Tournois.

---

Harfleur, Neuville, Valmont, and other captains of the
said bailliwick, from us, to let them know that they must
hold themselves ready to go in the service of the king,
our lord, as we have been commanded by my lord the
regent, whenever they should be informed thereof, xx. sols
Tournois.

Item, on the xij. day of the said month, to Raoulin
Fillaistre, for having carried from the siege of Torcy,
letters and commands from us to the vicomtes of Caudebec and Montivilliers, to cause to be brought certain
money which had been levied on the towns and parishes
of their vicomtés, to pay the workmen employed in the
said siege of Torcy, xx. sols Tournois.

Item, to Eliot, poursuivant, for having carried letters
from monsieur de Brinkeley, one of the captains of the
said siege, and from us, to our lords of the council of
the king, our lord, at Calais, for the good of the said
lord, and that of the said siege, iiij. sols Tournois.

Item, a Colin, trompete de Granville, pour avoir este du dit Torcy a Beauvaiz, savoir et enquerir de la venue des ennemis, lx. sols Tournois.

Item, a Raoulin Meriel, pour avoir porte de Longueville a Caudebec et Moustiervillier, devers les dits vicontes, mandemens de nous pour faire venir des charrettes, beneaulx et autres voictures pour la chaussee faicte au dessoubz du dit chastel de Torcy, laquelle etait rompue, xx. sols Tournois.

Item, au dit Fillaistre, pour avoir porte lettres du dit monsieur de Brinkeley et nous a nosseigneurs de conseil du roy, notre seigneur, a Rouen pour la dicte cause, xx. sols Tournois.

Item, a Pierre de Briligny, pour avoir porte du dit Torcy a Calaiz lettres closes du dit monseigneur de Brinkeley et nous devers nos diz seigneurs du grant conseil du roy, notre seigneur, pour le bien du siege, xl. sols Tournois.

---

Item, to Colin the trumpeter of Granville, for having gone from the said Torcy to Beauvais, to ascertain and enquire about the coming of the enemies, lx. sols Tournois.

Item, to Raoulin Meriel, for having carried from Longueville to Caudebec and Montivilliers, to the said vicomtes, commands from us, to cause carts, trucks, and other carriages to come about the causeway made below the said castle of Torcy, which was broken, xx. sols Tournois.

Item, to the said Fillaistre, for having taken letters from the said monsieur de Brinkeley and us to the lords of the council of the king, our lord, at Rouen, for the said cause, xx. sols Tournois.

Item, to Pierre de Briligny, for having carried closed letters from the said Torcy to Calais, from my said lord of Brinkeley and us to our said lords of the great council of our lord the king, for the good of the siege, lx. sols Tournois.

Item, au dit poursuivant, le xxij<sup>e</sup> jour de ce present mois de Juing, pour aller au dit Calaiz porter lettres de nous devers monseigneur le cardinal Dangleterre et de nos diz seigneurs du grant conseil, pour pourveoir a ce que certains Anglois, qui estoient logiez sur le pays du dit bailliage, fussent envoyez hors dicellui, pour les maux quilz y commettoient, lx. sols Tournois.

Lesquelles sommes, qui montent en somme toute a seize livres Tournois, nous certiffions avoir este paiez aux dessus dits messaigiers par le dit Golduit, par notre commandement et ordonnance.

Si vous mandons que la dite somme de xvj. livres Tournois vous paiez et delivriez au dit Golduit des deniers de votre recepte ; et par rapportant les presentes, avec quittance souffisant du dit Golduit, comme vous lui aurez paie la dite somme, ce vous sera alloue en vos comptes et rebatu de votre recepte par ceulx ou il appartendra.

---

Item, to the said poursuivant, the xxij. day of this present month of June, for going to the said Calais to carry letters from us to my lord the cardinal of England, and from our said lords of the great council, to arrange that certain English who were lodged in the country of tho said bailliwick should be sent away from the same, on account of the ills which they had committed there, lx. sols Tournois.

These sums, which amount in all to sixteen pounds Tournois, we certify to have been paid to the abovementioned messengers by the said Golduit, by our command and appointment.

Wherefore we command you that the said sum of xvj. pounds Tournois you shall pay and deliver to the said Golduit from the money of your receipt ; and by bringing these presents, along with a sufficient acquittance from the said Golduit that you have paid him the said sum, this shall be allowed you in your accounts, and struck off from your receipt by those to whom it shall belong to do so.

K 2

Date.

Donne, en tesmoing de ce, soubz le petit seel aux causes ou dit bailliage, le **xxix.** jour de Juing, lan mil cccc. et trente.

BOURSIER.

Given, in witness of this, under the little seal for the causes in the said bailliwick, the **xxix.** day of June, in the year one thousand cccc. and thirty.

BOURSIER.

1430.

LETTER from the duke of Bedford to the abbot of Mont Saint Michel, and Raoul le Saige, requesting them to hasten to him.[1]

A.D. 1430, July 20.

DEPAR le gouvernant et regent de France, duc de Bedforde.

The duke of Bedford summons the abbot of Mont S. Michel and Raoul le Saige.

TRESCHIERS et bien amez. Nous vous avons pieca mande et escript bien expressement depar monseigneur le roy, et depar nous, que, pour aucunes grans matieres touchans le bien general de ce royaume, vous

[TRANSLATION.]

BY the governor and regent of France, the duke of Bedford.

VERY dear and well beloved. We have already sent and written to you very expressly on the part of my lord the king, and on our own part, that for certain great matters touching the general good of this realm, you should come

---

[1] From the original letter, upon paper, in the MS. Gaignières, 266. fol. 95. A seal in red wax, perfect and in good preservation, remains, apparently the privy seal of the duke.

venissiez dedens la fin de ce mois pardevers nous. Et pour ce que les causes et raisons, pour lesquelles desirons voz presencez, croissent et se multiplient, nous vous prions et mandons derechief, que soiez au dit temps pardevers nous, sans y faillir. Et pour votre seurte, sommes daccord que prenez conduit ou besoing vous sera, aux despens de mon dit seigneur.

Treschiers et bien amez, notre Seigneur soit garde de vous.

Donne aux champs devant Laigni, le xx° jour de Date· Juillet.

RINEL.

(*Dorso.*) A noz treschiers et bien amez, labbe du Mont St. Michiel et le sire de Saint Pierre, conseillers de monseigneur le roy.

---

to us before the end of this month. And since the causes and reasons for which we desire your presence increase and multiply, we pray, and moreover command you, that you be, at the said time, with us, without failure therein. And for your safety, we have agreed that you should take a guard where you shall require it, at the expense of my said lord.

Very dear and wellbeloved, may our Lord be your protection.

Dated in the fields before Laigny, the xx. day of July.

RINEL.

(*Dorso.*) To my dear and wellbeloved, the abbot of Mont S. Michiel and the sire de Saint Pierre, counsellors of my lord the king.

1430.

LETTER from N. Braque to Jehan Gage, respecting the transmission of 1,600 francs.[1]

A.D. 1430.<br/>Sept. 3.<br/><br/>1,600<br/>francs to be<br/>delivered<br/>to the con-<br/>stable of<br/>France.

CHEIR et bon ami. Le roy et messeigneurs ont ordonne que vous bailliez et delivres a Estienne Braque, tresorier des guerres du roy, notre seigneur, ou a son certain commande, la somme de xvj. c. frans, pour le paiement de monseigneur le connestable de France. Si vous pri tant comme je puis, que icelle somme vous bailliez et delivrez hativement au dit Estienne, ou a son dit commande, en prenant de lui une cedule de Jehan Luissier a votre descharge de la dicte somme. Et gardez comment que ce soit, quelque chevanche que vous en doiez faire, tant des aides comme des fouages, par emprunt, ou autrement, que en ce nait

---

[TRANSLATION.]

DEAR and good friend. The king and my lords have ordained that you should give and deliver to Stephen Braque, treasurer of the wars of the king, our lord, or upon his certain command, the sum of xvj. c. francs, for the payment of my lord the constable of France. Wherefore I pray you as much as I can, that you give and deliver this sum hastily to the said Stephen, or upon his said command, taking from him a schedule of John Luissier for your discharge of the said sum. And take care whatever you do, whatever sum you must raise, either by aids or taxes, by borrowing, or otherwise, that herein there be no failure.

---

[1] From the original, upon paper, contained in the MS. Gaignières, 557. The seal is lost.

point de deffaut. Car aucunement il auroit faulte ou
dit paiement, il convendroit que je men excusasse sur
vous, et en seriez pugnie. Notre Seigneur vous gart.

Escript a Paris, le tiers jour de Septembre. Date.
N. BRAQUE.

(*Dorso.*) A mon chier et bon ami, Jehan Gaze,
receveur a Fescamp, sur les aides de la
guerre.

For if by any means there should be a failure in the said
payment, it would be necessary that I should therein excuse
myself at your cost, and you would therein be punished.
Our Lord keep you.

Written at Paris, on the third day of September.
N. BRAQUE.

(*Dorso.*) To my dear and good friend, John Gaze, receiver at Fescamp, for the aids of the war.

## 1430.

LETTER from Thomas de la Becque to Sir Raoul Campion respecting the transmission of 7,200 francs.[1]

A.D. 1430,
Sept. 27.

Letter from
Thomas de
la Becque
to Sir
Raoul
Campion,
respecting
the trans-
mission of
7,200
francs.

TRESCHIER sire et amis.

Mon maistre vous escript par ses lettres (les quelles il oublia a sceller, et les quelles jay scellees de mon seele), que vous apportez, ou envoiez, au Mans vij. M. ij. c. frans, demourans de xj. M. ij. c. francs assignez sur vous, si que vous verrez pleinement par les dictes lettres. Et aussi sur ce vous escrivent messeigneurs les generaulx. Si vous pri tant comme je puiz, quil vous plaise avancier la dicte somme, car il en est tres-grant besoing. Et je serai au Mans, au plaisir Dieu, dedens Mardi prochain, pour la recevoir, et la vous baillerai voz descharges de xj. M. ij. c. frans. Et

---

## [TRANSLATION.]

VERY dear lord and friend.

My master has written to you by his letters (which he has forgotten to seal, and which I have sealed with my seal) that you should convey or send to Le Mans vij. M. ij. c. francs, remaining out of xj. M. ij. c. francs affixed upon you, as you will see plainly by the said letters. And also my lords the generals write you upon the same subject. Wherefore I pray you as earnestly as I can, that it will please you to hasten the said sum, for there is very great need of it. And I shall be at Le Mans, if it please God, by Tuesday next, to receive it, and there I will give you your discharges for the xj. M. ij. c. francs. And I certify

---

[1] From the original, upon paper, contained in the MS. Gaignières, 557. It is sealed with a small seal in red wax, of which a portion still remains.

vous certify que les dictes lettres mon maistre les fist faire, et sont escriptes de la main Prinet, son clerc.

Je vous pri que vous me recommendez a monseigneur le chastellain de Caen, au bailli de Caen, et au bailli de Coustentin, se vous les veez. Et me commandez comme au votre. Le Saint Esperit vous ait en Sa saincte garde.

Escript a Savinny, ce Mecredi matin, xxvij. jour de Date. Septembre.

Votre clerc, THOMAS DE LA BECQUE,

Clerc sire Jacques Renart, tresorer des guerres.

(*Dorso.*) A mon treschier seigneur, sire Raoul Campion, receveur-general en la Basse Normandie des aides de la guerre.

———————

you that as to the said letters, my master has made them, and they are written with the hand of Prinet, his clerk.

I pray you recommend me to my lord the keeper of the castle of Caen, to the bailly of Caen, and to the bailly of the Cotentin, if you see them. And you may command me as your own. The Holy Spirit have you in His holy keeping.

Written at Savigny, this Wednesday morning, the xxvij. day of September.

Your clerk, THOMAS DE LA BECQUE,

The clerk of sire Jacques Renart, treasurer of the wars.

(*Dorso.*) To my dear lord, sir Raoul Campion, receiver-general in Lower Normandy of the aids of the war.

1430.

ACKNOWLEDGMENT by the city of Rouen for forty livres
Tournois advanced towards the payment of the
balance of the sum due by the said city to the
English, which has remained unpaid since the time
of its surrender.[1]

A.D. 1430.
Oct. 10.

Michiel
Basin has
advanced
40l. Tour-
nois to the
city of
Rouen.

LA ville de Rouen est tenue a Michiel Basin, demourant en la paroisse Saint Denis, en la somme de quarente livres Tournois, quil a ajourdhuy prestez au grant
besoin et necessite de la dite ville pour aidier a faire
certain paiement de xij. M. salus quil fault promptement faire sur la somme de xxiiij. M. salus encore
deubz de reste de la composition et rendue de la dite
ville de Rouen, avec autres choses a recouvrer avec
le dit reste. De laquelle somme de xl. livres Tournois le dit Michiel Basin sera paie sur les aides et
revenues de la dite ville, ou autrement, ainsi que

[TRANSLATION.]

THE city of Rouen is indebted to Michiel Basin, living
in the parish of Saint Denis, in the sum of forty pounds
Tournois, which he has this day lent in the great need
and necessity of the said town, to aid in making a certain
payment of xij. M. salus, which must promptly be made
towards the sum of xxiiij. M. salus still due from the
balance of the composition and surrender by the said city
of Rouen, with other things to be recovered along with
the said balance. Of which sum of xl. pounds Tournois the
said Michiel Basin shall be paid from the aids and revenues
of the said city, or otherwise, as shall be considered for

[1] From the MS. Fontanieu, 115–116.

len advisera pour le mieux, et le plus diligamment que faire se pourra. Et a ce tenir et paier, Pierres Daron, procureur general dicelle ville, obliga, par vertu de sa procuration, tous les biens et revenus de la dite ville, presens et advenir.

Donne soubz le petit seel aux causes du bailliage Date. de Rouen, le x. jour Doctobre, lan mil, cccc. et trente.

MARTIN.

---

the best, and as expeditiously as shall be possible to do it. And to observe and pay this, Pierres Daron, procurator-general of this city, pledges, in virtue of his procuration, all the goods and revenues of the said town, present and to come.

Dated under the little seal for the causes of the bailli-wick of Rouen, the x. day of October, in the year one thousand cccc. and thirty.

MARTIN.

1430.

LETTER from the duke of Burgundy to Henry the
Sixth, complaining of the non-payment of the
troops, and vindicating his own conduct.[1]

A.D. 1430.
Nov. 4.
———
The duke
of Bur-
gundy
complains
of Henry's
conduct,
and vindi-
cates his
own.
MON tres redoubte seigneur, je me recommande a
vous tant et si humblement que plus puis.

Mon tres redoubte seigneur, je tieng bien estre en
vostre noble memoire et de ceulx de vostre conseil,
comme a vostre grante requeste je me suis emploie ou
fait de vostre guerre de France ; et de mon coste et
de ma part ai fait et accompli jusque a ores ce quil
accorde et promis avoie par lendenture faite entre
tres reverend pere en Dieu, mon tres cher et tres
ame oncle, le cardinal Dangleterre, de nom de vous,
dune part, et de moy dautre.  Et est vray que a ceste

[TRANSLATION.]

MY very redoubtable lord, I recommend myself to you as
much and as humbly as I possibly can.

My very redoubtable lord, I am fully · persuaded that
it is your noble memory, and in that of those of your
council, how at your urgent request I have employed myself in the business of your war of France ; and on my
side and my part I have done and accomplished until this
present time all that I have agreed and promised by the
indenture made between the very reverend father in God,
my very dear and well-beloved uncle, the cardinal of England in your name, on the one part, and of myself on the
other.  And it is true that on this occasion all my lands,

---

[1] From the Supplément Franç., 292–10, p. 384.

occasion tous mes pais, tant de Bourgongne comme des marches de Picardie, ont este et sont en guerre et en voye de destruction, et aussi ma conte de Namur pour la plus grant partie destruite, comme il est notoire. Avecques ce, est vray que a vostre requeste et par vostre ordonnance je suis ale devant vostre ville de Compiengne, ja soit ce que lavis de moy et de ceulx de mon conseil ne fust pas tel, ains nous sembloit plus expedient de moy tirer a Crayl et Laonnois, ainsi que apparoir puet par les avis sur ce bailliez, envoiez a Calais par maistre Jehan Milet, vostre secretaire.

Est vray aussi, mon tres redoubte seigneur, que, par appointement fait depar vous avecques mes gens, (cest assavoir, les seigneurs de Santes et du Mesnil, et le provost de Saint Omer,) vous deviez paier pour chacun mois pour le paiement de mes gens estans devant la ditte ville de Compiengne, la somme de dix neuf mille cinq cent frans, monnoie royal, et aussi deviez paier lartillerie; et avecques ce, beau cousin le

---

as well those of Burgundy as in the marches of Picardy, have been and are at war and on the road to destruction, and also my comté of Namur is for the most part destroyed, as is well known. It is true, moreover, that at your request and by your appointment I went before your town of Compiègne, although my own opinion and that of my council was not to do so, but it seemed to us more expedient that I should go to Creil and the Laonnois, as may also appear by the advice hereupon given, which was sent to Calais by master Johan Milet, your secretary.

It is also true, my very redoubtable lord, that an agreement made on your part with my agents (that is to say, the lords of Santes and du Mesnil, and the provost of Saint Omer), you ought to pay during each month' for the payment of my men who are before the said town of Compiègne, the sum of nineteen thousand five hundred francs of royal money, and also you ought to pay the artillery; and, moreover, my good cousin the earl of Hun-

conte Hontenton et sa compaignie devoient demourer de lez moy en mes gens devant la ditte ville de Compiengne.

Et est vray que, soubz consideration ainsi deust estre fait de vostre part, et mesmement que le dit paiement deust estre fait et entretenu sans y faillir, comme accorde avoit este, jay toujours fait tenir mes gens devant la ditte ville de Compiengne.

Points in which Henry has failed. Mais, mon tres redoubte seigneur, de vostre coste na point este entretenu le dit paiement ; car il en est deu deux mois ou environ, et aussi dartillerie, pour la quelle jay fraye et debourse de mes propres deniers plus de quarante mille saluz, sans mon artillerie, que javoie de garnison, rien ne men a este restitue, jasoit ce que par plusieurs fois que je vous en ay escrit, et envoie devers vous, et fait touttes dilligences possibles ; et pareillement mes gens estans devant le dit Compiengne en mon absence en ont escrit souventes fois devers vous, en vous signifiant au vray lestat des

---

tingdon and his company, ought to remain with me among my people before the said town of Compiègne.

And it is true that, under the impression that this would be done on your part, and especially that the said payment would be made and kept without failing therein, according to agreement therein made, I have always caused my men to be kept before the said town of Compiègne.

But, my very redoubtable lord, the said payment has not been continued on your side; for it is due for two months or thereabouts, and also that of the artillery, for which I have paid and expended more than forty thousand saluz out of my own money, without speaking of my artillery, which I had in garrison, whereof nothing has been repaid to me, notwithstanding the many times that I have written to you about it, and sent to you, and used all diligence possible ; as likewise my men, who are before Compiègne aforesaid, in my absence have oftentimes written to you of it, signifying to you the true state of affairs, as well on the side

besoingnes, tant du coste des ennemis comme de leur, et les tres grans deshonneur, domages et inconveniens qui estoient tailliez den venir a vous se ny pourvoyez, et mesmement se ny envoiez hastivement argent pour fournir le dit paiement ; veu que journellement, par deffault dicelluy paiement, mes gens se departoient, et leur en convenoit departir et eulx se deschargant, se par faulte du dit paiement inconvenient en avenoit, ainsi quil puet apparoir par la minute de leurs lettres sur ce a vous envoiees,[1] dont sest ensuy que par faulte du dit paiement les gens qui estoient de mon coste ne se sont peu entretenir et les en a convenu departir. Par quoy par faulte de gens len na peu enclorre la ville, ainsi quil appartenoit. Et aussi le dit beau cousin de Hontenton ne povoit, comme il disoit, par faulte de paiement,

---

of the enemies as on their own, and the very great dishonour, damages, and inconveniences which were likely to happen to you therefrom if you do not provide for it, and especially if you do not hastily send money to provide for the said payment ; seeing that daily, in default of this payment, my men are going away, and they must of necessity depart and discharge themselves, if by default of the said payment any disadvantage should herein arise, as it may appear by the minute of their letters on this subject sent to you, whence it follows that, in default of the said payment, the men who were on my side have not been able to continue, and they have been forced to depart. Wherefore, for want of men, it has been impossible to surround the town, as ought to have been done. And also the said good cousin of Huntingdon could not, as he said, for want of payment, any longer keep his men together, so the

---

[1] *Envoiees*] This enclosure has not been preserved in the manuscript which furnishes the present letter.

plus entretenir ses gens, et tellement que linconvenient, dont len se doubtoit, est avenu, ainsi comme
je croy que vous et vostre conseil en povez estre
acertenez par la relation du dit beau cousin de
Hontinton et de ceulx de sa compaignie, lesquelles
gens du dit beau cousin de Hontinton, (ja soit ce
que apres la chose avenue, aient este fait requis
par mes gens deulx entretenir une espace de temps
a Pont Levesque, ou tenir les champs illec environ
jusques len eust peu envoier devers vous et devers
moy, a fin dy pourveoir plus avant,) ne lont voulu
faire, ains len sont alez.

Lesquelles choses venues a ma congnoissance mont
este et sont si desplaisans que plus ne peuent.  Et
a fin de obvier a plus grant inconvenient je, (qui
mestoye departi de devant la dite ville de Compiengne pour mon fait de Brabant, ainsi quil est
bien venu a vostre congnoissance, et men retournoye
de tire devant la dite ville, incontinent apres mon dit

--------

thing which was apprehended has come to pass, as I believe
you and your council can be assured by the relation of the
said good cousin of Huntingdon and those of his company.
And although the said followers of my said good cousin of
Huntingdon after this affair had occurred, had been requested by my men to tarry a space of time at Pont l'Évè-
que, to continue in the country thereabouts, until it might
have been possible to send to you and to me, in order to
make speedy provision for it, yet this they did not please to
do, but they took themselves off.

When these things came to my knowledge, they have
been and are so displeasing to me that nothing could be
more so.  And in order to obviate worse results, I (who
had set out from before the said town of Compiègne for
my affairs in Brabant, as you are well aware, and returned thence to go before the said town, immediately
after my said affairs in Brabant were completed) have

fait de Brabant expedie,) me suis arreste en ceste ma
ville, et diligamment ay escript et envoie lettres a vos
bonnes villes es marches de pardeca, pour les recon-
forter et entretenir en vostre obeissance, et aussi que
incontinent envoie gens darmes et de trait et establi
frontieres es villes et places prouchaines aux ennemis.
Et dautre part, (pour ce que iceulx ennemis tiennent
les champes et journellement gaignent places, et se
vantent dencores plus faire alencontre de vous et de
moy,) je fais mon mandement general a toute puissance au dixiesme jour de ce presente mois entour la
ville de Corbie, a fin de resister de ma part alencontre
des diz ennemis, et les combattre, alaide de nostre
Seigneur, se ils attendent ; esperans que de vostre part
y pourvoyez aussi en toute haste, ainsi que la chose
qui tant vous touche le requiert bien.

Et toutes voyes, mon tres redoubte seigneur, ces
choses je ne puis entretenir ne continuer de ma part
sans vostre bonne provision pour le temps a venir,

————————————

stopped at this my town, and have diligently written and
sent letters to your good towns in the marches on this side,
to encourage them and keep them in obedience to you, and
also have immediately sent men-at-arms and bowmen, and
established frontiers in the towns and places near to the
enemies. And on the other hand (because these enemies
hold the field, and daily gain strongholds, and boast that
they will do still more against you and me), I have
made my general summons of all my forces on the
tenth day of this present month in the neighbourhood of
the town of Corbie, in order to resist on my part the
said enemies, and to fight them, with the help of our
Lord, if they wait ; hoping that on your part you also
will make provision for the same in all haste, as this
thing, which concerns you so nearly, well requires.

And nevertheless, my very redoubtable lord, these things
I cannot support nor continue for my part without your
good provision, for the time to come, which should be

laquelle convient avoir grande et bien notable, et
aussi sans y avoir paiement de ce [que] deu mest
par vous, tant des diz deux mois, comme de lartillerie.   Pour quoy, mon tres redoubte seigneur, je vous
requiere et vous prie tres humblement quil vous plaise
delivrer, ou faire delivrer, a mes gens, par lour envoyez a Calais, et qui longuement y ont demore pour
ceste cause, les dis paiemens, incontinent, realment et
de fait, se deja fait ne lavez; et largent de quels
paiemens, (combien que deu me soit loyalment par
vous, et que en pourroie desposer a ma voulente,)
neantmoins le vueil je emploier et convertir en la
propre besoingne alencontre des diz ennemis.

Avecques ce, mon tres redoubte seigneur, vous re-
quier et prie que pour le temps avenir vueilliez pourveoir au fait de la guerre, tant de vostre coste comme
au regard de ce que me puet touchier, par telle maniere et si puissamment que les ennemis puissent estre
reboutez hastivement, et que ceulx de ce royaume et

---

very great and notable, and also without having payment
for that which is due to me from you, as well for the
said two months as for the artillery.   Wherefore, my very
redoubted lord, I require and pray you very humbly that
it may please you to deliver, or cause to be delivered, to
my men, by their envoys at Calais, who have long remained there for this cause, the said payments immediately,
really and truly, if you have not already done so; and the
money arising from these payments (although it be justly
due to me by you, and I might dispose of it at my will)
nevertheless I wish to employ it and expend in the special
business of opposition to the said enemy.

Moreover, my very redoubtable lord, I require and pray
you that for the future you will be pleased to provide for the
affairs of the war, as well on your own side as with regard
to what may touch me, in such manner and so powerfully as
that the enemies may be hastily repulsed, and that those of
this kingdom and all others may clearly perceive that your

tous autres apparcoivent clerement vostre puissance
estre plus grande que celle des diz ennemis, et que
ces choses ne soient point mises en delay ne dissimulation, mais soit trouvee manier de abregier ceste
guerre, et que ce que y aviserez soit chose brieve,
ferme, et entretenue sans faillir; ou autrement il est
a doubter de plus grans inconveniens, (que Dieu ne
vueille!) et mesmement de la perdicion des bonnes
villes de vostre obeissance, et ne devez, ne ceulx de
vostre conseil, doubter du contraire. Et au regard de
moy, de ma part, je vous en avise et adverti, et
vostre conseil, pour ma descharge et acquit.

Et pour ces choses et autres vous remonstrer plus
a plain, et a vostre conseil, jay entencion de prouchainement envoier devers vous aucuns de mes gens
et conseillers notables. Mais, mon tres redoubte
seigneur, je vous prie que sans attendre la venue de
mes dis gens, il vous plaise par ce messaige me
escrire vostre entencion et bon plaisir sur les choses
dessus dittes hastivement et le plus tost que bonne-

---

power is greater than that of the said enemies, and that
there may be no delay nor dissimulation about these things,
but that means of shortening this war be found, and that
what you determine about it be brief, firm, and carried out
without fail; or otherwise it is to be feared that there will
be greater disadvantage (which God forbid!), and even to
the loss of the good towns which are obedient to you; and
neither you nor those of your council should doubt to the
contrary. And with regard to myself and my part, hereof
I assure and advertise you and your council for my discharge and acquittal.

And to show these things and others more plainly to
you and your council, I intend to send to you shortly
some of my people and notable counsellors. But, my very
redoubtable lord, I pray you that, without waiting for the
arrival of my said people, it may please you to write your
intention and good pleasure on the things above mentioned

L 2

ment faire se pourra. Mon tres redoubte seigneur, je prie au benoist Fils de Dieu, qui vous ait en Sa sainte garde, et doint bonne vie et longue.

Escrit en ma ville Darras, le iv. jour de Novembre.

Vostre humble et obeissant oncle, Philipe duc de Bourgoingne et Brabant et de Lembourg.

A mon tres redoubte seigneur, monseigneur le roy.

**Date.**

---

by this messenger, hastily and the soonest that possibly may be.

My very redoubtable lord, I pray the blessed Son of God that He will have you in His holy keeping, and grant you a happy and long life.

Written in my town of Arras, the iv. day of November.

Your very humble and obedient uncle, Philippe, duke of Burgundy and Brabant and of Lembourg.

To my very redoubtable lord, my lord the king.

---

## 1430,

A.D. 1430.
Nov. 4.

Instruc-
tions to the
ambassa-
dors from
Burgundy

INSTRUCTIONS as to statements to be made upon the part of the duke of Burgundy to the king and council of England.[1]

INSTRUCTION pour messire Pierre Boffremont, seigneur de Charny, et messire Jehan de Tressy, seigneur

---

[TRANSLATION.]

INSTRUCTION for messire Pierre Boffremont, lord of Charny, and messire Jehan de Tressy, lord of Mesnil, knights,

---

[1] From the MS. Suppl'm. Franç., 292, 10, p. 302.

de Mesnil, chevaliers, conseillers, chambellan de mon- to the English court respecting
seigneur de Bourgoingne, ordonnez depar luy pour aler
devers le roy et son conseil estant devers luy.

Primo, presenteront leurs lettres de creance au roy,
a monseigneur le regent, monseigneur le cardinal, monseigneur de Warrwik et autres de son conseil, a cui
elles se adrecent; et apres les presentations des dittes
lettres et recommendations accoustumees pour leur
creance diront ce qui sensuit :—

Cest assavoir, que premierement ils remonstreront the duke's losses.
au roy et a son conseil comment, a la grant requeste du
roy, mon dit seigneur sest employe ou fait de sa guerre
de France, et de son coste et de sa part a fait et
accompli jusques a ores ce que accorde et promis avoit
par lendenture faite entre le dit monseigneur le cardinal, ou nom du roy, dune part, et de mon dit seigneur de Bourgoigne daultre ; et comment a ceste occasion tous ses pays, tant de Bourgoingne comme des
marches de Picardie, ont este et sont en guerre et en

---

counsellors, chamberlains of my lord of Burgundy, appointed
by him to go to the king and to his council being with him.

First, they shall present their letters of credence to the
king, to my lord the regent, my lord the cardinal, my lord
of Warwik and the rest of his council, to whom they are
addressed ; and after the presentations of the said letters
and the accustomed recommendations for their credit, they
shall say what follows :—

That is to say, that, firstly, they shall show to the king
and to his council how, at the urgent request of the king,
my said lord has employed himself in the business of his
war in France, and on his side and on his own part has
done and accomplished until this present time all that he
had accorded and promised by the indenture made between
my said lord the cardinal in the name of the king, on the
one part, and of my said lord of Burgundy, on the other ;
and how that on this occasion all his country, as well in
Burgundy as in the marches of Picardy, has been, and is

voye de destruction, et aussi sa conte de Namur pour
la plus grant partie destruitte, comme il est notoire.

his adher-
ence to his
engage-
ments,
Item, remonstreront apres, comment a la requeste
du roy et pour son ordonnance, mon dit seigneur ala
devant la ville de Compiengne, ja soit ce que lavis de
lui et de ceulx de son conseil ne fust pas tel, ains
leur sembloit plus expedient deulx tirer a Crayl et en
Laonnois, ainsi que apparoir puet par les avis sur ce
baillez, envoyez a Calais par messire Jehan Milet,
secretaire du roy.

Item, comment par appointement fait depar le roy
avecques les gens de mon dit seigneur (cest assavoir,
les seigneurs de Santes et du Mesnil, et le Prevost de
Saint Omer), le roy devoit paier pour chacun mois a
mon dit seigneur de Bourgoingne, pour le paiement de
ses gens estans devant la dite ville de Compiengne, la
somme [de] dix neuf mille cinq cents francs, monnoye
royal, et aussi devoit paier lartillerie. Et avec ce,

---

at war and in the road to destruction, and also his county
of Namur is for the most part destroyed, as it is well
known.

Item, they shall show afterwards how, at the request of
the king and by his command, my said lord went before
the town of Compiègne, although such was neither his
own opinion nor that of those of his council, but it seemed
more expedient to them to advance upon Creil and the
Laonnois, as may appear by the advice thereupon given,
sent to Calais by messire Jehan Milet, secretary of the
king.

Item, how that by the appointment made by the king
with the men of my said lord (that is to say, the lords of
Santes and Du Mesnil, and the Provost of Saint Omer),
the king ought to pay by each month to my said lord of
Burgundy, for the payment of his men being before the
said town of Compiègne, the sum of nineteen thousand five
hundred francs, of royal money, and also should pay the artillery. And moreover, my lord the earl of Huntingdon and

monseigneur le conte de Hontinton et sa compaignie devoient demourer delez mon dit seigneur et ses gens devant la dit ville de Compiengne ; et comment mon dit seigneur, confidant ainsi deust estre fait, et mesmement que le dit payement lui deust estre fait et entretenu sans y faillir, comme accorde avoit este, a tous jours fait tenir ses gens devant la ditte ville de Compiengne.

Item, comment le roy de son coste, na point entre-tenu le dit paiement, car il en est deu deux mois ou environ, et aussi de lartillerie ; pour la quelle mon dit seigneur a fraye et despence du sien propre plus de xl. M. salus, sans son artillerie quil avoit de garnison, rien ne lui a este restitue, ja soit ce que par pluseurs fois il en ait escript et envoie devers le roy et fait touttes diligences possibles, et pareillement ses gens estans devant le dit Compiengne en son absence en ont escrit souventes fois devers le roy, en lui signiffiant au vray lestat des besoingnes, tant du coste des enne-

*the king does not keep his arrangements ;*

his company should remain along with my said lord and his men before the said town of Compiègne ; and how my said lord, trusting that thus it would be done, and especially that the said payment would be made him and continued without failure therein, as had been agreed, has always kept his men before the said town of Compiègne.

Item, how that the king, on his part, has not observed the said payment, for it has been due for two months or there-abouts, and also for the artillery ; for which my said lord has defrayed and spent of his own money more than xl. M. salus, without mentioning his artillery which he had in garrison, whereof nothing has been returned to him, although many times he has written about it and sent to the king, and used all possible diligence, and likewise his men being before the said Compiègne in his absence have written many times about it to the king, signifying to him truly the state of affairs, as well on their own side as on that of

mis comme de leur, et les tres grans deshonneur et
dommaiges et inconveniens qui estoient taillez denvenir
au roy sil ny pourveoit, et mesmement sil ny envoioit
hastivement argent pour fournir les diz payemens, veu
que journellement par deffault dicelui paiement les gens
de mon dit seigneur departoient, et leur enconvenoit
departir, en eulx deschargant se par faulte du dit
paiement inconvenient en avenoit, ainsi quil puet apparoir par la minute de leurs lettres sur ce envoyees
au roy.

Item, comment par faulte du dit paiement, les gens
qui estoient du coste de monseigneur ne se sont peu
entretenir et les a convenu departir, par quoy par
faulte de gens len na peu enclorre la ville ainsi quil
appartenoit; et aussi mon dit seigneur de Hontinton
ne povoit (com il disoit) par faulte de paiement plus
entretenir ses gens, tellement que linconvenient dont
lon se doubtoit est advenu; ainsi comme le roy et son
conseil en peuent estre acertenez par la relation du

---

the enemies, and the very great dishonour and ills and evil
results which were likely to happen to the king if he did
not make provision for them, and especially if he did not
send money there hastily to provide for the said payments,
seeing that daily by default of this payment the men of
my said lord departed, and are compelled to go away, they
discharging themselves, if by failure of the said payment
misadvantage might arise, as may appear by the minute
of their letters sent about this matter to the king.

Item, how by default of the said payment, the men who
were on the side of my lord have not been able to continue,
and have been compelled to go; consequently for want of
men they have not been able to enclose the town as should
have been done; and also my said lord of Huntingdon could
not (as he said), for want of payment, retain his men any
longer, so that the ill results of which they were apprehensive had come to pass; as the king and his council may be
informed by the relation of my said lord of Huntingdon and

dit monseigneur de Hontinton et de ceulx de sa compaignie. Lesquelles gens de la compaignie du dit monseigneur de Hontinton, ja soit ce que apres la chose
avenue aient este fort requis par les gens de mon dit
seigneur deulx entretenir une espace de temps a Pont
Levesque, ou tenir les champs illec environ, jusques
len eust peu envoyer devers le roy et mon dit seigneur le duc, a fin dy pourveoir plus avant, ne lont
voulu faire, ains len sont alez.

Item, comment mon dit seigneur, lequel sestoit de- *the position*
parti de devant la ditte ville de Compiengne pour son *of the duke*
fait de Brabant, ainsi quil est bien venu a la congnois- *of Bur-*
sance du roy, tantost quil a eu expedie le dit fait de *gundy.*
Brabant, sen retournoit devant la dite ville, et comment en soy retournant en son chemin a sceu les
dittes nouvelles, qui tant lui desplaisent que plus ne
peuent. Et a fin de obvier a plus grans inconveniens,
a incontinent escript lettres aux bonnes villes du roy
des marches ,pardeca, dont les diz ambaisseurs por-

---

of those of his company. And those men of the company of
my said lord of Huntingdon, although after the thing had
happened, had been earnestly required by the men of my
said lord to continue for some space of time at Pont l'E-
vêque, or to keep in the country thereabouts, until they
could send to the king and my said lord the duke, so as to
make further provision for it, would not do so, but departed.

Item, how my said lord, who had gone from before the
said town of Compiègne on his affairs of Brabant, as
has come to the knowledge of the king, directly he had
finished the said business of Brabant, returned before the
said town, and how that in returning then on his road he
received the said news, which were so displeasing to him
that nothing could be more so. And in order to obviate
still greater misfortunes, he immediately wrote letters to the
good towns of the king of the marches here, of which the
said ambassadors carried the copy to show it, and also has

teront la copie,[1] pour la monstrer, et aussi a incontinent envoye gens darmes et de trait, et establi frontieres es villes et places prouchaines aux ennemis. Et
dautre part, pour ce que lon dit que iceulx ennemis
tiennent les champs, a lentencion dassembler gens de
son coste, pour y resister de sa part, esperant que le
roy y pourvoye en toutte haste de son coste en de-
laissant toutte autre chose, ainsi que la chose qui tant
lui touche le requiert bien.

Item, remonstreront au roy et a son conseil comment
mon dit seigneur a signiffie ces choses par lettres closes,
quil a escript sur ce au roy et son dit conseil, a fin
davoir sur se provision hastive ; et comment apres le
partement des messaiges pour les nouvelles continuelles,
que de jour en jour et de heure a heure venoient des
ennemis, et quils se boutoient fort avant et conqueroient
(comme ils font encores tous les jours), places et forte-

---

forthwith sent men-at-arms and archers, and established
frontiers in the towns and places near the enemies. And
further, because they say that these enemies hold the fields
with the intention of assembling men of their side, there
to offer resistance on their part, hoping that the king would
provide for the same in all haste on his side, leaving every
other business, as the matter which touches him so closely
well requires of him.

Item, they shall show the king and his council how my
said lord has signified these things by closed letters, which
he has written about this to the king and his said council,
in order to have speedy provision for the same ; and how
that after the departure of the messengers in consequence
of the continual news which from day to day and from
hour to hour come from the enemies, and that they were
pushing forward rapidly, and would conquer (as they still are
doing every day) strongholds and fortresses in the country

---

[1] *La copie*] This document has not been discovered.

resses ou pays du roy entre les riviers Doye et de
Somme, et sen vantent dencore plus faire, mon dit
seigneur a fait son mandement le plus brief quil a peu,
assavoir, au x. jour de ce mois de Novembre, entour
Corbie, a fin de resister de sa part alencontre des dis
ennemis et les combattre, sils tiennent la campagne, et
les rebouter a son povoir, esperant la dite provision
du roy estre brieve, et avec ce a establi frontieres en
trois ou quatre places prouchaines aus dis ennemis, et
envoye de ses gens, qui a este, et est, chose de grant
coustaige pour mon dit seigneur.

Item, remonstreront comment mon dit seigneur ne
puet ces choses entretenir ne continuer de sa part,
sans la provision du roy pour le temps a venir, laquelle convient avoir grande et bien notable; et aussi
sans avoir paiement de ce que deu lui est par le roy,
tant des dis deux mois comme de lartillerie.

Pourquoy requerront les diz ambaisseurs, premierement, quil plaise au roy delivrer, ou faire delivrer, a

The demands of the duke of Burgundy.

_____

of the king between the rivers of the Oye and the Somme,
and boast they will still do more, my said lord has issued
his summons for as early a period as possible, that is to
say, on the x. day of this month of November, in the
neighbourhood of Corby, so as to resist on his part the
said enemies, and to fight with them, if they keep in the
country, and to drive them back as well as he can, hoping
that the said provision of the king may be briefly made, and
besides this he has established frontiers in three or four places
near to the said enemies, and sent some of his men, which
has been, and is, a thing of great cost for my said lord.

Item, they shall state how that my said lord cannot
keep up nor continue these things upon his part, without
the provision of the king for the time to come, which ought
to be great and very notable; and also without having
payment of that which is due to him from the king, as
well for the said two months as for the artillery.

Wherefore the said ambassadors shall require, firstly, that
it may please the king to deliver or to cause to be delivered,

mon dit seigneur les diz paiemens incontinent, realment, et de fait, se deja nest fait ; largent desquels
paiemens (combien que deu soit par le roy a mon dit
seigneur, et quil en pouvoit disposer a sa voulente)
il est content de emploier et convertir en la presente
besoingne alencontre des dis ennemis.  Secondement,
que pour le temps a venir le roy pourvoye de fait de
sa guerre, tant de son coste comme au regard de ce
qui touche mon dit seigneur, par tele maniere et si
puissament que les ennemis puissent estre reboutez
hastivement, et que ceulx de ce royaume et tous
autres appercoivent clerement la puissance du roy
estre plus grande que celle des ennemis, et que ces
choses ne soient point mises en delay ne dissimulation,
mais soit trouvee maniere dabregier ceste guerre, et
que ce que le roy y avisera soit chose brieve, ferme
et entretenue, sans faillir.  Ou aultrement il est a
doubter de plus grans inconveniens (que Dieu ne
veuille !) et mesmement de la perdicion des bonnes

---

to my said lord the said payments immediately, really and
actually, if it be not done already ; the money of which
payments (although it be due from the king to my said
lord, and that he may employ it at his will), he is content
to employ and expend in the present matter against the
said enemies.  Secondly, that for the time to come the king
shall provide for the business of his war, as well upon his
side, as also regards what touches my said lord, in such
a manner and so powerfully, as that the enemies may be
hastily repulsed, and that those of this kingdom and all
others may perceive clearly that the power of the king is
greater than that of the enemies, and that these things
may not be delayed nor done in seeming only, but that
a means of shortening this war may be found, and that
the thing which the king shall therein advise may be brief,
firm, and carried out without fail.  If this be not done, it is
to be feared there will arise greater misfortunes (which
God forbid !) and especially the loss of the good towns

villes de lobeissance du roy, et ne doivent le roy ne
son conseil doubter du contraire. Et au regard de
mon dit seigneur de sa part, il en avise et advertist
le roy et son conseil pour sa descharge et acquit.

Item, au regard de ce qui est deu a monseigneur
de lartillerie, se largent nestoit prest, ou que len difficulte de le baillier ou envoier, les dis ambaisseurs
pouront secretement et discretement ouvrir comment
par monseigneur le cardinal a este autres fois offert
a mon dit seigneur de lui bailier monseigneur de
Bourbon en paiement de ce que le roy lui doit, et
que mon dit seigneur seroit asses content de prendre
icellui monseigneur de Bourbon pour le paiement de
son dit deu, ou la dite artillerie jusques a la somme
a lui deue pour ceste cause.

Item, remonstreront les dis ambaisseurs comment
les pays de mon dit seigneur sont en guerre et en voye
de perdition pour la dite guerre du roy, ainsi que
dessus est touchie, et especialment ses pays de Bour-

---

from the obedience of the king, and neither the king nor
his council should imagine the contrary. And as regards
my said lord, he, on his part, hereof informs and advertises
the king and his council for his discharge and acquittal.

Item, as regards what is due to my lord for the artillery, if money be not on hand, or there be difficulty in
paying it or sending it, the said ambassadors might secretly and discreetly open, how it has been formerly offered
to my said lord by my lord the cardinal, to surrender to
him my lord of Bourbon in payment of what the king owes
him, and that my said lord would be well satisfied to take
my said lord of Bourbon as payment of his said debt, or
for the said artillery, to the sum due to him on this
account.

Item, the said ambassadors shall show how the countries
of my said lord are in war and on the road to ruin in consequence of the said war of the king, as has been touched
upon above, and especially his country of Burgundy,

gongne, lesquels de tous costes sont enveronnez des
dis ennemis, excepte seulement du coste de Savoye;
et encores nouvellement sest allie le daulphin avec le
duc Dosteriche et les Allemans pour faire guerre es
dis pais de Bourgongne du coste Dallemaigne incontinent les abstinences faillies qui sont entre les dis
pais de Bourgongne et Dallemaigne, lesquelles fauldront
a la Saint Martin [1] prouchainement venant.

Et comment autresfois mon dit seigneur a fait requerir au roy quil voulsist ordonner gens de trait jusques
au nombre de deux mille, ou au de mille, paiez de ses
despens, pour faire guerre et resister aus dis ennemis
es dites marches, et comment de la part du roy la
dite requeste de mon dite seigneur fu mise en delay,
en donnant esperance dy pourveoir cy apres.

Et comment puis quatre jours est venu un messaige
de Bourgoingne devers mon dit seigneur depar son ma-

---

which are surrounded on all sides by the said enemies,
excepting only on the side of Savoy; and now the dauphin
has newly allied himself with the duke of Austria and the
Germans to make war on the said country of Burgundy
on the side of Germany directly the truce, which is between
the said countries of Burgundy and Germany, expires,
which will terminate on the feast of Saint Martin next
coming.

And how formerly my said lord made a request to
the king that he would be pleased to appoint archers
to the number of two thousand, or of one thousand, paid
at his expense, to make war and resist the said enemies
in the said marches, and how on the part of the king the
said request of my said lord was delayed, by giving hopes
of providing for this afterwards.

And how that four days ago a messenger from Burgundy
has come to my said lord from his marshal and his lords

---

[1] *La Saint Martin*]  November 11.

reschal et ses seigneurs et gens de son conseil depar
dela, lequel a dit et rapporte pour vray que le daulphin
en sa personne et grant puissance des dits ennemis
sont a Molins en Bourbonnois . . . . . . . . . . . . .[1]
et daultre part aultre grant puissance des dis ennemis
est arrive es marches de Masconnois et Aucerrois, et
requierent les gens de mon dit seigneur depar dela
que monseigneur voye en personne, ou aultrement y
pourveoie et envoie hastivement des gens, et par especial
des archers.

Et pour ce que le besoing y est plus grant que
devant, et la provision tres necessaire, requeront les
dis ambaisseurs au roy quil lui plaise ordonner et
bailler a mon dit seigneur le nombre de archers soubs
aucun capitaine notable, payez aus despens du roy, pour
(avecques les gens et subgiez de mon dit seigneur des
diz pays de Bourgoingne, dont il y a bon nombre et

---

and the members of his council in that part, who has
said and reported as a truth that the dauphin in person,
along with a large force of the said enemies, is at Moulins,
in Bourbonnois . . . . . . . . . . . and on the other hand,
that another large force of the said enemies has arrived
in the marches of the Maconnois and Auxerrois, and the
people of my said lord there require that my lord shall go
in person, or otherwise provide for the same, and send
hastily some troops, and especially some archers.

And because the need there is greater than before, and
the provision very necessary, the said ambassadors shall
require of the king that it would please him to appoint
and give to my said lord the number of archers under
some notable captain, paid at the expense of the king, in
order that they (along with the men and subjects of my
said lord, belonging to the said lands of Burgundy, of

---

[1] *Bourbonnois*] A blank space here occurs in the MS.

souffisant de gens darmes), resister et faire guerre aus diz ennemis, tant es dites marches de Bourgoingne comme aussi es autres marches du royaume illec environ.

Item, remonstreront comment maistre Robert Auclon, conseiller de monseigneur et son procureur en court de Rome, a este envoie depar nostre saint pere le pape devers monseigneur, et a raporte, entre autres choses, comment nostre dit pere avoit ordonne et depute deux cardinaulx, assavoir, le cardinal des Ursins et de Saint Pierre ad Vincula, pour venir en France pour le fait de la paix generale, et ne tenoit qua largent que les diz cardinaulx ne venissent, a este ordonne que les diz cardinaulx fussent paiez aux despens des parties, cest assavoir, le dit des Ursins aux despens du roy et le dit de Saint Pierre aux despens du daulphin et de la partie adverse. La quelle chose monseigneur sig- niffie au roy, a fin quil ait advis ; car (comme dient

------

which there is a good number and sufficient of men-at- arms), may resist and make war on the said enemies, as well in the said marches of Burgundy as also in the other marches of the kingdom contiguous thereto.

Item, they shall state how master Robert Auclon, coun- sellor of my lord and his procurator to the court of Rome, has been sent from our Holy Father the Pope to my lord, and has reported, among other things, how that our said father had appointed and deputed two cardinals, that is to say, the cardinal des Ursins and the cardinal of Saint Pierre ad Vincula, to come into France for the affairs of the general peace, and nothing but money prevented the said cardinals from coming, it has been arranged that the said cardinals should be paid at the expense of the parties, that is, the said des Ursins at the expense of the king and the said de Saint Pierre at the expense of the dauphin and of the adverse party. Which thing my lord signifies to the king, in order that he may have advice ; for (as some say) our said

aucuns) nostre dit saint pere seroit bien daccord que
len meist sur un demy dixiesme pour le paiement du
dit cardinal des Ursins; mais il lui fauldroit faire
prest dargent comptant, et le envoier par dela pour
le faire venir par deca, en attendant que largent du
dit demy dixiesme se levast.

Item, diront et exposeront au roy et a son conseil
comment mon dit seigneur a nagueres par lettres closes
escript au roy comment a la chose avenue devant la
ditte ville de Compiengne, le sire de Crequy, messire
Jacques de Brimeu, mareschal de lost, messire Florimond de Brimeu, et messire Waleran de Beauval, chevaliers, qui sont de lostel de mon dit seigneur le duc,
lesquels estoient en la bastille de la Leaue, laquelle
nestoit point encores achevee, et estoit comme non
tenable, ont este par assault, et apres ce quils se furent
vaillament et longuement deffendus, prins par les dis
ennemis et emmenez prisonniers, et que len a sceu par
aucuns prisonniers des dis ennemis, qui sen son venuz,

---

holy father would willingly agree that a half tenth should
be levied for the payment of the said cardinal des Ursins;
but he would be obliged to make an advance of ready
money, and to send it across to make him come hither,
and would have to wait until the money of the said half
tenth should be raised.

Item, they shall say and state to the king and to his
council how my said lord has formerly written to the king
by closed letters, how, in the affair that happened before the
said town of Compiègne, that the lord of Crequy, messire
Jacques de Brimeu, marshal of the army, messire Florimond
de Brimeu and messire Waleran de Beauval, knights, who
are of the household of my said lord the duke, who were
in the bastille de la Leaue, which was not yet finished, and
was (so to speak) untenable, were by assault, and after
they had valiantly and for a long time defended themselves,
taken by the said enemies and carried off as prisoners, and
that it has been made known by certain prisoners of the

que iceulx ennemis ont entencion de les tres durement
et griefment traiter en corps et en biens, et sont
taillez de perdre la vie, pour ce que les dis ennemis
les congnoissant, et quils savent bien quils sont vaillans chevaliers, et quils ont tousjours bien servi le roy
et mon dit seigneur alencontre des dis ennemis. Et
pour tant que le roy a et tient en son povoir aucuns
prisonniers de la partie des dis ennemis, comme le
sire de Rambure, le frere de La Hire, et aultres, par le
moien desquels lon pourroit bien parvenir a la delivrance des dessus dis chevaliers prisonniers, mon dit
seigneur a requis par ses dittes lettres closes au roy
que, en regard a lestat des dis prisonniers, qui sont
bons, vaillans et loyaulx chivaliers, et ont tousjours et
continuelment bien servi le roy en plusieurs besoignes,
tant a lassemblee des ennemis devant Senlis, ou les
aucunes deulx furent, et depuis a Paris, quant les
ennemis le vindrent assaillir, ou ils se porterent moult
vaillament, et en fu la ville en partie par leur moien

----

said enemies, who have come from thence, that these enemies
intend to treat them very harshly and severely in body and
goods, and they are like to lose their lives, because the
said enemies know them, and that they well know that they
are valiant knights, and that they have always well served
the king and my said lord against the said enemies. And
for as much as the king has and holds in his power certain
prisoners of the party of the said enemies, such as the lord
of Rambure, the brother of La Hire, and others, by the
means of whom one could easily procure the deliverance
of the above mentioned imprisoned knights, my said lord
has required by his said closed letters of the king that,
as regards the state of the said prisoners, who are good,
valiant and loyal knights, and have always and continually
served the king well in many ways, as well in the gathering
together of the enemies before Senlis, where some of them
were, and since then at Paris, when the enemies came to
assail it, where they behaved very valiantly, and the town
in part was preserved by their means, as also before the

preservee, comme aussi devant la ditte ville de Compiengne, ou ils ont toujours et continuelment este sans eulx en bougier. Et considere aussi que ils ont este prins en faisant la guerre du roy et pour son fait, que le roy vueille avoir compassion deulx, et non consentir la delivrance des dis prisonniers ennemis, ne dacun deulx, se nest que par leur moien les diz chevaliers prisonniers puissent estre delivrez, ou par aultre bonne voye et maniere, qui lon pourroit bien pratiquer et trouver avant la deslivrance des diz sire de Rambure et du dit frere de La· Hire et autres prisonniers, ennemis dessus diz. Les dis ambaisseurs lui feront encore depar mon dit seigneur semblable priere et requeste.

Item, diront comment aucuns de la ville et chastellenie de Cassel, subgiez de mon dit seigneur,· soubz umbre de certaine appellation quils ont en court de parlement a Paris, et aussi de certain mandement royal par eulx obtenu de la ditte court de parlement, soubs couleur de justice et par vertu dicelluy, iceulx

---

said town of Compiègne, where they have always and continually been without stirring from thence. And considering also that they were taken while making war for the king, and on his account, that the king would have compassion on them, and not consent to the deliverance of the said hostile prisoners, nor of any of them, unless it be that by their means the said captive knights may be delivered, or by some other good way or means, which might be easily managed and discovered, before the deliverance of the said lord of Rambure, and of the said brother of La Hire, and other prisoners, being enemies, above mentioned. The said ambassadors shall again make this same prayer and request from my said lord.

Item, shall say how certain persons of the town and district of the castle of Cassel, subjects of my said lord, under cover of a certain appeal which they may have in the court of parliament at Paris, and also of a certain royal writ obtained by them from the said court of parliament, under colour of justice and by virtue hereof, these inhabitants of

de Cassel, qui ja pieca se sont rebellez a lencontre de
mon dit seigneur et de ses officiers, se sont enfforciez
et se tiennent plus fermes et obstinez en leur rebellion
et desobeissance, en faisant de grans travaulx et oultrages aux bons subgiez de mon dit seigneur. Et ja
soit ce que par le roy eust este ordonne que la dite
court de parlement ne se melast plus de la ditte cause,
touttevoie rien nen a este tenu ; mais, que plus est,
soubs umbre et par vertu du dit mandement, duquel
est exceuteur un huissier de parlement, lequel les diz
de Cassel ont fait pardeca . . . . . .¹ et sont et per-
severent de pis en pis, en prenant et emmenant les
officiers et bons subgiez de mon dit seigneur, et leur
faisant beaucoup dautres maulx, oultrages et violences,
. . . . . .. nest a doubter . . . . . de peuple (que Dieu
ne veuille !) sont taillez dadvenir ou pais de Flandres.
Lesquelles choses mon dit seigneur (qui les a souffertes

---

Cassel, who some time ago rebelled against my said lord
and his officers, have strengthened themselves and hold
themselves firmer and more obstinate in their rebellion and
disobedience, making great molestations and outrages on
the good subjects of my said lord. And although it was
ordained by the king that the said court of parliament
should no more meddle in the said cause, nevertheless this
has not been at all observed ; but, what is more, under
shadow and by virtue of the said writ, the executor of which
is an officer of the parliament, whom the said men of Cassel
have here made . . . . . and are, and continue to be, going
on from worse to worse in taking and carrying away the
officers and good subjects of my said lord, and in doing
them many other ills, outrages and violences . . . . . . .
we fear . . . . . of people (which God forbid !) are certain to happen in the country of Flanders. These things,
my said lord (who has suffered them until now to his great

---

¹ *Pardeca*] This and the following blanks occur in the manuscript.

jusques a present a son grant desplaisir, esperant que
le roy y deust remedier, et non souffrir que ses officiers
continuassent tels explois desraisonnables contre et sur
les subgiez de mon dit seigneur), signiffie au roy et
a son conseil, en lui requerant tres accertes quil lui
plaise y mettre remede et provision, et faire faire
commandement a ceulx de son parlement a Paris et
au dit huissier, et aussi aux baillis Damiens, et le
prevost de Monstereul sur la Mer, et autres officiers
du roy de cy environ, desquels les diz de Cassel rebelles
et desobeissans se tiennent fors, que du fait des diz
de Cassel plus ne sentremettent, mais cessent par effect
doresnavant faire tels et semblables explois, comme
ils ont fait alencontre des bons subgiez et officiers de
mon dit seigneur.

---

dissatisfaction, hoping that the king would remedy them,
and not suffer his officers to continue such unreasonable
proceedings on and against the subjects of my said lord),
intimates to the king and to his council, requesting very
decidedly that it may please him to remedy and provide
against it, and to cause command to be given to those of
his parliament at Paris, and to the said officer, and also
to the baillies of Amiens and the provost of Montreuil sur
la Mer, and the other officers of the king in the neighbourhood, by whom the said rebels and disobedient persons
of Cassel are encouraged, that they would no further
intermeddle in the affairs of the said people of Cassel, but
would henceforward cease' from doing such and the like
actions as they have done against the good subjects and
the officers of my said lord.

## 1431.

MANDATE by king Henry the Sixth for the more regular inspection of the English troops in Normandy.[1]

A.D. 1431.
Feb. 1.

A previous mandate to the same effect having been neglected,

HENRY, par la grace de Dieu, roy de France et Dangleterre, au premier notre sergent qui sur ce sera requis, salut.

Comme pour congnoistre et savoir au vray sur le nombre de nos gens darmes et de trait, tant ordinaires comme de creue, ordonnes estre ez garnisons de notre duchie de Normendie et pais de conqueste, y sont entierement, ayons ja pieca voulu, commande et tres expressement enjoinct a notre ame et feal chevalier, Thomas Blount, tresorier de nos finances de Normendie, que en toute diligence envoyast et mandast depar nous aux commissaires sur ce ordonnez

---

### [TRANSLATION.]

HENRY, by the grace of God, king of France and England, to the first of our serjeants who shall be required about this matter, greeting.

Since, in order to know and correctly ascertain the total number of our men-at-arms and bowmen, as well the ordinary ones as the extra levy, appointed to be in the garrisons of our duchy of Normandy and our conquered country, we have some time ago willed, commanded, and very expressly enjoined our beloved and faithful knight, Thomas Blount, treasurer of our finances of Normandy, with all diligence to command and send from us to the commis-

---

[1] From the MS. Fontanieu, 115-116.

quilz prinssent les monstres de toutes icelles gens
de guerre; et il soit ainsi que notre dit tresorier nous
ait afferme que, (nonobstant que ainsi lait fait et
mande ja pieca par tout a tous les dits commissaires,
en leur enjoignant de par nous que en toute haste
envoyassent par devers nous, ou les gens de notre
grant conseil, soubz leurs sceaulx, les monstres ou revues de toutes les dits gens de guerre, tant ordinaires
que extraordinaires, et ainsi que acoustume est de
faire en tel cas), ce nonobstant en contempnant, comme
il semble, noz dits commandemens, iceulx commissaires
ny ont aucunement obey ne receu les dits monstres
ou revueus, ne certifie pourquoy ne les aient receues.
Car se trouve est que ce soit par la refus des capitaines, lieuxtenans, ou gens de guerre, notre intencion
nest pas que les reffusans soient paiez sinon du jour
quils auront faites leurs dits monstres. Parquoy
nous ne povons savoir ne cognoistre au vray de quel

---

sioners appointed for this purpose, that they should take
the musters of all these men-at-arms; and so it is that
our said treasurer has affirmed to us that, (notwithstanding
that thus he has done and commanded some time ago
in regard to all the said commissioners, enjoining them
from us that they should send in all haste to us, or the
members of our great council, under their seals, the musters
or reviews of all the said men-at-arms, as well the ordinary
ones as the extraordinary, as it has been the custom to do
in the like cases,) notwithstanding this, as it seems, holding
our said commands in contempt, these commissioners have
not by any means obeyed nor taken the said musters or
reviews, neither have they certified why they have not
taken them. For, if it be found that this is on account
of the refusal of the captains, lieutenants or men-at-arms,
our intention is that they who refuse should be paid only
from the day on which they shall have taken their said
musters. Wherefore we have not been able to know nor
ascertain truly upon what number of men of war we can

nombre de gens de guerre nous povons aidier, ne se
les dits garnisons et places sont souffisamment gardees;
en defaut de quoy grans inconveniens peuvent journelement avenir, se briefvement ny est remedie.

it is reim-<br>posed<br>under<br>penalties, Pourquoy nous, par ladvis des gens de notre grant
conseil, te mandons en commettant par ces presentes
que tu te transportes ez lieux ou tu pourras et devrais
trouver tous iceulx commissaires, par especial a ceulx
qui te ont ete baillez par escript en certain role, signe
de notre dit tresorier de Normandie, duquel voulons que
notre dit tresorier reteingne le double, collacionne par
lun de noz secretaires.    Et iceulx commissaires ad-
journe a certain brief jour et competent a comparoir
en personne par devant les gens de notre dit grand
conseil estans par devers nous, pour respondre a tout
ce que on leur vouldra dire, proposer et demander
depar nous; en leur faisant a chascune diceulx commissaires commandement expres depar nous que, sur
peine de confiscation de corps et de biens, ils com-

---

count, nor if the said garrisons and strongholds are sufficiently guarded; in default of which, great inconveniences
may arise daily, if it is not remedied immediately.

Wherefore we, by the advice of the members of our
great council, command you, commissioning you by the
present letters to go to those places where you might
and should find all these commissioners, more especially
those who have been given you by writing in a certain
roll, signed by our said treasurer of Normandy, of which
we desire that our said treasurer should retain a duplicate, examined by one of our secretaries.    And appoint
these commissioners a certain day, such as is early and
fitting, for them to appear in person before the members of
our said great council who are with us, to answer to all
that may be said, advanced, or asked of them from us;
giving to each of these commissioners an express command
from us that, under pain of confiscation of body and goods,
they shall appear on the days thus assigned to them by

parent aux jours a eulx par toi ainsi assignez, chascun
en sa personne ; en certiffiant des dits adjournemens
et commendemens les bailliz ou vicontes des dits lieux ;
ausquelz vous mandons et commettons par ces mesmes
presentes que sil leur appert que les diz commissaires,
ou aucuns deulz, ne soient venuz a leurs jours a eulx
assignez, comme dit est, que incontinent et sans autre
mandement attendre, prennent iceulx commissaires non
comparans, se trouver les puent, et mettent leurs corps
en noz prisons, et leurs biens, meubles et immeubles, en
notre main par bon et loyal inventaire, pour tout estre
gouverne soubz icelle et jusques a ce que autrement
y aions pourveu.   De tout lesquelz adjournemens, commandemens, et certifications faictes aux dits juges,
voulons que tu certiffies deuement les gens de notre
dit grant conseil, pour sur tout estre ordonne ainsi que
raison donra.

Donne en notre ville de Rouen, soubz notre seel Date.
ordonne en labsence du grant, lè premier jour de

---

you, each in person, certifying the baillies and sheriffs
of the said places of the said meetings and commands ;
whom we command and commission by these same present letters, that if it appears to them that the said commissioners, or any of them, do not come on the days assigned
to them, as has been said, immediately and without waiting
for another command, to seize these commissioners who
did not appear, if they can find them, and put their bodies
into our prisons, and their goods, both movable and im-
movable, in our hand, by a good and correct inventory,
that all may be arranged according to the same, and
until we may have otherwise provided.   Of all which appointments, commands and certifications made to the said
judges, we will that you certify duly the members of our
said grand council, that all may be arranged as reason
shall require.

Dated at our town of Rouen, under our seal appointed
to be used in the absence of the great seal, the first day

Fevrier, lan de grace, mil, cccc. et trente, et de notre regne le neufvieme.

Par le roi, a la relacion de son grant conseil etant a present pardevers luy.

L. CALOT.

CY APRES[1] ensuivent les noms et seurnoms des commissaires ordonnez par nous, Thomas Blount, chevalier, tresorier et general receveur des finances du roy, notre seigneur, ou pais et duchie de Normandie a prendre les monstres des gens darmes et de trait estans soubz les cappitaines des garnisons du bailliage de Caen, tant de leur retenue ordinaire comme de la creue a eulx ordonnee ; ausquels commissaires nous avons envoyees noz lettres de commission, comme chargie nous estoit par le conseil du roy, notre dit seigneur, en ce present mois de Janvier, mil, iiij. c. et trente.

---

of February, the year of grace, one thousand cccc. and thirty, and the ninth of our reign.

By the king, at the relation of his great council, being at this time with him.

L. CALOT.

HEREAFTER follow the names and surnames of the commissioners appointed by us, Thomas Blount, knight, treasurer and receiver-general of the finances of the king, our lord, in the country and duchy of Normandy, to take the musters of the men-at-arms and the bowmen being under the captains of the garrisons of the bailliwick of Caen, as well of their ordinary retinue, as of the extraordinary levy assigned to them ; to which commissioners we have sent our letters of commission, as it was charged us to do by the council of the king, our said lord, in this present month of January, one thousand, cccc. and thirty.

---

[1] This roll of the commissioners appointed to take the musters of the English troops is affixed to the previous document.

Guillaume Lude, grenetier, et Jehan Saint, vicomte de Faloyse, ont ete ordonnez commissaires pour la garnison du dit lieu de Faloyse.

Le vicomte de Vire et Jehan Fauquet ont ete ordonnez commissaires pour la garnison du dit lieu de Vire.

Guillaume Bosquet et Jehan Vanville ont ete ordonnez commissaires pour la garnison de Bayeux.

Giraud Desquay et Loys le Clire ont ete ordonnez commissaires pour le garnison de Caen.

Escript soubz notre signet et saing manuel pour laccomplissement des lettres du roy, notre dit seigneur, auxquelles ces presentes sont atachees soubs notre dit signet, le premier jour de Fevrier ou dit an, mil, iiij. c. et trente.

Date.

BLOUNT.

---

Guillaume Lude, keeper of the granary, and Jehan Sainte, vicomte of Falaise, have been appointed commissioners for the garrison of the said place of Falaise.

The vicomte of Vire and Jehan Fauquet have been appointed commissioners for the garrison of the said place of Vire.

Guillaume Bosquet and Jehan Vanville have been appointed commissioners for the garrison of Bayeux.

Giraud Dèsquay and Loys le Clire have been appointed commissioners for the garrison of Caen.

Written under our signet and sign manual for the accomplishment of the letters of the king, our said lord, to which these present letters are attached under our said signet, the first day of February in the said year, one thousand, cccc. and thirty.

BLOUNT.

## 1431.

THE answer made by the English council at Rouen to the articles sent to them by the duke of Burgundy.[1]

A.D. 1431.
May 28.
———
Answer
by the
council of
Henry VI.
to the
first eight
articles.

RESPONSE donnee depar le roy aux articles baillees par escript depar monseigneur le duc de Bourgoingne par messire Philibert Audrenet, chevalier, et Jehan Abonnel, dit le Gros, ses conseilliers, en la maniere qui sensuit.

Et primierement, au regard des huit premiers articles, es quels est faite mention des grans dommages, mises et despenses qui ont soustenues mon dit seigneur de Bourgoingne et ses pais Dartois, Picardie, Namur, Bourgoingne, Charolois, et le pays de Rethelois, a loccasion des guerres ; le roy en a tele desplaisance comme de ses propres pais, et a bien chacun congnoissance des grans diligences qui la fait faire ou temps

---

## [TRANSLATION.]

THE reply made on the part of the king to the articles given in writing on the part of monseigneur the duke of Burgundy by messire Philibert Audrenet, knight, and Jehan Abonnel, called le Gros, his counsellors, in the following manner.

And firstly, with regard to the first eight articles, in which is made mention of the great damages, outlays, and expenses which my said lord of Burgundy and his lands of Artois, Picardy, Namur, Burgundy, Charolois, and the country of the Rethelois, have sustained by occasion of the wars ; the king is as much annoyed therewith as if they had been in his own country, and has had ample information of the great diligence which he has caused to be done

---

[1] From the Supplément Franç., 292-10, p. 265.

passe, tant par monseigneur de Salisbury, (cui Dieux
pardoint!) comme par autres capitaines, de esloingner
la guerre qui estoit, sept et six ans a, sur les dis pais,
en tele maniere que deux ans a, ils estoient en bonne
disposition, se neust este la fortune que Dieulx a
voulu permettre. En faisant faire laquelle diligence,
et pour recouvrer les places qui faisoient nuysance aus
dis pais, a expose le roy sa puissance Dangleterre avec
grant somme de deniers, de saison en saison, ainsi que
encore fera au plaisir de Dieu si avant que bonnement
lui sera possible.

Item, quant au neufviesme article, faisant mention To the
de mil combatans, quil a ordonne soubs mon dit ninth.
seigneur de Guise pour les marches de Picardie, et de
mil autres combatans, quil envoiera en Bourgoingne
par son mareschal, lesquelz il entretendra pour deux
mois a ses despens, de la provision aussi quil a mise
sur la riviere de Somme, le roy len remercie de tout
son cuer. Et pour faire son devoir de son coste, il a

---

there in time past, as well by my lord of Salisbury (whom
may God pardon!) as by other captains, for driving away
the war, which has been for the last seven or six years
in the said countries, in such manner as that two years ago
things were in a good train, had not the issue been as
God was pleased to permit it to be. In causing this diligence to be done, and in order to recover the strongholds
which were injurious to the said country, the king, at a
considerable cost, from time to time, has shown what
England can do, as he will still do, if God permit, as
effectually as he possibly can.

Item, as for the ninth article, which makes mention of
a thousand men-at-arms, whom he has appointed under
the said lord of Guise for the marches of Picardy, and
of one thousand other men-at-arms, whom he shall send
into Burgundy, under his marshal, whom he shall keep
for two months at his own charges, and also as to the
provision which he has made for the river of Somme, the
king thanks him for the same with all his heart. And

appointie mon dit seigneur de Guise pour deux mois,
(cest assavoir, pour les mois de Juillet et Aoust prouchainement venans,) a la charge de dix huit cent combatans, dont il y aura six cent lances et douze cent
hommes de trait, qui seront paiez de ses deniers
Dangleterre, pour besoingner es marches de Picardie.
Et semble au roy que les diz dix huit cent combatans,
qui le roy paie pour les diz deux mois, pourront avec
les mil combatans ordonnez, comme dit est, par mon
dit seigneur de Bourgoingne, faire plus grant exploit
de guerre, et plus seurement et puissament rebouter les
diz ennemis, que ne feroient mil combatans seulement.
Et quant au pais de Bourgoingne, quant le provost de
Saint Omer vint en Angleterre, le conseil avoit ja
prins et advise touttes les conclusions pour le royaume
de France, tant au regard des finances comme de gens.
Et pour contemplacion de mon dit seigneur de Bourgoigne, et lui ader a diffendre son pays de Picardie,
ou len disoit lors les ennemis estre a puissance, le dit

---

in order to do his duty on his part, he has appointed my
said lord of Guise for two months (that is to say, for the
months of July and August next ensuing) with the charge
of eighteen hundred soldiers, of whom six hundred shall
be lances, and twelve hundred archers, who shall be paid
with his English money, to take care of the marches of
Picardy. And it appears to the king that the said eighteen
hundred soldiers, whom the king pays for the said two
months, shall be able, along with the thousand soldiers
appointed, as has been said, by my said lord of Burgundy
to make war more effectually, and more surely and powerfully repel the said enemies, than a thousand soldiers only
could do. And as for the country of Burgundy, when
the provost of Saint Omer came into England, the council
had already made and settled all its arrangements for the
kingdom of France, as well regarding money as troops.
And out of regard to my said lord of Burgundy, and to
help him to defend his country of Picardy, where it was
then said that the enemies were in strength, the said

conseil condescendi a baillir le dit nombre au dit monseigneur de Guise. Toutes voies, sil advient que, par
le plaisir de nostre Seigneur, on ait bonne briefve conclusion du siege que len mit devant Louviers, ainsi
que len espere, et aussi du pais den hault, par le moien
et bon aide de monseigneur de Bourgoingne, de monseigneur de Staffort, de mon dit seigneur de Guise, de
monseigneur de Salisbury, qui vendra prouchainement,
et dautres capitaines qui se trairont en hault, ou pourra
faire aide de gens pour Bourgoingne et aultres marches
par le bon advis et conseil de mon dit seigneur de
Bourgong ; a la quelle chose faire le roy sera bien enclin si avant que bonnement lui sera possible.

Au dixieme article faisant mention de ce que demand To the
mon dit seigneur de Bourgongne a cause de ses gens tenth.
qui ont este devant Compiengne, et de lartillerie qui
y a este employee, le roy fera voir les endentures et
appointemens qui ont este faiz et prins en ces matieres

---

council thought fit to assign the said number to the said
lord of Guise. Nevertheless, should it so happen that,
by the pleasure of our Lord, there were a good and
speedy conclusion to the siege which is before Louviers,
as is hoped, and also of the upper country, by the means
and good assistance of my lord of Burgundy, of my lord
of Stafford, of my said lord of Guise, of my lord of Salisbury, who will speedily come, and of other captains who
are coming up, troops may be provided for the assistance
of Burgundy and the other border lands by the good
advice and counsel of my said lord of Burgundy ; to do
which thing to the utmost of his ability the king will be
exceedingly well inclined.

To the tenth article, which makes mention of what is
demanded by my said lord of Burgundy in consequence of
his troops who have been before Compiègne, and the artillery which has been there employed, the king will cause to
be inspected the indentures and arrangements which have
been made and taken in these matters, as well at Bruges

tant a Bruges et a Gand, comme a Calais, lannee passee ; et sil plaisoit a mon dit seigneur de Bourgoigne envoier devers lui aucun de ses gens, il y fera tellement appoincter que par raison en devra estre content.

*To the eleventh.*  Au onziesme volume, faisant mencion des ambaxadeurs de lempereur, il est vray quils sont presentement devers le roy, et ont este ois en audience publique, et veulent encore aucunes choses dire en particulier, ce que le roy oira tres voulentiers ; et ce quils diront fera savoir a mon dit seigneur de Bourgoingne. Et est lentencion du roy dentendre a la matiere de tres bon cuer par le bon conseil et advis de mon dit seigneur de Bourgoigne, sans le quel il ne veult entrer, ne riens faire en la matiere, ainsi que le traitie de la paix final le contient.

*To the twelfth.*  Au douziesme article, faisant mencion de monseigneur le prince Dorenges, le roy a ordonne de faire communiquer avec les gens de mon dit seigneur le prince,

---

and at Gand as at Calais, during the past year ; and if it shall be agreeable to my said lord of Burgundy to send to him some of his people, he will cause such an arrangement to be made as ought reasonably to be satisfactory.

To the eleventh article, which makes mention of the ambassadors of the emperor, it is true that they are at this time with the king, and have already had a public audience, and still have some private communications to make, which the king will hear very willingly ; and what they shall say he will cause to be made known to my said lord of Burgundy. And it is the intention of the king to give heed to the matter most willingly, by the good counsel and advice of my said lord of Burgundy, without which he will neither enter upon or do anything in the matter, as is contained in the treaty of final peace.

To the twelfth article, which makes mention of my lord the prince of Orange, the king has arranged that communication be had with the people of my said lord

qui sont a Rouen, et de y faire tel appointement qui bonnement sera possible.

Au treziesme article, faisant mention de monseigneur To the thirteenth. de Savoye, pour le fait de la delivrance de monseigneur de Bourbon, il a este parle de ceste matiere a monseigneur le cardinal, qui freschement vient Dangleterre. Le quel dit quil na point sceu que conclusion soit prinse par dela ou fait de mon dit seigneur de Bourbon. Bien est vray que on a eu autrefois parle et y prins aucuns appointemens, mais de la partie de mon dit seigneur de Bourbon nont este aucunement entretenus, et aussi est la chose demouree. Toutes voics ou saura se depuis le partement Dangleterre de mon dit seigneur le cardinal se aucune chose y ait este conclue; et sil est ainsi, le roy le fera savoir a mon dit seigneur de Bourgoingne.

Ce fu fait a Rouen, ou grant conseil du roy, nostre Date. dit seigneur, le xxviij. jour de May, lan M. cccc. xxxj.

---

the prince, who are at Rouen, and to make there the best arrangement that may possibly be done.

To the thirteenth article, which makes mention of my lord of Savoy, for the matter of the deliverance of my lord of Bourbon, there has been some conversation upon this affair with my lord the cardinal, who has lately returned from England. He says that he did not know that any conclusion had been arrived at there upon the business of my said lord of Bourbon. It is quite true that this has been talked about previously, and that some arrangements have been therein made, but they were not at all entertained on the side of my lord of Bourbon, and so the matter has stood over. Nevertheless, it shall be ascertained whether, since the departure from England of my said lord the cardinal, any conclusion has been arrived at therein; and if it be so, the king will cause my said lord of Burgundy to be acquainted therewith.

This was executed at Rouen, in the great council of the king, our said lord, the xxviij. day of May, in the year M. cccc. xxxj.

## 1431.

LETTER from cardinal Beaufort to the duke of Burgundy, sent by the bearer of the previous despatch.[1]

A.D. 1431.
May 28.
———
The cardinal refers to the bearer, Jehan de Groos, for further intelligence.

HAULT et puissant prince, mon tres honneure et tres ame neveu, je me recommande a vous tant affectueusement que je plus puisse.

Et pour ce que de vostre bonne estat et prosperite me suis desirans savoir et ouir en bien, vous plaise souvent men ascertenner, dont je suis tres rejouix tant et si souvent que je en pourra ouir bonnes nouvelles.

Et quant aux matiers pour les quelles a besoigne par de ca, ou nom de vous, vostre recepveur, Jehan de Groos, vous plaise du response que sur icelles matieres vous rapportera le dit de Groos a lui commise parentre nous du conseil de monseigneur le roy prendre

———

## [TRANSLATION.]

HIGH and powerful prince, my most honoured and most beloved nephew, I recommend myself to you as affectionately as I best can.

And because I am anxious to know and hear good news of your good estate and prosperity, may it please you often to inform me thereof, of which I am very joyful as much and as often as I can hear good tidings thereof.

And as to the matters on which your receiver, Jehan de Groos, has here been employed in your name, may you be pleased to take as agreeable the answer which the said de Groos will convey to you upon these matters, committed to him by us, who are of the council of my lord the king,

———

[1] From the Supplément Franç., 292-10, p. 267.

agreablement, et vous en tenir content a ceste fois pour ce que icellui vostre receveur, sil vous plest, vous dira plus au long.

Et hault et puissant prince, mon tres honneure et tres ame neveu, si chose soit que pour vous faire puisse par deca, ou aillieurs, vous plaise moy en certiffier vos bonnes plaisirs, pour les accomplir a mon povoir voulontiers et de bonne coeur. En priant que nostre Seigneur par Sa saincte grace vous doint tousjours tres bonne vie et longue.

Escrit a Rouen, le xxviij. jour de May. Date.

Vostre loyal oncle,

H., CARDINAL DANGLETERRE.

A hault et puissant prince, mon tres honneure et tres ame neveu, le duc de Bourgogne, de Brabant et de Lymbourg, conte de Flandres, Dartois, de Bourgogne, et de Namur.

---

and hold yourself pleased therewith at this time, in respect to what this your receiver, if you please, will tell you more at length.

And high and powerful prince, my most honoured and well-beloved nephew, if there be anything which I can do for you here, or elsewhere, may it please you to certify me therein of your good pleasure, so that I may accomplish them with pleasure, according to my power, and with a good will. Praying that our Lord, by His holy grace, would give you always a very good and long life.

Written at Rouen, the xxviij. day of May.

Your faithful uncle,

H., CARDINAL OF ENGLAND.

To the high and powerful prince, my most honoured and wellbeloved nephew, the duke of Burgundy, of Brabant and of Lembourg, count of Flanders, of Artois, of Burgundy, and of Namur.

---

## 1431.

LETTER from the duke of Burgundy to Henry the Sixth respecting a truce with France.[1]

A.D. 1431.
12 Dec.

The duke of Burgundy, not having had help from Henry,

MON tres redoubte seigneur, tant et si tres humblement que plus puis, je me recommande a vous.

Mon tres redoubte seigneur, je tieng bien estre en vostre noble memoire comment par plusieurs fois jay fait remonstrer a vous et a vostre conseil de France et Dangleterre lestat ou mesme pays de Bourgoingne estoient et sont a loccasion de la guerre, et comment ils estoient de toutes pars environnez de vos ennemis et des mien ; et aussi la grant guerre que les dis ennemis faisoient journelement en nos pays Dartois, et autres pardeca es marches de Picardie, et pareillement de pays de Rethelois, es marches de Champaigne ; et comme, pour y pourveoir le plus avant que possible,

---

[TRANSLATION.]

MY most dread lord, I recommend myself to you as much and as most humbly as I am best able.

My most redoubted lord, I am well convinced that it is in your noble memory how that I have several times caused to be shown to you and your council of France and of England the condition in which the said countries of Burgundy were, and are, in consequence of the war, and how they were on all sides surrounded by your enemies and mine ; and also the great war which the said enemies made daily in our countries of Artois and others on this side, in the marches of Picardy, and likewise in the country of the Rethelois, in the marches of Champagne ; and how, in order that I might make the speediest provision there that

---

[1] From the Supplément Franç., 292-10, p. 388.

me seroit avoie entention de mettre sus es dittes
marches et pays le plus grant nombre de gens darmes
et de trait que pourroye, a lencontre des dis ennemis,
lespace de deux mois ; ce que jay fait et accompli.
Car tant es marches de mes diz pays de Bourgongne
soubz mon mareschal, comme es marches de mes diz
pays de Picardie, soubs beau cousin de Luxembourg,
et aussi ou pays de Rethelois soubs le sire de Cernant,
mon conseillier et chambellan, ay fait mettre ses
grandes et notables armees qui grandement se sont
emploiees a lencontre des diz ennemies, et telles
armees ay entretenues a mes frais et despens le dit
espace de deux mois et plus.

Et pour ce, mon tres redoubte seigneur, vous ay fait
requerer tres instament que, pour entretenir les dittes
armees et resister a iceulx ennemis, il vous plaise me
faire aide et secours de gens, dargent, ou au moins
dargent, tellement que par faulte de votre dit aide
et secours, il ne convenist les dittes armees desem-

---

is possible, it was my intention to raise in the said marches
and countries the greatest possible number of men-at-arms
and archers in opposition to the said enemies, for the space
of two months ; which I have done and accomplished. For
as well in the marches of my said countries of Burgundy,
under my marshal, as in the marches of my said countries
of Picardy, under my good cousin of Luxemburg, and also
in the country of the Rethelois, under the sire de Cernant,
my councillor and chamberlain, I have caused to be sent
those great and notable armies which have employed themselves to good purpose against the said enemies, and have
supported these armies at my charges and expenses for the
said space of two months and more.

And for this cause, my most dread lord, I have required
you very earnestly that, in order to support the said armies
and to resist these enemies, it would please you to assist
and succour me with troops and money, or at the least
with money, in such wise that from want of your said aid
and succour, it was not necessary to disband the said armies

parer, et prendre et accepter autre provision pour la
seurte de mes dis pays; ce que faire me convenoit
au deffault de vostre dit secours. Et ces choses vous
ay je fait exposer et a vostre dit conseil par diverses
ambassades, lettres, et messaiges. Cest assavoir, premierement, par le sire de Chauney, mon chambellan,
et messire Jehan de Pressy, mes conseillers; et depuis
par messire Philibert Audrenet, aussi mon conseiller
et chambellan, et Jehan Gros, mon receveur general
de mes finances, que pour ceste cause ay envoye
devers vous a vostre cite de Rouen; et aussi par
le prevost de S. Omer, mon conseillier, et maistre
Christian Hautain, mon secretaire, qui semblablement
ay envoie pour ceste cause par devers vostre conseil
en vostre royaume Dangleterre. Et avecques ce, lay
dit de bouche assez au long a beau cousin reverend
pere en Dieu levesque de Therouenne, vostre chancelier de France.

has entered
into a truce
with
France,

Lequel secours et aide, non obstant toutes lettres,
expositions, requestes et supplications, nay pou avoir

---

and to take and accept another arrangement for the safety of
my said countries; which I would have to do for want of your
said succour. And these things have I caused to be shown
to you and your said council by different embassies, letters,
and messengers. That is to say, in the first place, by the
sire de Chauny, my chamberlain, and messire Jehan de
Pressy, my councillors; and then by messire Philibert
Audrenet, likewise my councillor and chamberlain, and
Jehan Gros, my receiver-general of my finances, whom for
this cause I have sent to you to your city of Rouen; and
also by the provost of S. Omer, my councillor, and master
Christian Hautain, my secretary, whom in like manner I
have sent for this cause to your council, in your realm of
England. And moreover, I have stated it verbally, at con-
siderable length, to my good cousin the reverend father in
God the bishop of Therouanne, your chancellor of France.

Which succour and aid, notwithstanding all letters, statements, requests, and supplications, I have been unable to ob-

de vous, non mie encore le payement de ce que me
devez clerement par compte fait avecques vos gens,
montant a grant somme, que jeusse volontiers emploie
en lentretenement des dittes armees, se leusse peu
recouvrer de vous; par quoy a convenu de samparer
les dittes armees. Et finablement a ceste cause, par
deffault du dit vostre secours, et afin de . . . . . la[1]
destruction de mes diz pays et subgiez, ay estre con-
traint de consentir estre mises sus certaines treves et
abstinances de guerre de mes diz pays, et mesmement de mes pays de Bourgoingne, avecques vos
diz ennemis et les miens. Lesquelles treves et abstinances ont este par mes gens prinses et accordees
par certaine forme et maniere, qui est bien venue a
vostre cognoissance et de vostre conseil, comme je
croy. Et pour les asseurer et amplier, se mestier est,
sont venue perdeca aucuns ambaisseurs de votre dit

---

tain from you, not even the payment of what you clearly owe
me by the account made with your people, which amounts
to a large sum, which I would willingly have employed in
the support of the said armies, if I could have recovered
it from you; in consequence of which I have been compelled to disband the said armies. And finally, from this
cause, by default of your said succour, and in order to
[avoid] the destruction of my said countries and subjects,
I have been constrained to consent that certain truces
and abstinences of war should be made in my said countries, and especially in my countries of Burgundy, with
your said enemies and mine. The which truces and
abstinences have been by my people taken and agreed to
by a certain form and manner, which has assuredly come
to your knowledge and that of your council, as I believe.
And in order to confirm them, and extend them, if need
be, there have come hither certain ambassadors of your

---

[1] *Et afin de . . . . . la*] This blank occurs in the MS.

adversaire et le mien; cest assavoir, larcevesque de Reims, qui se nomme son chancelier, Christofle de Harrecourt, et maistre Adam de Cambray; lesquels sont en la ville de Tournay, et prouchainement doivent venir en ceste ville pardevers moy.

*in which certain towns wish to be comprehended.*   Et si est vray que nagueres ont este devers moy les deputtes des gens des trois estats de mon pais Dartois avecques les deputez de vos bonnes villes de pardeca, voisines de mes diz pays, comme Amiens, Abbeville, Noyon, S. Quintin, Chauny, et autres; que mont requis tres instament que je les veuille faire comprendre es dittes abstinences; eulx griefment complaignans, et disans que autrement ils seroient perduz.

Lesquelles choses, mon tres redoubte seigneur, je vous signiffie afin que sachiez la verite de ce que de ma part y a este fait jusques a present; et tout ce que plus avant ou aultrement y sera fait et besoigne cy apres vous signiffeiray et feray savoir diligemment;

---

said adversary and mine; that is to say, the archbishop of Rheims, who calls himself his chancellor, Christofle de Harcourt, and master Adam de Cambray; who are in the city of Tournay, and shortly will come into this town to me.

And it is indeed true that of late there have come to me the deputies of the people of the Three Estates of my country of Artois, with the deputies of your good towns on this side, contiguous to my said country, as Amiens, Abbeville, Noyon, S. Quintin, Chauny and others; who have requested of me most urgently that I would be pleased to cause them to be included in the said abstinences; complaining bitterly, and affirming that otherwise they will be ruined.

Which things, my most dread lord, I signify to you, to the end that you may know the truth of that which upon my part has been done up to this present time; and all that shall be done or proceeded with further, or otherwise, therein after this time, I will signify to you, and will dili-

en vous priant, mon tres redoubte seigneur, que de ce que y ay fait et feray, veuilliez estre contant, et que a ceste cause ne veuilliez concevoir aucune suspicion ou ymaginacion sinistre a lencontre de moy.  Car ou dit fait dicelles abstinences, ne aultrement, je nay fait, ne feray, chose que ne doye et puisse faire par honneur ; et ce que jen ay fait et feray se plus avant, men convient faire touchant les dites abstinences, a este et sera pour ce que ne puis plus supporter a mes frais et despens la charge de la guerre, et que de vous nay peu avoir laide et secours que faire me deviez de raison, et que si souvent et tres instament requis vous ay.

Mon tres redoubte seigneur, tousjours vous plaise moy mander vos bons plaisirs pour les a mon povoir accomplir tres volontiers et de tres bon cuer, a laide de nostre Seigneur, qui, mon tres redoubte seigneur,

---

gently take care that you are made aware of it ; praying you, my very dread lord, that with what I have done, and shall do herein, you would be pleased to be satisfied, and that on this account you would be pleased not to conceive any suspicion or evil surmise against me.  For neither in the said matter of these abstinences, nor otherwise, have I done, nor shall I do, anything which I ought not, or may not do with honour ; and what I have herein done, and shall do further, it was necessary for me to do touching the said abstinences, and has been and shall be because I could no longer support at my cost and expenses the charge of the war, and because I could not have of you the aid and succour which is rightfully due by you to me, and which I have so often asked of you, and that most urgently.

My very dread lord, may it always please you to send me your good pleasure, that I may accomplish it most willingly and with a right good will, by the aid of our Lord, Who, my most dread lord, I pray to keep you in

vous ait en Sa sainte et especiale garde, et doint bonne vie et longue.

Date.	Escript en ma ville de Lisle, le xij. de Decembre.

Vostre tres humble et obeissant cousin, le duc de Bourgoingne, de Brabant, et de Lembourg.

A mon tres redoubte seigneur, mon seigneur le roy.

His holy and especial protection, and give you a good life and long.

Written in my town of Lille, the xij. day of December.

Your most humble and obedient cousin, the duke of Burgundy, of Brabant, and of Lembourg.

To my most dread lord, my lord the king.

### 1432.

A.D. 1432.
March 6.

100 gunstones to be sent from Vernon to Rouen.

LETTER from the English council at Rouen to the governor of Vernon respecting the transmission of some gun-stones to be used in the siege of the tower of Rouen.[1]

TRESCHIER et grant ami. Il est necessite pour le recouvrement de la tour de Rouen avoir grant nombre

[TRANSLATION.]

VERY dear and great friend. It is necessary for the recovery of the tower of Rouen to have a great number of

[1] From the original, upon paper, in the MS. Gaignières, 649-6, fol. 19. Being pasted down upon a sheet of paper, the watermark cannot be ascertained, and from the same cause the address is somewhat uncertain.

de pierres de la grandeur et mesure [1] donc nous vous envoions la forme en ung filet ; et pour ce que len dit que Philibert de Molans en fist faire ung cent pour le roy, pour le siege de Louviers, que on dit estre en lieu de lescuirie, nous vous mandons depar le roy et depar monseigneur le regent, que vous les envoies en toute haste, par les porteurs de ces presentes. Et en cas que les dits pierres auroient este faictes et appartendront a autres que au roy, si les prenes, en les paiant a pris raisonnable, ou en faictes la debte votre, se mestier est, et nous vous promettons vous en faire avoir bonne descharge et garant. Et gardes que en ce nait faulte, sur tant que poves mesprendre envers le roy, notre dit seigneur, et mon dit seigneur le regent.

Donne a Rouen, soubs le singnet du conseil, le vj. Date. jour du Mars, lan de grace, mil iiij. c. **xxxj.**

------

stones of the size and measure of which we send you the form in a loop ; and as it is stated that Philibert de Molans caused a hundred of them to be made for the king, for the siege of Louviers, which are said to be in place of l'Ecurie, we command you, on the part of the king and on that of my lord the regent, to send them in all haste, by the bearers of these present letters. And in case that the said stones shall have been made for and belong to others than the king, take them, paying a reasonable price for them, or make the debt your own, if necessary, and we promise to make you have good discharge and warrant for them. And take care there be no failure herein, by as much as you can forfeit to the king, our said lord, and my said lord the regent.

Dated at Rouen, under the signet of the council, the vj. day of March, in the year of grace one thousand iiij. c. **xxxj.**

------

[1] *Mesure*] The reading of this word is doubtful.

Faites baillier bastel, et ce quil appertendra, pour ycelle apporter.

Escript comme dessus.

> Les gens du conseil du roy, notre
> seigneur, en Normandie.
>                               SEBIRE.

(*Dorso.*) A notre tres chier et grant ami, Jehan le Saige, gouverneur de Vernon.

---

Cause a boat to be sent, and what shall be necessary for the carriage of the same.

Written as above.

> The members of the council of the king
> our lord, in Normandy.
>                               SEBIRE.

(*Dorso.*) To our very dear and great friend, Jehan le Saige, governor of Vernon.

---

## 1432.

A.D. 1432.
May 27.

Directions
respecting
the levying
and appro·
priation
of a tax
voted by
the Estates
of Nor-
mandy.

MANDATE from king Henry the Sixth and the English council in Paris, respecting the levying and application of a tax voted by the three estates of Normandy.[1]

HENRY, par la grace de Dieu, roy de France et Dangleterre, a nostre ame et feal Jean Stanlawe, es-

---

[TRANSLATION.]

HENRY, by the grace of God king of France and of England, to our beloved and faithful Jean Stanlawe, esquire,

---

[1] From the MS. Fontanieu, 115–116.

cuyer, tresorier et general gouverneur de noz finances, ou pays et duchie de Normandie, et a nostre bien ame Pierre Surreau, receveur general des nos dits finances, salut et dilection.

Comme, environ le vij. jour Doctobre derrenier passe, nous, par ladvis et deliberacion des gens de nostre grant conseil etans lors par devers nous, nous eussions convoque et fait assembler en nostre ville de Rouen les gens des Trois Estatz de nos dits duchie de Normandie et pays de conqueste, et leur fait dire et exposer le grant desir et affection que avons de conserver, a laide de nostre Createur, noz villes, places, et forteresses diceulx duchie et pays, recouvrer par sieges ou autrement celles que y occupoient et detenoient noz ennemis et adversaires, et les rebouter a toute puissance. Pourquoy faire, avions advise continuer es dits places et fortresses le nombre de gens darmes et de trait que ordinairement y avoit este lannee precedent, finie a la Saint Michiel derrenier passe, montant ix. c. lances et

---

treasurer and governor-general of our finances in the country and duchy of Normandy, and to our wellbeloved Pierre Surreau, receiver-general of our said finances, greeting and love.

As, about the vij. day of October last past, we, by the advice and deliberation of the members of our great council being then with us, we had convoked and caused to assemble in our said city of Rouen the members of the Three Estates of our said duchy of Normandy and the conquered country, and caused to be told and shown to them the great desire and affection that we have to keep, by the aid of our Creator, our towns, strongholds, and fortresses of the said duchy and country, to recover by sieges or otherwise those which our enemies and adversaries occupy and retain there, and to repulse them effectually. To do which we have determined to continue in the said places and fortresses the number of men-at-arms and archers which there were generally there during the last year, which ended on St. Michael's day last, amounting to ix. hundred lances and ij. M. vij.c.

ij. M. vij. c. archiers, ou environ, tant a cheval comme
a pie, avec autre grant nombre, pour tenir les champs
et pour le recouvrement des places et forteresses de
Bosmoulins, Aimon, Hoe, Chaillonel, Saint Celerin,
Mauson, et Montaudain, occupee par les dits ennemis,
afin que nos bons, vrayz et loyaulx sujetz, manans et
demourants en iceulx duchie et pays, puissent vivre
en paix et transquillite, en bonne justice et police, et
faire paisiblement leurs labours, ouvrages, et marchandises.  Le paiement desquelles lances et archiers et
autres gens de guerre, ne porons pour ceste presente
annee, commencant a la Saint Michiel derrenier passe,
supporter ne fournir, attendu la paurete de noz finances.
Et pour ce eussions fait requerir a ceulx des dits estaz,
que pour le paiement des dits gens ils nous baillissent
octroys pour la dite armee la somme de ij. c. M. livres
Tournois, considere que en ce faisons convertir tous
les deniers de nos aides et greniers, excepte le paie-

---

archers, or thereabouts, as well on horseback as on foot,
with another great number for keeping the country and
for recovering the places and fortresses of Bosmoulins,
Aimon, Hoe, Chaillonel, Saint Celerin, Manson, and Montaudain, occupied by the said enemies, to the end that our
good, true, and loyal subjects, residing and living in the
said duchy and country, may be able to live in peace and
tranquillity, in good justice and government, and peaceably
to carry on their labours, work, and merchandise.  The
payment of which' lances and archers and other soldiers
we cannot for this present year, beginning on St. Michael's
day last past, either support nor furnish, on account of the
poverty of our finances.  And on this account we have
caused a request to be made to the members of the said
Three Estates, that for the payment of the said men they
should give us, as an assessment for the said army, the sum
of ij. c. M. pounds Tournois, upon the understanding that
in this we should cause to be expended all the money of
our aids and stores, excepting the payment of xlviij. pounds

ment de xlviij. livres Tournois par an, ordonnes pour
nostre tres chier et tres ame oncle Jehan, gouvernant
et regent nostre dit royaulme de France, duc de Bedfort, a icelle somme cueillir et lever a trois ou quatre
termes durant lannee.

Les quelz, comme bons, vraiz, et loyaux subgetz, oye
nostre dit requeste, et apres ce quilz eurent eu sur ce
deliberacion et advis entre eux, considerant les grans
charges tant de la guerre comme autres, qui nous
survenoient et pourroient survenir de jour en jour, nous
eussent liberalement octroye, et accorde prendre et
lever sur eulx, a trois ou quatre termes en icelle annee,
ce qui nous seroit necessaire pour le payement dicelles
gens des garnisons ordinaires de nos dit duchie et pays,
jusques a la somme de ij. c. m. livres Tournois, ou autre
somme au dessoubz telle, comme besoing seroit pour
le paiement dicelles garnisons ordinnaires, pour convertir et emploier ou dit paiement, et non ailleurs, ce
qui en seroit cueilli et leve sur eulx; en paiant bonne-

Tournois, yearly, assigned to our very dear and well beloved
uncle, John, governor and regent of our said kingdom of
France, duke of Bedfort; this sum to be collected and
raised at three or four terms during the year.

And they, like good, true, and loyal subjects, having heard
our said request, and after having had deliberation and counsel upon the same among themselves, considering the great
charges, as well for the war as for other things, which press
upon us, and may daily press upon us, have liberally granted
to us and given us authority to take and levy from them, at
three or four terms during this year, what will be necessary
for us for the payment of the said troops of the ordinary
garrisons of our said duchy and land, to the sum of ij. c. m.
pounds Tournois, or such other lower sum as shall be
necessary for the payment of the said ordinary garrisons,
to convert and employ in the said payment, and for no
other purpose, what shall be raised and levied on them;
justly paying in each vicomté, with the money which may be

ment en chacune viconte de largent qui en soit cueilli
a cause du dit octroy, les garnisons des villes ou forteresses etant en icelles. Et avec ce, nous eussent requis
que le nombre de iij. c. lances, et ix. c. archiers fust
mis sus pour recouvrement des dits places de Bosmoulins, Aimon, Hoe, Chaillonel, Saint Celerin, Mausson,
et Montaudain, occupee par noz dits annemis, lesquelles
places sont situees et assises es mettes et prochaines
de nostre dite paiis; et que les derniers quil con-
viendroit pour le payement diceulx fussent cueillis et
levez sur eulx en une ou plusiers fois avec loctroy
dessus dit, oultre et par dessus icellui, pour troys moys,
ou autre plus long tems, se pour le cas dessus dit
besoing en etoit. Oye laquelle requeste, icelle eusmes
agreable.

Pour quoy, et aussi pour consideracion des grans
volentes et bonnes loyaultez de nos dits subgiez, avons
pieca ordonne et mis sus icellui nombre de iij. c. lances
et ix. c. archiers, et avec ce cent lances et les archiers

---

gathered on account of the said tax, the garrisons of the
towns or fortresses being in the same. And moreover,
they have required of us that the number of iij. c. lances
and ix. c. archers should be raised for the recovery of the
said places of Bosmoulins, Aimon, Hoe, Chaillonel, St. Clerin,
Mausson and Montaudain, occupied by our said enemies ;
which places are situated and located on the border of and
near to our said country ; and that the money which shall be
required for their payment thereof should be gathered and
levied on them, once or more frequently, along with the
tax above-mentioned, over and above the same, for three
months, or some other longer period, if need be, for the cause
above-mentioned. Having heard this request, we assented
thereto.

For this cause, and also out of regard to the good wishes
and good loyalty of our said subjects, we have some time
since ordered and raised the said number of iij. c. lances
and ix. c. archers, and besides these a hundred lances and

ou nombre des garnisons ordinaires de noz dits duchie
et pays dessus dits pour tenir les champs et recouvrer
par sieges et autrement les places dessus declarees;
lesquelles gens y avoient servy par cinq mois, et encores
servent de present. Pour le paiement des quelx et aussi
de ceulx des dits garnisons ordinaires, pour les tiers
quartz de ceste dite presente annee, soit besoing et
necessite de asseoir et imposer sur noz dits subgiez
partie diceulx octroys, ou autrement le dit paiement
ne pourroit estre fait, ne les dits gens entretenuz; qui
seroit au retardement du fait de nostre guerre et de la
recouvrance des dits places.

Nous, qui desirons et voulons a ce pourveoir, par
ladvis et deliberation de nostre dit oncle, vous mandons et expressement enjoignons, en commettant par
ces presentes, que a toute diligence vous imposez et
assees sur les bourgeois, manans et habitans de noz
dits duchie de Normandie et pays de conqueste, la
somme de cinquante mille livres Tournois pour le tiers

---

archers to the number of the ordinary garrisons of our
said duchy and country above-mentioned, to keep the country
and recover by sieges and otherwise the strongholds above
declared; which troops have served there for five months,
and still at present are serving. For whose payment, and
also for those of the said ordinary garrisons, during the third
quarter of this said present year, it is needful and necessary
to assess and impose on our said subjects a part of these
taxes, or otherwise the said payment could not be made, nor
the said men continued; which would retard the progress of
our said war and the recovering of the places aforesaid.

We, who wish and desire to provide against this, by the
advice and deliberation of our said uncle, command and
expressly enjoin you, commissioning you by these present
letters, that with all diligence you levy and impose upon
the burgesses, residents, and inhabitants of our said duchy
of Normandy and the conquered country, the sum of fifty
thousand pounds Tournois, for the third payment of the

paiement de ij. c. M. livres Tournois, par bailliages, vi-
comtez, eslections et villes, le plus egalement que faire
pourres, non comprintz en ce les gens deglise, nobles
vivans noblement, frequentans les armes, ou qui par
vieillesse et impotence de corps en sont excuses, et
semblables personnes, qui selon la coustume du pays en
sont exemptes. Et oultre avec la dite somme asseez aussi
et imposes la somme de trente mil livres Tournois sur
iceulx bourgeois, manans et habitants pour continuer ce
paiement jusques au premier jour de Juillet prouchain
venant. Iceulx iij. c. hommes darmes et ix. c. archiers
estans soubz le dit sire de Willingtby Festass[1] pour
le mois de May derrennier passe, et ce present moys
de Juing, et se il ne besongne ce dit present mois de
Juing, sera tourne ou tems subsequant, et pour convertir en la demolicion de certaines places ordonnees
estre abatues en noz dits duchie et pays de conqueste,

---

ij. c. M. pounds Tournois, by bailliwicks, vicomtés, divisions
and towns, as equally as it can be done ; without comprehending in this churchmen, nobles living like nobles, frequenting arms, or persons who by age or infirmity of body
are exempt from this, and the like persons, who according
to the custom of the country, are exempt therefrom.
And moreover, with the said sum, you shall also levy and
impose the sum of thirty thousand pounds Tournois, on the
said burgesses, residents, and inhabitants, to continue this
payment until the first day of July next coming. These
iij. c. men-at-arms and ix. c. archers being under the said
lord Willingtby Festass for the month of May last past, and
this present month of June, and if this present month of
June be not needed, it shall be carried on to some subsequent time, and shall be employed in the demolition of
certain places appointed to be pulled down in our said
duchy and the conquered country, and for the payment of

---

[1] *Festass*] We should probably read,—soubz les sires de Willoughby
et Fastolf.

et au paiement de certaine creue de gens darmes et de
trait ordonnes a Mantes, Verneuil, Dreux et autres
places faisans frontiere en Normandie, contre le Chartrain, Beauvais et Rembures; et avec icelles sommes
asseez sur les dits bourgois, manans et habitans des
bailliages de Caen et Constantin, la somme de trois mil
livres Tournois pour faire le paiement de certaines
choses advisees pour le fait du Mont Saint Michiel.
Et au cas que le dit advis ne sera mis a effect, la dite
somme sera tournee en lentretenement de larmee du dit
sire de Willingtby, ou de la creue que demande le dit
sire de Willingtby pour les deux derrenieres places de sa
charge, qui encores sont a recouvrer. Et cinq cens livres
Tournois pour parfaire lemparement et fortiffication de
la ville Davranches; et six cens quarante cinq livres
Tournois sur les habitans de la viconte de Coustances,
pour convertir au payement de une lance et quarante
archiers a cheval, quilz mettent sus pour rebouter les
brigantz pour troys moys.

---

certain additional men-at-arms and bowmen appointed at
Mantes, Verneuil, Dreux, and other places which constitute
the frontiers in Normandy opposite the Chartrain, Beauvais
and Rambures; and with these sums levied on the said
burgesses, residents and inhabitants of the bailliwicks of
Caen and the Cotentin, the sum of three thousand pounds
Tournois, to make the payment of certain things decided on
for the affair of Mont Saint Michiel. And in case the
said plan shall not be carried into effect, the said sum
shall be employed upon the keeping up of the army of the
said lord of Willingtby, or of the extra troops which the
said lord of Willingtby demands for the two last places
under his charge, which are still to be recovered. And
five hundred pounds Tournois to accomplish the taking and
fortification of the town of Avranches; and six hundred and
forty-five pounds Tournois on the inhabitants of the vicomté
of Coutances, to employ it in the payment of one lance
and forty archers on horseback, whom they have raised to
repulse the brigands for three mouths.

Et les dits assiettes faictes, les renvoyes par devers les esleuz de la vicomte, et autres officiers des lieux quil appartiendra, pour les imposer par paroisses, si comme il est accoustume. Et icelles sommes faictes cueillir et lever par ceulx qui a la requeste des dits Estats ont receu et cueilli laide de lannee passee, ou les premier et second paiement du dit octroy, tellement et si diligemment que dedens le viij$^e$our de Juillet prouchainement venant elles sont cueillies, levees et apportees par devers vous, Pierre Surreau, receveur general de Normandie, ausquelles sommes recevoir nous vous avons commis, et commettons par ces presentes, pour les convertir et employer aux choses dessus dites, et non ailleurs. Pourveu quil y ait au devant de quelconque contrainte, trois jours de marchie depuis la publication de lassiette en chascun des bailliages ou vicontez dessus dits. Et contraingnez, ou faictes contraindre, a ce tous ceux qui pour ce seront a contraindre par toutes

----

And when the said assessments have been made, you shall send them to the assessors of the said vicomté, and the other officers of the places as required to levy them by parishes, as is customary. And these sums you shall cause to be collected and raised by those persons who at the request of the said Estates have received and collected the aid for the last year, or the first and second payment of the said tax, in such manner and so diligently, that before the viij. day of July next coming they may be collected, levied, and brought to you, Pierre Surreau, receiver-general of Normandy, which sums we have commissioned you, and do commission you by these present letters, to receive, to spend them and employ them in the things above-mentioned, and not otherways. Provided that before any distress whatsoever, there be three market days after the publication of the tax in each of the said bailliwicks or vicomtés above-mentioned. And you shall distrain, or shall cause to be distrained, all those persons whom it shall be necessary to distrain by all

voyes deues et raisonnables, ainsi que accoustume est
de faire pour nos propres debtes.

De toutes lesquelles choses faire, avec leurs circonstances et dependances, vous avons donne et donnons
par ces presentes povoir, auctorite et mandement especial.
Mandons et commandons a tous nos justiciers, officiers
et subgiez que a vous, vos commis et deputtez en ce
faisant, obeissent et entendent diligemment.

Donne en nostre ville de Paris, le xxvij. jour de May, Date.
lan de grace mil cccc. et trente deux, et de nostre regne
le dixieme.

Par le roy, a la relacion de monsieur le gouvernant
et regent de France, le duc de Bedfort.

DE RINEL. .

————————

right and reasonable means, as it is customary to do to
recover our own debts.

We do give you by these present letters, and have given
you, power, authority, and special command to do all these
things with their circumstances and dependances; and we
command and order all our justices, officers, and subjects,
diligently to obey and assist you, your commissioners and
deputies, in so doing.

Given in our town of Paris, the xxvij. day of May, the
year of grace M. cccc. and thirty-two, and the tenth year
of our reign.

By the king, at the relation of my lord the governor
and regent of the kingdom of France, the duke of Bedford.

DE RINEL.

## 1432.

MANDATE, by Peter Cauchon, bishop of Beauvais, re-
ducing by one half the payment to be made by
the convent of the Holy Trinity at Caen.[1]

A.D.1432.
July 14.

The bishop
of Beau-
vais,

PETRUS, miseratione divina, Belvacensis episcopus,
judex et executor unicus certarum litcrarum aposto-
licarum super impositione duarum integrarum decimarum in ducatu Normanniæ dudum illustrissimo
principi, domino duci Bedfordiæ, regnum Franciæ tunc
regenti, concessarum, venerabilibus et discretis viris,
receptoribus particularibus primo dictarum duarum
decimarum in diœcesibus Baiocensi, Constanciensi, Abrin-
censi et Sagiensi, a nobis commissis et deputatis, et
eorum cuilibet in solidum, salutem in Domino.

in conse-
quence of
the poverty
of the
convent of
the Holy
Trinity at
Caen,

Audita per nos humili et devota supplicatione vene-
rabilium et religiosarum abbatissæ et conventus monasterii Sanctæ Trinitatis de Cadomo, [ordinis] Sancti
Benedicti, dictæ Baiocensis diœcesis, continente quod, licet
ædificia ejusdem monasterii fuerint in captione dictæ
villæ de Cadomo, in primo descensu in dicto ducatu Nor-
maniæ felicis recordationis domini Henrici regis Angliæ,
ultimo defuncti (cui Deus parcat !), pro majori parte tam
igne cremata quam aliter obruta et destructa, ac omnia
bona mobilia ejusdem, vasa etiam argentea et aurea, libri
et calices ,aliaque ecclesiæ dicti monasterii jocalia ablata
et deperdita, necnon postmodum fructus, redditus et
proventus in præmissis diœcesibus consistentes, occasione
guerrarum ibidem (proh dolor !) ex tunc incessanter
urgentium, adeo attenuati et diminuti, quod præfati
abbatissa et conventus non habent unde præmissa et
alia sua ædificia iu dictis diœcesibus consistentia, quæ

---

[1] From the MS. Fontanieu, 115–116.

ruinam permaximam patiuntur, et ad totalem desolationem tendunt, reædificare, reparare, vel substinere, neque suos servitores necessarios, etiam divinis obsequiis insistentes, manutenere et substentare ; — iis tamen non obstantibus, dictos abbatissam et conventum ad solvendum vobis integraliter dictam primam decimam, juxta commissionem nostram vobis datam, compellatis, quod, ut asserunt, sine omissione divini servitii facere non possunt, supplicantes humiliter de remedio opportuno.

Quocirca, quia debita informatione primo facta de prædictis debite informati, attento etiam mandati apostolici nobis transmissi tenore, et quod de tribus aliis integris decimis ultimo in dicto ducatu impositis et levatis, licet temporalia et redditus dicti monasterii pro tunc essent multo meliora, dicti abbatissa et conventus, propter gravia onera ex tunc sibi incumbentia, medietas trium dictarum decimarum per commissarios ad hæc deputatos et potestatem habentes, relaxata est et penitus remissa, prout per authenticas litteras super hoc confectas nobis constitit, dictam integram decimam per abbatissam et conventum sæpedicti monasterii in supradictis diœcesibus debitam, ad medietatem dictæ decimæ moderamus ; et per præsentes mandamus vobis omnibus et vestrum cuilibet, mandantes quatenus, facta solutione de dicta medietate dictæ primæ integræ decimæ per prædictos abbatissam et conventum, aut alium vel alios eorum nomine, de hacce prima integra decima eosdem abbatissam et conventum quietos, immunes et pacificos teneatis, et quilibet vestrum, pro quanto eum tangit, teneat et habeat ; ipsos in posterum nullatenus super hoc inquietantes seu molestantes. Volumus autem medietatem hujus decimæ sic relaxatam et remissam in vestris compotis allocari, et de receptis vestris deduci et defalcari.

In quorum præmissorum testimonium, sigillum nostrum de camera præsentibus litteris duximus apponendum.

*reduces by one-half the contribution due by that convent.*

Date.    Datum Parisius, die Lunæ, xiiij. mensis Julii, anno
Domini millesimo, quadringentesimo, tricesimo secundo.

Ita signatum, TEXTOR.

Sic signatum, Collatio fit per me, R. LATAGNEL.[1]

W. OGIER.

———— ————

1432.

MANDATE from the bishop of Laon, ordering the payment to Guillaume Faverot of twenty-five moutons
for expenses incurred by him.[2]

A.D. 1432.
Nov. 13.
———

GUILLAUME evesque et duc de Laon, per de France,
president de la chambre des comptes du roy, notre
sire, et general conseiller sur le fait et gouvernement
de toutes ses finances es pays de Languedoc et duchie
de Guyenne, a maistre Guillaume Faverot, secretaire
du dit seigneur et receveur general du don equivalent

————

[TRANSLATION.]

GUILLAUME, bishop and duke of Laon, peer of France,
president of the chamber of accounts of the king our lord,
and general counsellor about the affairs and government
of all his finances in the countries of Languedoc and the
duchy of Guienne, to master Guillaume Faverot, secretary
of the said lord, and receiver-general of the gift equiva-

————

[1] Appended are the attestations of
two notaries public, dated 31 July,
1431, namely, of Simon Joliet
and Nicolas Ogier, who vouch for
the accuracy of the above transcript.

[2] From the MS. Fontanieu, 115–
116.

au dixieme entier fait au dit seigneur par les gens
du clergie du dit pays, a lassemblee des gens des Trois
Estatz dicellui pais tenue a Besiers, ou mois de Juillet,
mil cccc. xxxi., salut.

Nous vous mandons que des deniers de votre recepte, vous payez, baillez et delivrez a Jehan Brunet,
escuier, la somme de vingt cinq moutons dor, que
tauxee et ordonnee lui avons, tauxons et ordonnons
par ces presentes, pour avoir este par lordonnance de
monsieur le comte de Foix, lieutenant general du roy,
notre sire, es diz pays et duchie par devers aucuns
seigneurs, barons, et nobles du dit pays de Languedoc, pour les faire assembler et mettre sus en armes
pour aller, avec autres gens darmes et de trait, ou
mon dit seigneur et comte les mandoit; et [son] lieutenant les mandoit aler a lencontre des Anglois, qui
tenoient Castelnau et Ratier, sur les marches du pays
Dalbigeois. Et par rapportant ces presentes, avec quit-

---

lent to the entire tenth made to the said lord by the
ecclesiastics of the said country at the assembly of the
members of the Three Estates of this country, held at
Beziers during the month of July, one thousand cccc. xxxi.,
greeting.

We command you that, out of the money which you have
received, you pay, give, and deliver to Jehan Brunet, esquire,
the sum of twenty-five moutons of gold, which we have
allowed and awarded, and do award and allow him by these
present letters, for having been, by the appointment of
monsieur count de Foix, lieutenant-general of the king our
lord, in this said country and duchy, with certain lords,
barons, and nobles of the said country of Languedoc, to
cause them to assemble and place themselves under arms
to go with the other men of war and the bowmen wherever
my said lord and count should command them; and his lieutenant ordered them to march against the English, who held
Chateauneuf and Rattieres, upon the marches of the country
of the Albigeois. And upon the production of these pre-

tance du dit escuier sur ce tant seulement, la dite
somme de xxv. moutons dor sera passee et allouee
en voz comptes, et rabatue de votre dite recepte par
tout ou il appartendra.

Donne soubz notre signet, le treiziesme jour de
Novembre, lan mil cccc. trente et deux.

PASQUOT.

sent letters, with an acquittal from the said esquire hereupon, the said sum of xxv. moutons of gold shall be past
and allowed in your accounts, and struck off from your
said receipt wherever it may appear.

Given under our signet, the thirteenth day of November, in the year one thousand cccc. thirty-two.

PASQUOT.[1]

1433.

LETTERS from Hue de Lannoi and the Treasurer of the
Boulennois, in which they give a history of their
embassy into England.[2]

NOSTRE tres redoubte seigneur; nous noz recom-
mendons a vous si tres humblement que plus povons.

[TRANSLATION.]

OUR very redoubtable lord, we recommend ourselves to
you as humbly as we best can.

*Margin notes:* Date. — A.D. 1433. July 18. — Outline of the following correspondence.

---

[1] To this piece was attached the receipt for the above sum by Jehan, Brunet, bearing the same date.

[2] From the MS. Supplém. Franç. 292–10, p. 436.

En accomplissant vostre commandement et ordonnance, avons este devers le roy en son royaulme Dangleterre. Et pour ce que devons rescripre en unes lettres tout ce que avons besoingnie, vu et oy pardela, ne se pourroit pas bien faire, (car la chose seroit trop longue,) nous le vous escripvons avec cestes en trois parties ce qui y avons besoingnie et trouve. Dont la premiere lettre contient ce que avons expose au roy au regard de nostre charge principal, et des responses que sur ce avons eues.

La seconde contient comment nous avons parle a monseigneur Dorleans; ce que il nous a dit, ce que avons peu sentir de lui et de son fait.

La tierche contient plusieurs choses de divers propos que avons oyes et entendues pardela, dont il nous semble estre bon que soyez adverti.

Si vous supplions, nostre tres redoubte seigneur, quil vous plaise recevoir en gre ce que avons peu ou sceu faire, car a nos povoirs la vous fait loyalment. Et au

---

In accomplishing your command and appointment, we have been to the king in his kingdom of England. And as we ought to write all that we have seen and heard there, it could not well be done in one letter (for the matter would be too long), we will write to you herewith in three parts, what we have done there and found. Of this, the first letter contains what we have stated to the king with regard to our principal charge, and the answers which we have had thereto.

The second contains how we have spoken to my lord of Orleans; what he has said to us, what we have been able to discover about him and his affairs.

The third contains many things of divers matters which we have heard and understood there, of which it seems good to us that you should be apprised.

Wherefore we entreat you, our very redoubtable lord, that you would be pleased to take in good part what we have been able to do or ascertain, for we have done it as faithfully for you as we were able. And as regards

regard de moy, Hue de Lannoy, garde les termes, a
vostre correction, de ce que me deistes ou prayel de
vostre hostel en vestre ville Darras le plus pres que
jay peu ; mais en proposant a vous. En regard a la
disposition en quoy avons trouve generalment tous
ceulx du royaume, qui en verite a nostre venue
estoient generalment comme tous malcontens, et avons
este de prime face asses cruement receuz. Mais apres
ce que avons este oye, il nous est advis que les choses
se sont tres bien adouchies ; et a vous veritablement
escripre, navons point trouve quils aient entention de
faire quelques traitties ne entreprinses au prejudice de
vous, ou de vos pays ; mais tenons pour verite quils
desirent entretenir amour et bienveuillance a vous et
vos diz pays ; ainsi que tout ce vous pourra plus a
plain apparoir par les lettres du roy et la response,
dont dessus est faite mention. Nostre tres redoubte
seigneur, nous prions au Benoit Filz de Dieu, quil
vous donist bonne vie et longue.

---

me, Hue de Lannoy, I have kept the terms, under your
correction, as to what you told me in the lawn of your
residence in your town of Arras, as near as I could, but
yet submitting it to you. As regards the disposition in
which we have for the most part found all those of the
kingdom, truly at our arrival they were generally almost
all of them ill-affected, and we were received at the first
unkindly enough. But, after what we have heard, we
have come to the conclusion that things have become
considerably softened down ; and to write to you truly,
we have not by any means found that they intend to
make any treaties or enterprises to the prejudice of you
or your country : but we hold it as a truth that they
desire to continue in love and good-will towards you and
your said country ; all which may more plainly appear by
the king's letter and the answer, of which mention is
made above. Our very dread lord, we pray the Blessed
Son of God, that He give you a good and long life.

Escript en vostre ville de Lisle, le xviij. jour de <sup>Date.</sup> Juillet.

Vos humbles et obeissans serviteurs,

HUE DE LANNOY, SEIGNEUR DE SANTES, et le TRE-SORIER DE BOULENOIS.

Nostre tres redoubte seigneur; nous vous prions que les lettres que nous vous escripvons avec ces presentes, apres ce que les aures veues, soient arses, rompues, ou gardees par tel de vos gens que nul inconvenient nen puissent venir; car vous veez bien quelles touchent a plusieurs personnes.

Mon tres redoute seigneur; jai oublie de mettre en mes lettres comment nous avons bien oi en Engle-terre parler ke le mariage du roi et de la fille du Daufin a este mis avant par aukuns; mes nous navans point peu sentir ke rien en soit fet, et osi ce seroit, comme on nous a dit, en faisant pais generalle.

HUE DE LANNOY.

---

Written in your town of Lille, the xviij. day of July.

Your humble and obedient servants,

HUE DE LANNOY, LORD OF SANTES, and the TREASURER OF THE BOULENOIS.

Our very redoubtable lord; we pray you that the letters which we write you with these presents, after you have seen them, may be burnt, torn, or kept by such persons of yours as that no mischief may arise therefrom; for you well see that they relate to several persons.

My very redoubtable lord; I have forgotten to put in my letters how we have heard it said in England that the marriage of the king and of the daughter of the Dauphin has been hurried on by certain persons; but we have not been able to ascertain that anything will be done therein, and also that this would be, as we have been told, by making a general peace.

HUE DE LANNOY.

A nostre tres redoubte seigneur et prince, monseigneur le duc de Bourgoingne et de Brabant, etc.

--------

### ACCOUNT OF THEIR ARRIVAL IN ENGLAND.

Account
of their
arrival in
England.

Nostre tres redoubte seigneur, nous nous recom-
mandons a vous si tres humblement qui plus povons.
Et vous plaise savoir que nous, arrive en Angleterre,
entre Sandewids et Cantorbie, encontrasmes plusieurs
prelas et princes, qui sen alloient au devant de monseigneur le regent et madame la regente, en laquelle
compaignie estoit monseigneur le comte de Suffort,
auquel aviesmez lettres adrechans depar vous, lesquelles lui presantasmes, et avec ce lui priasmes que il
se voulsist emploier ad ce que peussions avoir audience
devers le roy, et quil nous vaulsist aidier en nostre
expedition, en lui recommendant vous et vos affaires.
Et lui dismes depar vous tout ce quil nous sembloit
qui povoit prouffiter selon nostre charge.     Lesquelles

--------

To our very redoubtable lord and prince, my lord the
duke of Burgundy and Brabant, &c.

--------

Our very redoubtable lord, we recommend ourselves to
you as humbly as we best may.  And may it please you
to know that on our arrival in England, between Sandwich
and Canterbury, we met several prelates and princes who
were going to meet my lord the regent and madame his
wife, in which company was my lord the earl of Suffolk,
to whom we had letters addressed from you, which we
presented to him, and at the same time prayed him that
he would be pleased to employ himself so that we might
have an audience with the king, and that he would be
so good as to aid us in bringing our mission to an end,
recommending to him you and your affairs.  And we said
from you to him all that seemed likely to be profitable to
us, in advancing our business.  These said letters of yours

vos dites lettres rechut tres liement, et demanda tres
fort de vous, et nous dist quil est tout a vostre commandement, et quil se sentoit plus tenus a vous qua
prince du monde, et pour qui il vouldroit le plus faire
apres le roy, son seigneur.

Et dillec tout droit nous tirasmes a Londres; et incontinent nous arrive en allasmes devers le conte de
Warewic, qui estoit en son hostel, et lui presentasmes
vos lettres, et lui dismes depar vous en substance ainsi
que aviesmez fait au dit conte de Suffort. Le quel
conte de Warewic nous rechut gracieusement, un peu
plus sombrement que aultre fois navoit fait. Touttes
voyes il nous demanda de vostre estat; et a la parfin
nous lui demandasmez ou nous pourriesmez trouver le
roy, car nous avions lettres depar vous adrechans a
lui. A quoy nous respondy que prestement ne nous
en savoit respondre, car le roy estoit alle en chaches
et deduis; mais le lendemain nous feroit savoir le jour
et lieu ou nous le pourriens trouver.

---

he received very joyfully, and asked after you very
anxiously, and he said to us that he is quite at your
command, and that he felt himself more beholden to you
than to any prince in the world, and for whom he
would do the most after the king, his lord.

And from thence we went straight to London; and immediately on our arrival we went to the earl of Warwick,
who was in his house, and we presented to him your
letters, and said to him from you in substance the same
that we had said to the said earl of Suffolk. The said
earl of Warwick received us graciously, a little more
gravely than he had done before. Still, however, he
asked how you were; and at the last we asked him
where we should be able to find the king, for we had
letters from you addressed to him. To which he replied
that at that present time he could not answer about that,
for the king had gone on a hunting and pleasure ex-
cursion; but that on the morrow he would let us know
the day and the place when we should be able to find him.

Et le lendemain bien matin en alasmes a la messe de monseigneur le cardinal, lui presentasmez vos lettres, et deismez tout ce quil nous sembloit qui povoit proufiter au bien et expedition de nostre charge. Lequel mon dit seigneur le cardinal nous rechut bien gracieusement, et demanda beaucoup de vous, en soy presentant de semployer a tout ce qui senteroit qui vous pourroit venir a plaisir, et a nostre delivrance. Mais a la verite nous le trouvasmes aucunement plus estrange que par cy devant navons accoustume de faire. Et en ceste mesme journee nous fist savoir mon dit seigneur de Warewic que nous trouveriemez le roy en une ville xxv. miles pardela Londres, apelle Gildevorde, et que fussiens le Vendredy ensuivant bien matin devers lui a lessue de la messe, ce que nous fusmes ; et illec trouvasmes le roy, et en sa compaignie les ducs de Bedfort, de Glocestre, et Dyork, et le joisne duc de Noortfolk, le conte de Warewic, le conte de Salseberi, de Notonberlant, et de Souffort, et plusieurs autres grans

---

And very early on the next morning, as we were going to the mass of my lord the cardinal, we presented to him your letters, and said to him all that we thought would be profitable for the good and expedition of our charge. The said lord cardinal received us very graciously, and asked a great deal about you, promising to employ himself in all that he thought likely to forward your pleasure and our discharge. But, truly, we did find him somewhat stranger than before this we have been accustomed to do. And this same day my said lord of Warwick told us that we should find the king in a town xxv. miles on the other side of London called Guilford, and that we should be with him the next Friday very early in the morning, as he came from his mass ; and this we did, and there we found the king, and in his company were the dukes of Bedford, of Gloucester, and of York, and the young duke of Norfolk, the earl of Warwick, the earls of Salisbury, of Northumberland, and of Suffolk, and many other great

seigneurs. Et illec presentasmes au roy vos lettres, et feismes les recommendations le mieulx que nous sceusmez ne peusmez. Le quel roy (qui est ung tres bel enfant, et de belle venue) nous demanda tres gracieusement et en langaige Francois, comment vous le faisies, et ou vous estiez; et nous lui respondymes que vous estiez, a nostre partement, en tres bon point, et pensiesmez que lors esties en la Champaigne avec grant compaignie de gens darmes pour resister alencontre de ses ennemis et des vostres. Et apres aucunes menues gracieuses paroles que eusmes avec lui, nous fist retraire, et appella tous les princes dessus nommez, qui autour de lui se mirent a genoulz, et illec fist lire vos lettres; et apres quils eurent parle ensemble aucune espace, feusmes rappelle, et nous fu dit par monseigneur le conte de Warewic que les lettres que aviesmes apporte depar vous contenoient creance, lequel le roy vouloit estre exposee pardevant son grant conseil en sa ville de Londres le Mardi, ou Merquedi, ensuivant.

---

lords. And there we presented your letters to the king, and made the recommendations as best we knew and were able. The said king (who is a very beautiful child, and well grown,) asked us very graciously, and in the French language, how you were, and where you were; and we replied that at our departure you were in excellent health, and we thought that you then were in Champagne with a great company of men-at-arms, to resist his enemies and your own. And after some gracious conversation which we had with him, he caused us to retire, and he called all the above-mentioned princes, who knelt around him, and there he caused your letters to be read; and after that they had spoken together for some time, we were recalled, and my lord the earl of Warwick told us that the letters which we had brought from you contained a credence, which the king would wish to have reported before his great council in his city of London, on the Tuesday or Wednesday following.

and the
council.

Et illec, apres que eusmes prins congie ainsi quil
appartient, retournasmes a Londres ; et le Merquedi,
ainsi que assigne nous estoit, venismes a Westmoustre
devers les seigneurs qui estoient assemblez du grant
conseil.   Cest assavoir, les ducs de Bedford, de Glocestre, monseigneur le cardinal, les archevesques de
Cantorbie et Dyork, le chancellier Dangleterre, les
contes de Warewic, de Nontonberlant, de Salseberi, et
de Suffort, et chinq ou six autres grans seigneurs.   Et
illec fu par moy, Hue de Lannoy, expose la creance,
tele que chargie maviez a vostre correction ; apres laquelle oye, me dirent que je le baillasse par escript,
pour sur ce avoir le roy son bon avis, dont nous nous
excusasmes beaucop, et par beaucop de moiens.   Mais
finablement nous avons este constrains de le bailler par
escript, ce que tres enuis avons fait ; pour ce princi-
palement que nous naviesmes aultre instruction que ce
que vous, mon tres redoubte seigneur, en aviez dit de
bouce a moy, Hue de Lannoy.   Et le landemain leur

---

And from thence, after we had taken leave as ought to be
done, we returned to London, and the Wednesday, as had
been appointed us, we came to Westminster before the
lords of the great council, who were assembled.   That is
to say, the dukes of Bedford, of Gloucester, my lord the
cardinal, the archbishops of Canterbury and York, the
chancellor of England, the earls of Warwick, Northumberland, Salisbury, and Suffolk, and five or six other great
lords.   And there by me, Hue de Lannoy, were exhibited
the credentials, such as I had been charged with at your
correction ; after hearing which, they told me to deliver it
in writing, in order that the king might have good deliberation upon it, for which we excused ourselves a great
deal, and in many ways.   But finally we were constrained
to deliver it in writing, which we were much provoked to
do ; principally because we had had no other instruction
except what you, my very redoubtable lord, had told me,
Hue de Lannoy, verbally.   And the next day we carried

apportasmes par escript, ainsi que veoir pourrez par le semblable que avec ces presentes vous envoyons; et lors nous fu dit que pour ce que aviesmes expose que vous, mon tres redoubte seigneur, aviez sceu daucunes seigneurs certaines choses de quoy le roy povoit avoir grant aide et confort, et dont les aucuns pouroient avoir ung tres grant dommaige, comme il povoit sembler, que ce vaulsissions dire apart a monseigneur le cardinal, monseigneur larcevesque Dyork, et monseigneur le conte de Warewic, et ce fait, le plus brief que bonnement pourroient, feroit le roy response sur tout. Et le lendemain a lostel de monseigneur le cardinal leur deismes ce que aviesmez senti de monseigneur le duc de Bretaigne et monseigneur le conte de Richemont, et la maniere bien au long comment le roy sen pourroit aidier, en y gardant tousjours les meilleurs termes a lonneur de mes diz seigneurs de Bretaigne et de Richemont que faire se pourroit. Et aussi leur deismes que vostre entencion

---

it to them in writing, as you may see by the duplicate which we send you with these present letters; and then we were informed that, as we had stated, that you, my very redoubtable lord, had been informed by certain lords of certain things, through which the king might have great aid and comfort, and by which some others might sustain a very great damage, as it might appear, we would have the goodness to state this matter privately to my lord the cardinal, my lord the archbishop of York, and my lord the earl of Warwick, and when this was done, the king would make answer as speedily as possible on all points. And the next day, at the house of my lord the cardinal, we told them what you had ascertained from my lord the duke of Bretaigne and my lord the count of Richemont, in detail, and the manner how the king could help himself herein, keeping always the best terms possible for the honour of my said lords of Bretaigne and of Richemont. And we also told them that

P 2

estoit de parler a monseigneur le duc de Savoye, pour savoir si de luy le roy pourroit avoir quelque ayde ; veu que len vous avoit rapporte quil estoit malcontent des ennemis du roy et des vostres ; et quil vous sembloit que le roy devoit fort contendre davoir lametee du dit duc de Savoye. Les quelles choses ils rechurent tres bien en gre ; et apres plusieurs interrogatoires a nous faites, et aussi plusieurs responses sur ce, leur deismes quil sembloit a plusieurs sages et notables que, se le roy vouloit venir a fin de sa guerre, il convenroit quil se aidast des grans et puissans seigneurs du royaume de France et pays denviron, et quil trouvast avec sa puissance Dangleterre maniere de les contenter de terres, seignouries et finances, etc.

Apres les quelles choses faites, et plusieurs diligences pour avoir nostre response, laquelle nous fu baillee le Mardy, vij. jour de Juillet. Cest assavoir, tous les princes dessus nommez presens, et le conte de Staffort,

---

it was your intention to speak to my lord the duke of Savoy to know if the king could have some assistance from him ; since it had been told you that he was displeased with the enemies of the king and of yourself ; and that it appeared to you that the king ought to make every effort to have the friendship of the said duke of Savoy. These things they took in very good part ; and, after many questions had been put to us, and after many answers thereupon made, we told them that it appeared to many wise and notable men that, if the king wished to put an end to his war, it would be necessary that he should be assisted by the great and powerful lords of the kingdom of France and the neighbouring countries, and' that with his power in England he should find means of contenting them with lands, estates, and money, &c.

After these things had been done, and we had used much diligence to have our answer, it was given to us on Tuesday the vij. day of July. That is to say, all the princes above-mentioned being present, and the earl of

nous fut dit que le roy estoit tres contens de tres
gracieuses lettres que lui aviez envoyees, et de la
creance par nous exposee. Et pour ce que il avoient
entendu que nul de nous ne devoit retourner devers
vous, le roy vous escriproit ses lettres closes, et nous
bailloit par escript la response sur ce que expose lui
avions, le quel vous envoions avec ces presentes.

Et quant aux choses particulierement exposees par
lordonnance du roy a monseigneur le cardinal, monseigneur larcevesque Dyork, et conte de Warewik, le
roy de ce avoit chargie mon dit seigneur le cardinal
nous en faire la response.

Et en icellui jour meismes allasmes devers mon dit Their
seigneur le cardinal, lequel nous dit en effect que le second interview
roy vous prioit que vaulsissies toujours entretenir les with the
besoignes entre les ducs de Savoye et de Bretaigne et cardinal.
conte de Richemont, et y faire le mieulx que pourriez
pour le bien du roy; et que de dessus, adonc que
le parlement, que le roy a presentement assemble a

---

Stafford, it was told us that the king was very well
pleased with the very gracious letters which you had sent
him, and for the credence exhibited by us. And as he
had heard that none of us were to return to you, the
king would send his closed letters to you, and give us
in writing the answer to what we had opened to him,
which we send you along with these presents.

And as to the things particularly stated by the command of the king to my lord the cardinal, my lord the
archbishop of York, and the earl of Warwick, the king
had charged my said lord the cardinal to give us the
answer to this.

And on the same day we went to my said lord the
cardinal, who told us in effect that the king prayed you
that you would always be so good as to carry on the
business between the dukes of Savoy and of Bretagne and
the count of Richemont, and do the best therein that
you could for the good of the king. And that, moreover,
until the parliament, which the king has at present as-

Londres, seroit fine, le roy ne povoit et impossible lui
estoit de rien presenter, poursuir ne promettre envers
les diz seigneurs ; mais incontinent le dit parlement
fine, mon dit seigneur le cardinal tenoit pour certain
que le roy envoieroit aucune notable ambaxade devers
vous, pour avec vous en ce, et en plusieurs autres
grans matieres qui presentement ne povoient estre
declairez, traitter et besoigner.    Et ce fait, allasmes
prendre le congie du roy pour retourner pardeca.

Nostre tres redoubte seigneur, nous prions au Benoit
Filz de Dieu, quil vous doinst bonne vie et longue.

Escript.—Voz humbles et obeissans serviteurs,

Hue de Lannoy, Seigneur de Santes, et le
Tresorier de Boulenois.

---

### Account of their Interview with the Duke of Orleans.

Nostre tres redoubte seigneur, nous nos recom-
mandons a vous si tres humblement que plus povons.

sembled at London, shall be finished, the king could not,
and it was impossible for him, to present, procure, or
promise anything whatever to the said lords ; but that
immediately the said parliament should be finished, my
said lord the cardinal thought it certain that the king
would send a notable embassy to you, along with you to
treat of and consider this and many other great matters
which at present could not be declared.    And this being
done, we went to take leave of the king to return home.

Our very redoubtable lord, we pray the blessed Son of
God that He may give you a good and long life.

Written.—Your humble and obedient servants,

Hue de Lannoy, Lord of Santes, and The Treasurer
of Boulenois.

---

Our very redoubtable lord, we recommend ourselves to
you as humbly as we best can.    And may it please you

Et vous plaise savoir que apres ce que fusmes retournez a Londres de devers le roy, nous venismes
a lostel dou conte de Souffort au lever de son disner,
lou nous trouvasmes monseigneur Dorleans avec le dit
comte, aus quelx nous feismes le reverence. Et incontinent monseigneur Dorleans nous prist par les
mains, et nous demanda tres fort comment vous le
faisies et ou vous esties, dont nous lui en deismes la
verite, et comment vous voz recommandiez a lui tres
fort, et esties desirant savoir de son bon estat, etc.
A quoy il nous respondy quil estoit en bon point
de corps, en desplaisance de ce quil usoit le meilleur
temps de son eage prisonnier. A quoy je, Hue de
Lannoy, luy respondy que encores, au plaisir de
Dieu, en pourra bien yssir et par bonne maniere.
Car se par son bon moien Deiux lui donnoit la
grace que il peust traittier et estre moyen de la
paix des deux royaulmes, et de faire paix generale
entre les royaulmes et princes diceulx, il ne de-
veroit point plaindre les paines et dangiers quil a

---

to know that after we had returned to London, from having
been before the king, we came to the house of the earl of
Suffolk, as he was rising from his dinner, where we found
my lord of Orleans with the said earl, to both of whom we
made obeisance. And immediately my lord of Orleans took
us by the hand, and asked us very anxiously how you were,
and where you were, and we told him the truth, and how
that you recommended yourself very earnestly to him, and
that you desired to know of his good health, &c. To
which he answered us that he was in good bodily health,
but that he was distressed because he was spending the best
part of his life in prison. To which I, Hue de Lannoy,
answered, that still, by the pleasure of God, good might
result from it, and in a good way. For if by his good agency
God should give him the grace to treat and be the mediator
of a peace between these two kingdoms, and to make a
general peace between the realms and princes of the same,
he ought not to complain of the pains and dangers he has

portees. A quoy il respondy, " Vecy beau cousin de
Suffort, qui sceut comment devers le roy Dangleterre et les seigneurs de son conseil je me suy
presentez tousjours de my y employer, et encores fay ;
mais je suy ainsi comme une espee qui est enfermee
dedens une huge, dont len ne se peut aidier, qui ne
le tire dehors ; et je ay tousjours dit, et encore diz,
que je ny puis bonnement prouffiter se je ne parloye
a aucuns de mes amis de France, par qui moien je
peusse aidier a conduire la besongne ; et me semble
que se je poveie avoir parle a aucuns especiaulx amis
que jay, je y prouffiteroia beaucop.    Car je cuide
avoir des plus grans seigneurs dautour de monseigneur
le roy de France, et de ceulx qui tiennent son party,
qui feroient et vauldroient beaucop user par mon conseil au regart de paix generale.   Et par la foy de mon
corps, je desire tant la dite paix que je voudroye que
je fusse cause et moyen de le avoir bien faite, et que
icelle se deust bien entretenir, et sept jours apres lac-

---

gone through.  To which he replied, " Here is my good cousin
of Suffolk, who knows how I have always offered myself to
the king of England and the lords of his council, to be employed therein, and I still do so ; but I am like a sword, shut
up in a sheath, of which a man cannot avail himself unless he
draws it ; and I have always said, and still do say, that I
can be of no real use unless I speak to some of my friends
of France, by which means I might help to advance the
business ; and it appears to me that if I might have a conference with some of the especial friends that I have, I might
therein be of much service.   For I believe that there are
among the greatest lords in the court of my lord the king
of France, and those of his party, persons who would act,
and who would be very pleased to act, according to my
counsel with regard to the general peace.   And by the
faith of my body, so much do I desire the said peace,
that I wish, provided I might be the cause and means of
having it fully accomplished, and of its assured continuance,

complissement de ce je deusse recevoir la mort. Et
je oze bien dire devant vous, beau cousin de Suffort,
que mon beau cousin de Bourgoingne et de Bretaigne
y pevent plus, apres les parties principalles, que prince
qui vive."

Et lors je, Hue de Lannoy, respondy que je savoye
de certain que vous, mon redoubte seigneur, estiez
tant desirant la paix que chose qui fust en ce monde,
pour obveir aux grans maulx qui journelment se font,
et relever le poure peuple de France, qui a loccasion
de la guerre est tout destruit ; et que a vous ne tenroit
point, mais que plus y aideriez de tout vostre povoir.
Et lors dit le conte de Suffort au dit monseigneur
Dorleans, "Monseigneur, je vous ay bien toujours dit
que monseigneur de Bourgoingne est bien dispose a
paix." Et lors respondy monseigneur Dorleans, "De
ce je ne fay nulle doubte ; car je say bien que lui ne
moy ne sommes point cause des maulx advenus ou
royaulme de France ; et de ce vous ay je autrefois

---

seven days after this were brought about, I would be willing
to suffer death. And I venture to say before you, my fair
cousin of Suffolk, that my good cousins of Burgundy and of
Bretaigne could do more herein, after the principal parties,
than any prince who lives."

And then I, Hue de Lannoy, replied, that I knew for
certain that you, my redoubtable lord, were as desirous
of this peace as of anything in this world, so as to obviate
the great evils which arise daily, and to relieve the poor
people of France, which on account of the war is totally
ruined ; and that the blame was not with you, but that you
rather would aid therein with all your might. And then
said the earl of Suffolk to my said lord of Orleans ; "My
lord, I have always told you that my lord of Burgundy is
well disposed towards peace." And then my lord of Orleans
replied, "Of this I have no doubt ; for I well know that
neither he, nor I, are the cause of the evils which have
come upon the kingdom of France ; and of this I formerly

parle, messire Hue, et creez que je suis encores en ce propos." Et lors me estraint la main et, qui plus est, me pincha par le bras tres fort, et par deux fois ; et veoye bien quil ne ozoit point dire ce quil eust bien voulu dire. Et lors derechief commenca a dire, "Je vouldroye que le roy Dangleterre me vaulsist emploier en ces besoingnes, en se tenant seur de ma personne. Car je ne desire point tant a traittier ma delivrance que je fay la dite paix. Et oze bien dire tout hault que je y puisse estre aussi grant moien, ou plus, que homme qui vive." Et lors monseigneur de Suffort lui dit, "Orcha, monseigneur, le roy a bonne voulente dentendre a la ditte paix, et de vous y employer, car encores savez vous quil a de present donne sauf conduit a aucuns de vos gens pour venir devers vous." A quoy monseigneur Dorleans respondy, "Vous dites veoir, beau cousin, car je envoie briefment Camail, mon herault." Alors derechief il me commencha tres fort a demander de vous et de vostre estat ; et en verite il ne

---

spoke to you, messire Hue, and believe me, I am still of this mind. And then he pressed my hand (and what is more) he squeezed me by the arm very strongly, and this he did twice ; and I very well saw that he did not dare to say what he would much have wished. And then he began to say again, "I wish that the king of England would employ me on these affairs, making himself sure of my person ; for I do not in the least desire so much to treat of my own deliverance as of this said peace. And I dare to say aloud, that I could therein be of as great an assistance, or greater, than any man alive." And then my lord of Suffolk said to him, "Well, my lord, it would be a pleasure to the king to hear of this said peace, and employ you in it, for you know that he has now given safe conduct to certain of your people to come to you." To which my lord of Orleans replied, "You speak truly, fair cousin, for I shall shortly send Camail, my herald." Then he began to ask me once more very anxiously about you and your health ; and truly he could not refrain

se povoit appaisier de en parler ; en vous tres fort loant et souhaidant tres fort quil vous eust peu veoir et parler a vous.

Et apres toutes ces bonnes et gracieuses parolles presimes congie de lui et du dit conte de Suffort, au quel congie prendre me dist mon dit seigneur Dorleans, "Je vous prie, messire Hue, que me revenes encores veoir;" et le dit conte prist la parolle en disant, "Ils vous verront avant quils partent." Et en verite, nous noz sommes parcheuz par beaucop de manieres de moyens que les dis Engles ne prendrent point bien en gre que nous, ne aucuns de vos gens ayent gaires de parolles au dit monseigneur Dorleans.

Et environ deux jours apres ce, vint devers nous ung appelle Jennin Cauvel, barbier du conte de Suffort, et une des gardes depar le dit conte mon dit seigneur Dorleans, et nous dist, "Jay toujours este vray et loyal Bourguignon, et aussy je suis natif du pays de monseigneur de Bourgoingne, de sa ville

---

from speaking thereof, praising you very much and wishing very earnestly that he might be able to see and speak to you.

And after all these good and gracious words, we took leave of him and of the said earl of Suffolk, at which leave-taking my said lord of Orleans said to me, "I pray you, messire Huc, come again and see me;" and the said earl began to speak, saying, "They will see you before they leave." And of a truth we perceived, by many ways and means, that the said English do not take it with good will, that either we, or any of your people, have any communication whatever with my said lord of Orleans.

And about two days after this came to us one called Jennin Cauvel, the barber of the earl of Suffolk, and one of the guards appointed by the said earl over my lord of Orleans, and he said to us, "I have always been a true and loyal Burgundian, and moreover I am a native of the country of my lord of Burgundy, of his town of Lille, and therefore I love

de Lisle, et si layme de tout mon cuer comme mon seigneur naturel. Et pour vous advertir, pour ce quon a fort parli que monseigneur Dorleans haoit fort monseigneur de Bourgoingne, et que sil povoit widier quil lui feroit de grans guerres et dommages, je vous promets par my foy pour ce que je parle Francois il se confie de sa grace plus a moy que en nulles de ses gardes, ne en personne qui soit en nostre hostel. Mais avant vostre venue, autant que jay este autour de lui, je lui ay oy dire tant de bien que merveilles de monseigneur de Bourgoigne, en monstrant quil layme de tout son coer, et men a parle le plus que de tout le remanant des seigneurs de France ; et povez dire hardiement a monseigneur de Bourgoigne quil se teingne tout assure que monseigneur Dorleans ne veult que tout amour et amistie avec lui. Et se bon vous semble, et je puisse sentir que ce soit le plaisir de monseigneur de Bourgoingne par vous, tresorier de Boulenois, qui demourez pres Dangleterre, je me

---

him with all my heart as my natural lord. And that I may caution you, since it has been openly said that my lord of Orleans thoroughly hates my lord of Burgundy, and that if he could escape, he would make fierce war on him, and do him much damage, I assure you on my faith, because I speak French, he is pleased to put more trust in me than in any other of his guards, or in any one whatever in our house. Before your arrival, as long as I have been near him, I have heard him say marvellously much good of my lord of Burgundy, showing that he loves him with all his heart, and he has spoken to me more of him than of all the rest of the lords of France ; and you may boldly tell my lord of Burgundy that he may hold himself perfectly assured that my lord of Orleans wishes nothing but perfect love and friendship with him. And if it seem good to you, and I may understand that it be the pleasure of my lord of Burgundy, by you, treasurer of Boulonois, you who live near England, I am very confident that I shall find good

fay bien fort que je trouveray bien maniere de aler devers mon dit seigneur de Bourgoingne, et lui porter lettres de mon dit seigneur Dorleans, par lesquelles il poura savoir sa bonne voulente. Et monseigneur de Bourgoingne ne vous ne prendez nulle deffiance sur moy, car, en verite, je suis vray Bourguignon; et se je sentoye chose qui fust au dommaige de mon dit seigneur le duc, je men vauldroie acquitter de lui faire savoir comme a monseigneur."

Ce de quoy nous le merchiasmes beaucop depar vous, et lui chargeasmes quil deist a monseigneur Dorleans quil se tenist tout asseur que vous seriez toujours prest de vous emploier a sa delivrance et faire tous les plaisirs que vous pourrez; et quil nestoit point deceu sil vous aymoit, car aussi faisiez vous lui.

Et le lendemain presismes congie des diz monseigneur Dorleans et conte de Suffort; lequel monseigneur Dorleans nous dist que le voulsissons recommander envers vous, en disant, "Beau cousin de Suffort, pour-

---

means of going to my said lord of Burgundy and carry letters to him from my said lord of Orleans, by which he may know of his good will. And neither my lord of Burgundy nor you need feel any apprehension about me, for assuredly I am a true Burgundian; and if I discovered anything that was to the hurt of my said lord the duke, I would wish herein to do my duty by letting him know, since he is my lord."

For this we thanked him much from you, and we charged him that he should say to my lord of Orleans that he should consider it as a certainty that you would always be ready to employ yourself for his deliverance, and do him all the pleasure possible; and that he was not at all deceived if he loved you, for you do the same towards him.

And the next day we took leave of my said lord of Orleans and the earl of Suffolk; and my lord of Orleans asked me to be so good as to recommend him to you, saying, "My fair cousin of Suffolk, might I not write a letter to

roie je point escripre unes lettres a beau cousin de
Bourgoingne?" A quoy le dit conte de Suffort respondy: "Monseigneur, vous y adviserez encore nuit;"
et lendemain nous envoya monseigneur de Suffort par
le dit Cauvel unes lettres a vous adrechans, lesquelles
nous vous envyons; mais le dit Cauvel nous dist que
mon dit seigneur Dorleans ne pot lors avoir license de
vous escripre.

Vos humbles et obeissans serviteurs,
HUE DE LANNOY,
SEIGNEUR DE SANTES, et LE TRESORIER LE BOULENOIS.

---

## ACCOUNT OF VARIOUS INCIDENTS WHICH OCCURRED TO THEM DURING THEIR RESIDENCE IN ENGLAND.

Intelligence about the parliament,

NOTRE tres redoubte seigneur, nous noz recommen-
dons a vous si tres humblement que plus povons.
Et pour vous advertir de plusieurs materes qui par

my good cousin of Burgundy?" To which the said earl
of Suffolk replied, "My lord, you shall deliberate upon it
before night;" and on the morrow my lord of Suffolk sent
us by the said Cauvel a letter addressed to you, which we
send you, but the said Cauvel told us that my said lord of
Orleans could not then have leave to write to you.

Your humble and obedient servants,
HUE DE LANNOY,
LORD OF SANTES, and THE TREASURER OF BOULENOIS.

---

### [TRANSLATION.]

OUR very redoubtable lord, we recommend ourselves to
you as humbly as may be possible. And to advertise you
on many matters which at many times and from divers

pluseurs fois et diverses personnes avons oyes en nostre voyage Dangleterre, il vous plaise savoir ;—

Premiers, le roy fist commenchier son parlement le viij. jour de ce presente mois de Jullet ; auquel parlement sont toz assemblez les princes, prelas et estas du royaulme, et sans faulte ilz y sont en tres grant nombre ; et ainsi que nous avons peu sentir, il est taillie de durer pour tout le mois Daoust, ou plus. Et adceque nous avons peu sentir, entre autres materes ils mettront avant ou de prendre paix avec le daulphin, telle quelle pourront avoir, ou de trouver finance pour mettre sus aucune tres grant et puissant armee. Car ad ce que nous porons parcevoir, il ont bien congnoissance que le fait de France ne puet pas longuement durer en lestat ou il est de present.

Item, quant nous eusmes prins congie du conte de Suffort, il dist a moy, Hue de Lannoy, a part, " Faittes savoir, ou dittes, a monseigneur de Bourgoingne har-

*conversation with the earl of Suffolk,*

---

persons we have heard in our journey to England, may it please you to know ;—

Firstly, the king caused his parliament to begin on the viij. day of this present month of July ; at which parliament are assembled all the princes, prelates and estates of the kingdom, and without failing they are there in very great numbers ; and from what we have been able to discover, it is likely to continue the whole month of August, or longer. And from what we have been able to learn, among other things, they exert themselves either to make peace with the dauphin, upon whatever terms they can obtain it, or to find money to raise a very large and powerful army. For from what we can perceive, they very well know that the affairs of France cannot long continue in the state in which they are now.

Item, when we had taken leave of the earl of Suffolk he said to me, Hue de Lannoy, apart, " Let my lord of Burgundy know decidedly (or tell him yourself,) that I

diment que je ay plus grant esperance en paix generale que je neuch oncques mais ; et les gens que
monseigneur Dorleans fait venir presentiment arrivez
pardeca devers lui, auxquels le roy a donne sauf
conduit, jen pense a savoir plus avant." Et lors lui
demandais qui estoient lez diz ambaxadeurs. Il me
nomma les noms ; mais en verite je nen ay retenu
que lun, cest assavoir, Hue de Saint Marcq, lautre
est un maistre Dorleans, et le tiers ung des secretaires du daulphin. Et encore me dist, "Se les choses
se portent ainsi que journee de paix soit prinse, y
convendra que monseigneur de Bourgoingne y viengne ;
car se la chose doit venir a bien, il fauldra que plusieurs grans seigneurs en soient assemblez." A quoy
je luy respondy que jesperoye quant la venroit que
vous feriez toujours tellement vostre devoir que len
en devroit estre bien contens. Et me dist oultre que
incontinent que aucune chose en sera deliberee, len
le vous fera savoir.

---

have greater hope of a general peace than I ever had before ;
and on the arrival of the people, whom my lord of Orleans
presently shall cause to come from hence to him, to whom
the king has given a safe conduct, I hope to know still more
about it." And then I asked him who were the said ambassadors. He mentioned their names to me, but in truth I
have only remembered one, that is to say, Hue de Saint
Marcq, the other is a master of Orleans, and the third one
of the secretaries of the dauphin. And he also said to me,
" If things are so settled that a conference is fixed for the
peace, it would be necessary that my lord of Burgundy
should come there ; for if the thing is to come to any good,
it would be necessary that many great lords should be
assembled." To which I replied that I hoped that when
it should happen, you would always do your duty in such
a way that they would be well content with it. And he
told me moreover that directly anything should be determined on, they would let you know.

Item, au prendre congie de monseigneur le cardinal, *with cardinal, and with the earl of Warwick.* il nous dist, "Vous povez seurement faire savoir a beau nepveu de Bourgongne que ce parlement departy, (lequel se departira ou sur paix ou sur troubles, ou pour faire plus forte guerre que oncques mais,) incontinent jespoire que le roy envoiera devers beau nepveu vostre maistre pour apointier avec lui telement que len entendra li ungs lautre, et que chascun scara ce quil aura a faire, et comment on se pourra et aura a gouverner."

Item, et quant nous preismes congie de monseigneur *Intelligence respecting Bretagne.* de Warewic, qui se recommandoit a vous, il nous dist entre plusieurs parolles, "Si Dieux me ayt, entre nous Englois (a vous feablement dire,) avons prins une tres grant desplaisance et merancolie de ce que tandis que le roy a este en France, monseigneur de Bourgoingne, vostre maistre, ne la onques veu ne venu devers lui. Et par le foy de mon corps, je vouldroye avoir perdu le moiete de ma revenue pour ung an, et monseigneur de Bourgongne fust pardeca

---

Item, on taking leave of my lord the cardinal, he said to us, "You can assuredly make known to my good nephew of Burgundy that when this parliament rises, (which it will do whenever there is either peace, or trouble, or in order that a greater war than ever before be made), I hope that the king will immediately send to my good nephew, your master, to arrange with him so that they shall mutually understand each other, and that each one will know what he has to do, and how they shall be able to arrange.

Item, and when we took leave of my lord of Warwick, who recommended himself to you, he said to us, among many words, "As may God have me! we English, to tell you the truth, are exceedingly displeased and disappointed that, whilst the king was in France, my lord of Burgundy, your master, has neither seen him nor visited him. And by the faith of my body, I would willingly have lost the half of my revenue for a year, if my lord of Burgundy came here for fifteen days, for

quinze jours, car certes il ny trouveroit que bien et
honneur, et tout en vaulroit mieulx." A quoy je
lui dis, entre autres choses, puis quil parloit france-
ment, que aussi feriesmes nous a lui; et lors deismes
comment se pourroit telle chose faire selon les cruelles
parolles que len ot journellement par ceste ville, en
disant tous les maulx que len povoit dire de monseigneur de Bourgoingne, en le manechant lui et ses
pays. A quoy il repundy, "Ce ne sont que menues
gens qui dient telz parolles, mais il ne trouveroit
nulle faulte es princes, ne en ceulx qui ont le puissance ou gouvernement du dit royaulme; et monseigneur son pere en plaine guerre vint bien devers
le roy en sa ville de Calais, ou len ne lui fist que
tout bien et honneur." Sur quoy nous respondimes
que le roy devenoit grant, et venoit au plaisir de
Dieu brief en France, et lors, se Dieu plaist, venriez
devers luy.

**Intelli-
gence
respecting
Bretagne.**  Item, monseigneur le duc de Bretaigne a tousjours
eu, tandis que nous avons este la, trois ambaxadeurs

---

surely, he would only find good and honor, and all would
be the better for it." To which I answered, among
other things, that since he had spoken frankly we would
do the same to him; and then we asked how could such
a thing be done after the harsh words that one heard daily
in this town, where was said all the evil that could be
spoken of my lord of Burgundy, menacing him and his lands.
To which he replied, "They are only low people who speak
such words, but he would find no fault with the princes,
nor with those who have the power or government of
the said kingdom, and my lord his father in open war
went to the king in his town of Calais, where they
offered him nothing but all good and honor." Upon which
we replied that the king was growing up, and if it were
the will of God would shortly come to France, and then
if it please God you would come to him.

Item, my lord the duke of Bretaigne has always had,
while we have been there, three ambassadors with him.

depar lui. Cest assavoir ; messire Thomas Thissac, chevalier du pays Dirlande, maistre Jehan Pregent, docteur en loix, du pays de Bretaigne, et maistre Jehan Godart, secretaire de mon dit seigneur de Bretaigne. Mais onques ils nont parle a nous, et si estiesmes logie bien pres li uns de de lautre. Et ad ce que avons peu sentir, ils y sont pour aucuns traittiez tendans a la delivrance de monseigneur Dorleans, et aussi poursievant certain grant dommaige que leur ont fait les Englois sur la mer, et plus avant nen savons a la verite. Et avons veu empres le roy Gilles, monseigneur, fil le duc de Bretaigne, qui se recommande humblement a vous, et en verite cest un tres gracieux et habille enfant.

Item, Camail, herault de monseigneur Dorleans, et Respecting the duke of Orleans. aussi dautre part Jennin Cauvel, barbier de monseigneur le conte de Suffort, lun en labsence de lautre, ont dit a moy, Hue de Lannoy, entre plusieurs parolles, et de leur mouvement, que se le

---

That is to say, messire Thomas Thissac, a knight of the country of Ireland, master Jehan Pregent, doctor in laws, of the country of Bretaigne, and master Jehan Godart, secretary of my said lord of Bretaigne. But they have spoken nothing to us, although we were lodged very near the one to the other. And from what we have been able to perceive, they are there for some treaties tending to the deliverance of my lord of Orleans, and also they are prosecuting for some great damages that the English have done to them on the sea ; but more hereof we do not know certainly. And we saw in the king's company my lord Gilles, son of the duke of Bretaigne, who humbly recommends himself to you ; and truly he is a very gracious and clever child.

Item, Camail, the herald of my lord of Orleans, and also on the other hand Jennin Cauvel, the barber of my lord the earl of Suffolk, the one in the absence of the other, has said to me, Hue de Lannoy, among many words, and of their own free will, that if the dauphin

Q 2

daulphin et les seigneurs dautour de lui ne veuellent entendre a paix, et par ce moien a la delivrance de mon dit seigneur Dorleans, pourtant mon dit seigneur Dorleans na pas entention de soy laissier perdre ne demourer toujours ou point ou il est. Mais lui ont oy dire que sil pouvoit avoir parle a vous, mon tres redoubte seigneur, a monseigneur le duc de Bretaigne, et ou bastard Dorleans, son frere, que encore trouvera il bien maniere de sa delivrance; et plus avant ne men ont declarez.

**Respecting the intentions and proceedings of Charles VII.** Item, et nous arrive a Calais a nostre retour Dangleterre, trouvasmes Jehan de Saveuse, qui tout droit venoit Dorleans, et nous dist quil avoit este devers le daulphin. Et nous luy demandasme quel apparence de paix generale len avoit par dela. Il nous dist que moiennant la delivrance de monseigneur Dorleans, sans laquelle rien ne sen seroit, tout tendroit bien a paix, mais ce seroit par ainsi que les Englois navoient point la couronne, car de ce ne failleroit il

---

and the lords of his party will not hear of peace, and (by this means) of the deliverance of my said lord of Orleans, nevertheless my said lord of Orleans has no intention to allow himself to be ruined, nor will he always live in the state in which he now is. But they have heard him say that if he could have spoken to you, my very redoubtable lord, to my lord the duke of Bretaigne, or to the bastard of Orleans, his brother, he would still find ample means for his deliverance; and more than this they have not declared to me.

Item, and when we arrived at Calais on our return from England, we found Jehan de Saveuse, who had come straight from Orleans, and he told us he had been with the dauphin. And we asked him what appearance there was of general peace there. He told us that if my lord of Orleans were delivered, without which nothing could be, all would be tending towards peace, provided that the English should not have the crown, for on this point he

tenir nulles parolles ; mais aultrement len trouveroit
tous bons traittiez. Et nous dist que presentement le
daulphin avoit fait une grant assemblee des estats de
ses pays ; et y estoient devers lui le duc Dalenchon,
le conte de Fois, le conte de Clermont ; et encores
disoit on que le comte de Richemont y devoit venir,
et ny estoit point le seigneur de la Trimoille, car il
lavoit laissie a Sully, environ a huit jours, et disoit
quil esperoit que le dit seigneur de la Tremoille
nauroit plus tel auctorite autour du daulphin quil
souloit. Et entre autres paroles me dist que apres
le siege de Montargies leve, le dit seigneur de la
Tremoille dist au Bastard Dorleans, "Pourquoy nalez
vous au devant du duc de Bourgoingne, qui sen
vient en Bourgoingne? on ne lara jamais en meilleur
place." A quoy le dit Bastard respundy, quil ne lui
vouloit nul mal, car il savoit bien que monseigneur
de Bourgoingne ne haoit point monsieur son frere, et
aussi son frere ne haioit point mon dit seigneur de

---

(the dauphin) would admit of no compromise ; but otherwise
good terms might easily be obtained  And he told us that
at this time the dauphin had made a great assembly of the
estates of his country ; and there were with him the duke
of Alençon, the count of Fois, the count of Clermont.
And it was also said that the count of Richemont would
come thither, and the lord de la Trimoille was not there,
for he had left him at Sully about eight days ago, and
he said that he hoped that the said lord de la Tremoille
would no longer have such authority with the dauphin as
he used to have.  And among other things he told me
that after the raising of the siege of Montargis, the said
lord de la Tremoille said to the bastard of Orleans,
" Why do you not go to the duke of Burgundy, who is
coming to Burgundy ? you will never have a better place."
To which the said Bastard replied, that he did not wish
him any ill, for he well knew that my lord of Burgundy
does not hate my lord his brother, and also his brother

Bourgoingne. Et demanda le dit Jehan de Saveuse a moy, Hue de Lannoy, quel chiere mon dit seigneur Dorleans nous avoit faite, et je lui respundy que tres bonne. Et lors il dit, " Certes monsieur le duc de Bourgoingne se puet tenir seur que mon dit seigneur Dorleans laime de tout son coer, et a parfaitte fiance en lui."

Conversation with the regent of France, Item, et pour advertir de toutes les parolles que durant nostre ambaxade avons eu avec monsieur le regent, il est vray que ainsi que nous arrivasmes a Calais, mon dit seigneur le regent, et madame, et leur compaignie widoient les portes pour aler monter en la mer pour passer en Angleterre, et lors luy feismes la reverence ; et incontinent demanda a moy, Hue de Lannoy, " Dont venez vous, et ou voulez vous aler?" Et lui dis que vous nous envoiez en Angleterre, ou nous vaulriesmes desja estre, se pooresmes trouver passage. Et lors il dist, " Je vous ferai delivrer

---

did not hate my said lord of Burgundy. And the said Jehan de Saveuse asked me, Hue de Lannoy, what cheer my said lord of Orleans had made us, and I replied that it was very good. And then he said, "Certainly my lord the duke de Burgundy may hold himself quite assured that my said lord of Orleans loves him with all his heart, and has perfect confidence in him.

Item, and to advertise you of all the conversation which we have had with my lord the regent during our embassy ; true it is that as we arrived at Calais, my said lord the regent, and madame, and their company, were leaving the port to embark to cross the sea for England. And then we made him our reverence ; and immediately he asked me, Hue de Lannoy, "Whence came you, and where are you going?" And I told him that you were sending us into England, where we would have been already if we could have found the means of crossing. Then he said " I will cause a transport to be delivered to you," which

vaissel," ce que incontinent nous fist ; car il nous fist
mettre ou ballenjer de Calais.

Item, nous a este certiffie par les contes de Warwic who speaks
et Souffort, que quant nous presentasmes vos lettres kindly of
the duke
au roy, et que len nous fist retraire, mon dit seigneur of Bur-
le regent fist au´ roy tres grans recommendations de gundy.
vous, en vous tres fort loant, et en disant plusieurs
biens et honneurs de vous. Et semblablement nous
ont jure et afferme par leurs fois que ens ou grant
conseil il sest acquittez de dire beaucoup de biens
et de honneurs de vous, en disant, "Combien quil y
ait aucunes manieres de malveillance entre beau frere
et moy, pourtant ne veul je pas laissier a me acquitter
envers monseigneur le roy, en entre vous, de dire les
grans biens et services que lui a fait beau frere de
Bourgoingne, et fait de jour en jour," en parlant de
vous en tres grant honneur.

Item, le jour avant nostre partement je, Hue de
Lannoy, men alay devers lui pour dire adieu, et aussi

---

immediately he did, for he caused us to be despatched in
a balenger of Calais.

Item, it has been certified to us by the earls of Warwick and Suffolk that when we presented your letters to the
king, and we were required to withdraw, my said lord the
regent made great recommendations of you to the king, praising you very greatly, and speaking of you much to your
honour. And likewise they have sworn and affirmed to us
by their faith that in a great council he did his duty in
saying much that was to your good and honor, saying,
" Although there may be some appearance of ill-will
between my good brother and me, nevertheless I will not
refrain from discharging my duty towards my lord the king,
to say among you, how great have been the good deeds
and services that my good brother of Burgundy has done
to him, and still does from day to day ;" speaking of
you with very great honor.

Item, the day before our departure, I, Hue de Lannoy,
went to him to say farewell, and also to madame his

a madame la regente, savoir sils vouloient riens mander
es marches de Picardie; et apres plusieurs parolles
gracieuses me dist mon dit seigneur le regent a part,
" Messire Hue, je say bien que vous amez beau frere
de Bourgoingne, aussi croy je que vous ne me haez
point. Je vous promets par ma foy, quil me desplaist
bien que beau frere a tel ymagination contre moy;
car je ne le hech point ; est lun des princes de
ce monde que jai toujours le plus ame. Et ay bien
congnoissance que les maniers que tenons sont grandement prejudiables a monsieur le roy et a la chose
publique. Et non obstant tout, je ne delaisseray je
a faire le bien du roy, ne aussi des pays et subgez
de beau frere ; car encores, se Dieu plaist, serons en
tel amiste que avons este par cy devant et ce devons
estre."

Vos humbles et obeissans serviteurs,

HUE DE LANNOY, SEIGNEUR DE SANTES, et LE
TRESORIER DE BOULENOIS.

---

wife, to know if they wished to send anything to the
marches of Picardy ; and after many gracious words my
lord the regent said to me apart, " Messire Hue, I know
well how much you love my good brother of Burgundy ;
I also believe that you do not hate me. I assure you,
by my faith, that it displeases me much that my good
brother has such an ill opinion against me; for I do not
hate him, he is one of the princes of this world whom
I have always loved the most. And I well know that the
attitude we have assumed is very prejudicial to my lord the
king and the public good. And notwithstanding all this, I
shall not discontinue to act for the good of the king, nor
for the country and subjects of my good brother ; for yet, if
it please God, we shall enjoy such friendship as we have
before this time, and still ought to enjoy."

Your humble and obedient servants,

HUE DE LANNOY, LORD OF SANTES, and THE TREASURER
OF BOULENOIS.

Monsieur de Varembon est a Londres, ou il pour-
sieut aucune besongne devers le roy et les seigneurs,
le quel, pour honneur de vous, nous a fait accom-
paigner et faist tout honneur quil a peu; et ma dit
quil ne peut finer davoir Nogent ne Montigny. Et
lui retourne par deca, il vous pourra dire plusieurs
menues nouvelles, car len ne se garde pas si pres de
lui par dela comme on fait de plusieurs autres, et
si se recommande a vous tres humblement; et en
verite, il se presente tres fort de vous faire service.

Monsieur de Varembon is in London, where he is pursu-
ing some business with the king and the lords; who,
out of honour to you, accompanied us and did us all the
honour that he could; and he said to me that he could
not succeed in having Nogent or Montigny. And when
he returns home, he will be able to tell you much news, for
they do not watch him so closely there as they do many
others; and he recommends himself to you very humbly,
and truly he is very anxious to do you service.

## 1433.

ANSWER by Henry the Sixth and his Privy Council
to the articles presented by the ambassadors of
the duke of Burgundy.[1]

A.D. 1433.
July.

CI sensuit la response donnee depar le roy, nostre
seigneur, et son conseil en Angleterre, a certains

The answer by the English

[TRANSLATION.]

HERE follows the answer given by the king, our lord,
and his council in England, to certain articles exhibited

---

[1] From the Supplement Franç., 292-10, p. 356.

Privy
Council to
the Articles
sent by
the duke of
Burgundy.
To the 1, 2,
3 and 4.
articles exposez et baillez par escript par messire
Hue de Lannoy, seigneur de Santes, chevalier, et le
tresorier de Boulenois, ambaxadeurs envoyez devers
le roy, nostre dit seigneur, par monseigneur le duc de
Bourgongne.

Quant au premier, second, tiers et quart articles;
le roy, nostre dit seigneur, remercye mon dit seigneur
de Bourgongne, son bel oncle, de ce quil lui a signifie
et fait savoir lestat de son royaume de France, et des
advertissement et conseil que il lui donne, pour remedier et pourveoir aux inconveniens et afflictions que
sueffre le peuple de son dit royaume a loccasion des
guerres dicellui. Les quels inconveniens mon dit seigneur de Bourgongne supplie et desire estre ostez par
paix, ou longue abstinence generale; au aultrement,
pour faire tele et si forte guerre que lorgueil des ennemis puist estre abatus, et par ce moien contrains de
venir a la dite paix, ou abstinence. Et quant a ce
matiere, pieca feu nostre saint pere pape Martin exhorta

and given in writing by messire Hue de Lannoy, lord of
Santes, knight, and the treasurer of the Boulenois, ambassadors sent to the king, our said lord, by my lord the duke
of Burgundy.

As to the first, second, third and fourth articles; the
king, our said lord, thanks my said lord of Burgundy,
his good uncle, for having signified and made known to
him the state of his kingdom of France, and for the advice
and counsel which he has given him to remedy and provide
against the damages and afflictions which the people of
his said kingdom suffer on account of his said wars.
Which damages my said lord of Burgundy supplicates and
desires should be taken away by peace, or a long general
truce; or, on the other hand, to make such and so terrible
a war, that the pride of the enemies may be lowered, and
by this means they be compelled to come to the said peace
or truce. And as to this matter, some time ago our late
holy father, pope Martin, exhorted my lord the cardinal

monseigneur le cardinal Dangleterre a ce quil se
voulsist emploier envers le roy, dentendre au bien
dicelle paix, et ainsi le fit mon dit seigneur le cardinal a Calais; lequel trouva le roy en ceste partie
tres enclin et bien dispose; et depuis, mon dit seigneur de Bourgongne a ce mesme effet en supplia au
roy, lui estant a Rouen, au quel temps monseigneur
le cardinal de Sancte Croix vint pardevers lui pour
celle mesme cause; et par grant avis et meme deliberacion de conseil, en consideracion a la requeste et
conseil de mon dit seigneur de Bourgongne, lui fu
respondu depar le roy quil estoit toujours prest et
enclin de bonne voulente entendre a tous bons, amiables,
et raisonnables moiens de paix, ou de bonne, seure
et ferme abstinence de guerre, sans communicacion de
la quelle response fu tres content icelui cardinal. Et
ceste response fist le roy incontinent savoir a mon
dit seigneur, devers lequel ala le dit cardinal de
Sainte Croix, et peu de temps apres retourna a Paris
et a Corbueil, ausquels lieux communiquerent ensemble

-----

of England to employ himself in causing the king to
listen to this peace, as did my said lord the cardinal
at Calais; who found the king well inclined and disposed
thereto; and since then, my said lord of Burgundy sup-
plicated the king to the same effect, he being at Rouen,
at which time my lord the cardinal de Sancte Croix came
to him for this same cause, and by great advice and even
by deliberation of council, in consideration of the request
and advice of my said lord of Burgundy, it was replied to
him by the king that he was always ready and inclined to
hear, with good will, all good, amiable, and reasonable means
of peace, or of good, sure, and firm abstinence from war;
without the communication of which reply the said cardinal
was very well pleased. And the king made this reply known
immediately to my said lord, to whom the said cardinal de
Saint Croix went, and a short time after he returned to
Paris and to Corbeil, at which places my lord the regent,

monseigneur le regent, duc de Bedford et lui, et furent
offers au dit cardinal de Sancte Croix, comme media-
teur dicelle paix, plusieurs lieux notables et seurs
pour convenir les ambaxadeurs des parties ; et apres
grant longueur de temps, le dauphin refusa, et ne
voult prendre ou choisir quelconque lieu se non Nevers
ou Aucerre tant seulement ; et non obstant que ung
chascun des diz lieux de Nevers et Aucerre fut diffi-
cile et dangereux au regard des chemins pour les gens
du roy, qui estoient ordonnez pour convenir, neantmoins pour le bien de paix, a la quelle le roy est toujours incline, et se mettre en tout devoir, envoia ses
dits gens au dit lieu Daucerre, et pareillement mon
dit seigneur de Bourgongne et monseigneur de Bretaigne y envoyerent les leurs, lesquels longuement
attendirent les gens du dit daulphin. Et finablement
eulx venus, il ne firent quelconque ouverture de paix,
ne vouldrent entendre a quelconque abstinence ; mais
dirent sil estoit aucune esperance de paix, il estoit
besoing que les seigneurs de France, prisonniers en

---

the duke of Bedford and he communicated with each other ;
and many well-known and safe places for convening the ambassadors of the parties were offered to the said cardinal as
the mediator of this peace ; and after a considerable length
of time the dauphin refused, nor would he take nor choose any
place except Nevers or Auxerre, only ; and notwithstanding
that each of the said places, Nevers and Auxerre, were
difficult and dangerous as regards the roads for the king's
men who were appointed to meet there, nevertheless, for the
good of the peace, for which the king is still inclined, and
to do his duty to the utmost, he sent his said men to the
said town of Auxerre, and in like manner my said lord
of Burgundy and my lord of Bretaigne sent theirs thither,
where they waited a long time for the men of the said
dauphin. And when at last they did come, they made no
overture of peace whatever, nor would they hear of any
truce ; but they said if there was any hope of peace, it was
necessary that the lords of France, who are prisoners in

Angleterre, feussent menez en aucun lieu oultre la
mer, pour avoir leur conseil et advis en la dite
matiere. Et quant a la traittie ou abstinence, ils nen
bailleroient point ; et sils la balloient, elle seroit de
petit effect ; disans aulcuns deulx que se leur maistre
avoit cent mille escus, si ne la pouverent il faire garder,
pour ce quil nestoit servi en sa guerre que destran-
giers, ausquels il a abandonne le pais, et non obeissent
a lui en ceste partie. Et a fin que en la dite matiere
neust rupture, fu prise a lexortation du dit cardinal
une aultre journee entre eulx pour convenir a Corbueil et a Melun vers la fin de Mars derrenierement
passe, au quel lieu de Corbueil compairerent les diz
cardinal et gens du roy, notre dit seigneur, et ceulx
de mon dit seigneur de Bourgongne. Et si fist savoir
a mon dit seigneur le regent mon dit seigneur de
Bretaigne quil estoit prest de tenir, garder, et accepter
tout ce que par le roy seroit conclu et accorde en la
dicte matiere ; et dillec en certain village entre Cor-

England, should be conducted to some place across the sea,
that their advice and counsel in the said matter might be
had. And as to the treaty or truce, they would give none ;
or if they did give it, it would be of little effect; some of
them saying that if their master had a hundred thousand
crowns, he could not make them keep it, because he had
only employed strangers in his war, to whom he abandoned
the country, and they would not obey him in this thing.
And in order that there should be no rupture in this said
matter, by the advice of the said cardinal another day was
settled between them to meet at Corbeil and at Melun,
towards the end of March last, at which town of Corbeil
the said cardinal and the men of the king, our said lord,
appeared, and also those of my said lord of Burgundy.
And my said lord of Bretaigne made known to my said
lord the regent, that he was ready to hold, keep, and accept, all that might be concluded and accorded by the
king in the said matter; and from thence the said men of

bueil et Melun comparerent les dittes gens du roy
avec les ambaxadeurs du dit daulphin, ausquels ils
signifierent de plus au plus la bonne voulente et disposition du roy, nostre dit seigneur, et comment il
faisoit mener a Douvre, qui est le plus prouchain
port vers France, les dis seigneurs prisonniers, offrans
baillir a ceulx de partie adverse, qui vouldroient venir,
saufs conduiz et seurtes pour parler a eulx ; a quoy
ne firent aucune response les gens du dit daulphin,
mais dirent quils le raporteroient a leur maistre, et en
feroient savoir sa voulente, pour laquelle avoir a este
longuement le dit cardinal de Sainte Croix pardevers
lui, qui finablement a reporte son consentement et offre
pour avoir trieve seulement pour quatre mois, sans ce
que mention ait este faitte de sa venue ne communicacion des diz seigneurs prisonniers qui longuement
ont este a Dovere, et monseigneurs le regent, de Gloucestre, et cardinal Dangleterre, les chancelliers et
conseils de France et Dangleterre a Calais aussi par

---

the king met with the ambassadors of the said dauphin at
a certain village between Corbeil and Melun, to whom
they signified more and more the good will and disposition
of the king, our said lord, and how that he caused the said
captive lords to be conducted to Dover, which is the
port nearest to France, offering to provide those of the
adverse party, who wished to come, with a safe conduct and
sureties, to speak with them; to which the men of the said
dauphin made no answer, but said that they would report
it to their master, and would make known his will about
it, to have which the said cardinal de Sainte Croix has
been a long time with him, who finally brought back his
consent, and offer to have a truce for four months only,
without any mention being made of his coming, nor the
communication of the said captive lords, who had been a
long while at Dover. And my lord the regent, my lord of
Gloucester and the cardinal of England, the chancellors and
councillors of France and England, have also been for a long

long temps, en esperance que le dit adversaire deust
envoier ses dittes gens pour parler aus diz seigneurs
prisonniers, ainsi quil avoit desire, pour le bien dicelle
paix. Les quels seigneurs prisonniers ont este moult
troublez et desplaisans de ce que on nest venu devers
eulx pour le dit bien ; au quel bien le roy les treuve
tres despose et presta deulx emploier en toutes manieres pour icelui bien, ainsi que les diz seigneurs,
mesmement le duc Dorleans, a fait savoir a ses gens
et officiers en France.

Les quelles choses considerees, puet chacun congnoistre comment le roy, nostre dit seigneur, sest mist
et met grandement en son devoir, et na pas tenu, ne
tient a lui, que len nait entendre au bien de paix, et
que encore on ny entende ; mais a tenu et tient au
dit daulphin. Et voit len bien que la trieve de
quatre mois, quil a offert, est pour advitailler, le temps
pendant dicelle, les places et lieux a lui obeissans, qui
en ont grand besoing, et rompre et empescher les sieges,

---

time at Calais, hoping that the said adversary would send
his said agents to speak with the said captive lords, as it
had been desired, for the good of this said peace. And
these captive lords have been much troubled and displeased,
because no one has come to them, on the subject of the
said peace ; for which good the king finds them well disposed and ready to employ themselves in every manner
for this end, as the said lords, especially the duke of
Orleans, has made known to his men and officers in France.

These things being considered, every one may know how
the king, our said lord, has acted and acts for the best
according to his duty, and that it is not, nor was it, to be
attributed to him that no heed had been given to the
matter of the peace, and that no attention is yet being given
thereto ; but that all this was to be, and still is to be, attributed to the said dauphin. And one sees very well that
the truce of four months, which he has offered, is, that
during this period he may provision the places and towns
obedient to him, which have great need of it, and to break

armees et enterprises du roy, notre dit seigneur, et de mon dit seigneur de Bourgongne, qui ne sont pas de petit frait; comme le siege de Saint Walery, larmee de monseigneur de Huntyngton, la charge de monseigneur de Arondel, et la finance baillee pour la France.

Puet on aussi considerer que la trieve des diz quatre mois ne puet estre pour le roy et ses subgiez daucun effect prouffitable. Car en si petit de temps pou de bien en si haulte matiere se pourroit ensuivir, et a peine souffiroit le dit temps pour choisir et eslire lieu de ouverir et entendre aux seurtez qui pour la dite trieve seroient necessaires; mais en plus grant longueur de trieve se pourroient trouver moiens de paix, se en la partie adverse ne tient.

To the 5, 6, 7, & 8. Item, au regard des v., vj., vij., et viij. articles, le roy, nostre dit seigneur, considere bien que continuation de guerre est destruction de pais, et si considere bien aussi les grans diligence, frais et despences qui fait

---

and hinder the sieges, armies and enterprises of the king, our said lord, and of my said lord of Burgundy, which are not of little expense; such as the siege of Saint Valery, the army of my lord of Huntingdon, the charge of my lord of Arundel, and the finance given for France.

One may also consider that the truce of the said four months cannot be of any profitable effect for the king and his said subjects. For in so short a time very little good could be done in so important a matter, and the said time would scarcely suffice to choose and select a place to open and hear the sureties who were necessary for the said truce; but if the truce were longer, means might be found for making peace, if the adverse party was not against it.

Item, with regard to the v., vj., vij. and viij. articles, the king, our said lord, considers well that a continuation of the war is the destruction of the country, and he considers well also, the great diligence, outlay, and expen-

de present mon dit seigneur de Bourgongne pour resister aux diz ennemis, qui ne luy ont tenu aucune
promesse de abstinence, de quoy il le remercie de tout
son cuer, et lui prie que semblablement il ait regard
et consideration a son jeune aage, et aux tres sump-
tueuses et grans charges quil a eues a supporter depuis
le premier an de son dit aage jusques a ores, et sup-
porte encores de jour en jour. Car pour bouter la
guerre oultre, et esloigner les dis ennemis de Picardie,
France et Normandie, il souldoie maintenant pour
quatre mois le nombre de gens qui sensuivent. Cest
assavoir, pour recouvrer Saint Walery, qui a este de
nouvel pris en la trieve de mon dit seigneur de Bourgongne, et autres forteresses a lenviron, seize cent combatans, soubz monseigneur de Saint Pol, avec cinq
cent combatans que mon dit seigneur de Bourgongne a
accorde y mettre a ses despens pour la deffense de la
France ; douze cent combatans soubz monseigneur de
Huntyngton, pour tenir les champs es basses marches

---

diture which at present my said lord of Burgundy is making to resist the said enemies, who have not kept any
promise of truce ; for which he thanks him with all his
heart, and prays him in like manner to have regard and
consideration to his youth, and the very heavy burdens he
has had to bear since the first year of his said life until
the present time, and still bears from day to day. For
to make an end of the war and to drive the said enemies
from Picardy, France, and Normandy, he is now paying
for four months the following number of men. That is to
say, to recover St. Valery, which has been newly taken
during the truce of my said lord of Burgundy, and other
fortresses thereabouts, sixteen hundred men-at-arms under
my lord of Saint Pol, along with five hundred men-at-arms,
whom my said lord of Burgundy has agreed to place there
at his expense for the defence of France ; twelve hundred
men-at-arms under my lord of Huntingdon, to hold the
country of the lower borders of Normandy ; nine hundred

de Normendie ; neuf cent combatans soubz monseigneur
Darondel, sans les garnisons gisans en forteresses de
France, Normendie, Anjou et Le Maine ; qui sont plus
de six mille combatans. Par la diligence des quelz,
et de larmee que a mise sus presentement mon dit
seigneur de Bourgongne, le roy, nostre dit seigneur, a
esperance que en ceste saison notables explois de guerre
et grans recouvrances de pais se feront, al aide de
mon dit seigneur. Porquoy grant nombre des subgiez
de roy et de mon dit seigneur de Bourgongne pourront
vivre en plus grant repos et seurete quils nont fait par
cy avant.

To the 9,
10, 11 and
12.

Item, en tant que touche les ix., x., xj. et xij. articles ; pour ce que en aulcuns diceulx mon dit seigneur
de Bourgongne requiert avoir quatre cent combatans,
ou la finance pour les paier, a fin de les joindre avec
larmee ordonnee par mon dit seigneur de Bourgongne
soubs messire Jehan de Luxembourgh, conte de Liney,
pour la seurte de la Picardie, se offre aussi de bonne

---

men-at-arms under my lord of Arundel, exclusive of the
garrisons lying in the fortresses of France, Normandy, Anjou
and Le Maine ; which are more than six thousand men-at-
arms. By whose diligence, and by that of the army which
my said lord of Burgundy has lately raised, the king, our
said lord, hopes, that during this season, notable exploits
of war and a great recovery of the country will take place,
with the aid of my said lord. Whereby a great number
of the subjects of the king and of my said lord of Burgundy will be able to live in greater repose and surety
than they have hitherto done.

Item, in so much as regards the ix., x., xj. and xij.
articles ; because that in some of them my said lord of Burgundy requires to have four hundred men-at-arms, or the
sum for paying them, so that he may join them with the
army appointed by my said lord of Burgundy under messire
Jehan de Luxembourgh, count de Ligny, for the surety of
Picardy, my said lord of Burgundy also offers himself with

voulente mon dit seigneur de Bourgongne au service
du roy, et de se exposer, ses subgiez et aliez, et tout
ce que Dieux lui a preste, et en porter la charge autant
et si avant que possible lui sera ; ou cas toutes voyes
que ce sera le plaisir du roy de mettre sus une tres
grande et notable puissance pour rebouter les diz
ennemis et leur donner a faire en plusieurs lieux,—
le roy, nostre dit seigneur, recoit joyeusement et en
grant gre les belles et notables offres que lui fait
mon dit seigneur de Bourgongne, de quoy il le remercie tant comme il puet. Et pour ce est son entencion
de faire exposer et remonstrer lestat de son royaume
de France, et les choses dessus dites aux Trois Estas
de son royaume Dangleterre, presentement assemblez
pardevers luy, pour y prendre et avoir bon advis et
conclusions eues nouvelles du dit cardinal de Sainte
Croix et des ambaxadeurs du roy et de mon dit
seigneur de Bourgoingne, vacans de present au bien
dicelle paix; dont depend partie de ce qui sera a faire,
soit pour parvenir a paix, ou a guerre, se paix ou abs-

---

good will to the service of the king, both to expose himself,
his subjects and allics, and all that God has given him, and
to bear the cost of it as much and so far as he is able ; provided however that the king shall be pleased to raise a
very great and notable power to drive back the said enemies,
and give them something to do in several places,—the king,
our said lord, receives joyously and most willingly the good
and handsome offers which my said lord of Burgundy has
made him, for which he thanks him as much as he can. And
consequently it is his intention to make known and declare
the state of his kingdom of France, and the things above mentioned, to the Three Estates of his kingdom of England now
assembled with him, to take and have therein the good advice
and conclusions newly had from the said cardinal de Sainte
Croix and the ambassadors of the king and of my said
lord of Burgundy, who are occupied at this time in the
business of this peace ; which partly depends upon what
will have to be done, whether to come to peace, or to war,

tinence ne ce puent avoir ; et ce qui sera advise et
se poura faire en ceste matiere, le fera le roy savoir a
mon dit seigneur de Bourgoingne. Et sil advient que
le dit daulphin ne vueille entendre a paix generale, ou
a trieve de trois aus, de deux, ou dun a tout le moins,
et que journee soit prise pour besoigner au bien dicelle
paix, le temps pendant de labstinence, le roy na pas
pourtant entencion de habandonner sa coronne et
seigneurie de France, mais la veult garder et defendre
a laide de nostre seigneur, et au bon confort de mon
dit seigneur de Bourgoingne, et de ses autres bons
parens, amis, vassaulx, aliez et subgiez, par tous les
moyens qui lui seront possibles. Et neantmoins sera
tousjours prest de entendre a tous amiables et bons
moiens de paix en temps si long, convenable, et raisonnable que homme ny soit deceu ; et aussy de y commettre de sa part gens de si grant et bonne auctorite
quil doit souffire, pourveu que ainsi soit fait dautre
coste.

---

if peace or truce cannot be had ; and what shall be advised
or can be done in this matter, the king will make known
to my said lord of Burgundy. And if it so happen that
the said dauphin will not hear of a general peace, or a
truce of three years, or of two, or one at the least, and that a
day should be fixed to see to the business of this peace, during
the time of the abstinence, the king, nevertheless, has no intention of abandoning his crown and sovereignty of France,
but will keep and defend it, by the aid of our Lord, and
with the good help of my said lord of Burgundy, and
of his other good relations, friends, vassals, allies, and
subjects, by all the means possible to him. And nevertheless he will be always ready to hear all amiable and good
means of peace for a period so long, convenient and
reasonable, as that one should not be therein deceived ;
and also on his part to commission thereto men of so good
and great authority as ought to suffice, provided that the
same be done on the other side.

Item, en tant que touche le xiij. article, le roy a To the 13.
bien regard aus grans pouretez et meschiefs qui ont
longuement souffert, et suiffrent, ses loyaulx subgiez
de son dit royaume de France, et la grant charge que
mon dit seigneur de Bourgoingne et ses pais portent
a la occasion de la guerre, dont il a grant pitie et compassion. Mais il a grant esperance en nostre Seigneur,
que lui, qui de sa grace le met et fait approuchier laage
de plus grant congnoissance, ses affaires auront plus
grant prosperite. Car au plaisir de Dieu il y vacquera
en sa personne et aura souvenance de ceulx qui luy
auront aide et secouru en son tendre aage, pour recongnoistre leurs services, labours, et grans charges
selon ce que bonnement luy sera possible; et lui semble
que le service que on lui fait en tel temps ne doit
jamais estre oublie.

Et quant a ce que mon dit seigneur de Bourgoingne Compli-
requiert que le roy ait sa personne, ses terres, seig- mentary
neuries et paix en recommendation, et ne vueille ad- conclusion,

Item, as to what concerns the xiij. article, the king regards
well the great poverty and miseries which his loyal subjects
of his said kingdom of France have long suffered, and suffer
still; and of the heavy charge which my said lord of
Burgundy and his country have borne by occasion of the
war, for which he has great pity and compassion. But
he has great hope in our Lord, that He, who of His grace
makes and causes him to approach the age of greater wisdom,
will cause his affairs to be more prosperous. For, by God's
pleasure, he will attend thereto in person, and will have
a recollection of those who shall have aided and assisted
him in his tender age, by remembering their services, labours
and great charges as far as he well may; and it seems to
him that the service which has been done for him at such
a time ought never to be forgotten.

And because my said lord of Burgundy requires that
the king would have his person, his lands, lordships and
country in recommendation, and will not give faith to evil

jouster foy a sinistres rappors que on lui feroit de sa personne, le roy a eu tousjours, comme chascun scet, et veult encores avoir, mon dit seigneur de Bourgoingne que son oncle, et ses pais et subgiez a lui obeissance, en bonne recommendacion, en toute faveur gracieuse. Et en oultre, na sceu ne veu aucuns grans ou petits qui lui aient fait sinistres rapors de sa dite personne. Et se aucunes lui en faisoient, il le vouldroit de ce advertir, comme son bon oncle, et le oir de tres bonne voulente. Mais il croit et tient certainement quil est tel prince, et aime le roy et sa seigneurie si tendrement, quil ne vouldroit ne daigneroit faire chose qui ne feust loyale et honnourable, et que noble et loyal prince ne deust faire.

COUDRAY.

reports which may be herein made of him, the king has always regarded, as every one knows, and wishes still to regard, my said lord of Burgundy as his uncle, and to have his lands and subjects obedient to him, in good recommendation and in all gracious favour. And further, he has neither known nor seen any persons, great or little, who have made evil reports of his said person. And if any such persons should make any such to him, he would willingly let him know thereof, as his good uncle, and to hear him willingly. But he holds and certainly believes, that he is such a prince, and that he loves the king and his lordship so tenderly, that he would not do so, but would disdain to do a thing which was unloyal and dishonourable, and such as a loyal and honourable prince ought not to do.

COUDRAY.

## 1433.

MANDATE of Katherine, queen dowager of England, ordering her receiver-general in France to send her 30*l.* sterling.[1]

### DEPAR LA ROYNE.

CHIER et bien ame, nous vous saluons. Et vous envoions par notre bien ame escuier, Fook Eyton, porteur de cestes, unes lettres de mandement, chargant a lui bailler et delivrer la somme de xxx. livres esterlings, pour certaines choses que nous lavons chargie a ordonner pour nous, et icelles nous envoier le plus tost que faire se pourra. Si voulons et vous chargons, ja soit ce que notre bien ame secretaire, Guillem Gedney, nous a expose de votre part comment vous avez fait finance par emprunt pour le paiement de la plus grant partie de noz vins de ceste annee, (dont

A.D. 1433
Dec. 18.
_____
Thirty pounds sterling to be paid to the bearer.

### [TRANSLATION.]

### BY THE QUEEN.

DEAR and well-beloved, we salute you. And we send you by our well beloved esquire, Fook Eyton, the bearer of these, a letter of command, charging you to give and deliver to him the sum of xxx. pounds sterling, for certain things for which we have charged him to settle for us, and to send them to us as soon as possible. Wherefore we will and charge you that (although our very dear secretary, Guillaume Gedney, has informed us from you how you have made up your money by borrowing for the payment of the greater part of our wines for this year, for which we are

---

[1] From the original letter, upon paper, in the MS. Gaignières, 557.

vous savons tres bon gre,) que vous faites finance de
la dicte somme de xxx. livres, et la delivrer, comme
dit est ; affin que les ditz choses pour deffaulte de
paiement ne soient nullement retardees, comme vous
desirez notre bonne seigneurie.   Et notre Seigneur soit
de vous garde.

Date.    Donne a Londrez, desoubz notre signet, le xviij. jour
de Decembre.

KATHERINE.

(*Dorso.*) A notre chier et bien ame Jehan le. Sac,
receveur general de noz finances en France et
Normandie.

---

much indebted to you) you raise the said sum of xxx.
pounds, and to deliver it, as has been said ; so as that the
said things should in no way be retarded by default of payment ; as you desire our good lordship.   And may the Lord
have you in His keeping.

Given at London, under our signet, the xviij. day of
December.

KATHERINE.

(*Dorso.*) To our very dear and beloved Jehan le
Sac, receiver-general of our finances in France
and Normandy.

1434.

CERTIFICATE of the employment of Jehan Lesac in the service of Katherine, queen dowager of England.[1]

NOUS, Pierre, par la permission divine evesque de Lisieux, chancellier de tres hault et tres puissant princesse, la royne Dangleterre, certiffions a tous a qui il appartient, que en ce present mois de May, M. cccc. xxxiiij., Jehan Lesac, receveur general dicelle princesse, est venu de la ville de Vernon en ceste ville de Rouen devers nous, pour adviser et pourveoir a plusieurs choses necessaires, touchantes les terres et seigneuries dicelle princesse; et y a vaque depuis le Samedi, viij. jour du dit mois, quil parti du dit Vernon, jusques au Dimenche, xxiij. du dit mois de May, quil retournera en son dit hostel.

A.D. 1434. May 21. Jehan Lesac has been employed in the service of the queen of England.

[TRANSLATION.]

WE, Pierre, by divine permission, bishop of Lisieux, chancellor of the most high and mighty princess, the Queen of England, certify to all those whom it concerns, that in this present month of May, M. cccc. xxxiiij., Jehan Lesac, receiver-general of the said princess, has come from the town of Vernon to this town of Rouen to us, to advise and provide for several necessary things, touching the lands and lordships of the said princess; and stayed there from Saturday, the viij. day of the said month, when he set out from the said Vernon, until Sunday, the xxiij. of the said month of May, when he shall return to his said home.

[1] From the original, in the MS. Gaignières, 155, f. 27.

Date.  Escript au dit Rouen, le xxj. jour de May, lan mil cccc. trent quatre.

---

Written at Rouen aforesaid, the xxj. day of May, the year one thousand, cccc. and thirty-four.

---

## 1434.

WRIT from the duke of Bedford, ordering the bailly of Caux to be present at the meeting of the Three Estates at Rouen.[1]

A.D. 1434.
Sept. 2.

Summons to the bailly of Caux to attend the meeting of the Three Estates at Rouen.

DE par le gouvernant et regent le royaume de France, duc de Bedford.

Treschier et bien ame. Pour aucunes causes qui touchent tres grandement monseigneur le roy et le bien de ses pais et duchie de Normandie et de conqueste, nous vous mandons depar mon dit seigneur le roy et depar nous, que dedens le xx. jour de ce present mois de Septembre, vous soiez pardevers nous en

---

[TRANSLATION.]

BY the governor and regent of the realm of France, the duke of Bedford.

Very dear and well-beloved. For certain causes which very greatly affect my lord the king and the good of his country and duchy of Normandy, and the conquered districts, we command you, upon the part of my said lord the king and ourselves, that by the xx. day of this present month of September, you be with us in this city of Rouen;

---

[1] From the original, upon paper, in the MS. Gaignières, 557.

ceste ville de Rouen, densquelz jour et lieu nous mandons estre les deputez des Troiz Estaz des dits pais,
pour deliberer et conclurre sur ce qui sera expose et
requis depar mon dit seigneur le roy au bien de lui
et des dits pais ; et gardez que en ce nait aucune faulte.
Tres chier et bien ame, notre Seigneur soit garde de
vous.

Donne a Rouen, soubz notre signet, le second jour de Date.
Septembre.

*Signe*, MILET.

A notre tres chier et bien ame, Clement Bourse, lieutenant du bailli de Caux.

---

at which day and place we order the deputies of the Three
Estates of the said country to be present, to deliberate and
conclude upon what shall be presented to and demanded
of them on the part of my said lord the king, for the good
of himself and his said country ; and take care that herein
there be no shortcoming. Very dear and well-beloved, our
Lord be your keeper.

Dated at Rouen, under our signet, the second day of
September.

*Signed*, MILET.

From my dear and well-beloved, Clement Bourse, lieutenant of the bailly of Caux.

### 1434.

WRIT from the duke of Bedford, ordering the election of one or two representatives of the nobility in the parliament at Rouen.[1]

A.D. 1434.
Sept. 2.

The duke of Bedford orders the election of one or two persons to represent the nobility.

DEPAR le gouvernant et regent le royaume de France, duc de Bedford.

Tres chier et bien ame. Pour aucunes causes qui touchent tres-grandement monseigneur le roy et le bien de ses pais et duchie de Normandie et de conqueste, nous vous mandons, de par mon dit seigneur le roy et depar nous, que, par les nobles de votre viconte, vous faittes eslire un ou deux notables chevaliers, ou escuiers, de votre ditte viconte pour venir et estre pardevers nous en ceste ville de Rouen, le xx. jour de ce present mois de Septembre, avecques povoir souffisant pour les diz nobles pour deliberer et conclurre

---

[TRANSLATION.]

By the governor and regent of the kingdom of France, the duke of Bedford.

Dear and well-beloved. In consequence of certain causes which very greatly affect my lord the king and the good of his country and duchy of Normandy, and the conquered districts, we command you, on the part of my said lord the king and ourselves, that, by the nobles of your vicomté, you cause to be chosen one or two knights or esquires of your said vicomté, of reputation, to come and to be with us in this city of Rouen by the xx. day of this present month of September, with sufficient power for the said nobles to deliberate and conclude upon what shall be presented to

---

[1] From the original, upon paper, in the MS. Gaignières, 557.

sur ce qui leur sera expose et requis depar mon dit seigneur, au bien de lui et des diz pais. Et pour celle mesme cause vous mandons en oultre que a ce jour vous soiez pardevers nous au dit lieu de Rouen, et gardez que en ce nait aucune faulte. Tres chier et bien ame, notre Sire soit garde de vous.

Donne a Rouen, soubz notre signet, le second jour de Septembre. Date.

*Signe*, MILET.

A notre treschier et bien ame, le viconte Darques.

---

and demanded of them by my said lord, for the good of himself and of the said countries. And for this same cause we command you further, that by that day you be with us at the said place of Rouen; and take care that herein there by no shortcoming. Very dear and well-beloved, our Lord be your keeper.

Dated at Rouen, under our signet, the second day of September.

*Signed*, MILET.

To our very dear and well-beloved, the vicomte of Arques.

1434.

MANDATE of Katherine, queen dowager of England,
respecting the transmission of wines from France
for her use in England.[1]

A.D. 1434.
Oct. 6.
———
Queen
Katherine
gives di-
rections
respecting
the pur-
chase and
shipping
of wine for
the use of
her house-
hold in
England.

KATHERINE,[2] par la grace de Dieu, royne Dangleterre, fille a Charles roy de France, mere au roy
Dangleterre et de France, et dame Direland, a notre
chier et bien aime Jehan Le Sac, receveur general de
noz finances en France et Normandie, salut.

Nous avons delibere, par ladvis de nostre conseil,
avoir ceste annee, pour la provision et despense de
notre hostel, soixante queues de vin vermeil du creu
de France, et six poincons de vin blan dicellui creu ;
et voullons, vous chargeons et expressement enjoignons

[TRANSLATION.]

KATHERINE, by the grace of God, queen of England,
daughter of Charles, king of France, mother of the king of
England and of France, and lady of Ireland, to our dear and
well-beloved Jehan le Sac, receiver-general of our finances
in France and Normandy, greeting.

We have determined, by the advice of our council, to
have this year, for the provision and use of our household,
sixty pipes of red wine of the growth of France, and six
puncheons of white wine of the same growth ; and we will,
charge, and expressly command you that, with all diligence

---

[1] From the MS. Fontanieu, 117–
118.

[2] Appended to this document was
an indenture between the said Le
Sac and Newburgh, by which it

appears that the wine mentioned in
the said letters, together with the
money necessary for the transit
thereof, had been paid by the former
to the latter, 13 November 1434.

que, pour toute dilligence et cellerite possible, incontinent aprez la veue de cestes, faites finance des dits
soixante queues et six poincons, et les choisez vous
mesmes ; gardant que yceulx vins soient telz et si
comme vous en voullez respondre, et avoir honneur
et gre ou tempz advenir ; en payant pour iceulx des
deniers de notre recepte aux marchans qui les vendront,
ainsi que pourrez accorder avecques eulx. Et aprez la
provision des diz vins faitte, les admener a Rouen, et
illec les faictes mettre et chargier en nef et vessel
sceure, pour estre admenez par devers nous en Angleterre par notre ame serviteur, Jehan Newburgh, ung
de nos bouteillers, porteur de cestes, lequel envoions
presentement par de la pour ceste meme cause.

Et en oultre, pour ce que icellui Jehan na la pra-
tique a soy gouverner et de mener en la conduite des
diz vins par la riviere de Rouen jusques a Harrefleu,
voullons que, pour la sceurete diceulx vins, ordonnez

---

and expedition possible, immediately upon sight of these
presents, you provide for the purchase of the said sixty
pipes and six puncheons, and choose them yourself ; taking
care that the wines aforesaid be of such a quality as that
you can answer for them, and have therefrom honour and
satisfaction in time to come ; paying for the same out of the
money of our receipt to the merchants who sell them, as you
may agree with them. And after having laid in the same
wines, you convey them to Rouen, and there cause them
to be placed and shipped in a safe ship and vessel, that
they may be conveyed to us in England by our beloved
servant, John Newburgh, one of our butlers, the bearer
of these, whom we send at this time thither for this same
cause.

And moreover, since the said John has had no experience how to arrange things there, and how to provide
for the conveyance of the said wines by the river from
Rouen to Harfleur, it is our will that, for the safety of

aucune personne saige et suffisant a venir avec luy au
dit Harfleu, lequel soit chargie a parler aux maistres
dautres nefs, qui lors vendront en Angleterre, afin que
notre dit bouteillier puisse venir en leur compaignie
plus sceurement par dessa. Et aussy voullons et vous
chargons que baillez et delivrez par endentures faites
par entre vous et notre dit bouteillier pour les frais
des diz vins de Rouen jusques en Angleterre ; et
avecques ce, pour ses couts et depenses en admenant
les diz vins, ainsy que par votre discretion vous sem-
blera estre bon a faire. Et ces presentes, avec certiffi-
cation soubz les signes des diz marchans de tout ce
que leur aurez paye pour les diz vins, avecques les
endentures par entre vous et les dits boutellier, vous
en font garant et allouance en vos comptes devant les
gens et auditeurs de noz comptes, ausquelz nous mandons quainsy le facent sans contredit, car ainsy nous
plaist il estre fait.

———————

the said wines, you appoint some discreet and sufficient
person to come with him to Harfleur aforesaid, who shall
be charged to speak with the captains of the other ships
who shall then be coming into England. so that our said
butler may come hither in their company the more safely.
And also it is our pleasure, and we charge you, that you
give and deliver, by indentures made between you and
our said butler, money for the expense of the said wines
from Rouen into England ; as also for his costs and expenses in conveying the said wines, as it shall seem good
to you at your discretion to be done. And these presents,
along with a certificate under the signatures of the said
merchants as to the entire amount of what you shall have
paid them for the said wines, with the indentures between
you and the said butler, shall make your warrant and
allowance herein in your accounts before the accountants
and auditors of our accounts ; whom we order to do this
without gainsaying ; for it is our pleasure that it should
be done.

Donne a notre chastel de Hartford, soubz notre seel, Date.
le vj. jour Doctobre, lan de grace, mil, quatre cent,
trente quatre.

KATHERINE.

*Et plus bas :* Par la royne.

*Signe,* VEDNER, *avec griffe.*

---

Dated at our castle of Hertford, under our seal, the vj.
day of October, in the year of grace, one thousand, four
hundred and thirty-four.

KATHERINE.

*And lower :* By the Queen.

*Signed,* VEDNER, *with a flourish.*

## 1434.

RECEIPT by Gilles de Duremont, abbot of Fécamp, for
 money awarded to him while upon an embassy
 to the duke of Gloucester.[1]

A.D. 1434.
Nov. 3.

Receipt for
150*l.* T.
by the
abbot of
Fécamp.

NOUS, Gilles, par la permission divine abbe de
Fescamp, congnoissons avoir eu et receu de Pierre Surreau, recepveur general des finances de Normendie, la
somme de cent cinquante livres Tournoiz, sur nos

---

### [TRANSLATION.]

WE, Gilles, by divine permission abbot of Fécamp,
acknowledge that we have had and received from Pierre
Surreau, receiver-general of the finances of Normandy, the
sum of one hundred and fifty pounds Tournois, for our wages

---

[1] From the original, in the MS. Gaignières, 262.

gaiges de six livres Tournoys, a nous ordonnes pour
chacun jour que nous vaquerons en certain voyage en
ambaxade ou de present sommes envoyes devers monseigneur le duc de Gloucestre, cy comme il appert par
les lettres du roy, notre seigneur, donnees a Paris,
le xxviij. jour Doctobre, derrenier passe, expediees
par les tresorier et generaulx gouverneurs des finances
du royaume de France, cy comme il appiert par leurs
lettres atachees a icelles. De la quelle somme de cent
cinquante livres Tournois nous nous tenons contens ;
et en quittons le roy, notre seigneur, le dit recepveur,
et tous autres.

Date.    En tesmoing de ce, nous avons signees ces presentes,
le iij. jour de Novembre, lannee cccc. xxiiij.

G. DE FESCAMP.[1]

---

of six pounds Tournois, appointed to us for each day that
we shall spend in a certain journey on an embassy in which
we are at this present time despatched to my lord the
duke of Gloucester, as it appears from letters of the king
our lord, dated at Paris, the xxviij. day of October last,
expedited by the treasurers and governors-general of the
finances of the kingdom of France, as appears by their letters
attached to these. Of which sum of one hundred and fifty
pounds Tournois we hold ourselves content ; and thereof
we acquit the king, our said lord, the said receiver, and all
others.

In witness of this, we have signed these present letters,
the iij. day of November, the year cccc. xxiiij.

G. DE FÉCAMP.

---

[1] This signature is autograph.

## 1435.

Mandate of Katherine, queen dowager of England, for the payment of twenty-six pounds sterling for purchases to be made in Paris.[1]

A.D. 1435.
20 Feb.
___
Repayment for purchases in Paris for the queen.

Katherine, par la grace de Dieu royne Dangleterre, fille a Charles, roy de France, mere au roy Dangleterre et de France, et dame Direland, a notre chier et bien ame, Jehan le Sac, receveur general de noz finances en France et Normandie, salut.

Nous voulons et vous chargons que incontinent aprez la vue de ceste, baillez et delivriez a Jehan Chienart, orfevre, demourant a Paris, la somme de vint six livres esterlinges, monnoye Dangleterre, cest a scavoir, trois nobles pour chacun livre de la dite monnoye, le noble au prix de soixante quatre escus Parisis, monnoye de France, pour ycelle somme de vingt six livres esterlings employer en une paire de flacons dargent, que nous lavons chargie ordonner pour nous

---

[Translation.]

Katherine, by the grace of God queen of England, daughter of Charles, king of France, mother of the king of England and of France, and lady of Ireland, to our dear and well-beloved Jehan le Sac, receiver-general of our finances in France and Normandy, greeting.

We will and charge you that, immediately after the sight hereof, you give and deliver to Jehan Chienart, goldsmith, dwelling in Paris, the sum of twenty-six pounds sterling, of English money; that is to say, three nobles for each pound of the said money, the noble at the rate of sixty-four ecus of Paris, of the money of France, in order to employ this sum of twenty-six pounds sterling upon a pair of flagons of silver which we have charged him to make for us, together

---

[1] From the MS. Fontanieu, 117-118.

s 2

avec autres noz bescoingnes, gardant que en ce nail aulcun deffault. Et ces presentes, avecq quittances de la dite somme payee au dit Chienart, vous en font garant et allouance en vos comptes devant les gens et auditeurs de noz comptes, ausquelz nous mandons que ainsi le facent sans contredit, car ainsy nous plaist il estre fait.

Date.   Donne soubz notre seel, a notre chastel de Hartford, le xxᵉ jour de Fevrier, lan de grace, mil, quatre cent, trente et quatre.

Et en outre, voulons et vous chargons que vous nous envoyez par Raufwaller, escuyer, mareschal de notre salle, six livres de cire vermeille sucree; et ces presentes vous en sont garant.

Donne comme dessus,

KATHERINE.

Par la royne,

VEDNER, *avec paraphe.*

---

with our other affairs, taking care that herein there be no short-coming. And these presents, together with the acquittances for the said sum paid to the said Chienart, shall be your warrant and authority in your accounts before the accountants and auditors of our accounts, whom we command to do so without gainsaying; for it is our pleasure that so it should be done.

Dated, under our seal, at our castle of Hartford, the xx. day of February, in the year of grace one thousand, four hundred and thirty-four.

And moreover we will and charge you to send us, by Ralph Waller, esquire, marshal of our hall, six pounds of sugared red wax; and these presents shall be your warrant therein.

Dated as above,

KATHERINE.

By the queen,

VEDNER, *with a flourish.*

## 1435.

CERTIFICATE of the payment of 8*l.* Tournois to the pursuivant of the bastard of Saint Pol for carrying certain letters respecting the meeting at Arras.[1]

LAN de grace mil, quatre cent, trente cinq, le xvj$^e$ jour de May, devant nous, Jehan Gresille, lieutenant general de honnourable homme et sage, Guy de la Villette, viconte de Rouen, fut present Bien-Ame, poursuivant darmes du bastard de Saint Pol, lequel cognut avoir eu et receu de lhonnourable homme et saige, Michiel Durant, receveur general de Normandie, la somme de huit livres Tournois, que deubz lui etoient et a lui ordonnes par marchie fait pour certain sejour quil a fait en cette ville de Rouen par lespasse de xiij. jours, par lordonnance de monsieur le chancelier de France, attendant lexpedition de pleusieurs sauf-conduis en-

---

[TRANSLATION.]

IN the year of grace one thousand, four hundred and thirty five, the xvj. day of May, before us, Jehan Gresille, lieutenant general of the honourable and discreet man, Guy de la Villette, vicomte of Rouen, was present Bien-Ame, the pursuivant of arms of the bastard of Saint Pol, who acknowledged that he had had and received of that honourable and discreet man, Michiel Durant, receiver general of Normandy, the sum of eight pounds Tournois, which were due and appointed to him by an agreement made for a certain stay which he has made in this city of Rouen for the space of xiij. days, by the appointment of monsieur the chancellor of France, while waiting for the copying of several safe-conducts sent, by the said pursuivant, to the

---

[1] From the MS. Fontanieu, 117, 118.

voyez par le dit poursuiant devers les adversaires du
roy, notre sire, pour ceulx qui iront a la journee prinse
Darras pour le fait du traitie de la paix final.

De la quelle somme de viij. livres Tournois dessus
dite, le dit poursuiant se tint pour content et bien
paye, et en quitta le roy, notre dit seigneur, le dit
receveur general, et tous autres.

Date.          Donne comme dessus.

DOMPIERRE.

adversaries of the king, our lord, for those persons who
are about to go to the meeting to be held at Arras upon
the business of the treaty of final peace.

Of which sum of eight pounds Tournois aforesaid, the
said pursuivant declares himself satisfied and well paid;
and thereof he has acquitted the king, our said lord, the
said receiver general, and all others.

Dated as above.

DOMPIERRE.

## 1436.

A.D. 1436.
9 May.
LETTER from Queen Katherine to Jehan le Sac,
explaining the circumstances which have interrupted the transaction of business.[1]

The
queen's af-
fairs have
been de-
layed by
the pressure
of public
business,

DEPAR LA ROYNE.

CHIER et bien ame, nous vous saluons souvent; et
avons receues les lettres, instructions, exposition, et

[TRANSLATION.]

BY THE QUEEN.

DEAR and well beloved, we greet you frequently; and
we have received the letters, instructions, statement, and

[1] From the original, on paper, contained in the MS. Gaignières, 557,
fol. 7.

autres choses que vous, et autres noz officiers depar
de la, envoiees nous avez par votre serviteur, Jaquet
Lubin, dont vous savons tresgrant gre, tant des dictes
instruccions, que de la dicte exposition ; et le tout avons
veu bien au long, et apres ce envoiees devers notre
conseil, qui le tout semblablement ont bien veu et
examine, et le contenu estre honnourablement fait et
tres raisonnable, par especial la dicte exposition. La
quelle alors de la venue de votre dit clerc ne presentasmes point a notre treschier et tresaime filz, le
roy, pour certaines causes touchans pareille matiere
que avions a poursuir devers notre dit filz pour reste
de certaine somme qui nous este encore a assigner a
cause de notre douaire depar deca, dont navons peu
avoir aucune response ou expedicion, pour les empeschemens et diversities intervenues en la seigneurie de
France et Normandie de notre dit filz. Pour lesquelles arising
from the
causes nous avons fait retenir et sejourner devers nous disturbed
votre dit clerc par long temps, et jusques a ores, en state of
France and
Normandy.

---

other things which you, and our other officers on your side
have sent to us by your servant, Jaquet Lubin, for which
we thank you very much, as well for the said instructions
as for the said statement; and we have examined the whole
at length, and afterwards have sent it to our council, who
in like manner have carefully seen and examined it, and
have decided that the contents are honourably and most
reasonably made, and especially the said statement. But
since the arrival of your said clerk we have not presented
this to our very dear and well-beloved son, the king, for
certain causes touching a like matter which we have to
bring before our said son for the balance of a certain sum
which still remains to be assigned to us in consequence of
our dower here, to which we cannot obtain any answer or
settlement in consequence of the hindrances and differences
which have sprung up in our said son's lordship of France
and Normandy. For these reasons we have caused your
said clerk to be detained and to tarry with us for a long
time, and until this present, in the hope of having from our

esperance davoir de icellui notre filz, ou de son conseil, response et ottroy du contenu en notre exposition ; ce que navons peu, ne ne povons avoir, pour les tres-grans empeschemens tousjours intervenuz, et qui ung chacun jour interviennent depar dela, comme dit est, de mal en pis, a quoy, devant toutes autres besongnes, il a esconvenu entendre et vacquer pour y remedier et donner resistence, comme de ce pourriez en brief avoir congnoissance.

Pourquoy, par ladviz et deliberacion de notre conseil pardeca, avons conclue de non plus traittier de ceste matiere, jusques a ce que les choses soient revenues et mises en meilleur termes et estat que a present ne sont, et que, (au plaisir Dieu,) esperons estre de brief, moiennant sa grace, et laide de ses loyaulx vassaulx et subgiez. Et ces choses acomplies, comme dicelles vous pourrez advertir par escripture, notre voulente et entiere affection est de nous emploier et entendre de tout notre cuer a avoir response et conclusion du

---

said son, or his council, an answer and a grant of the matter contained in our statement; and this we have not been able, nor are we yet able, to obtain, in consequence of the very great obstacles which have always intervened, and which daily do intervene, on that side, as has been said, going on from bad to worse, to which, before everything else, it is necessary to attend and give heed in order to provide a remedy and resistance thereto, as you will speedily discover.

Wherefore, by the advice and deliberation of our council here, we have determined to treat no further about this matter, until affairs are settled and placed on a better footing and condition than they are at present, and this (if it be God's pleasure) we hope will speedily be the case, by His favour, and by the assistance of the king's loyal vassals and subjects. When these things have been accomplished, whereof you can inform us by writing, our will and entire wish is to employ and devote ourselves with our whole heart to have an answer to and to complete the matter contained

contenu en icelle exposition, et dautres choses, tellement que, Dieu devant, ce sera au bien et augmentacion de notre seigneurie et subgietz depar dela. Et pour les causes que dessus, a present ne vous envoions touchant ce que signiffie nous avez par les dits instruccions que lettres adresans depar nous aux tresorier et receveur generaulx de Normandie, narratives tant du fait de notre assignement pour ceste presente annee, que des tailles, sauçunes en sont accordees pour le temps present, ou advenir. Lesquelles lettres vous presenterez en notre nom aus dits tresorier et receveur, ainsi que verrez bon estre, affin que ilz soient plus inclins de vous bailler la dicte assignation sans plus y delaier; et de ce que faire en vouldront, nous certiffier par les premiers entrevenans par deca.

Chier et bien ame, notre Seigneur soit de vous garde.

---

in the said statement, and our other business, in such a way as, before God, shall be for the good and advantage of our lordship and our subjects on that side. And for the said causes we do not at this present time send you any further answer as to the matter on which you have given us information by the said instructions, than letters addressed by us to the treasurer and receiver-general of Normandy, and these refer as well to the matter of our assignment for this present year, as to the taxes, if any of them are granted for the present time, or the future. These letters you will present in our name to the said treasurer and receiver, as you shall see to be good, in order that they may be the better inclined to give you the assignation aforesaid, without any further delay therein; and what they desire to do herein, certify us by the first persons who are crossing over hither.

Dear and well beloved, our Lord have you in His keeping.

Date.        Donne a notre chastel de Hartford, soubz notre signet,
le ix. jour de May.

KATHERINE.[1]

*Dorso.*—A notre chier et bien ame, Jehan le Sac,
notre receveur general de France et Normandie.

•

Given at our castle of Hertford, under our signet, the
ix. day of May.

KATHERINE.

*Dorso.*—To our dear and well beloved, Jehan le Sac,
our receiver-general of France and Normandy.

## 1436.

A.D. 1436. WRIT ordering the payment of the wages of the garrison of Gisors under lord Talbot.[2]

The king,
after re-
citing the
import of    HENRY, par la grace de Dieu, roy de France et
the petition Dangleterre, a nos amez et feaulx conseillers, les tre-
of John,     soriers et generaulx gouverneurs de nos finances en
lord Tal-
bot, orders  France et Normandie, salut et dilection.
his prayer
to be
granted.

[TRANSLATION.]

HENRY, by the grace of God, king of France and England, to our beloved and faithful councillors, the treasurers
and governors-general of our finances in France and Normandy, greeting and love.

---

[1] This signature is autograph.    [2] From the MS. Fontanieu, 117–
118.

Receu avons humble supplication de notre ame
et feal cousin, Jehan, sire de Talbot, contenant que
depar nous il fut ordonne garde et capitaine des ville[1]
et chastel de Gisors pour le temps commencant a la
Saint Michiel, mil, cccc.xxxiiij., et finissant a la Saint
Michiel, mil, ccccxxxvj., a la charge de certain nombre
de gens darmes et de trait, et que le dit jour de Saint
Michiel, mil ccccxxxvj. venu, (ou quel lendenture sur ce
faicte failloit,) le dit sire de Talbot, par lettres closes de
notre tres chier et tres ame cousin, Richard duc Dyork,
comme lors notre lieutenant et general gouverneur de
par nous de nos royaume de France et duchie de
Normandie, fut continue en la dite garde et capi-
tainerie ; lequel nostre cousin le duc Dyork lui promist
faire payement pour le tempz quil serviroit en la dit
qualite. En confiance de laquelle promesse le dit
sire de Talbot tint au dit lieu de Gisors en notre

---

We have received the humble petition of our beloved and
faithful cousin, John, lord Talbot, containing that he was
appointed by us governor and captain of the town and
castle of Gisors for the period beginning at Michaelmas,
one thousand cccc.xxxiiij., and ending at Michaelmas, one
thousand cccc.xxxvj., with the charge of a certain number
of men-at-arms and archers ; and that upon the said Michaelmas day, one thousand cccc.xxxvj. having come, (at which
the indenture hereupon made expired,) the said lord Talbot,
by the closed letters of our very dear and well-beloved
cousin, Richard duke of York, our then lieutenant and
governor-general in our kingdom of France and duchy of
Normandy, was continued in the said custody and captaincy ;
and our said cousin, the duke of York, promised to pay
him for the time during which he should serve in the said
quality. Upon the faith of which promise the said lord
Talbot kept, at the said place of Gisors, in our service, the

---

[1] *Ville*] Villes, MS.

service les nombre et quantite de quarante lances a
cheval et de dix a pie, et de six vingt dix huit archers,
pour le temps et espace de quarante deux jours entiers,
commencant le vingt neufiesme de Septembre, jour
du dit Saint Michiel, mil cccc.xxxvj. inclus, et finissans
le dixiesme jour du moys de Novembre prouchain
ensuyvant, exclud ; desquelles lances et archers monstres
furent faictes le xviij⁰ jour de moys Doctobre au dit an
mil cccc.xxxvj., devant Jehan Chief Dostel, grenetier de
Gisors, et Jehan de la Mare, receveur des aides au dit
lieu, a ce commis. Et toutes foys, obstant ce quil ne
vous est apparu par nos lettres patentes de la charge,
retenue, et continuation du dit sire de Talbot pour
les dit quarante deux jours, et aussi quil devoit avoir
payement, a la cause avant dite, sur les appatiz, gains
de guerre, prouffit de scel et signet, et autres choses
sur le dit pays, vous avez este, et estes, reffusans de
luy en faire faite compte et payement ; par quoy de

---

number and amount of forty lances on horseback and ten on
foot, and six score and eighteen archers, for the time and
space of forty-two entire days, beginning on the twenty-
ninth of September, Michaelmas day, one thousand cccc.xxxvj.
included, and finishing on the tenth day of month of November next following, excluded ; of which lances and archers
the musters were taken on the xviij. day of the month of
October in the said year one thousand cccc.xxxvj., before
Jehan Chief Dostel, salt-store keeper of Gisors, and Jehan de
la Mare, receiver of the aids of the said place, commissioned
thereto. Yet on the objection that it does not appear to you by
letters patent as to the charge, retinue, and continuance of
our the said lord Talbot for the said forty-two days, and also
because he ought to have been paid, for the cause above
said, from the contributions and gains of the war, the profit
of the seal and signet, and other matters from the country
aforesaid, you have refused, and do refuse, to cause an account
and payment to be made ; in consequence of which he is

son dit service, fait de bonne foy en la qualite dicte, il
seroit et demourroit frustre et endommage, se par nous
ne lui estoit sur ce pourveu de remede, dont il nous
a tres humblement supplie.   Pour ce est il que, les
choses dessus dites considerees, voulans le dit service recongnoistre, attendue mesmement la necessite
quil etoit pour lors de  .  .  .  a la bonne garde et
seurete du dit lieu de Gisors, nous, par ladvis et deliberation de noz amez et feaux les gens de notre[1]  .  .  .  .

and continues to be disappointed and endamaged by his said
service, which he has done in good faith in the capacity
aforesaid, unless remedy be hereupon provided by us for
him, for which he has most humbly petitioned us.  Wherefore,
considering the things above said, desiring that the said service should be acknowledged, considering especially the
necessity which there existed at that time  .  .  .  for the
safe keeping and security of the said place of Gisors, we, by
the advice and deliberation of our well-beloved and faithful
accountants  .  .  .  .  .

[1] The conclusion is mutilated, but enough remains to show that the
petitioner's prayer was granted.

## 1437.

A.D. 1437.
Jan. 26.

——

Four scouts
to watch
by night
outside
Rouen.

WRIT for the payment of four English scouts to watch by night outside the city of Rouen.[1]

HENRY, par le grace de Dieu, roy de France et Dangleterre, a notre ame et feal Jehan Stanlawe, escuier, tresorier et general gouverneur de toutes noz finances, tant en France que en Normandie, salut et dilection.

Comme, par la deliberacion de notre tres chier et tres ame cousin, Richard, duc Dyork, notre lieutenant general et gouverneur pour nous de noz diz royaumes de France, pays et duchie de Normandie, ayons, pour la sauve garde de notre bonne ville de Rouen, et affin que on fust mieulx adverty des embusches et venues des enemis environ icelle, ordonne que quatre Anglois facent doresenavant et jusques a notre plaisir, les escoutes

---

[TRANSLATION.]

HENRY,[2] by the grace of God, king of France and of England, to our beloved and faithful John Stanlawe, esquire, treasurer and governor-general of all our finances, as well in France as in Normandy, greeting and love.

Since, by the advice of our very dear and well-beloved cousin, Richard, duke of York, our lieutenant-general and the governor upon our behalf of our said realms of France and country and duchy of Normandy, we, for the safe keeping of our good city of Rouen, and in order that better warning may be had of the ambuscades and approaches of the enemies of the same, have appointed that four Englishmen should henceforth, and as long as it is our pleasure, keep

---

[1] From the MS. Fontanieu, 117-118.

[2] To this document is affixed the order of the said John Stanlawe to Guy de la Villette, vicomte of Rouen, for the execution of the same, dated 1 February 1436.

par nuyt hors les portes de notre dite ville de Rouen
aux champs et a lenviron dicelle, ausquelz quatre
Anglois a ceste cause ayons, par ladvis que dessus,
tauxe, et tauxons par ces presentes a chacun diceux,
la somme de trois soulz quatre deniers Tournois pour
chacun nuyt que ilz feront les dits escoutes, vous mandons que, par le vicomte dicelle ville de Rouen, vous
faictes, des deniers de sa recepte, paier, baillier, et
delivrer a chacun des dits escoutes la dite somme de
iij. s. iiij. d. Tournois pour chacune nuyt quilz auront
vacque a faire icelles escoutes, dont voulons que le dit
viconte soit certiffie de moys en moys par notre tres
cher et ame cousin, le sire de Talbot, ou son lieutenant ou dit lieu de Rouen. Et par rapportant ces
presentes, ou Vidimus dicelles, fait soubz scel royal,
avecques quittance de notre dit cousin de Talbot, ou
de son dit lieutenant, par laquelle le dit viconte sera
certiffie du nombre des nuyts esquelles iceulx Anglois

---

watch by night outside the gates of our said city of Rouen
in the open country and contiguous thereto, to which four
Englishmen we for this cause have, by the advice above said,
awarded, and do award by these presents to each of them,
the sum of three sols and fourpence Tournois for each night
on which they shall keep the said watch, we command you
that by the vicomte of the said city of Rouen you cause,
out of the money which he has on hand, to be paid, given,
and delivered to each of the said scouts the said sum
of iij. s. iiij. d. Tournois for each night on which they
shall have been employed in making the said watches,
of which it is our will that the said vicomte should be
certified from month to month by our very dear and well-
beloved cousin the lord Talbot, or his lieutenant in the said
place of Rouen. And upon the production of these presents,
or the Vidimus of the same, made under our royal seal, with
the acquittance of our said cousin Talbot, or his lieutenant,
by which the said vicomte shall be certified of the number

auront fait icelles escoutes, nous voullons tout ce qui
a ceste cause aura este paie par le dit visconte aus
dits quatre Anglois estre alloue en ses comptes et rabatu de sa recepte par noz amez et feaulx gens de
noz comptes a Rouen, ausquelz nous mandons par ces
mesmes presentes que ainsi le facent sans contredit ; car
ainsi par ladvis de notre beau cousin le duc nous plaist
il estre faict.

Date.        Donne en notre dite bonne ville de Rouen, le vingt
sixieme jour de Janvier, lan de grace mil quatre cent
trente et six, et de notre regne le quinzieme, soubz
notre scel ordonne en labsence du grant.

Par le roy, a la relacion de monsieur le duc Dyork,
lieutenant general et gouverneur de France et Normandie.

CALOT.

of the nights during which the said English have made
the said watches, we will that all that for this cause shall
have been paid by the said vicomte to the said four Englishmen ·
shall be allowed in his accounts and deducted from his
receipt by our beloved and faithful accountants at Rouen,
whom we command, by these same presents, to do this without gainsaying ; for, by the advice of our said good cousin
the duke, it is our pleasure that so it should be.

Dated in our said good city of Rouen, the twenty-sixth
day of January, in the year of grace one thousand four
hundred thirty and six, and of our reign the fifteenth, under
our seal appointed in the absence of the great.

By the king, at the relation of my lord the duke of York,
lieutenant-general and governor of France and Normandy.

CALOT.

## 1437.

LETTER from Richard, duke of York, to lord Scales, requesting him to retain the custody of Vire.[1]

A.D. 1437.
June 20.

Lord Scales is requested to continue to act as captain of Vire.

DEPAR le duc de York, lieutenant general et gouverneur de France et de Normandie.

Treschier et ame cousin, pour ce que la fin du temps de voz endentures, par lesquelles estes tenu et obligie garder pour monseigneur le roy les ville et chastel de Vire, aproche fort, et quil est besoing de continuer la dicte garde, nous vous prions et requerons, et neantmoins mandons et chargons tres expressement depar mon dit seigneur et nous, que les gens darmes et de trait de votre charge et retenue, tant pour la garde et seurte de . . . . . , comme[2] pour les champs, vous continuez et entretenez encores pour ung moys,

---

[TRANSLATION.]

BY the duke of York, lieutenant-general and governor of France and Normandy.

Very dear and beloved cousin, since the end of the period mentioned in your indentures, by which you are holden and bound to keep, for my lord the king, the town and castle of Vire, is very near at hand, and since it is necessary that the said custody should be continued, we pray and require you, and nevertheless command and charge you very expressly on the part of my said lord and ourselves, still to continue and keep the men-at-arms and archers of your charge and retinue, as well for the keeping and security of . . . . . as also for the open country, for one month, to begin on the day on which your said enden-

---

[1] From the original in the MS. Gaignières, 557.

[2] *Seurte de . . . , comme*] This blank occurs in the original.

a commencier du jour de la fin de voz dites endentures, a tel et semblable nombre de gens darmes et de trait que avez eu et tenu a la dicte cause ce present quartier, et par les conditions et conveus contenuz es dictes endentures.  Desquelles gens darmes et de trait faces monstres pardevant les commiz qui derreinerrement les receverent, pour vous valoir au regard du payement des gaiges, regards, et soldees de vous et ceulx de votre dicte charge et retenue, comme raison est, si ne faces en ce aucune fault.

Treschier et ame cousin, notre Seigneur vous ait en sa saincte garde.

Date Escript a Rouen, soubz notre signet, le **xx.** jour de Juing.

DROSAY.

(*Dorso.*) A notre tres chier et amie cousin, le sire de Scales, cappitaine de Vire, ou a son lieutenant au dit lieu.

---

tures end, with such and a similar number of men-at-arms and archers as you have had and kept for the said cause during this present quarter, and according to the conditions and covenants contained in the said endentures.  Of which men-at-arms and archers make musters before the commissioners who received them last, that they may serve you in regard to the payment of the wages, rewards and pays of yourself and the persons of your said charge and retinue, as is reasonable, so that there be no shortcoming herein.

Very dear and beloved cousin, our Lord have you in His holy keeping.

Written at Rouen, under our signet, the **xx.** day of June.

DROSAY.

(*Dorso.*) To our very dear and beloved cousin, the lord Scales, captain of Vire, or to his lieutenant at the same place.

## 1437.

LETTER from Richard, duke of York, to the earl of Suffolk, requesting him to retain the custody of Tombelaine.[1]

A.D. 1437.
June 20.
——
The earl of Suffolk is requested to continue captain of Tombelaine.

DEPAR le duc de York, lieutenant general et gouverneur de France et de Normandie.

Treschier et ame cousin ; pour ce que la fin du temps de voz endentures, par les quelles estes tenu et obligie garder, pour monseigneur le roy, le lieu et place forte de Tombelayne aprouche, pour ce quil est besoing de entretenir la dicte garde, nous vous prions, et neantmoins mandons et chargons tres expressement depar mon dit seigneur et nous, que la dite garde et cappitainnie vous continuez et entreteniz encores pour ung moys, a commencer du jour de la fin de voz dictes endentures, a tel et semblable nombre de gens darmes et de

——

[TRANSLATION.]

BY the duke of York, lieutenant general and governor of France and Normandy.

Very dear and beloved cousin ; since the end of the period mentioned in your endentures, by which you are holden and bound to keep the place and stronghold of Tombelayne for my lord the king, approaches, and since it is necessary that the said guard should be continued, we pray you, and nevertheless command and charge you very expressly, on the part of my said lord and ourselves, that you still continue and carry on the said custody and captainship for a month, to begin from the day on which your said endentures end, with such and a similar number of men-

[1] From the original in the MS. Gaignières, 557.

T 2

trait que aves eu et tenu a la dite cause en ce present quartier, et par les condicions et conveus contenuz es dictes endentures. Des quelles gens darmes et de trait faites monstres par devant les commiz que derrenerement les receuprent pour vous valoir au regart du paiement des gaiges, regardz, et soldees a vous et a voz compaignons, comme raison est. Si ne faces en ce aucune faulte.

Treschier et ame cousin, notre Seigneur vous ait en sa saincte garde.

Date. Escript a Rouen, le xx. jour de Juing.

DROSAY.

(Dorso.) A notre treschier et ame cousin, le comte de Suffolk, capitaine de Tombelaine, ou a son lieutenant au dit lieu.

---

at-arms and archers as you have had and kept for this cause during this present quarter, and according to the conditions and covenants contained in the said endentures. Of which men-at-arms and archers make musters before the commissioners who last received them, that they may serve you in regard to the payment of the wages, rewards, and pay for yourself and your companions, as is reasonable. Let there be herein no shortcoming.

Very dear and beloved cousin, may our Lord have you in His holy keeping.

Written at Rouen, the xx. day of June.

DROSAY.

(Dorso.) To our very dear and beloved cousin, the earl of Suffolk, captain of Tombelaine, or to his lieutenant in the said place.

## 1437.

LETTER from Richard, duke of York, to the captain of Tombelain, requesting him to retain his post during the month of September.[1]

A.D. 1437. Sept. 1.

The captain of Tombelain is requested to continue his custody.

DEPAR le duc de York, lieutenant et gouverneur general de France et Normandie.

Treschier et bien ame. Pour certaines causes et consideracions nous, par ladvis des gens de monseigneur le roy, avons continu, pour cest mois de Septembre, les capitaines, hommes darmes et de trait, estans es garnisons de Normandie et pais de conquest, ainsi et par la forme et maniere que continuez. ont este pour les mois de Juillet et Aoust derreinierement passes. Si vous mandons, depar mon dit seigneur le roy et depar nous, que entertenez les gens de votre retenue pour ce dit mois ; en faisant diceulx monstres par devant les

---

## [TRANSLATION.]

By the duke of York, lieutenant and governor general of France and Normandy.

Very dear and wellbeloved. For certain causes and considerations we, by the advice of the councillors of my lord the king, have continued, for this month of September, the captains, men-at-arms, and archers who are in the garrisons of Normandy and the conquered country, in the way and according to the form and manner in which they have been continued for the months of July and August last past. Wherefore we command you, on behalf of my lord the king and ourselves, that you continue your retainers for this said month ; making musters of them before the commissioners

---

[1] From the original, on paper, in the MS. Gaignières, 557.

commissaires qui pour les dits mois de Juillet et Aoust ont este ordonnes a les veoir et recevoir, affin davoir paiement.

Treschier et bien ame, notre Seigneur soit garde de vous.

Date.        Donne a Rouen, le premier jour de Septembre.

RINEL.

(*Dorso.*) A notre treschier et bien ame, le capitaine de Thombelaine, ou a son lieutenant.

---

who have been appointed to view and receive them for the said months of July and August, so that they may have payment.

Very dear and wellbeloved, may our Lord be your keeper. Dated at Rouen, the first day of September.

RINEL.

(*Dorso.*) To our very dear and wellbeloved, the captain of Tombelaine, or to his lieutenant.

---

## 1438.

A.D. 1438. June 30.

The abbot of Fécamp is repaid his expenses incurred in the English service.

RECEIPT by the abbot of Fécamp, for the repayment of money expended by him while employed in an embassy into Britanny, in the service of Henry the Sixth.[1]

NOUS,[2] Gilles, abbe de Fescamp, conseillier du roy, notre seigneur, confessons avoir eu et receu de Pierre

[TRANSLATION.]

WE, GILLES, abbot of Fécamp, councillor of the king, our lord, acknowledge that we have had and received of Pierre

---

[1] From the original, in the MS. Gaignières, 262.

[2] The same volume contains the

following documents connected herewith :—

Letters of Henry VI. addressed

Baille, receveur general de Normandie, la somme de cinquante livres, six soulz, trois deniers, Tournois, pour restitution de semblable somme que nous affermons avoir loyalment paiee, tant en salaire de guides, conduis, poursuivans, messagers, comme en autres menue despenses, a cause et pour raison de certain ambassade par nous naguaires fait par lordonnance dicellui seigneur en la compagnie de monseigneur Jehan Popham, chevalier, seigneur de Thorigny, maistre Raoul Roussel, tresorier de leglis de Notre Dame de Rouen, et maistre Jehan de Rinel, conseilliers et secretaire dicellui seigneur, pardevers monseigneur le duc de Bretaigne, pour le bien de paix. De la quelle somme les parties ensuivient.

---

Baille, receiver general of Normandy, the sum of fifty pounds, six sols, three deniers, Tournois, as the repayment of a similar sum which we affirm we have honestly paid, as well in the hire of guides, conductors, poursuivants, and messengers, as also in other petty expenses, in consequence and by reason of a certain embassy by us recently undertaken by the direction of the said lord in the company of my lord John Popham, knight, lord of Thorigny, master Raoul Roussel, treasurer of the church of Our Lady of Rouen, and master Jehan de Rinel councillors and the secretary of the said lord, to my lord the duke of Bretagne, upon the matter of a peace. Of the which sum the parcels follow.

---

to the treasurers and governors-general of his finances in France and Normandy, reciting that the abbé of Fécamp was about to proceed into Bretaigne, "pour en-" tendre et besongner sur la matiere " de preparer plusieurs choses ne-" cessaires touchans le bein de la " paix final de noz royaume de " France et d'Angletere," and ordering them to pay the necessary expenses. Dated at Rouen, 3 May, 1438. *Orig.*

A further receipt of Giles, the same abbé, for 259*l.* Tournois paid by Pierre Baille for the above embassy, extending for 39 days, namely, from 13 May, when the ambassadors left Rouen, until the 20 June, when they returned. Dated, Monday, 30 June, 1438.

Premierement, pour notre part et portion de xl. salus
dor, distribues par le dit monseigneur Jehan Popham,
tant a poursuivants, trompetes, comme autres gens,
pour le fait du dit ambassade, depuis le xiij. jour de
May, derrenier passe, commencement du dit ambassade,
jusques au dixieme de cest present mois de Juing, que
de ce feismes compte ensemblez,

xviij l̃. xv s̃. Tournois.

Item, a Mondoubleau, poursuivant, sur le voiage par
lui fait de Vennes a Rouen devers monseigneur le
conte de Warwyk, lieutenant general et gouverneur de
France et Normandie, et monseigneur le chancellier de
France, leur apporter lettres touchants le fait du dit
ambassade ; son dit voiage commencant le second jour
de ce dit present mois de Juing,

quatre salus dor, valent cxvij s̃. Tournois.

Item, a ung des gens de lostel de mon dit signeur
le duc, pour plusieurs services quil nous fist,

ung salut dor, vault, xxix s̃. iij d̃. Tournois.

---

In the first place, for our part and portion of xl. salus
of gold, distributed by the said lord John Popham, as well
to pursuivants and trumpeters as to other persons, upon the
business of the said embassy, from the xiij. day of May
last past, the beginning of the said embassy, to the tenth
of this present month of June, when we reckoned together
as to the same.          xviij l̃. xv s̃. Tournois.

Item, to Mondoubleau, pursuivant, for the journey by him
made from Vannes to Rouen, to my lord the earl of Warwick, lieutenant-general and governor of France and Normandy, and my lord the chancellor of France, to convey to
them letters touching the business of the said embassy ;
his said journey beginning on the second day of this present month of June,

four salus of gold, which are worth cxvij s̃. Tournois.

Item, to one of the household of my said lord the duke,
for many services which he did us,
one salut of gold, which is worth xxix s̃. iij d̃. Tournois.

Item, aux archiers de Coustances, pour nous avoir conduit au retour du dit ambassade jusques a Saint Lo,                                         xl s̃. Tournois.

Item, aux archiers de Saint Lo, pour nous avoir conduit au dit retour depuis le dit lieu de Saint Lo jusques a Bayeux,                          lx s̃. Tournois.

Item, [aux] archiers Dargences, pour nous avoir conduit de Caen a Dives,                   xl s̃. Tournois.

Item, aux archiers de Caen, pour nous avoir conduiz jusques a Honnefleu,             iiij l̃. Tournois.

Item, a trois messagiers envoiees de Pontaudemer ; lun a Caudebec, lautre a Lisieux, et lautre a Ourbec, pour avoir du conduit,           xxx s̃. Tournois.

Item, a deux hommes darmes et huit archiers de la garnison du dit Ponteaudemer, pour nous avoir conduit du dit lieu jusques a Rouen,     c s̃. Tournois.

Item, a xij. archiers de Caen, qui nous condurent du dit lieu de Ponteaudemer jusques a Rouen, avec les deux hommes darmes et viij. archiers dessus dits, vj l̃.

---

Item, to the archers of Coutances, for having conducted us on our return from the said embassy as far as Saint Lo,                          xl s̃. Tournois.

Item, to the archers of Saint Lo, for having conducted us on our said return from the said place of Saint Lo to Bayeux,                      lx s̃. Tournois.

Item, to the archers of Argences for having conducted us from Caen to Dives,         xl s̃. Tournois.

Item, to the said archers of Caen, for having conducted us to Honfleur,         iiij l̃. Tournois.

Item, to three messengers sent from Pont Audemer ; the one to Caudebec, the second to Lisieux, and the third to Orbec, in order to obtain guides,      xxx s̃. Tournois.

Item, to two men-at-arms and eight archers of the garrison of Pont Audemer aforesaid, for having conducted us from the said place to Rouen,       c s̃. Tournois.

Item, to xij. archers of Caen, who conducted us from the said place of Pont Audemer to Rouen, with the two men-at-arms and eight archers aforesaid,         vj l̃.

Et a ung batellier, pour nous avoir amenez par eaue en vaissel depuis la Bouylle jusques a Rouen, pour estre plus seurement, a lui pour ce paie,

xl s̃. Tournois.

Toutes lesquelles parties valent et se montent ensem-blez la dicte somme de cinquante livres, six soulz, trois deniers, Tournois ; dont nous sommes et nous tenons pour bien contens, et en avons quittie et quittons le roy, notre dit seigneur, le dit receveur general et tous autres.

Date.       En tesmoing de ce, nous avons scelle de notre scel ceste presente quittance et signee de notre saing ma-nuel, le dernier jour de Juing, lan de grace mil, cccc. et trente huit.

G. DE FESCAMP.

---

And a boatman for having conveyed us by water in a boat from La Bouille to Rouen, that we might be in greater safety ; paid to him on this account,        xl s̃. Tournois.

The whole of these particulars reach and amount collec-tively to the said sum of fifty livres, six sols, three deniers, Tournois, of which we are and hold ourselves to be well satisfied, and thereof we have acquitted and do acquit the king, our said lord, the said receiver general and all others.

In witness whereof we have sealed with our seal this pre-sent acquittance and signed it with our sign manual, the last day of June, in the year of Grace one thousand, cccc. and thirty-eight.

G. DE FÉCAMP.

## 1439.

WRIT of Henry the Sixth for the payment of additional troops required for the safety of Rouen.[1]

A.D. 1439.
April 4.

Additional
troops
being re-
quired for
the defence
of Rouen,

HENRY, par la grace de Dieu roy de France et
Dangleterre, a noz amez et feaulx, les tresoriers et
generaux gouverneurs de noz finances en France et
Normandie, salut et dillection.

Comme, pour aucunes nouvelles qui survenues nous
sont du connive de noz ennemis et adversaires, soit
expedient pourveoir a la seurte et sauvegarde de ceste
notre ville de Rouen, nous ayons ordonne estre mis
en icelle de creue, oultre et par dessus les gens de la
garnison dicelle, le nombre de six vings combattans,
tant en hommes darmes que en gens de trait, en ce
compris notre ame et feal Thomas Gryffin, chevalier
bachelier, les quelz combatans seront sous la conduitte

---

## [TRANSLATION.]

HENRY, by the grace of God king of France and of England, to our beloved and faithful, the treasurers and governors-general of our finances in France and Normandy, greeting and love.

Since, in consequence of certain news which has reached
us respecting the plots of our enemies and adversaries, it
is expedient to provide for the security and safeguard of
this our city of Rouen, we have ordained that there be
placed within the same, as an additional force, over and
above the troops of the garrison of the same, the number
of six score fighting men, as well men at arms as archers,
including therein our beloved and faithful Thomas Gryffin,
knight bachelor, which fighting men shall be under the

---

[1] From the MS. Fontanieu, 117–118.

et gouvernement du dit Griffin, et dautres qui ad ce serviront et se employront pour notre service en la ditte ville, ou ailleurs, se mestier est, jusques ad ce que par nous en soit autrement ordonne, dont voulons que le plus brief que faire se pourra soient faictes monstres ; nous vous mandons et enjongnons que par notre ame Pierre Baille, receveur general des dits finances, vous faictes payer, bailler et delivrer des orders are given for their payment. deniers des a[1] recepte au dit Greffyn et aux autres, qui auront le gouvernement des dits gens, les gaiges et regards deulx et des gens de la dite charge, pour quinze jours, ou autre tel temps que adviserez. Cest assavoir, a chacun deulx, incontinent ses monstres faittes, pour lui et les gens de sa charge jusques au dit nombre, ou au dessoubz, a commencer le jour dicelles monstres, aux pris, cest assavoir, pour le dit chevalier, deux solz Esterlings par jour ; pour homme darmes a cheval, douze deniers Esterlings par jour, avec regards accous-

---

command and governance of the said Griffin and others who shall serve in this matter and shall employ themselves in our service in the said town, or elsewhere, if need be, until it be otherwise provided by us, of which troops we will that musters be made as speedily as possible ; we command and enjoin you that by our beloved Pierre Baille, receiver-general of the said finances, you cause to be paid, given and delivered, out of the money which he has in hand, to the said Griffyn and to the others who shall have the command of the said troops, their wages and rewards, and those of the people thus put in charge, for fifteen days, or such other time as you shall think fit. That is to say, to each of them, immediately upon the passing of his musters, for him and for the troops under his charge, up to the said number, or under, to begin on the day of the said musters, that is to say, at the rate, for the said knight, of two shil-

---

[1] *Des a*] De sa (?)

tumez ; et pour chacun homme de trait, six deniers Esterlings par jour, tout monnoye Dangleterre ; en prenant le Noble Dangleterre pour six solz huit deniers Esterlins, ou autre monnoye a la valeur coursable en France, en la maniere accoustumee. Et dillec en avant de temps en temps semblablement, jusques a leur cassement, selon leurs monstres ou revues qui sur ce seront faittes.

Et par rapportant ces presentes, les dits monstres ou revues, et quittances souffisans seulement, tout ce que par le dit receveur sera paie a ceste cause voulons estre aloe en ses comptes et rebatu de sa recepte, par noz amez et feaulx les gens de nos comptes a Rouen ; ausquelz nous mandons que ainsi le facent, sans contredit ou difficulte quieuxconques.

Donne a Rouen, le iiij. jour Davril, avant Pasques, Date. lan de grace mil cccc. trente huit, et de notre regne le dix septiesme.

---

lings Sterling daily ; for a man-at-arms on horseback, twelve pence Sterling by the day, with the usual rewards ; and for each archer, six-pence Sterling daily, the whole in English money ; taking the English Noble at six shillings and eight pence Sterling, or other money at the rate current in France, in manner accustomed. And so on from time to time in like manner, until their discharge, according to their musters, or reviews, which shall hereupon be made.

And on the production of these presents, with the said musters or reviews, and sufficient acquittances only, we will that all that shall have been paid by the said receiver for this cause shall be allowed in his accounts and deducted from his receipt by our beloved and faithful our accountants at Rouen ; whom we command so to do, without any gainsaying or difficulty whatever.

Dated at Rouen, the iiij. day of April, before Easter, in the year of grace one thousand, cccc. thirty-eight, and of our reign the seventeenth.

Par le roy, a la relacion de monsieur lo contc de Warrewy[k], le lieutenant general et gouverneur de France et de Normandie.

DROSAY.

---

By the king, at the relation of my lord the count of Warwick, lieutenant-general and governor of France and Normandy.

DROSAY.

---

## 1439.

A.D. 1439. May 13.

MANDATE for the payment of the garrison of Gisors under John Lord Talbot.[1]

Mandate for the payment of the garrison of Gisors.

LES tresoriers et generaulx gouverneurs des finances du roy, notre sire, en France et Normandie.

Pierres Baille, receveur general des dits finances, accomplissez le contenu es lettres royaulx, ausquelles ces presentes sont attachees soubz lun de noz signetz, en faisant compte et paiement, des deniers dicelles

---

[TRANSLATION.]

THE treasurers and governors-general of the finances of the king, our lord, in France and Normandy.

Pierres Baille, receiver-general of the said finances, perform that which is contained in the royal letters to which these presents are attached under one of our signets, by making account and payment, from the money of the said

---

[1] From the MS. Fontanieu, 117–118.

finances, au sire de Talbot, naguerres garde et cappitaine des ville et chastel de Gisors, des gaiges et
regards de xv. lances a cheval, x. a pie, et vj$^{xx}$. xviij.
archiers, quil a entretenuz en la sauvegarde du dit
lieu de Gisors pour le temps declaire es dits lettres,
tout ainsi pour les causes et par la fourme et maniere
que le roy le veult et mande par icelles.

Donne a Rouen, soubz noz signets, le xiij. jour de Date.
May, lan mil cccc. trente neuf.

DUFFOUR.

---

finances, to the lord de Talbot, late warden and captain
of the town and castle of Gisors, for the wages and rewards
of xv. mounted lances, x. on foot, and vj$^{x}$. xviij. archers,
whom he has kept for the safe custody of the said place
of Gisors during the time mentioned in the said letters,
just as the king has willed and commanded it to be done
for the causes and in the form and manner specified in the
said letters.

Dated at Rouen, under our signets, the xiij. day of May,
in the year one thousand cccc. thirty-nine.

DUFFOUR.

## 1440.

RECEIPT by John Beaufort, earl of Somerset, for his allowance, as lieutenant-general of France and Normandy, during the month of July, A.D. 1440.[1]

NOUS, Jehan, comte de Somerset, lieutenant general de monseigneur le roy sur le fait de la guerre en ses royaume de France et duchie de Normendie, confessons avoir eu et receu de Pierre Baille, receveur general de Normendie, la somme de six cens livres, Tournois, pour notre etat ou pension de ce present moys de Juillet, a nous ordonnee par mon dit seigneur le roy pour nous aydier a supporter les frais et charges que faire nous convient a loccasion et estat du dit office de lieutenant general. De la quelle somme de six cens livres, Tournois, nous sommes contens et bien paies; et en quittons mon dit seigneur le roy, le dit receveur general, et tous autres.

---

[TRANSLATION.]

WE, John, earl of Somerset, lieutenant-general of my lord the king, in the matter of the war in his realm of France and duchy of Normandy, acknowledge that we have had and received of Pierre Baille, receiver-general of Normandy, the sum of six hundred livres, Tournois, for [keeping up] our dignity, or our pension, for this present month of July, appointed to us by my said lord the king, to help us to support the expenses and charges which we are compelled to incur in consequence and from the dignity of the said office of lieutenant-general. Of which sum of six hundred livres, Tournois, we are satisfied and well paid; and thereof we acquit my said lord the king, the said receiver-general, and all others.

---

[1] From the MS. Fontanieu, 117–118.

En tesmoing de ce, nous avons scellees ces presentes, Date.
le xxj. jour de Juillet, lan mil cccc. quarante.

Du commandement de mon dit seigneur le conte.

BRUCELLES.

In witness whereof we have sealed these presents, the
xxj. day of July, in the year one thousand cccc. forty.

By commandment of my said lord the earl.

BRUCELLES.

## 1440.

LETTER from Isabella Milles to William Milles, merchant A.D. 1440.
at Rouen, upon family affairs.[1] Sept. 3.

Intelligence respecting his relations,

WORSCHEPFULLE and right enterly welbelovyd sone,
I commande me unto yow with alle my herte, desyrynge alle tymes to here and knowe of youre good
prosperyte and welfare, whiche I praye to Almyghtye
God send yow ever after youre owene hertes desire, to
His plesaunce. And plese hit yow to knowe of my
welfare; the daye of this letter makynge I was in
good helthe of body, blessede be oure Lorde Gode.
Furthermore, I lete yow wyte that youre fader ys
dede, whiche passede of this wordle at Cresmasse was
xij. yere; on whos soule Almyghty Gode have mercy,
for his heye Godhede! Also William Myles youre uncle,

---

[1] From the original in the MS. Gaign. 557. This letter is written, upon paper, in a good bold hand, and is considerably soiled on the outside. It is endorsed, "Rec'. at " Rouen, this Monday, xvij. day of " Octobre, 1440."

and Janet Brokhamptone, youre suster, ben dede bothe, on whos saules God have mercye! And Richard Milles youre brother,[1] and Jonet youre suster, ben alyve and faren welle, and recommaundethe hem unto yow with alle here hole hertys. And Cristyan Artoure, youre cosyn, lyvethe and farethe welle, blessede be Gode.

and his property. And also I lete yow wyte that the place in Corylonde, the whech scholde falle unto yow by dessent after deses of youre fader forsayde, ys sesyde in to the cheffe lordes handes of the fee for defaute of claym of yow; the whiche youre frendes wolde have sewede ouȝt, yf theye hadde wyst or knowen that ye hadde been alyve. Wherfore and hit plese yow to wryte youre letters of atorney unto Thomas Mucheldever and to Johne Wydecombe, my hosebande, dwellynge in the parische of Mertoke in Somersetshire, to sewe for the seyde place in Corylonde in youre name, and also a letter of youre wylle what schal be done therto, and they wollen bothe done here trewe dyligence therto with alle here hertys, with ouȝte feynynge. And, righte worschepfulle sone, I beseke yow of alle gentelnesse, and hit plese yow, to sende me a letter of youre welfare, and how hit standythe with yow, the wheche I hertely desyre to knowe, as Gode wote, wheche have yow in His blessede kepynge, to His plesaunce ever-more durynge.

Wryten at Mertoke forsayde, the iij. day of Sep-tembre.

By youre moder,<br>Isabelle Milles.

(*Dorso.*) To my ryghte worschipfulle and enterly welbelovede sone, Willyam Miles, dwellyng at Rone, be this letter take in haste.

---

[1] *Youre brother*] An interlineation in the original.

1440.

LETTER from Sir Robert Laidamis, parson of Saint
Martin's of Wareham, to William Mylys, merchant
at Rouen, upon family and personal matters.[1]

A.D.1440.
Sept. 19.

Remembrances and requests from the writer.

WORSYPFULLE and reverent frend and mayster, Y
recommande me to ȝoue wyth alle my hert, desyrynge
to here and to knowe of ȝoure wellfare by letter, how
hyt stondyth wyth ȝoue. Doynge ȝoue to understond
that ȝe and Y where scollfelaus sumtyme at Hylmyster,
ȝe beynge at borde att More ys howse, the wyche he
recomaunde me to ȝoue. Also, Y pray ȝoue that ȝe
wolde be gode mayster and frend to me for a mylstone,
for Y have ypray John Penylle to by one for my
mayster. Wherefore Y pray ȝoue that ȝe wylle be gode
mayster and frend there to. Also Y pray ȝouc that
ȝe wylle sende me worde, yn the most secre wyse,
what yt costyth; for trwly Y wulle chentylmanly
aquyte ȝoure labour by that nex messangere that
comyth by twyne ȝoue and me. Also yff ȝe wulle
sende eny worde to ȝoure modyr, sendyth to me to
Warhiam, and Y wylle trewly do ȝoure erant. Nomore
to ȝoue att thys tyme, but the Wholy Trynyte have
ȝoue in ys kepynge.

Ywrytyne at Warham, the Monday nex byfore Sent
Mathew ys day.

Date.

Also Y have ysende ȝoue to letterys fro ȝoure
modyre wyth this letter.

By ȝoure owne frend,
Sir ROBERT LAIDAMIS,
Parsone of Martyne of Warham.

(*Dorso.*) Thys letter be take to M. Wyllam
Mylys, dwellynge yne Rone.

---

[1] From the holograph letter, upon paper, in the MS. Gaignières, 557. It is thus endorsed, " Rec'. at Rouen, " this Monday, xvij day of Octobre, " 1440."

1440.

A.D. 1440.
Sept. 24.
———
Gun-
powder re-
quired for
the siege of
Harfleur.

LETTER from Edmund Beaufort, earl of Dorset, to Symchyne Walere, requesting him to forward gunpowder for the siege of Harfleur.[1]

CHIER et bien ame.   Nous vous chargons que, incontinent ces presentes par vous receues, vous nous envoyez en ce present siege deux barilz de notre pouldre a canon, estans en nostre chastel de Harecourt; et chargez a notre viconte du lieu quil face finance dune charrete pour iceulx amener; et gardez y deffaire nyent.

Chier et bien ame, notre Seigneur soit garde de vous.

Escript au siege devant Harfleu, le xxiiij. jour de Septembre.

---

[TRANSLATION.]

DEAR and well beloved.   We charge you that as soon as you receive these presents you forthwith send to us for this present siege two barrels of our gunpowder for cannon, which are in our castle of Harcourt, and direct our vicomte of the same place to provide a cart to bring them; and take care that herein you fail not.

Dear and well beloved, our Lord be your keeper.

Written at the siege before Harfleur, the xxiiij. day of September.

---

[1] From the original, upon paper, in the MS. Gaignières, 557.

Le conte de Dorset, de Mortaing, et de Hare-court.

DORSET.[1]

(*Dorso.*) A notre chier et bien ame, Symchine Walere, lieutenant de notre chastel de Hare-court.

---

The earl of Dorset, of Mortagne, and of Harcourt.

DORSET.

(*Dorso.*) To our dear and well-beloved Symchine Walere, lieutenant of our castle of Harcourt.

===

## 1440.

LETTER from Edmund Beaufort, earl of Dorset, to Andrieu Beauquesne, directing him to obtain the services of certain Englishmen.[2]

A.D. 1440. Oct. 17

Twenty or thirty Englishmen to be added to the garrison of the castle of Harcourt.

LE conte de Dorset, de Mortaing, and de Hare-court.

CHIER et bien ame. Nous escripvons presentement a Waler, lieutenant de notre chastel de Harecourt, entre aultres choses comment sil peult retruuver de vingt ou xxx. bons compaignons Anglais, que pour ung temps il les reteingne en notre dit chastel, et que

---

[TRANSLATION.]

THE earl of Dorset, of Mortagne, and of Harcourt.

DEAR and well beloved. We write at this present time to Waler, the lieutenant of our castle of Harcourt, among other matters, that if he can find from twenty to xxx. good English fellows, he should engage them for a while in our said castle, and that for the sum of xl. or l. francs to help

---

[1] This signature is autograph.
[2] From the original, upon paper in the MS. Gaignières, 557.

pour leur aider de xl. ou L francs ne soit lesse. Si voullons, et vous chargons, que ou cas que il, ou vous, en pourrez finer daucuns, que jusquez a la dicte somme et audessoubz vous y emploiez, et en ce faictez pour le mieulx que porrez. En attendant que de nous ayez aultres nouvelles, quelle chose nous esperons en Dieu que bien brief aurez tres bonnes nouvelles. Et en faictez tant que vous en doyons savoir gre ; et tout ce que par vous sera mis a vacance dessusdicte, jusquez a la dicte some de cinquante livres, vous sera alloue en voz comptes et rebate de votre compte par tout ou il appartendra.

Chier et bien ame, notre Seigneur soit garde de vous.

Date.      Escript au siege devant Harfle, le xvij. jour Doctobre.

DORSET.[1]

(Dorso.) A notre chere et bien-ame, Andrieu Beauquesne, notre viconte de Harccourt.

---

them with, he lose not the opportunity. Wherefore it is our will, and we charge you, that in case he, or you, can obtain any of them, you employ yourselves therein up to the said sum or there under, acting herein to the best of your ability. You may anticipate other news from us, and we hope in God that within very short time you will have very good tidings. Act in this matter in such wise that we shall have cause to thank you herein ; and all that shall be expended by you as above, as far as the said sum of fifty livres, shall be allowed to you in your accounts and deducted from your account whenever it shall be fitting.

Dear and well-beloved, our Lord be your keeper.

Written in the siege before Harfleur, the xvij. day of October.

DORSET.

(Dorso.) To our dear and well-beloved Andrieu Beauquesne, our vicomte of Harcourt.

---

[1] The signature is autograph.

## 1440.

LETTER from Edmund Beaufort, earl of Dorset, to Simmequin Waller, giving directions respecting the custody of the castle of Harcourt.[1]

LE conte de Dorset, de Mortaing, et de Harecourt.

CHIER et bien ame. Nous vous prions et tres estroictement chargons que vous faictez faire bon guet de jour et de nuit, et en si grant diligence que en deffault de ce nul inconvenient nen adviengne, (que Dieu ne vueille!) et tant que vous en doyons savoir gre, et nous le recongnoistrons envers vous et nous. Saluez tous les gentilz hommes et compaignons, leur priant et chargant que chacun face bon devoir de bien garder la place; et au plaisir de notre Seigneur, vous et eulx aurez bien brief bonnes nouvelles.

*A.D. 1440. Oct 17.*

*The castle of Harcourt to be carefully watched, and the garrison increased.*

---

### [TRANSLATION.]

THE earl of Dorset, of Mortagne, and of Harcourt.

DEAR and well beloved. We pray you, and charge you very strictly, that you keep good watch, day and night, and with such diligence that from failing herein no mischief may arise (which may God forbid!) and in such manner as that herein we may have cause to thank you, and we will acknowledge the same towards you and ourselves. Salute all the gentlemen and our comrades, praying them and charging them that each should do his duty to the best for the safe custody of the fortress; and by the permission of our Lord, you and they shall very speedily have good tidings.

---

[1] From the MS. Gaignières, 557. The letter is original, and is written upon paper.

Nous escripvons presentement a notre viconte de Harecourt que sil treuve vingt ou trente Anglois qui vueillent estre dedens notre place pour ung temps, que pour xl. ou l. frans il ne espargne pour que ne les ayez; si essais se daucuns en pourrez retruuver, et en tout faictez le mielx que vous pourrez, ainsi que en vous est notre confidence.

Chier et bien ame, notre Seigneur soit garde de vous.

Date.        Escript au siege devant Harfleu, a Lundi, xvij. jour Doctobre,

DORSET.[1]

> (*Dorso.*) A notre chiere et bien-ame Simmcquin Waller, escuier, lieutenant de notre chastel de Harecourt.

---

We write at the present time to our vicomte of Harcourt, that if he can find twenty or thirty Englishmen who are willing to reside within our fortress for a time, he should not grudge xl. or l. francs for you to secure them ; try, therefore, if you can find any such, and in all matters do the best that you can, as our trust is that you will do.

Dear and well beloved, our Lord be your keeper.

Written at the siege before Harfleur, on Monday, the xvij. day of October.

DORSET.

> (*Dorso.*) To our dear and well beloved, Simmcquin Waller, esquire, lieutenant of our castle of Harcourt.

---

[1] An autograph signature.

## 1440.

MANDATE for the repayment of certain sums advanced by the earl of Dorset during the siege of Harfleur.[1]

HENRY, par la grace de Dieu, roy de France et Dangleterre, a noz amez et feaulx, les tresoriers et generaulx gouverneurs de toutes noz finances en France et Normandie, salut et dillection.

Notre tres chier et ame cousin, le conte de Dorset, nagaires commis et ordonne a mettre et tenir de par nous le siege devant notre ville de Harrefleu, lors occupee par noz adversaires, nous a faict exposer que pour certaine assemblee faicte par noz diz adversaires, en grant puissance, cuidant lever icellui siege, notre tres chier et tres ame cousin Jehan, conte de Sommerset, lors notre lieutenant et general gouverneur sur le fait

*A.D. 1440 Nov. 10.*

*The earl of Dorset having advanced certain sums of money during the siege of Harfleur,*

---

[TRANSLATION.]

HENRY, by the grace of God, king of France and England, to our beloved and faithful, the treasurers and governors-general of all our finances in France and Normandy, greeting and love.

Our very dear and beloved cousin, the earl of Dorset, late commissioned and appointed to undertake and carry on the siege, on our part, before our town of Harfleur, at that time held by our adversaries, has caused it to be made known to us that, in consequence of a certain gathering together made by our said enemies in great power, who intended to raise the said siege, our very dear and right well-beloved cousin, John earl of Somerset, at that time our lieutenant

---

[1] From the MS. Fontanieu, 117-118.

de la guerre en France et Normendie, se tira au dit siege, et mena en icellui avec lui Mathieu Go et autres capitaines de gens de guerre du nombre de larmee que lui avons ordonnee, pour nous servir sur les champz et autrement durant ycellui siege, tant de resister a lentreprinse de noz diz adversaires, lesquieulx vindrent a Moustervillier, et mesme assaillir et courir sur icellui siege tant per mer comme par terre, et illec se tindrent pour certain tempz en grosse puissance, durant le quel temps les gaiges des dits Mathieu Go et cappitaines dessus dits et des gens estans soubz eulx finrent, par quoy convint a icelui notre cousin de Dorset, pour la sceurete dycellui siege, trouver maniere de les entretenir. A laquelle chose faire, leur presta et paia de ses deniers jusques a la somme de quatre vint dix livres, Tournois, pour leur aydier a vivre.

Et en oultre, nous a semblablement fait exposer que pour tousjours scavoir au certain du couraige diceulx adversaires, a envoie par diverses foys chevaucheurs,

---

and governor-general in the matter of the war in France and Normandy, advanced towards the said siege and brought to the same along with him Mathieu Go and other captains and troops from the force of the army which we had provided for him to serve us in the field and in other ways during the siege aforesaid, as well to resist the enterprise of our said enemies, who came to Montivilliers and even attempted to attack and raise the siege aforesaid, as well by sea as by land, and there continued for a certain time in great power, during which time the pay of the said Mathieu Go and the captains aforesaid and the troops under them expired, whereupon it was necessary for our said cousin of Dorset, for the safety of the said siege, to find the means of retaining them. To do this he advanced and paid of his own money as much as the sum of fourscore and ten livres, Tournois, to enable them to live.

And moreover, he has in like manner caused it to be made known to us that, in order to have uninterrupted and certain knowledge of the plans of the said adversaries,

messagiers et espiez sur les marches de Picardie, dautre part, ausquelz il a semblablement paie de ses deniers jusqua la somme de cent cinquante livres, Tournois, et plus; en nous requerant que lui veuillons faire paier et restituer icelles sommes de quatre vingt dix livres, Tournois, dune part, et de cent cinquante livres, Tournois, dautre part.

Pourquoy nous, considerans les bons et agreables services a nous fait par notre dit cousin en icelui siege, et que tout estoit pour le bien de nous et du dit siege, vous mandons et expressement enjoignons que, par notre bien ame Pierre Baille, receveur general des dits finances, vous faictes paier et restituer a icelui notre cousin de Dorset les dites sommes de quatre vingt dix livres, Tournois, dune part, et de cent cinquante livres Tournois, dautre part, par lui payee ainsi et pour les causes dessus dictes. Et par rapportant ces presentes et quictance, ou quictances, de

*the king orders the repayment of the same.*

---

ho has sent at different times couriers, messengers and spies to the borders of Picardy, on the other part, to whom he has in like manner paid, out of his own money, as much as the sum of one hundred and fifty livres, Tournois, and more; and he has requested of us that we would be pleased to cause to be repaid to him those sums of fourscore and ten livres, Tournois, on the one part, and of one hundred and fifty livres, Tournois, on the other part.

Wherefore, considering the good and acceptable services to us rendered by our said cousin in this siege, and that the whole was for the advantage of ourselves and of the said siege, we command you and expressly enjoin you that by our well-beloved Pierre Baille, receiver-general of the said finances, you cause to be paid and returned to our said cousin of Dorset the said sums of fourscore and ten livres, Tournois, on the one part, and of a hundred and fifty livres, Tournois, on the other part, by him thus paid and for the causes aforesaid. And upon the mere production of these presents, along with the acquittance, or acquittances, of our

notre dit cousin tant seulement, voulons que tout
ce que paie et restitue aura este par le dit receveur
general a icellui notre cousin estre alloe en ses comptes
et rabatu de sa recepte par noz amez et feaulz les
gens de noz comptes a Rouen; ausquels nous mandons que ainsi le facent sans aucun contredit ou difficulte, non obstant quil nappert de la declairation des
personnes et parties auxquelles notre dit cousin a delivree les dictes sommes.

Date.     Donne a Rouen, le dixieme jour de Novembre, lan
de grace, mil cccc. quarante, et de notre regne le
xix.

Par le roy, a la rellacion du grant conseil.

I. RINEL.

---

said cousin, we will that all that shall have been paid
and returned by the said receiver-general to our said cousin
shall be allowed in his accounts and deducted from his receipt
by our beloved and faithful accountants at Rouen; whom
we command thus to do without any gainsaying or difficulty,
notwithstanding that the persons (and the particulars) to
whom our said cousin has delivered the said sums do not
appear in the declaration.

Dated at Rouen, the tenth day of November, in the year
of grace one thousand cccc. and forty, and of our reign
the xix.

By the king, at the relation of the great council.

I. RINEL.

## 1440.

MANDATE for the payment of a pension to John lord Talbot, until he should be more amply provided.[1]

A.D. 1440.
Dec. 3.

A payment to be made to John, lord Talbot.

HENRY, par la grace de Dieu, roy de France et Dangleterre, a nos amez et feaulx les tresoriers et generaulx gouverneurs de nos finances en France et Normandie, salut et dilection.

Savoir vous faisons que pour consideration de ce que puis certain temps en ca, notre ame et feal cousin et mareschal de France, Jehan, sire de Talbot, na eu depar nous aucune charge de cappitainerie et garde de places en noz royaume de France ou duchie de Normandie, et que encores il na de present aucune autre cappitainerie depar nous que cette de Lisieulx et la garde de Harfleu et Monstiervilliers, qui baillee lui a este de nouvel et incontinent apres la reddition di-

## [TRANSLATION.]

HENRY, by the grace of God, king of France and England, to our beloved and faithful the treasurers and governors-general of our finances in France and Normandy, greeting and love.

We give you to know that in consideration that for a certain time past our beloved and faithful cousin and marshal of France, John, lord de Talbot, has not had from us any charge as a captain or warden of fortresses within our realm of France or duchy of Normandy, and that at this present time he has none, from us, except that of Lisieux and the custody of that of Harfleur and Montivilliers, which have been delivered to him of late and immediately upon the surrender of the same unto our jurisdiction, to

[1] From the MS. Fontanieu, 117–118.

celles en notre obeissance, en attendant quil ait autre
plus haute et ample provision, nous, pour lui aider a
maintenir son estat en notre service plus honnorable-
ment, lui aider a supporter les fraiz que faire lui convendra a loccasion dicelle, et affin de lentretenir ainsy
que plusieurs foiz a este fait avant le jour dhuy par
de ca la mer en nostre service, luy ayons ordonne
avoir et prendre de nous la somme de trois cens salus
dor pour ung quartier dan, commencant a la feste
Saint Michiel derrenier passee, oultre et par dessus les
gaiges, pension, ou estat de certains fraiz joings a iceluy
estat quil prend de nous.

Si vous mandons et expressement injoingnons que,
par notre bien ame Pierre Baille, receveur general de
noz dits finances, vous faites payer, bailler et delivrer
des deniers de sa recepte au dit sire de Talbot, ou a
son certain commandement, la dite somme de iij. c.
salus dor, ou monnoye a la valeur, au pris de xxix. s̃.
iij. đ. piece, pour le dit quartier commencant a la dite

---

hold until he shall have some other higher and more ample
provision, we, (to assist him in maintaining his position in
our service more honourably, to aid him in supporting the
charges which he must necessarily incur by occasion of the
same, and in order to retain him, as oftentimes has been
done before this present day on this side the sea in our
service,) have appointed him to have and take of us the
sum of three hundred salus of gold for one quarter of a
year, beginning on the feast of Saint Michael last past, over
and above the wages, pension, or estate of certain charges
incident to the same estate which he receives of us.

Wherefore we command and expressly enjoin you that, by
our well-beloved Pierre Baille, receiver-general of our said
finances, you cause to be paid and delivered, out of the
money by him received, to the said lord de Talbot, or to
his certain order, the said sum of iij. c. salus of gold, or
money to that amount, at the rate of xxix. s̃. iij. đ. each,
for the said quarter, commencing at the said Michaelmas ;

Saint Michiel; et par rapportant ces presentes et quittance souffisant seulement, tout ce que par le dit receveur aura este paye a ceste cause sera aloe en ces [1]
comptes et rebatu de sa recepte par nos amez et feaulx
les gens de noz comptes a Rouen; aus quels nous mandons que ainsy le facent sans difficulte ou tardement
aucun.

Donne a Rouen, le iij. jour de Decembre, lan de grace Date.
mil cccc. et quarante, et de notre regne le xix.

Par le roy, a la relation du grand conseil.[2]

---

and upon the sole production of these presents and a sufficient acquittance, all that which shall have been paid by
the said receiver on this account shall be allowed in his
accounts and deducted from his receipt by our beloved and
faithful accountants at Rouen; whom we command so to do
without any difficulty or delay.

Dated at Rouen, the iij. day of December, in the year of
grace one thousand cccc. and forty, and of our reign the
xix.

By the king, at the relation of the great council.

---

[1] *Ces*] So the MS.
[2] Then follows a copy of the order of governors-general of the finances for the payment of the said sum, dated on the same day, which is succeeded by the receipt for the same, dated on 10 January, A.D. 1441, and signed " R. Stafford."

## 1441.

A.D. 1441.
Aug. 28.

Certain
sums to be
paid to
Henry
Amoure
and Rich-
ard Ver-
non.

CERTIFICATE of the payment of certain sums to two messengers employed in the service of John lord Talbot.[1]

LAN mil cccc. quarante et ung, le **xxviij.** jour Daoust, devant nous, Thomas Her,[2] chevalier, bailly de Mante, furent presens en leurs personnes Henry Amoure et Richart Vernon, hommes de guerre, les quelx cogneurent et confessent avoir eu et receu de Pierre Baille, receveur general de Normandie, la somme de quatorze livres, dix sols, Tournois, que monseigneur de Talbot, mareschal de France, leur a en notre presence ordonnee estre payee par le dit receveur pour les causes cy apres desclariees. Cest a scavoir : le dit Henry, dix livres, Tournois, poùr ses peinnes et salaires de presentement aller hastivement de ceste ville de Mante en la ville de Pontoise, savoir de lestat des seigneurs et autres

---

[TRANSLATION.]

IN the year one thousand cccc. forty and one, the **xxviij.** day of August, before us, Thomas Her, knight, bailly of Mantes, appeared personally Henry Amoure and Richard Vernon, men-at-arms, who owned and acknowledged that they had had and received of Pierre Baille, receiver-general of Normandy, the sum of fourteen livres, ten sols, Tournois, which monseigneur de Talbot, marshal of France, had, in our presence, commanded to be paid to them by the said receiver for the causes hereafter declared. That is to say : to the said Henry, ten livres, Tournois, for his trouble and pay in having at this time gone hastily from this town of Mantes to the town of Pontoise, to ascertain the condition

---

[1] From the MS. Fontanieu, 117-118.    [2] *Her*] An error of the scribe for Hoo.

gens du roy, notre seigneur, qui y sont, et du dit lieu
de Pontoise a Conflans pour enquerir, veoir et scavoir
de lestat et armee du principal adversaire du roy, notre
dit seigneur, estant au dit lieu de Conflans, et de tout
rapporter response a mon dit seigneur de Talbot, afin
quil peust mielx employer larmee estant soubz luy en
ceste dicte ville pour lavitaillement du dit lieu de Pontoise, et faire plusieurs autres exploitz de guerre ; et
le dit Richart, quatre livres, dix sols, Tournois, pour
ses peinnes et salaires daller de ceste dicte ville au dit
lieu de Pontoise enquerir de lestat des seigneurs et
autres gens du roy, notre dit seigneur, y estans, et en
rapporter hastivement response a mon dit seigneur de
Talbot. De la quelle somme de xiiij. ł. x. ŝ. Tournois
les dits Henry et Richart se tindrent pour contens
et bien payez, et en quicterent, et quictent par ces
presentes, le roy, notre dit seigneur, le dit recevoir
general, et tous autres.

----

of the lords and other subjects of the king, our lord, who
are there, and from the said place of Pontoise to Conflans
to enquire, see and ascertain the condition and the army
of the chief adversary of the king, our said lord, who is
at the said place of Conflans, and to report upon the whole
to my said lord de Talbot, in order that he may the better
dispose the army under him in this said town for the vic-
tualing of the said place of Pontoise and perform many
other exploits of war ; and to the said Richard, four livres,
ten sols, Tournois, for his trouble and wages in going from
this said town to the said place of Pontoise to enquire
about the condition of the lords and other subjects of the
king, our said lord, who are there, and to convey a speedy
answer to my said lord de Talbot. Of which sum the
said Henry and Richard consider themselves satisfied and
well paid, and thereof they would acquit, and do acquit
by these presents, the king, our said lord, the said receiver-general, and all others.

Date.        Donne a Mante, soubz nostre signet, lan et jour dessus dits.

Et a greigneur confirmation et approbation de ce,
y avons faict mettre le scel de la ville et chastellenie
de Mante par la garde dicelluy, lan et jour dessus
dit.

LE COMTE.

Dated at Mantes, under our signet, in the year and day
above written.

And for the greater confirmation and security hereof, we
have hereto caused to be affixed the seal of the town and
jurisdiction of the castle of Mantes, by the keeper of the
same, on the year and day abovesaid.

LE COMTE.

## 1442.

A.D. 1442. SUMMONS to the inhabitants of Pont Audemer to send
March 20.        a representative to the Parliament at Rouen.[1]

Summons
to the        DEPAR le duc de York, lieutenant general et gouver-
Parliament   neur de France et de Normandie.
at Rouen.
TRES chier et bien amez.  Pour avoir bon conseil et
adviz sur certaines choses touchans grandement la

[TRANSLATION.]

By the duke of York, lieutenant-general and governor of
France and Normandy.

Very dear and well-beloved.  In order to have good counsel and advice upon certain matters which greatly concern

---

[1] From the original, in the MS. Gaignières, 557.

bonne entretenu de la seigneurie de monseigneur le
roy et votre bien propre, mandons venir pardevers
nous en ceste ville de Rouen plusieurs prelas et autres
gens deglise, nobles et bourgois des bonnes villes de
ceste seigneurie, et y estre le seiziesme jour du mois
Davril prouchainement venant, pour la matere y estre
communiquee.

Si vous mandons depar mon dit seigneur le roy et
nous, que pour estre depar nous au dit lieu de Rouen,
le dit xvij. jour Davril prouchain, vous eslisez et
envoyez une personne dentre vous, garni de procuration et pouvoir souffisant, pour adviser, deliberer, accorder et conclurre tout ce qui sera advise en la matere.
Et en ce ne faittes aucune faulte, sur la loyaute que
devez a mon dit seigneur et a nous. Tres chiers et bien
amez, notre Sire vous ait en sa sainte garde.

Donne a Rouen, soubz notre signet, le xx. jour de Date.
Mars.

Signe, DROSAY.

---

the good preservation of the sovereignty of my lord the
king, and your own personal interest, we have commanded
to come to us at this city of Rouen, many prelates and
other churchmen, nobles and burgesses of the good towns of
this lordship, and that they be there on the sixteenth day
of the month of April next coming, for the business which
shall be there communicated to them.

Wherefore we command you, upon the part of my said lord
the king and our own, that you elect and send a person from
among you, so that he may be with us at the said place of
Rouen on the said xvj. day of April next, provided with a
proxy and sufficient power, to advise, deliberate, agree
and conclude on all that shall be decided on in the business. And make no failure herein, by the loyalty which you
owe to my said lord and to us. Very dear and well-beloved,
our Lord have you in His holy keeping.

Dated at Rouen, under our signet, the xx. day of March.

Signed, DROSAY.

x 2

A noz tres chiers et bien amez, les bourgoiz, manans
et habitans de la ville de Pontaudemer.[1]

To our very dear and well-beloved, the burgesses, residents and inhabitants of the town of Pont Audemer.

## 1442.

The expenses of Jehan de Luxembourg are to be repaid.

MANDATE for the repayment of expenses incurred by
Jehan de Luxembourg during a mission from the
duchess of Burgundy to the duke of York at
Rouen.[2]

HENRY, par le grace de Dieu roy de France et
Dangleterre, a noz amez et feaulx les tresoriers et
generaulx gouverneurs de noz finances en France et
Normandie, salut et dillection.

Comme, pour certaines besoingnes et matieres touchans le bien de nous, de noz pays et subgetz de France

### [TRANSLATION.]

HENRY, by the grace of God king of France and England, to our beloved and faithful the treasurers and governors-general of our finances of France and Normandy,
greeting and love.

Since, for certain business and matters touching the welfare of us and our country and subjects of France and

---

[1] On the back of the instrument is a Certificate stating that these present letters were presented to, and opened and read in the presence of the inhabitants of Pontaudemer, on

Thursday, 29 March, 1441, before Easter, in the presence of Thomas Haliday, vicomte of the said place.
[2] From the MS. Fontanieu, 117-118.

et Normandie, Jehan de Luxembourg, bastard de Saint
Pol, chevalier, soit de notre congie et licence venu depar
notre tres chiere et tres amee cousine, la duchesse de
Bourgoigne, en notre ville de Rouen pardevers notre
tres chier et tres ame cousin Richard, duc de York,
notre lieutenant general et gouverneur depar nous de
noz royaume de France et duchie de Normandie, et
illec ait demoure des le unzieme jour de ce present
mois jusques au vingtsixiesme jour dicellui moys in-
cludz, le quel chevalier ayons, par ladvis et deliberacion de notre dit cousin de York, pour certaines causes
voulu et ordonne estre, des deniers de nos dits finances,
deffraye des despens par lui, ses gens et chevaulx, faiz
pendant le dit tems en hostelleries en notre ville de
Rouen, et aussi lui estre pourveu a noz despens de
gens de guerre pour lui conduire de ville en autre
jusques ou party de noz adversaires ;—nous vous mandons et commandons que, par notre bien ame Pierre
Baille, receveur general de nos dits finances, vous des ·

---

Normandy, Jehan de Luxembourg, bastard of Saint Pol,
knight, by our leave and licence came, on the part of our
very dear and entirely beloved cousin, the duchess of Burgundy, to our city of Rouen, to our very dear and well-
beloved cousin Richard, duke of York, our lieutenant general and the governor on our part of our kingdom of France
and duchy of Normandy, and has tarried there from the
eleventh day of this present month until the twenty-sixth
day of the same month inclusive ; and by the advice and
judgment of our said cousin of York, for certain reasons, we
have willed and appointed that the said knight be repaid,
out of our said finances, the expenses incurred by himself,
his servants and horses during the said time within the inns
within our said city of Rouen, and also that he be provided,
at our expenses, with soldiers to escort him from one town
to another, as far as the district of our adversaries ;—we
command and order that, by our well-beloved Pierre Baille,
receiver-general of our said finances, you, out of the money

deniers de sa recepte faites paier, bailler et delivrer a
Pierre Cordier, hostellier et bourgoiz du dit lieu de
Rouen, la somme de deux cens soixante livres, cinq
sols, Tournois ; cest assavoir, deux cens trente livres,
Tournois, a quoy monte la despense de bouche faite par
icellui chevalier, ses dits gens et chevaulx, en icelle
notre ville de Rouen durant le dit temps quil a este,
comme dit est, et trente livres, cinq solz, Tournois, tant
pour le louage de certains chevaulx sur quoy ont este
montez aucuns gens de guerre, comme pour le salaire
daucuns archers davoir conduit icelui chevalier et sa
compaignie du dit lieu de Rouen jusques au Neufchatel.

Et par rapportant ces presentes et quittance du dit
Pierre Cordier tant seulement, nous voulons icelle
somme de deux cens soixante livres, cinq solz, Tournois,
estre aloee es comptes et rabatue de la recette du dit
receveur general par noz amez et feaulx les gens de
nos comptes a Rouen ; aus quelx nous mandons que
ainsy le facent, sans contredit ou difficulte quelconques.

---

by him received, cause to pay, give and deliver to Pierre
Cordier, innkeeper and burgess of the said place of Rouen,
the sum of two hundred and sixty livres, five sols, Tournois ; that is to say, two hundred and thirty livres, Tournois, the amount of the personal expenses of the said knight,
his said servants and horses, in this our city of Rouen,
during the time he has been there, as aforesaid, and thirty
livres, five sols, Tournois, as well for the hire of certain
horses for the mount of certain soldiers, as also for the pay
of certain archers who escorted the said knight and his
company from the said place of Rouen as far as Neufchâtel.

And upon the simple production of these presents and
the acquittance of the said Pierre Cordier, it is our will that
this sum of two hundred and sixty livres, five sols, Tournois, shall be allowed in the accounts and deducted from
the receipt of the said receiver general by our beloved and
faithful accountants at Rouen ; whom we command so to do,
without any contradiction or difficulty whatsoever

Donne a Pont de Larche, le vingtyesme jour de Date.
Juillet, lan de grace, mil cccc. quarante deux, et de
notre regne le vingtyesme.

Par le roy, a la relacion de monsieur le duc Dyork,
lieutenant general et gouverneur de France et Normandy.[1]

DE RINEL.

Dated at Pont de l'Arche, the twentieth day of July, in
the year of grace one thousand cccc. forty-two, and of our
reign the twentieth.

By the king, at the relation of my lord the duke of
York, lieutenant-general and governor of France and Normandy.

DE RINEL.

1442.

RECEIPT by Henry lord Bourgchier for three thousand
pounds, Tournois, paid to him for services rendered.[2]

A.D. 1442.<br>Aug. 11.<br><br>3,000l. T.<br>paid to<br>Henry lord<br>Bourg-<br>cheir.

NOUS, Henry, conte de Eu, seigneur de Bourgchier,
confessons avoir eu et receu de Pierre Baille, receveur

[TRANSLATION.]

WE, Henry, count of Eu, lord Bourgchier, acknowledge
that we have had and received of Pierre Baille, receiver-

---

[1] Affixed is the mandate of the Generals of the Finances addressed to Pierre Baille, ordering the execution of the order, dated 27 July, 1442, together with the acquittance of the said Pierre Cordier on the payment of the above sum, dated 29 July, in the same year.

[2] From the MS. Fontanieu, 117–118.

general de Normandie, la somme de trois mil livres, Tournois, que le roy, notre sire, par ses lettres donnees le xxvj. jour de Juillet derrenier passe, expediees par les tresoriers de Normandie, a ordonnee nous etre paiee pour aucunement nous recompenser de plusieurs services par nous faits au dit roy, notre seigneur, dez le penultime jour de Mars derrenier passe, includ, jusques au xxix. jour de Juing, aussi derrenier passe, exclude. De la quelle somme de trois mil livres, Tournois, nous sommes contens et bien payez, et en quittons par ces presentes le roy, notre dit seigneur, le dit receveur et tous.

Date.  En tesmoing de ce nous avons scelle ces presentes de notre scel, le xj. jour Daoust, lan mil cccc. et quarante deux.

BOURGCHIER.

---

general of Normandy, the sum of three thousand livres, Tournois, which the king, our lord, by his letters dated the xxvj. day of July last passed, and despatched by the treasurers of Normandy, had decreed to be paid to us as a recompense in some sort for many services by us rendered to the said king, our lord, from the last day but one of March last past, inclusive, to the xxix. day of June, also last past, exclusive. Of which sum of three thousand pounds, Tournois, we are satisfied and well paid, and thereof we acquit, by these presents, the king, our said lord, the said receiver, and all people.

In testimony whereof we have sealed these presents with our seal, this xj. day of August, the year one thousand cccc. and forty-two.

BOURGCHIER.

## 1442.

MANDATE for the payment of the expenses of Toison d'Or, while at Rouen with the duke of York.[1]

A.D. 1442.
Oct. 26.

The expenses of Toison d'Or to be repaid.

HENRY, par la grace de Dieu, roy de France et Dangleterre, a nos amez et feaulx les tresoriers et generaulx gouverneurs de toutes nos finances en France et Normandie, salut et dilection.

Nous voulons et, par ladvis et deliberation de notre tres chier et tres ame cousin, Richard, duc Dyork, nostre lieutenant general et gouverneur de nos royaume de France, pays et duchie de Normandie, vous mandons expressement par ces presentes que, a Toison Dor, roy darmes, (qui pour aucunes matieres et besongnes touchants grandement le bien de nous et de nostre seigneurie, est nagaires venu pardevers nostre dit cousin en ceste nostre ville de Rouen, ou il est encores,

---

[TRANSLATION.]

HENRY, by the grace of God, king of France and England, to our beloved and faithful the treasurers and governors-general of all our finances in France and Normandy, greeting and love.

It is our pleasure and, by the advice and deliberation of our very dear and well-beloved cousin, Richard, duke of York, our lieutenant-general, and the governor of our realm of France and country and duchy of Normandy, we expressly command you by these presents, that, to Toison d'Or, king of arms, (who, for certain matters and business which closely concern the welfare of ourselves and our lordship, has of late come to our said cousin in this our city of Rouen, where he

---

[1] From the MS. Fontanieu, 117–118.

de par nostre tres chiere et tres amee tante et cousine, la duchesse de Bourgongne,) vous faites paier, bailler et delivrer par nostre ame Pierre Baille, receveur general de nos dits finances, la somme de vint saluz dor, ou trente solz, Tournois, pour chacun salut, qui est a present leur cours. La quelle somme nous avons ordonne etre baillee au dit Toison Dor pour le aidier et deffraier des despens par lui faiz en ceste nostre dite ville, attendant sa response et expedicion. Et par rapportant ces presentes et quittance sur ce tant seulement du dit Toison Dor, nous voulons la dite somme estre allouee es comptes et rebatue de la recette de nostre dit receveur general par noz amez et feaulx, les gens de noz comptes a Rouen; ausquels nous mandons que ainsi le facent, sans contredit ou aucune difficulte.

Date.    Donne a Rouen, le xxvj. jour Doctobre, lan de grace mil cccc. quarante deux, et de notre regne le vingt ungniesme.

---

still is, on the part of our very dear and right well-beloved cousin, the duchess of Burgundy,) you cause to be paid, given and delivered by our beloved Pierre Baille, receiver-general of our said finances, the sum of twenty salus of gold, or thirty sols, Tournois, for each salu, which is at this time their current value. This sum we have appointed to be given to the said Toison d'Or, to assist him and to defray the expenses by him incurred in this our said city, while waiting for his answer and despatch. And upon the simple production of these presents, and the discharge thereof by the said Toison d'Or, we will that the said sum shall be allowed in the accounts and deducted from the receipt of our said receiver-general by our beloved and faithful our accountants at Rouen, whom we command to do this, without opposition or any difficulty.

Dated at Rouen, the xxvj. day of October, in the year of grace one thousand cccc. and forty-two, being the twenty-first of our reign.

Par le roy, a la relacion de monseigneur le duc
Dyork, lieutenant et gouverneur general de France et
Normandie.

DE RINEL.

By the king, at the relation of my lord the duke of York,
lieutenant and governor-general of France and Normandy.

DE RINEL.

## 1442.

RECEIPT for 2,900 salus of gold paid by the count de
Dunois.[1]

A.D. 1442.
Oct. 30,

Receipt for
2,900 salus
of gold
paid by the
count de
Dunois.

Nous, Francoix de Suryenne, dit Larragonnoiz, chevalier, Mathieu Goth, Thomas Gerard, et Thomas
Stonnes, escuiers, confessons avoir au jour duy eu et
receu de noble et puissant seigneur, monseigneur le
bastart Dorleans, conte de Dunoys, la somme de deux
mil neuf cens saluz de bon or et de bon poix, ou la

### [TRANSLATION.]

WE, Francoix de Suryenne, called l'Arragonnoiz, knight,
Matthew Goth, Thomas Gerard, and Thomas Stonnes, esquires, acknowledge that we have this day had and received
of the noble and powerful lord, monseigneur the bastard
of Orleans, comte of Dunois, the sum of two thousand nine
hundred salus of good gold and of good weight, or their

---

[1] From the original, upon vellum, in the MS. Fontanieu, 117–118.

valleur, sur et en deduction du premier payement de
la somme de unze mil saluz dor, dont mon dit seigneur
le bastart est tenuz de paier et fournir, sur lappoinct-
ment fait par luy avecques nous, Mathieu Goth et
Thomas Gerard dessus diz, touchant le demoliement de
Gallardon et wydange de Tourville, ainsi que plus
aplain est contenu ou dit appoinctment.   De laquelle
somme de ij. M. ix. c. saluz dor, telz que dessus, nous
tenons pour contens et bien paiez, et en quitons mon
dit seigneur le bastart et tous aultres quelzconques, a
qui quittance en puet ou doit appartenir.   Et promettons chascun de nous, par la foy et serement de noz
corps, et sur noz honneurs et loyaultez, deduire et faire
deduire et rabbatre la dite somme de ij. M. ix. c. saluz
a mon dit seigneur le bastart sur la dite somme de
unze mil saluz sans nul contredit ; et tout sans fraulde,
baralt ou mal engin.

Date.       En tesmoing de ce nous avons signe ces presentes

---

value, towards and in reduction of the first payment of
the sum of eleven thousand salus of gold, which my said
lord the bastard is bound to pay and furnish, according
to the agreement made by him with us, Matthew Goth and
Thomas Gerard abovesaid, touching the demolition of Gallardon and district of Tourville, as is more fully contained
in the said agreement.   And of this sum of ij. M. ix. c.
salus of gold as abovesaid, we hold ourselves satisfied and
well paid ; and thereof we acquit my said lord the bastard
and all others whomsoever, to whom a discharge can or
ought to belong.   And each of us promises by his faith
and oath, upon his body and by his honour and troth, to
deduct and cause to be deducted and withdrawn the said
sum of ij. M. ix. c. salus of gold due by my said lord
the bastard from the said sum of eleven thousand salus,
without any opposition ; and all this without fraud, debate,
or deceit.

In witness whereof we have signed these presents with

de noz seingz manuelz, le peneultysme jour du moys
Doctobre, lan mil quatre cens quarente et deux.

F. LARAGONOYS,                     MATHEU,
GERARD,                            T. STONES.

our signs manual, the last day but one of the month of
October, in the year one thousand cccc. forty and two.

F. LARAGONOYS,                     MATHEU,
GERARD,                            T. STONES.

### 1442.

MANDATE from the duke of York to the captain of
Honfleur respecting the garrison of that place.[1]

A.D. 1442.
Nov. 4.

DEPAR le duc Dyork, lieutenant et gouverneur general de France et Normandie.

Tres chier et bien ame.  Pour certaines causes et consideracions nous avons continue les capitaines, hommes
darmes et de trait, estans es garnisons de Normandie

The gar-
rison of
Honfleur to
be con-
tinued.

### [TRANSLATION.]

BY the duke of York, lieutenant and governor-general
of France and Normandy.

Very dear and well-beloved.  For certain causes and considerations we have continued the captains, men-at-arms,
and archers, which are in the garrisons of Normandy, for

---

[1] From the original, in the MS. Gaignières, 557.

pour ce present mois de Novembre, ainsi que continuez ont este pour le mois Doctobre derrainement passe.

Si vous mandons et commandons, de par monseigneur le roy et depar nous, que les gens de votre retenue vous entretenez pour ce dit mois ; en faisant voz monstres devant les commisses sur ce ordonnez, et il vous sera pourveu de paiement selon icelles. Tres chier et bien ame, notre Seigneur soit garde de vous.

Date.      Donne a Rouen, le iiij. jour de Novembre.

RINEL.

(*Dorso*.)   A notre tres chier et bien ame, le capitaine de Honneflou, ou a son lieutenant.

---

this present month of November, just as they have been continued for the month of October last past. Wherefore we order and command you, on behalf of my lord the king and ourselves, to continue during the said month the people of your retinue ; making your musters before the commissioners thereto appointed, and provision shall be made for your payment according to the same. Very dear and well-beloved, our Lord be your keeper.

Dated at Rouen, the iiij. day of November.

RINEL.

(*Dorso*.)   To our very dear and well-beloved, the captain of Honfleur, or to his lieutenant.

## 1443.

PAYMENT of 200*l.* Tournois to be made to the bishop
of Bayeux, for services rendered to king Henry.[1]

A.D. 1443.
Feb. 5.

200*l.* T.
to be paid
to the
bishop of
Bayeux.

HENRY, par le grace de Dieu roy de France et
Dangleterre, a nos amez et feaulx conseilliers, les
tresoriers et generaulx gouverneurs de noz finances en
France et Normandie, salut et dilection.

Comme par notre ordonnance notre ame et feal
conseilleur, Zanon, evesque de Bayeux, ait vacque et
se soit grandement employe pour le bien de notre
seigneurie et la chose publique dicelle, (mesmement en
fait touchant la recoeuvre des villes et places de Dyepe
et de Grant Ville,) a la quelle cause il est ale et soy
transporte, avecques lui et en sa compaignie autres
gens commis a ce par nous, en divers lieux, esquelz il
a grandement fraye et liberalement despendu du sien

---

[TRANSLATION.]

HENRY, by the grace of God king of France and England,
to our beloved and faithful councillors, the treasurers and
governors-generals of our finances in France and Normandy,
greeting and love.

Since, by our appointment, our faithful and beloved
councillor, Zano, bishop of Bayeux, has occupied himself
and been greatly employed for the good of our lordship and
the public benefit of the same (especially on the business
touching the recovery of the towns and strongholds of
Dieppe and Granville), in consequence of which he has
travelled and journeyed, together with many others in his
company, who were thereto commissioned by us, into divers
places, in doing which he has largely expended and liberally

---

[1] From the original, in the MS. Gaignières, 151.

en notre service, savoir vous faisons que, eue consideracion a ce, voulons le dit evesque aucunement
estre recompense de ses ditz fraiz et despens en ceste
partie. Nous a icellui evesque de Bayeux, par ladviz
et deliberacion de notre tres chier et tres ame cousin,
Richart, duc de York, lieutenant general et gouverneur
depar nous de noz royaume de France et duchie de
Normandie, avons ordonne et tauxe, ordonnons et
tauxons par ce presentes, avoir et prendre de nous
pour une et ceste foiz seulement, la somme de deux
cens livres, Tournoiz.

Si vous mandons que par notre bien ame Pierre
Baille, receveur general de noz dites finances, et des
deniers de sa recepte, vous faites payer, baillier et
delivrer au dit evesque de Bayeux la dicte somme de
deux cens livres, Tournois. Et par raportant ces presentes et quittance souffisant du dit evesque de Bayeux,
seulement, icelle somme de deux cens livres, Tournois,

---

advanced his own money in our service, we make known
to you that, having regard hereto, it is our pleasure that
the said bishop should in some sort be recompensed for his
said charges and expense in this behalf. We, therefore,
by the advice and deliberation of our very dear and well-
beloved cousin, Richard, duke of York, lieutenant-general
and governor on our behalf of our realm of France and
duchy of Normandy, have appointed and awarded, and by
these presents do appoint and award, to the said bishop of
Bayeux to have and take of us, for once and for this time
only, the sum of two hundred livres, Tournois.

Wherefore we command you that, by our well-beloved
Pierre Baille, receiver-general of our said finances, and out
of the money which he has on hand, you cause to be paid,
given and delivered to the said bishop of Bayeux the said
sum of two hundred livres, Tournois. And on the simple
production of these presents and a sufficient acquittance of
the said bishop of Bayeux, this sum of two hundred livres,

nestoit ne pour votre honneur ne pour votre prouffit,
ne pour bien que on peust congnoistre qui en peust
ensuir, aincois, comme est vraysemblable par les ap-
parances et demonstrances quilz faisoient, estoit plus
pour perturber et empeschier le bien de paix dessus
dit, ce que tenons pour certain, et ne revocquons point
en doubte quil ne venoit ne procedoit aucunement de
votre vouloir, entencion ne consentement,) ont estes
faiz certains appoinctemens pour le bien des dictes
matieres, lesquelz, comme pensons, vous ont este notiffiez
et faiz savoir par iceulx gens de vestre conseil residens
au dit lieu de Rouen, et ausquelz appoinctemens ne
aux commandemens par vertu diceulx faiz de votre
part, ne aux sommacions et requestes faictes de la
notre aus diz Mathieu Go, Heton, Mundeford, et autres
qui tiennent les places, na aucunement par iceulx este
obey ne obtempere. A la quelle cause, selon la teneur
des ditz appoinctemens, ilz sont demourez desobeissans
envers vous, et desadvouez de votre part comme indig-

---

neither to your honour or profit, nor for any conceivable
advantage which may result from it, but, as is probable by
the show and demonstration which they make, is rather to
disturb and hinder the blessing of the peace above-mentioned, as we hold for certain, and will never consider it
questionable that this neither came nor proceeded in anywise
of your will, intention nor consent,) there have been made
certain arrangements for the good of the said matters, which,
as we think, have been notified and intimated to you by
the members of your council resident in the said town of
Rouen, and neither to these arrangements nor to the com-
mandments by virtue of them made on your part unto the
summons and requests made on our part to the said Matthew
Go, Heton, Mundeford and others who keep those fortresses,
has any obedience or submission whatever been made. In
consequence whereof, according to the tenor of the said
arrangements, they have become disobedient towards you,
and are disavowed upon your part as unworthy of being

nes destre comprins ou benefice des treues, et reservez expressement dicelles ; et en ceste qualite, et pour le tort en quoy ilz se sont mis, et la grant faulte quilz ont faicte, et obvier aussi aux inconveniens qui estoient fort adoubter de advenir, mesmes en la matiere principale de paix, se provision ny eust este mise, avons este meuz de proceder alencontre deulx en la maniere que faisons.

Charles sends R. Regnault with further information.

Mais pour ce, tres hault et puissant prince, notre treschier nepveu, que ne savons se on vous auroit donne a entendre aucune chose touchant les matieres dessus diz en autre maniere que ainsi que dit est, et que a ceste cause vous et ceulx depardela eussies par aventure ymaginacion que ne feussions pas si enclins et disposez, ne en si bon vouloir et affection envers vous et au bien de paix comme nous sommes, ne faites doubte que la verite des choses dessus dictes est telle comme devant est dit. Et a ce que en soies encore plus amplement informe, nous envoions presentement

---

included within the benefit of the truce, and are expressly excluded therefrom ; and in this capacity, and in consequence of the wrong in which they have put themselves, and the great error which they have committed, and in order also to obviate the mischiefs which there is much cause to dread will ensue, even in the principal matter of the peace, unless provision be made against it, we have been moved to proceed against them in the way we have done.

But, most high and powerful prince, our very dear nephew, because we do not know whether you have in any way been informed of anything touching the matters abovesaid otherwise than is stated above, and on this account you and the people in England possibly imagine that we are not so inclined and disposed, nor that we have the same goodwill and affection towards you, and for the prosecution of the peace, as we really have, be assured that the truth of the circumstances above-mentioned is such as we have stated it to be. And in order that herein you may be still more fully

par devers vous pour ces causes notre ame et feal
eschancon, Raoulin Regnault, escuier, porteur de ces
presentes, par lequel en oultre avons voulu que nos
diz ambaxeurs, qui ont conduit et manie les dictes
matieres, vous escrevissent bien au long tout leffect en
abrege de ce quilz ont veu et fait en ceste matiere.
Car croiez que nous navons fait, ne ne voudrions faire,
chose touchant les matieres dessus dictes, ne autres
quelzconques, que quant auries au telz appoinctemens
avecques nous en quelque matiere que ce soit comme
nous avons avecques vous sur les dictes matieres, nous
ne feussions contens que feissies le semblable.

Si vous prions, tres hault et puissant prince, notre
treschier nepveu, que icellui notre eschancon dessus
nomme es matieres dessus dictes vous vueilliez benignement oir et escouter, et adjouster plaine foy et creance
a tout ce quil vous dira de notre part sur ce ; en nous
signiffiant se chose vous plaist que faire puissons pour

---

informed, we send to you at this time for these causes our
beloved and faithful cupbearer, Raoulin Regnault, esquire,
bearer of these present letters, by whom we have moreover
willed that our said ambassadors, who have conducted and
managed the said matters, should write to you at length
an outline of the whole proceedings, what they have seen
and done in this business. For we would have you believe
that we neither have done, nor wish to do, anything touching
the matters aforesaid, nor any others whatsoever, otherwise
than that you should have the same advantages in these
arrangements in regard to us, whatsoever that may be, as
we have with you in the said matters, nor would we be
pleased were it otherwise.

Wherefore we pray you, most high and powerful prince,
our very dear nephew, that you would be pleased graciously
to hear and give heed to this our cupbearer above-named
in the matters specified above, and to give him faith and
credence in all that he will say to you on our part herein ;
letting us know if there is anything which it is your pleasure

nous y emploier de tres bon cuer, au plaisir de Dieu, qui vous vueille avoir et maintenir en Sa saincte et benoite garde.

Donne, etc.

(*Dorso.*) Copie de lettres Dangleterre.

---

that we should do for you, that we may heartily employ ourselves herein, to the pleasure of God, Whom may it please to have and keep you in His holy and blessed keeping.

Dated, &c.

(*Dorso.*) Copy of the letters for England.

---

## 1446.

### LETTER from Henry VI. to Charles VII., expressive of a desire for peace.[1]

A.D. 1446. Jan. 2.

Henry and queen Margaret are in good health.

A TRESHAULT et puissant prince, notre treschier oncle de France, Henry, par la grace de Dieu, roy de France et Dangleterre, salut, avec cordiale dileccion.

Treshault et puissant prince, notre treschier oncle, comme naguaires vous avons escript, nous avons sceu par voz ambaxadeurs que derreinerement avez envoye devers nous et autrement le bon estat et prosperite

---

To THE most high and powerful prince, our very dear uncle of France, Henry by the grace of God king of France and England, greeting, with cordial love.

Most high and powerful prince, our very dear uncle, as we lately have written to you, we have understood by your ambassadors whom recently you have sent to us and by other means

---

[1] From the original, upon paper, in the MS. Baluze, 9037/7. No. 38. The watermark resembles a | staff fixed upright in a rock with a double pennon at top.

de votre personne, de quoy avons este tres joyeux, et
prenons plaisir bien grant toutes les foiz que en
sommes acertenez en bien.  Si vous prions que souvent nous en vueillez faire savoir, pour notre singulier
resjoyssement.  Et se des notres desirez semblablement
oir, nous et notre treschiere et tresamee compaignee
la royne, votre niepce, estions alescripture de cestes
en tresbonne convalescience et disposicion de noz
personnes, graces au doulz Jhesu Christ, qui le semblable, par son plaisir, vous vueille tout temps octroier, ainsi que de joyeux courage et de bon vouloir
le desirons.

Et treshault et puissant prince, notre treschier *He is de-*
oncle, pour ce que loiaument et de bonne foy voulons *sirous of*
de notre part sans dissimulacion proceder en la matiere *peace,*
de paix generale dentre vous et nous, et que de
entiere affection desirons que elle soit conduicte et
conclute en toute bonne perfection pour le relievement
du pouvre peuple qui tant longuement par guerre a

---

the good estate and prosperity of your person, whereof we
have been right joyous, and we take great pleasure whenever we are informed of your welfare, wherefore we pray
you that you would be pleased often to make us acquainted
herewith, for our singular rejoicing.  And if you desire in
like manner to hear of ours, we and our very dear and
well-beloved companion, the queen, your niece, at the
writing of these present letters were in excellent bodily
health, thanks to the gentle Jesus Christ, Whom may it
please to grant you the like always as you would most
heartily wish it for yourself.

And, most high and powerful prince, our very dear uncle
because we truly and in good faith desire, upon our part,
without dissimulation, to proceed in the business of a
general peace between you and us, and whereas we with
entire affection desire that it should be conducted and concluded in all good perfection for the relief of the poor
people who so long have been troubled and ruined by war,

este perturbe et desole, aussi que les conclusions que
avons prinses sur le fait de notre passage pardela pour
faire et tenir la convention mutuele entre nous
deulx, voulons, moyennant la grace notre Createur,
tenir et accomplir, tant pour le cordial et entier
desir que nous avous au bien dicelle paix, comme
pour la singulier amour et affection que nous avons
a votre personne en tout desir de bonne concorde,
and for this nous envoyons presentement devers vous Gartier, roy
purpose
sends
darmes, afin de vous exposer a votre plaisir bien a
Garter. plain aucunes choses touchans la dite matiere, et
mesmes ce qui par nous a este appointie et conclud
touchant notre dit passage. Si vous prions de rechief
que le dit Gartier vueillez benignement oyr, et adjouster plaine foy et credence a tout ce quil vous
dira de nostre part, et par lui nous signifier se chose
vous est aggreable qui faire puissons, et nous lacom-
plirons tres voulentiers et de bon cuer.

Treshault et puissant prince, notre treschier oncle,

---

and because we wish also to keep and observe (by the help
of God's favour) the conclusions which we have taken
upon the business of our passage across the water, to
hold and keep the mutual meeting between our two selves,
as well for the cordial and entire desire which we have
for the good of this peace as for the singular love and
affection which we have for your person in all desire of
good concord, we send at this present time to you Garter,
king of arms, as well fully to explain to you, with your
permission, certain things touching the said matter, and
especially what we have arranged and concluded touching
our said passage. Wherefore we pray you moreover to be
pleased favourably to hear the said Garter, and to give full
faith and credence to all that he will say to you on our
part, and by him to let us know if there is anything which
we can do for your satisfaction, and it shall be done most
willingly and cordially.

Most high and powerful prince, our very dear uncle,

nous prions le Benoist Filz de Dieu quil vous ait et teingne en Sa tres digne garde.

Donne en notre chastel de Wyndesore, le second Date. jour de Januier.

HENRY.<br>PARIS.

(*Dorso.*)—A treshault et puissant prince, notre treschier oncle de France.

Lettres closes du roy Dangleterre, apportes par Jarretier le heraut, et receus le xvij. jour de Fevrier, cccc. xlv.[1]

———

we pray the Blessed Son of God to have you in His most worthy keeping.

Dated in our castle of Windsor, the second day of January.

PARIS.<br>HENRY.

(*Dorso.*)—To the most high and powerful prince, our very dear uncle of France.

Closed letters of the king of England, brought by Garter the herald, and received the xxvij. day of February, cccc. xlv.

═══════════

## 1446.

ACKNOWLEDGMENT by Zano de Castiglione, bishop of Bayeux, of the receipt of 220*l.* Tournois, for accompanying the duke of York into Lower Nomandy.

Nous Zanon, par la permission divine evesque de Bayeux, conseilleur du roy notre seigneur, confessons

A.D. 1446.<br>July 27.

———

[TRANSLATION].

We, Zano, by the divine permission bishop of Bayeux, councillor of our lord the king, acknowledge that we have had

Receipt of<br>the bishop<br>of Bayeau<br>for 220*l.*<br>Tournois.

———

[1] This entry is in a different hand.

[2] From the original, in the MS. Gaignières, 151. The seal no longer exists.

avoir eu et receu de Pierre Baille, receveur general du
Normandie, la somme de deux cens vingt livres Tournois,
pour la parpaye de certain voyage par nous fait de ceste
ville de Rouen a Caen et ailleurs en la Basse Normendie,
en la compaignie du treshault et puissant prince, monseigneur le duc de York, lieutenant general et gouverneur
de France et Normendie, semblablement que autres gens
du grant conseil du roy, notre dit seigneur ; icelui voyage
fait a pourveoir aux necessitez du pays, au bien et honneur du roy, notre dit seigneur, de sa justice, et a la
transquilite de ses subgetz. Ou quil voyage nous affirmons en notre conscience avoir vaque par cent douze
jours, commencans le vingt septieme jour de Mars, lan
mil cccc. quarante trois, avant Pasques, que nous partismes du dit lieu de Rouen pour le fait du dit voyage,
et finie le scizesme jour de Juillet ensuivant, inclus,
qui montent, au pris de dix livres Tournois pour chacun
diceulx jours, unze cent vingt livres Tournois. Sur la
quelle somme paiement nous a este fait par le dit

---

and received of Pierre Baille, receiver-general of Normandy,
the sum of two hundred and twenty pounds Tournois, in full
payment for a certain journey by us made from this city of
Rouen to Caen, and elsewhere in Lower Normandy, in the
company of the most high and powerful prince, my lord the
duke of York, lieutenant-general and governor of France and
Normandy, in like manner as other members of the great
council of the king, our sovereign lord ; this journey being
made to provide for the necessities of the country, for the good
and honour of the king, our said lord, for his justice, and for
the quiet of his subjects. In this journey we affirm in our
conscience that we have been employed for one hundred and
twelve days, beginning on the twenty-seventh day of March
in the year one thousand cccc. and forty-three, before Easter,
when we set out from the said place of Rouen upon the
business of the said journey, and finishing on the sixteenth day
of July following, included, which, at the rate of ten pounds
Tournois for each of these days, amounts to eleven hundred
and twenty pounds Tournois. Of the which sum payment has

receveur general de quatre cens livres Tournois, et par
Remon Monfault, nagueres, et par aucun temps, receveur
general de Normendie, de cinq cens livres Tournois.
Ainsi nous restoit la dicte somme de deux cens vingt
livres Tournois ; de la quelle nous sommes contens et
bien paiez, et en quittons par ces presentes le roy, notre
dit seigneur, le dit receveur general, et tous autres.

En tesmoing de ce nous avons escript a ces dites Date.
presentes notre nom, lesquelles nous avons scellees de
notre signet, a Rouen, le xxvij. jour de Juillet, lan mil
cccc. et quarante six.

Ita est ; Zanonus, episcopus Bayocensis,[1] manu propria.

___

been made to us by the said receiver-general of four hundred
pounds Tournois, and by Remon Monfault, formerly, and for
some time, receiver-general of Normandy, of five hundred
pounds Tournois.  So there remained to us the said sum of
two hundred and twenty pounds Tournois ; of the which we
are content and well paid, and thereof we acquit by these
presents the king, our said lord, the said receiver-general, and
all others.

In witness of this we have written our name to these
presents, which we have sealed with our signet, at Rouen, the
xxvij. day of July, in the year one thousand cccc. and forty-
six.

___

[1] *Ita . . . Bayocensis*] These words are in the bishop's writing.

tenues au dit mandement, touchans grandement le bien
du roy, notre dit seigneur, et de sa seigneurie. Icelle
voyage faict pour ce que alors les dits sergens nestoient pas presens en ceste dite ville de Caen, et que
la chose requeroit celerite ; auquel, tant en allant, sejournant que retournant, le dit messagier a vacque par
de six jours entiers, commencans le dixiesme jour de
cest moys, pour chascun desquelz lui avons tauxe, et
tauxons par ces presentes, la somme de xij. livres vj. d.,
Tournois, auquel prix valleut la dite somme de xxv.
livres, Tournois. Et par raportant ces presentes et
quittance du dit messagier, icelle somme sera alloee en
voz comptes et rabatue de votre recepte ou et par qui
il appartiendra, sans contredit ou difficulte aucune.

Donne a Caen, le xvij. jour de Decembre, lan mil <sup>Date.</sup>
cccc. quarante troys.

LE HENRIE.

---

affairs which are specified in the said order, which closely
concern the welfare of the king, our said lord, and his government. This journey was undertaken because the said
sergeants were not then present in the said town of Caen,
and the matter required expedition ; in which, as well in
going, as in tarrying and returning, the said messenger was
engaged for six entire days, beginning on the tenth day of
this month, for each of which we have awarded him, and
by these presents do award him, the sum of xij. livres vj.*d.*
Tournois, at which rate the said sum amounts to xxv. livres,
Tournois. And on the production of these presents and the
acquittance of the said messenger, this sum shall be allowed
in your accounts and deducted from your receipt, whenever
it shall be fitting, without any contradiction or difficulty.

Dated at Caen, the xvij. day of December, in the year
one thousand cccc. and forty-three.

LE HENRIE.

1444.

MANDATE for the levying of a tax in Languedoc for
the expulsion of the English.[1]

A.D. 1444.
March 25.
—
The dau-
phin Louis

LOYS, aisne filz du roy de France, Daulphin du
Viennois, aux castellain de Pezanas, ou son lieutenant,
et consulz de la ville Dagde et Pezanas, et a chacun
deux, ou a leurs lieutenants, salut.

Comme les gens des trois estats de la seneschausee
de Carcassonne assemblez en la ville de Beziers par
notre mandement et ordonnance, apres que leur avons
fait dire et montrer les grans charges, frais et despens
qui nous a convenu et convient encores plus porter et
soustenir pour reduire et mettre a lobeissance et subjection de monseigneur aucuns cappitaines et gens de
guerre vivans es marches voisines de ce pays de Languedoc, les garder et empescher de entrer, vivre, et sejourner ou dit pays aussi quilz avoient propose a la
totale destruction dicellui, contre le voloir et deffense

[TRANSLATION.]

LOYS, eldest son of the king of France, Dauphin of
Vienne, to the castellan of Pezanas, or his lieutenant, and
to the consuls of Agde and Pezanas, and to each of them,
or to their lieutenants, greeting.

The Three Estates of the seneschalsy of Carcassonne,
assembled in the town of Beziers at our command and
ordinance, after we had caused them to be told and informed of the great charges, costs and expenses which it
was necessary, and still is necessary, for us to sustain and
endure, in order to reduce and bring into obedience and
subjection to our lord certain captains and soldiers living
in the borders contiguous to this country of Languedoc, to
watch them and to hinder them from entering, living and
residing in the said country, as they have proposed to do,
to the total destruction of the same, contrary to the will

[1] From the MS. Fontanieu, 119-120.

de mon dit seigneur et a sa tres grant desplaisance ;
lequel pour ce, entre autres choses, nous avoit envoye
es pays et marches depar deca, et aussi pour retraire
et esloigner dycellui pays les cappitaines et autres gens
de guerre que pour accomplir et mettre affin les choses
dessus dites, nous a este necessaire amener et faire
venir en notre service et compaignie ou dit pays, affin
de garder le dit pays de toute charge, foule et oppres- *orders the*
sion, comme est le plaisir de mon dit seigneur, ne *levying of* *a tax in*
povons fournir, obstant les autres grans despences que *the diocese*
convient faire a mon dit seigneur pour la garde de *of Agde* *and town*
son royaume et seigneurie, pour nous aucunement aidier *of Pezonas.*
apporter et soustenir les dits charges, nous aient donne
et octroye liberalement la somme de neuf mille livres
Tournois, a ycelle somme paier dedans le premier jour
de Septembre prouchain venant.   De la quelle somme
au dit diocese Dagde et ville de Pezanas apartient
pour leur quote et portion la somme de cinq cens
quatre livres, quinze solz, quatre deniers, Tournois ; et

---

and command of my said lord, and to his very great displeasure ; who, on this account, among other things, has
sent us into this country and the marches thereof, as well
to remove and withdraw from this country the captains
and other soldiers, as also to finish and put an end to the
things abovesaid, it has been necessary for us to bring and
to cause to come in our service and company into the said
country, so as to keep the said country from all charge,
crowd and oppression, as is the pleasure of my said lord,
which we cannot supply (being hindered by the great expenses
which my said lord must incur for the keeping of his
kingdom and lordship),—in order somewhat to assist us to
bear and sustain the said charges, have given and granted
us freely the sum of nine thousand livres Tournois, this
sum to be paid by the first day of September next coming.
Of this sum to the said diocese of Agde and to the town
of Pezanas belongs for their quota and proportion the sum
of five hundred and four livres, fifteen shillings, and four

est besoing de icelle somme asseoir, lever et cueillir
et faire promptement venir ens pour convertir es choses
dessus dites, et eviter les inconveniens et domaiges qui
autrement en pourroient ensuir, nous vous mandons
et commandons par ces presentes en commettent que
la dite somme de v$^c$ iiij. livres, vj. s̃. iiij. đ. Tournois,
ensemble les frais necessaires, vous divisez, imposez et
asseez sur tous les consuls, manans et habitans du dit
diocese au mieulx et le plus justement et esgalement
que faire se pourra, le fort portant le foible, et comme
est accoustume de faire, tellement que la dite somme
puisse venir franchement ens ; et la dite assiette faitte
baillez a Estienne Bandinel, lequel nous avons commis
recepveur particulier au dit diocese, et commettons par
ces presentes, sans ce que autre lettre lui en con-
vengne avoir de nous, de faire devoir et diligence de
recevoir la ditte somme, avec les fraiz raisonnablement
necessaires, et icelles sommes baillez a Orto Castellain,
tresorier de mon dit seigneur en la seneschausse de

---

deniers, Tournois, and it is necessary to assess, levy and
collect this sum, and to cause it speedily to be available,
so as to employ it in the matters abovesaid, and to avoid
the injuries and dangers which might otherwise ensue, we
command you by these presents, and put you in commission, to apportion, impose, and assess the said sum of
v$^c$ iiij.*l.* vj.*s.* iiij.*d.* Tournois, together with the necessary
expenses, upon the consuls, residents, and inhabitants of the
said diocese, as best, most justly and equitably may be done,
taking the strong and the weak together, and as it is usual
to do, in such wise that the said sum may arrive freely ;
and the said assessment you shall cause to be delivered to
Stephen Bandinel, whom we have appointed a special commissioner for the said diocese, and do commission him by
these presents, it being unnecessary for him to have any
other letter from us in this matter, for him to do his duty
and diligence in receiving the said sum, with the expenses
reasonably necessary, and these sums to give to Orto Castellain, the treasurer of my said lord in the seneschalry of

Tholouse, receveur general par nous sur ce ordonne de
ce faire, et de contraindre et compeller a payer la dite
somme tous ceux quil apartiendra par prinse, vente
et explectation de leurs biens, et arrestation de leurs
personnes, et par toutes autres voyes accoustumees
pour les propres debtes et affaires de mon dit seigneur
et notres. Et au dit Estienne Bandinel, receveur, a
chacun de vous, comme a lui touche et apartiendra,
avons donne, et donnons par ces presentes, plain povoir,
auctorite et mandement especial, mandons et commandons a tous justiciers, officiez et subgiez de mon dit
seigneur, que a vous et chacun de vous, comme dessus
est dit, obeissent et entendent diligemment, et prestent
et donnent conseil, confort, aide et prisons, ce mestier
est et requis en soit.

Donne a Baga, le xxv. jours de Mars, lan mil quatre Date.
cens, quarante trois.

 Par mon seigneur le Daulphin, le sire de Stissac,
  maistre Yves Desepeaulx, Jehan de Baillon, et
  plusieurs autres presents.

RIBOLE.

---

Tolouse, receiver-general by us herein appointed to do this,
and to constrain and compel to pay the said sum all those
persons to whom it shall appertain so to do, by the seizure,
sale, and exposure of their goods, the arrest of their persons, and by all other ways and means accustomed for the
debts and affairs of my said lord and our own. And to
the said Stephen Baudinel, receiver, and to each of you,
as to him belongs and appertains, we have given, and we
do give by these presents, full power, authority and especial
commandment, and we order and command all justices,
officers and subjects of my said lord, that to you and
each of you, as is abovesaid, to be diligently obedient to
you and attentive, and that they render and give you
counsel, comfort, aid, and prisons, if need be and they are
required so to do.

Given at Baga, the xxv. day of March, in the year one
thousand, four hundred and forty-three.

RIBOLE.

## 1444.

APPOINTMENT of two proctors to serve in the parliament
at Caudebec.[1]

A.D. 1444.
Aug. 19.

The abbot
of Vou,
near Cher-
bourg,
appoints
two proc-
tors.

A TOUS ceulx qui ces presentes lettres verront, Jehan,
par la permission divine, humble abbe du monstier de
Notre Dame de Vou pres Chierebourg, savoir faisons
que nous, en obtemperant aux lettres missives de tres
hault et tres puissant prince, monseigneur le duc Dyork,
lieutenant general et gouverneur de France et Normendie, donnees a Rouen, le xxij. jour de Juillet, et
signees . . . . Drosay, confiant a plain es grans sens et
bonne prudence de maistre Gires Lenglois, prestre, religieux du monstier, et de maistre Thomas Brebenchon,
eulx et chacun deulx par soy, advons commis, ordonne
. . . . et par ces presentes faisons, ordonnons, establissons

---

### [TRANSLATION.]

To all those persons who shall see these present letters,
we John, by divine permission the humble abbot of the
monastery of our Lady de Vou near Chierbourg, make
known that, in obedience to the letters missive of the most
high and most powerful prince, my lord the duke of York,
lieutenant-general and governor of France and Normandy,
dated at Rouen, the xxij. day of July, and signed . . . .
Drosay, fully trusting in the great discretion and good
judgment of master Gires Lenglois, priest, monk of the
monastery, and of master Thomas Brebenchon, have appointed
and ordained them, and each of them by himself, and by
these presents we do make, appoint, and establish them

---

[1] From the original, in the MS. Gaignières, 557.

noz procureurs et commiz pour nous et en notre nom,
pour ..... et comparer au premier jour de Septembre
prouchain, et aultres jours ensuivans, se mestier est, a
Caudebec, devers mon dit seigneur Dyork, en la compaignie de pluseurs prelas et aultres gens deglise,
nobles et bourgois des bonnes villes de Normendie,
affin pour avoir conseil, advis et deliberacion, et conclurre sur la maniere de pourvoier pour le temps
advenir a la garde et deffence et aultres affaires necessaires du dit pais de Normendie. Et aus dits maistre
Gires et maistre Thomas Brebenchon, et a chacun deulx,
advons donne et donnons povoir, puissance et auctorite
dy besongner et conclurre tout autant que nous mesmes
ferions, ou faire pourrions, si present en personne y
estions, sur le contenu et substance des dittes lettres
de mon dit seigneur Diorc. Promettant en bonne foy,
sur la caupcion e ypoteque des biens de notre ditte
eglise, tenir tous ce qui par nos diz procureurs, ou
commis, ou lun deulx, sera fait, advise, conclut et

---

to be our proctors and commissioners for us and in our
name, to ..... and appear on the first day of September
next, and on the other days ensuing, if need be, at Caudebec,
in the presence of my said lord of York, in the company of
many prelates and other churchmen, nobles and burgesses
of the good towns of Normandy, in order to have counsel,
advice and deliberation, and to conclude how to provide for
the future for the guard and defence and the other necessary
affairs of the said country of Normandy. And to the said master
Gires and master Thomas Brebenchon, and to each of them,
we have given, and do give, power and authority hereupon
to deliberate and conclude, as entirely as we ourselves could
or might do, if we were there present in person, upon the
contents and substance of the said letters of my said lord
of York. Promising in good faith, upon the caption and
hypothec of the goods of our said church, to observe all
that by our said proctors or commissioners, or by one of them,
shall be done, advised, concluded and deliberated, upon the

delibere sur le contenu aux dittes lettres, sans aller allencontre en aucune maniere.

Date. En tesmoing de ce, nous advons selle ces presentes de notre propre seel, le xix. jour Daoust, lan mil iiij. c. xliiij.

contents of the said letters, without gainsaying in any manner.

In witness whereof we have sealed these presents with our own seal, the xix. day of August, in the year one thousand cccc. xliiij.

## 1444.

LETTER from Henry VI. to Charles VII. respecting his intended marriage, and desiring peace with France.

A.D. 1444.
Aug. 21.

Thanks Charles for the kind reception of the English ambassadors,

TRESHAULT et excellent prince, notre treschier onole de France, Henry par la grace de Dieu roy de France et Dangleterre, salut, avec cordial desir de toute bonne et mutuele amour et concorde.

### [TRANSLATION.]

To the most high and excellent prince, our very dear uncle of France, Henry, by the grace of God, king of France and England, sends greeting, with the cordial desire of all good and mutual love and concord.

¹ From the original, upon paper (without watermark) in the Baluse MS. 9037-7, No. 24.

Treshault et excellent prince et notre treschier oncle, nouvellement sont retournez pardevers nous notre treschier et feal cousin le conte de Suffolk, grant maistre de notre hostel, et autres noz serviteurs que tant pour le bien de paix, comme pour avoir cognoissance et nous certiffier de voz bon estat et sante, et aussi pour vous ouvrir en announces grant confidence notre desir au regard du mariaige de his intended nous et de notre treschiere et tresamee compaigne la marriage, royne, fille de notre treschier et tresame pere le roy de Sicile, avions nagaires envoiez pardevers vous. Les quelz, apres ce que avons par eulx receu voz gracieuses lettres, que joyeusement avons veues, nous ont certiffie de voz bon estat et sante, et expose en quante doulceur et lonneur les avez, pour amour de nous, voulu recevoir et traictier, et faire par voz pais et subgietz gracieusement traictier et recevoir, et comment a leuvre du dit mariaige vous a pleu vacquer et entendre de grant voulente et bonne affection, et finablement faire vacquer, entendre et communiquer sur la

---

Most high and excellent prince, and our very dear uncle, our faithful cousin the earl of Suffolk, grand master of our household, and others of our servants, have lately returned to us, whom we have of late sent to you, as well as upon the matter of a peace as to have information and knowledge respecting your good estate and health, and also to open to you in great confidence our desire in regard to the marriage between us and our very dear and well-beloved companion, the queen, the daughter of our very dear and well-beloved father, the king of Sicily. These messengers, after we had received by them your gracious letters, which we saw with joy, have certified us of your good estate and health, and declared to us with what gentleness and honour you were pleased to receive them and treat them, out of love towards us, and how graciously you caused them to be treated and received by your country and subjects, and how it pleased you to employ and devote yourself to the business of the said marriage with great will and good affection, and finally devoted yourself to deliberate and discuss the matter of the

*and wishes peace.* matiere de la dicte paix, et pour le repos et aaise du povre peuple longuement afflict et languissant aloccasion des pestilensieuses guerres qui tant ont dure, prendre et conclure abstinence pour certain temps, pendant lequel on labourera efficacement de votre part, et de la notre, a trouver voies et manieres pour parvenir, moyennant la grace de notre Benoit Redempteur, a finale conclusion de paix perpetuele et amoureuse entre nous et les deux royaumes. Auquel bien vous sentons estre entierement, et pareillement sommes nous, enclinez et disposez, qui nous est le plus souverain bien que puissons en terre avoir et desirer.

De la quele votre disposicion, inclinacion et voulente, regracions notre Seigneur de ce et des autres choses dessus dictes, dont notre dit cousin et les autres devant diz nous ont fait agreable et plaisant relacion, et mesmement de ce que nous avez escript par vos dictes lettres, que, pour plus amplement nous declairer votre entencion, et traictier final appointement avecques

---

said peace ; and for the repose and ease of the poor people, long afflicted and languishing by occasion of these pestilential wars which have so long continued, to take and conclude an abstinence for a certain time, during which the strenuous effort shall be made on your part, and on ours also, to discover some way and means, by the grace of our Blessed Redeemer, to arrive at the final conclusion of a perpetual and living peace between us and the two kingdoms. To which blessing you feel entirely inclined and disposed, as do we in like manner ; for peace is the most sovereign good which we can have or desire upon earth.

For this your disposition, inclination and good will, we thank our Saviour, and for all other things above-mentioned, whereof our said cousin and the other persons above-named have made an agreeable and pleasant report, and especially as to the business about which you have written in your said letters, viz., that, in order more fully to declare to us your intention and to treat of a final arrangement with us respecting the business of the said

nous sur le fait de la dicte paix, et aussi pour nous visiter et savoir la certainete de notre bonne prosperite, avez delibere de briefment envoier pardevers nous de voz gens notables, sommes tresjoyeux, et vous en remercions si effectueusement et de cueur comme plus povons. Desqueles voz gens desirons la venue, et les verrons joyeusement, voulentiers et de cuer.

Si vous prions, treshault et excellent prince, notre treschier oncle, que pour le brief et bon accomplissement des choses commencees, vous plaise envoier les dessus diz pardevers nous, ainsi que nous escripvez, et par eulx et autres venans pardeca, nous certiffier de votre bon estat et prosperite, qui nous sera chose joyeuse a savoir et oyr ; et samblablement serons de temps en temps envers vous de tres bon cueur.

*Will be glad to see Charles' ambassadors.*

Treshault et excellent prince, et notre treschier oncle, nous prions le Benoist Filz de Dieu quil vous ait en sa sainte garde.

---

peace, and also to visit us to know for certain of our good prosperity, you have determined shortly to send to us some of your honourable people, whereof we are very glad, and hereof we thank you as effectively and cordially as we best may. We desire the arrival of your people, and will see them joyfully, willingly aud cordially.

Wherefore we pray you, most high and excellent prince, our very dear uncle, that for the speedy and good accomplishment of the matters thus begun, it would please you to send the persons abovesaid to us, as you have written to us, and by them and by others coming into England to certify us of your good estate and prosperity, which to us will be a joyful thing to know and hear ; and in like manner from time to time we shall be right heartily glad to have tidings of you.

Most high and excellent prince, and our most dear uncle, we pray the Blessed Son of God to have you in His holy keeping.

Date. Escript soubz notre signet, en notre parc de Woude-
stok, le xxj.[1] jour Daoust.

HENRY.[2]

(*Dorso.*) A treshault et excellent prince, notre
treschier oncle de France.

---

Written under our signet, in our park of Woodstock, the
xxj. day of August.

HENRY.

(*Dorso.*) To the most high and excellent prince, our
very dear uncle of France.

---

## 1445.

RECEIPT by sir Thomas Hoo for 1,000 salus of gold
paid by the duke of Orleans for the demolition
of Galardon and Tourville.[3]

A.D. 1445.
March 18.

Receipt by
Thomas
Hoo.

NOUS, Thomas Hoo, chevalier, chancellier en France
et Normandie, confessons avoir eu et receu de tres honnore seigneur Jehan bastard Dorleans, conte de Dunois, la somme de mil salus dor par les mains de Noel
Labarge, notre serviteur, en vins et drap de soye;
de la quelle somme de mil salus nous nous tenons

---

[TRANSLATION.]

WE, Thomas Hoo, knight, chancellor in France and Normandy, acknowledge that we have had and received of the
most honourable lord, John bastard of Orleans, count Dunois,
the sum of one thousand salus of gold by the hands of Noel
Labarge, our servant, in wines and silk cloth ; of the which
sum of one thousand salus we hold ourselves as accounted

---

[1] From the original receipt, preserved in the MS. Fontanieu, 117-
118. A small round seal in red
wax remains.

[2] The numerals are inserted in a
blank left when the letter was
copied.

[3] This signature is autograph.

pour comptes, et promettons deduire et rebattre sur
les scellez que tenons de hault et puissant prince, monseigneur le duc Dorleans, du dit tres honnore seigneur
le conte de Dunois et du Vidame de Chartres, pour
partie de la somme contenue es dits scellez, a cause
de la demolition de Galardon et Tourville.

Tesmoing notre signe manuel et signet, cymis, a Date.
Paris,[1] le dixhuitieme jour de Mars, lan mil cccc.
quarante quatre.

Hoo.[2]

---

withal, and we promise to deduct and withdraw them from
the bonds which we hold of the high and powerful prince
my lord the duke of Orleans, of the said most honourable
lord the count of Dunois, and of the vidâme of Chartres, as
part of the sum contained in the said bonds, in consequence of the demolition of Galardon and Tourville.

Witness our sign-manual and signet hereunto placed, at
Paris, the eighteenth day of March, in the year one thousand
cccc. forty-four.

Hoo.

## 1445.

LETTER of Charles VII. to Henry VI., complaining of
the delay in the surrender of Maine.[3]

A TRESHAULT et puissant prince, notre treschier A.D. 1445.
nepveu Dangleterre, Charles, par la grace de Dieu,

Complains
of the con-
duct of Go,
Heton and
To the most high and powerful prince, our very dear Munde-
nephew of England, Charles, by the grace of God, king of ford.

---

[1] *A Paris*] Written on a blank.

[2] The signature is autograph.

[3] From the Baluze MS. 9037-7,

No. 36. A fair copy, written upon
paper by a contemporary hand. The
watermark is cow with very large
horns.

roy de France, singuliere affection damour et parfait
vouloir a toute vraye paix, entiere union, et bonne
concorde.

Treshault et puissant prince, notre tres chier nep-
vieu, ainsi que par plusieurs foiz vous avons escript,
oir de voz nouvelles en bien et estre acertenez du
bon estat, sante, et prosperite de votre tres noble
personne, nous est grant liesse et consolation.  Pourquoy vous prions que souvent nous en faciez savoir
pour notre singulier resjoissement.  Et si de nous vous
plaisoit savoir le semblable, nous estions a la facon
de cestes en tresbonne disposition, graces a notre Seigneur, qui le pareil tous temps vous vueille octroier,
ainsi que de bon cuer le desirons et que pour notre
propre personne mieulx le saurions souhaitier.

Au surplus, tres hault et puissant prince, notre
treschier nepveu, vous savez les promesses par vous a
nous faictes touchans la delivrance du Mans, et des
autres places qui estoient en votre obeissance ou conte

---

France, wishes singular affection and love and a perfect
desire for all true peace, entire union, and good concord.

Most high and powerful prince, our very dear nephew,
as we have oftentimes written to you, it is to us great
pleasure and comfort to hear good tidings of you, and to
be ascertained of the good estate, health and prosperity, of
your most noble person.  Wherefore we pray you that you
would often let us know hereof for our singular rejoicing.
And if it please you to hear the like of us, we were at the
making of these present letters in very good health, thanks
to our Saviour, whom may it please always to grant the like
to you, which we desire as heartily as we could wish it for
our own person.

Moreover, most high and powerful prince, our dear
nephew, you know the promises made by you to us touching the deliverance of Le Mans, and the other places which
were in subjection to you in the comté of Maine, and the

du Mayne, et les causes pour les quelles avez este meu
de ce faire ; qui sont pour mieulx et plus de legier
pervenir au bien de paix entre vous et nous. Car,
comme tousjours vous a este dit et par nous souventes
foiz escript, la dicte delivrance mise a execution effec-
tuelment est ung des meillieurs et plus convenables
moitees pour y pervenir. Et en laquelle matiere con-
cernant le fait de la dicte delivrance, auparavant et
depuis le temps quelle se devoit faire, tant envers
Mathieu Go et Foulques Heton, commissaires par vous
ordonnez a icelle faire, comme envers Moundeford et les
autres qui tenoient les dits places, nous nous sommes
mis en tous les devoirs qui convenablement faire se
est peu, et plus avant quil ne sembloit a beaucop le
gens que faire se deust, ne que vous mesmes lentendies.
A quoy toutes voies les dessus diz nont aucunement
voulu obtemperer. Et voians les subterfuges, cautelles
et dissimulacions quilz faisoient, (pour plus encore nous
mettre en notre devoir, et a ce que par vous et eulx

---

causes by which you have been moved to do this ; which
are that you might the better and more easily attain the
advantage of a peace between you and us. For, as it has
always been said to you and oftentimes written by us, the
said deliverance effectively put in execution is one of the
best and most fitting means to attain peace. And in this
matter concerning the business of the said deliverance, both
before and since the time when it ought to have been done, as
well in regard to Matthew Go and Foulques Heton, commissioners appointed by you to do this, as also in regard to Mundeford and the others who held the said places, we have done
our duty in every way in which it could possibly be done, and
indeed we have herein done more than in the opinion of many
people we ought to have done, or than you yourself know.
To these the persons abovesaid would in no wise obey.
And seeing the subterfuges, pretences and dissimulations to
which they resorted, (in order that we might still further
perform our duty, and that you and your subjects might

de votre obeissance feussent sceuz et entenduz les bons
termes que avons tenuz en ceste partie, et les devoirs
dessus dits, en quoy nous sommes mis, et que chacun
congneust la bonne entencion que avons au bien des
matieres principales, et a ce quelles sentretenissent et
peussent estre conduictes a bonne fin et conclusion,
et que a notre deffaulte nous ne vouldrions que aucune
roupture ou inconvenient y advensist, ne que lon peust
dire que voulsissions faire aucune surprinse alencontre
de vous, ne de chose qui soit en votre obeissance, a
votre tort,) a vous envoie noz solempnelz messaiges et
ambaxeurs devers les gens de votre grant conseil estans
a Rouen, pour bien amplement leur remonstrer les
choses dessus dits.   Entre lesquelz voz conseilliers dune
part, et nos diz ambaxeurs dautre, (veuz premierement
et bien entenduz les subterfuges, cautelles et dissimulacions dessusditz que faisoient les diz Mathieu Go,
Heton, Mundefort et autres, qui tenoient les places, qui

---

know and understand the good faith which we have kept
in this matter, and have discharged the aforesaid duties
which we have undertaken as incumbent on us, and that
everyone should know the good intention which we have
towards the accomplishment of the chief matters, and that
they might be preserved and come to a good end and issue,
and that we would not have it that by any shortcoming
on our part the matter should be broken off, or any mischief should arise, nor that it might be said that we would
take any undue advantage over you to your harm, nor avail
ourselves of any occurrence which might arise within your
jurisdiction,) we sent our accredited messengers and ambassadors to the members of your great council which are at
Rouen, to show them at full length the matters abovesaid.
Between which your said councillors on the one part, and our
said ambassadors on the other (having in the first place seen
and well considered the subterfuges, pretences and dissimulations abovesaid made by the said Matthew Go, Heton,
Mundeford and others, who hold the strongholds, which is

sera allouee es comptes du dit receveur general et rabatue de sa recepte par noz amez et feaulx les gens de nos comptes a Rouen ; ausquelz nous mandons que ainsi le facent, sans dificulte ou contredit.

Donne a Rouen, le cinquiesme jour de Fevrier, lan Date. de gracé mil, quatre cens, quarante deux, et de notre regne le vingtunzieme.

> Par le roy, a la relacion de monseigneur le duc de York, lieutenant general et gouverneur de France et Normandie.[1]
>
> DROSAY.

---

Tournois, shall be allowed in the accounts of the said receiver-general and deducted from his receipt by our beloved and faithful accountants at Rouen, whom we command so to do, without difficulty or opposition.

Dated at Rouen, the fifth day of February, in the year of grace one thousand, four hundred and forty-two, and of our reign the twenty-first.

> By the king, at the relation of my lord the duke of York, lieutenant-general and governor of France and Normandy.
>
> DROSAY.

---

[1] The original receipt, signed, "Ita est, Zanonig, episcopus Bayo- "censis, manu propria," and dated 29 May, 1443, is also contained in the same manuscript.

---

## 1443.

A.D. 1443.
Feb. 11.

———

92l. 6s. 10d.
to be paid
to the
English
garrison at
Villedieu.

MANDATE for the payment of troops in the garrison of
Villedieu.[1]

THOMAS, sire de Scalles et de Nucelles, vidame de
Chartres et seneschal de Normandie, au viconte de
Villedieu, salut.

Comme, par vertu de notre mandement, en dabte le
quart jour de derrain Janvier passe, ait este assis sur
les vicontes de Avrenches, Vire, Mortaing et Conde,
la somme de xiij.c. lxx. livres, Tournois, pour le paiement des gages des gens darmes et de trait estans au
dit lieu de Villedieu, tenans frontiere aux adversiers du
roy, notre seigneur, occupans les places de Granvelle et
le Mont Saint Michiel ; et il soit ainxi que Jehan
Blacet, Jehan Parquer, lances a cheval, et xxxj. archiers
en leur compaignie, aient ete passes et alloues aux mon-

---

[TRANSLATION.]

THOMAS, lord Scales and of Nucelles, vidame of Chartres
and seneschal of Normandy, to the vicomte of Villedieu,
greeting.

Since, by virtue of our command, dated the fourth day of
January last past, there have been assessed upon the vicomtés of Avranches, Vire, Mortain and Condé, the sum of
xiij.c. lxx. livres, Tournois, for payment of the wages of
the men-at-arms and archers who are in the said place
of Villedieu, guarding the frontier against the adversaries of
the king our lord, who occupy the strongholds of Granvelle
and the Mont Saint Michel ; so it is that Jehan Blacet,
Jehan Parquer, mounted lances, and xxxj. archers in their
company, have been passed and allowed at the musters

---

[1] From the original in the MS. Gaignières, 557.

stres faittes au dit lieu de Villedieu devant maistre Robert Byotte, viconte de Coustances, et vous, a ce commis, le xij. jour du dit moys de Janvier, comme par la roulle des dittes monstres nous est apparu, pour les dits xv. jours ensuivans le dit xij. jour de Janvier, sans de ce avoir eu paiement, parce que la ditte somme de xiij.c. lxx. livres, Tournois, ne suffisoit pas a payer le nombre des gens contenues et declaires ou dit roulle de monstres ; vous mandons que, des deniers y estans de lassiette que aujourduy y a este faitte sur les dittes vicontes par vertu de notre mandement, vous paies, bailles et delivres aux dites lances et archiers la somme de iiij$^{xx}$. xij. livres, v s̃. x d̃. Tournois, que pour leur gaiges des dittes xv. jours leur compettent et appartiennent. Et par rapportant ces presentes avecques quittance des dittes lances, la ditte somme de iiij$^{xx}$. xij l̃. v s̃. x d̃. vous sera allouee et rabatue sur ce que recevres des deniers de la ditte presente assiette, partout ou il appartiendra. Ce faittes sans deffault.

---

made at the said place of Villedieu before master Robert Byotte, vicomte of Coutances and yourself, commissioners for the same, on the xij. day of the said month of January, as by the roll of the said musters is clear to us, for the said xv. days following the said xij. day of January, without having had payment for the same, because the said sum of xiij.c. lxx. livres, Tournois, was not sufficient to pay the number of the troops who were contained and declared on the said muster-roll ; we command you that, out of the money arising from the assessment which has to-day been made upon the said vicomtés by virtue of our mandate, you pay, give, and deliver to the said lances and archers the sum of iiij$^{xx}$. xij. livres, v s̃. x d̃. Tournois, which are due and belong to them as their wages for the said xv. days. And upon the production of these presents, together with the acquittance of the said lances, the said sum of iiij$^{xx}$. xij l̃. v s̃. x d̃. shall be allowed to you and deducted from what you shall receive of the money of the present assessment, wherever it shall appear. This do without fail.

**Date.**

Donne au dit lieu de Villedieu, le xj. jour de Fevrier, lan mil, iiij.c. xlij.

*Signe,* MAILLART.

---

Dated at the said place of Villedieu, the xj. day of February, in the year one thousand, iiij.c. xlij.

*Signed,* MAILLART.

---

### 1443.

**A.D. 1443.**
**Mar. 2.**

**300*l*. T. to be paid to the captain of Gisors.**

PARTICULARS respecting the settlement of a dispute between the English captains of Gournay and Gisors.[1]

HENRY, par le grace de Dieu, roy de France et Dangleterre, a noz amez et feaulx conseilliers, les tresoriers et generaulx gouverneurs de noz finances en France et Normandie, salut et dilection.

Comme, sur le debat et discord qui estoit meu entre noz bien amez Guillaume Chambrelain, chevalier, capitaine de Gournay et Gerberoy, dune part, et Guillaume Corwen, escuyer, capitaine de Gisors, dautre

---

[TRANSLATION.]

HENRY, by the grace of God, king of France and England to our beloved and faithful councillors, the treasurers and governors-general of our finances in France and Normandy, greeting and love.

Since, in the matter of the dispute and disagreement which has arisen between our well-beloved Guillaume Chambrelain, knight, captain of Gournay and Gerberoy, on the one part, and Guillaume Corwen, esquire, captain of Gisors,

---

[1] From the MS. Fontanieu, 119–120.

part, pour [et] a cause des apastis des dits lieux et places de Gournay et Gisors, certain appoinctement ait este par nous fait, par moyen duquel appoinctement (dont les dits parties ont ete et sont daccord) au dit Guillaume Corwen, entre autres choses coutenues en icelui appoinctement, ayons ordonne et accorde, ordonnons et accordons par ces presentes, quil ait et pregne de nous, pour une et ceste foiz seullement, la somme de trois cens livres, Tournois, et ce oultre et par dessus autres payemens contenus en ces endenteurs faictes de la garde et cappitainerie du dit lieu de Gisors ; nous, (par ladvis and deliberacion de notre tres chier et tres ame cousin, Richart duc Dyork, notre lieutenant general et gouverneur depar nous de noz royaume de France et duchie de Normandie,) vous mandons et par ces presentes expressement enjoignons que, par notre bien ame Pierre Baille, receveur general de noz dits finances, et des deniers de sa recepte, vous

---

on the other part, for and in consequence of the contributions of the said places and fortresses of Gournay and Gisors, a certain agreement has been made by us, in consequence of which agreement (by means of which the said parties have been and are reconciled) we have appointed and ordained, and by these presents do appoint and ordain, to the said Guillaume Corwen, amongst other things contained in the same agreement, that he shall have and receive of us, for once and this time only, the sum of three hundred livres, Tournois, and this over and above the other payments contained in his indentures made concerning the guard and captainship of the said place of Gisors ; we, (by the advice and deliberation of our very dear and well-beloved cousin, Richard, duke of York, our lieutenant-general and the governor on our behalf of our realm of France and duchy of Normandy,) command, and by these presents expressly enjoin you that, by our well-beloved Pierre Baille, receiver-general of our finances, and out of the money by him received, you

faitez paier, baillier et delivrer au dit Guillaume Corwen la dite somme de trois cens livres, Tournois.    Et
par rapportant ces presentes et quictance souffisant du
dit Guillaume Corwen tant seullement, icelle somme
de trois cens livres, Tournois, sera allouee es comptes
du dit receveur general et rabatue de sa recepte par
noz amez et feaulz les gens de noz comptes a Rouen ;
aux quelz nous mandons que ainsi le facent sans difficulte ou contredit aucun.

Date.          Donne a Rouen, le second jour de Mars, lan de
grace, mil cccc. quarante deux, et de notre regne le
vint ungiesme.

Par le roy, a la relation de monseigneur le duc
Dyork, lieutenant general et gouverneur de France et
Normandie.

DROSAY.

---

cause to be paid, given and delivered to the said Guillaume
Corwen, the said sum of three hundred livres, Tournois.
And upon the simple production of these presents, along
with a sufficient discharge of the said Guillaume Corwen,
the said sum of three hundred livres, Tournois, shall be
allowed in the accounts of the said receiver-general, and
deducted from his receipt by our beloved and faithful accountants at Rouen ; whom we command to do this without
any difficulty or opposition.

Dated at Rouen, the second day of March, in the year of
grace one thousand cccc. and forty-two, and of our reign
the twenty-first.

By the king, at the relation of my lord the duke of York,
lieutenant-general and governor of France and Normandy.

DROSAY.

## 1443.

MANDATE by Richard duke of York, that a representative from the city of Avranches do attend the
meeting of the Three Estates at Caudebec.[1]

A.D. 1443.
22 July.

Summons
to the Par-
liament at
Caudebec.

DEPAR le duc de York, lieutenant general et
gouverneur de France et Normandie.

Chiers et bien amez. Pour avoir bon conseil et advis
sur la matiere de pourveoir pour le temps advenir a
la garde et defense et autres affaires necessaires de
ceste seigneurie, nous mandons venir pardevers nous
plusieurs prelas et autres gens deglise, nobles et
bourgoiz des bonnes villes de ceste dicte seigneurie, si
vous mandons depar monseigneur le roy et nous que,
au premier jour du moys de Septembre prouchainement venant, vous envoyez pardevers nous en la ville de
Caudebec une personne notable dentre vous, qui y soit
garnie de pouvoir souffisant depar vous pour adviser,
deliberer et conclurre en la matiere dessus dicte.

---

### [TRANSLATION.]

By the duke of York, lieutenant-general and governor of
France and Normandy.

Dear and well-beloved. In order to have good counsel
and advice upon the business of providing during the time
to come for the protection and defence and for other the
necessary affairs of this lordship, we are commanding many
prelates and other churchmen, nobles and burgesses of the
good towns of this said lordship, to come to us ;—wherefore we command and charge you very expressly on the
part of my lord the king and ourselves, that upon the
first day of the month of September next coming you send
to us to the town of Caudebec, a person of repute from
among you, who shall be provided with sufficient power
upon your part to advise, deliberate and conclude in the
matter above said.

---

[1] From the original writ in the MS. Gaignières, 557.

Chiers et bien amez, notre Seigneur soit garde de vous.

Date. Donne a Rouen, soubz notre signet, le xxij. jour de Juillet.

DROSAY.

(*Dorso.*) A noz chiers et bien amez, les bourgoiz, manans et habitans de la ville Lavrenches.[1]

---

Dear and well-beloved, the Lord be your keeper.

Dated at Rouen, under our signet, the xxij. day of July.

DROSAY.

(*Dorso.*) To our dear and well-beloved, the burgesses, residents and inhabitants of the town of Avranches.

---

[1] Letters of summons (all of which exist in the same volume), were addressed to the following communities and individuals :—

A notre chier et bien ame, Robert de Fresville, escuier.

A notre chier et bien ame, Thomas Pellew, viconte de Carenton.

A noz chiers et bien amez les bourgoiz, manans et habitans de la ville de Valongnes.

A notre chier et bien ame, Guillem de Gaillon, escuier.

A noz chiers et bien amez,

les bourgoiz, manans et habitans de la ville de Bayeux (2 deputies).

A noz chiers et bien amez, les bourgois, manans et habitans de la ville de Coustances (2 deputies).

A noz chiers et bien amez, les bourgois, manans et habitans de la ville de Vernon.

A noz chiers et bien amez, les bourgois, manans et habitans de la ville de Lisieux (2 deputies).

---

[TRANSLATION.]

To our dear and well-beloved, Robert de Fresville, esquire.

To our dear and well-beloved, Thomas de Pellew, sheriff of Carentan.

To our dear and well-beloved, the burgesses, residents and inhabitants of Valognes.

To our dear and well-beloved, Guillem de Gaillon, esquire.

To our dear and well-beloved,

the burgesses, residents and inhabitants of the city of Bayeux (2 deputies).

To our dear and well-beloved, the burgesses, residents and inhabitants of the city of Coutances (2 deputies).

To our dear and well-beloved, the burgesses, residents and inhabitants of the town of Vernon.

To our dear and well-beloved, the burgesses, residents and inhabitants of the city of Lisieux (2 deputies).

## 1443.

SUMMONS to Durand de Thieville to attend the Parliament to be held at Caudebec.[1]

DEPAR le duc Dyork, lieutenant general et gouverneur de France et Normandie.

A.D. 1443.
July 24.

Summons
to attend
the Parlia-
ment at
Caudebec.

---

[TRANSLATION.]

By the duke of York, lieutenant-general and governor of France and Normandy.

---

A notre chier et bien ame Hue Spencier, escuier, bailli de Costentin. (Dated 17 August.)

A nos chiers et bien amez, les bourgoiz, manans et habitans de la ville de Vire.

A notre chier et bien ame Guillem Raison, esleu de Falloize. (Dated 22 August.)

A noz chiers et bien amez les bourgeoiz, manans et habitans de la ville de Conches.

A noz cheirs et bein amez, les bourgeoix, manans et habitans de la ville de Saint Lo.

---

To our dear and well-beloved, Hue Spencier, esquire, bailly of the Cotentin. (Dated 17 August.)

To our dear and well-beloved, the burgesses, residents and inhabitants of our town of Vire.

To our dear and well-beloved, Guillem Raison, elect of Faloise. (Dated 22 August.)

To our dear and well-beloved, the burgesses, residents and inhabitants of the town of Conches.

To our dear and well-beloved, the burgesses, residents and inhabitants of the town of Saint-Lo.

A notre treschier et bien ame messire Thierry de Robessart, chevalier.

A noz chiers et bien amez les bourgoiz, manans et habitans de la ville du Pontaudemer.

A notre chier et bien ame, Jehan Pipart, receveur des octroiz de la viconte Dauge. (Dated 7 August.)

A notre chier et bien ame Pierre de Rupall, escuier.

A notre chier et bien ame Guillem Poisson, viconte de Valongnes (Dated 7 August.)

---

To our dear and well-beloved, messire Thierry de Robessart, knight.

To our dear and well-beloved, the burgesses, residents and inhabitants of the town of Pont Audemer.

To our dear and well-beloved John Pipart, receiver of the dues of the vicomté of Auge. (Dated 7 August.)

To our dear and well-beloved, Pierre de Rupalle, esquire.

To our dear and well-beloved, Guillem Poisson, sheriff of Valognes. (Dated 7 August.)

[1] From the original, on paper, in the MS. Gaignières, 557.

Chier et bien ame. Pour avoir conseil et adviz sur la maniere de pourveoir pour le temps advenir a la garde et deffense et aux autres affaires necessaires de ceste seigneurie, nous mandons venir par devers nous plusieurs prelas et autres gens deglise, nobles et bourgois des bonnes villes de ceste dicte seigneurie, si vous mandons et chargons bien expressement depar monseigneur le roy et nous que, au xiiij. jour du mois Daoust prochainement venant, vouz soyez en votre propre personne pardevers nous en la ville de Caudebec pour adviser, deliberer et conclurre en de la matere dessusdit.

Chier et bien ame, notre Seigneur soit garde de vous.

Date.        Donne a Rouen, soubz notre signet, le xxiiij. jour de Juillet.[1]

DROSAY.

(*Dorso.*) A notre chier et bien ame, Durand de Thieville, escuier.

---

Dear and well-beloved. In order to have counsel and advice upon the business of providing, during the time to come, for the protection and defence and for other necessary affairs of this lordship, we are commanding many prelates and other churchmen, nobles and burgesses of the good towns of this said lordship to come to us ;—wherefore we command and charge you very expressly on the part of my lord the king and ourselves, that upon the xiiij. day of the month of August next coming, you in your proper person be with us in the town of Caudebec, to advise, deliberate and conclude in the matter above said.

Dear and well-beloved, our Lord be your keeper.

Dated at Rouen, under our signet, the xxiiij. day of July.

(*Dorso.*) To our dear and well-beloved, Durand de Thieville, esquire.

---

[1] The session was transferred to Rouen, as appears by the following memorandum, which is contained in the same manuscript :—

" Ce sont ceulx des estatz man- " dez au xiiij. jour Daoust, mil " cccc. quarante trois, a Caudebec, et " qui se sont presentez a Rouen,

## 1443.

MANDATE for the payment of a messenger employed to summon troops for the siege of Beaumont-le-Vicomte.[1]

A.D. 1443.
Dec. 17.

Mandate for the payment of a messenger.

EUSTACE QUENINET, lieutenant general de noble homme, messire Richart Haringthon, chevalier, bailly de Caen, au viconte du dit lieu, ou a son lieutenant, salut.

Nous vous mandons et enjoignons que, des deniers de votre recepte, vous payez et delivrez a Jehan Pain, messagier a cheval, la somme de vint cinq livres, Tournois, pour sa peinne, sallaire et despens davoir este, par commendement de justice, chevaulchie hastivement de ceste ville de Caen es sergenteries Deurecy, Preaulx, Villierz et Cheux, et de len alant devers les sergens

---

[TRANSLATION.]

EUSTACE QUENINET, lieutenant-general of the noble man, messire Richard Haringthon, knight, bailly of Caen, to the viconte of the said place, or to his lieutenant, greeting.

We command and enjoin you that, out of the money by you received, you pay and deliver to Jehan Pain, mounted messenger, the sum of twenty-five livres, Tournois, for his trouble, wage, and expense, in having, at the command of the law, ridden with speed from this town of Caen to the sergeantries of Evrecy, Preaux, Villers and Cheux, and for having gone to the sergeants of the said sergeantries,

---

" ou la convention en estoit trans-
" late le xviij. jour du dit moys
" Daoust."

Then follows a notice of the attendance, arranged as under—

"Du bailliage de Rouen :
  Gens deglise, Nobles, Bourgoiz.

Du bailliage de Caen :
  Gens deglise, Nobles, Bourgoiz de villes.

Du bailliage de Costentin :
  Gens deglise, Nobles, Officiers, Bourgoiz.

Du bailliage de Caulx :
  Gens deglise, Nobles, Bourgoiz.

Du bailliage Dalencon :
  Gens deglise, Nobles, Bourgoiz.

Du bailliage de Gisors.

Du bailliage de Mante."

[1] From the MS. Fontanieu, 119–120.

des dits sergenteries leur porter a chacun ung executoire du mandement de mon dit seigneur le bailly,
icellui executoire des lettres closes de tres hault et
puissant prince, monseigneur le duc de Sommerset, pour
par les dits sergens cryer et publier, chacun es mettes
de sa sergenterie accoustumez a faire crys et publications, que toutes gens de guerre, quelz quilz soient,
estans et vivans sur le pays, et tous autres qui sont
hors de garnisons et de gaiges, soient gardes de paroisse ou autres, se fassent pretz et se tirent devers
mon seigneur le bailly en ceste ville de Caen, dedans
Samedy ou Dimence prouchain venant, ou plus tard,
pour aller en la compaignie de mon dit seigneur le
bailly devers mon dit seigneur le duc, lequel avoit
assegie la forteresse de Beaumont le Viconte, occupee
par les ennemis et adversaires du roy, notre dit
seigneur, la quelle estoit en composition a rendre, ou
combatre, dedans certain terme, pour expulser les dits
ennemis, ainsi que mestier sera, et autres choses con-

---

to carry to each of them an official copy of the orders of my
said lord the bailly, the said being a copy of the closed letters
of the most high and mighty prince, my lord the duke of
Somerset, to the effect that an announcement and proclamation should be made by the said sergeants, each within
the limits of his sergeantry, where it is usual to make an-
nouncements and publications, that all fighting men, whoso-
ever they be, who are and live within the country, and all
others who are outside the garrisons and at wages, whether
they be guards of parishes or others, should make themselves ready and should come to my said lord the bailly into
this town of Caen by Saturday or Sunday next following, at
the latest, to go in the company of said lord the bailly
to join my said lord the duke, who has besieged the fortress
of Beaumont le Vicomte, which is held by the enemies and
adversaries of the king, our said lord, and which had agreed
to surrender, or fight, within a fixed term, to drive out the
said enemies, as shall be necessary, and for other certain

# LIST OF WORKS

PUBLISHED

By the late Record and State Paper Commissioners,
or under the Direction of the Right Honourable
the Master of the Rolls, which may be purchased of Messrs. Longman and Co., London;
Messrs. J. H. and J. Parker, Oxford and London; Messrs. Macmillan and Co., Cambridge and
London; Messrs. A. and C. Black, Edinburgh;
and Mr. A. Thom, Dublin.

---

## PUBLIC RECORDS AND STATE PAPERS.

---

ROTULORUM ORIGINALIUM IN CURIA SCACCARII ABBREVIATIO. Henry
III.—Edward III. *Edited by* HENRY PLAYFORD, Esq. 2 vols.
folio (1805—1810). *Price 25s.* boards, or 12*s.* 6*d.* each.

CALENDARIUM INQUISITIONUM POST MORTEM SIVE ESCAETARUM.
Henry III.—Richard III. *Edited by* JOHN CALEY and JOHN
BAYLEY, Esqrs. Vols. 2, 3, and 4, folio (1806—1808; 1821—1828),
boards : vols. 2 and 3, *price 21s.* each; vol. 4, *price 24s.*

LIBRORUM MANUSCRIPTORUM BIBLIOTHECÆ HARLEIANÆ CATALOGUS.
Vol. 4. *Edited by* The Rev. T. H. HORNE. (1812), folio, boards.
*Price* 18*s.*

ABBREVIATIO PLACITORUM, Richard I.—Edward II. *Edited by* The
Right Hon. GEORGE ROSE and W. ILLINGWORTH, Esq. 1 vol.
folio (1811), boards. *Price* 18*s.*

LIBRI CENSUALIS vocati DOMESDAY-BOOK, INDICES. *Edited by* Sir
HENRY ELLIS. Small folio (1816), boards (Domesday-Book,
vol. 3). *Price* 21*s.*

LIBRI CENSUALIS vocati DOMESDAY-BOOK, ADDITAMENTA EX CODIC.
ANTIQUISS. *Edited by* Sir HENRY ELLIS. Small folio (1816),
boards (Domesday-Book, vol. 4). *Price* 21*s.*

STATUTES OF THE REALM, large folio. Vols. 4 (in 2 parts), 7, 8, 9, 10, and 11, including 2 vols. of Indices (1819—1828). *Edited by* Sir T. E. TOMLINS, JOHN RAITHBY, JOHN CALEY, and WM. ELLIOTT, Esqrs. *Price 31s. 6d.* each; except the Alphabetical and Chronological Indices, *price 30s.* each.

VALOR ECCLESIASTICUS, temp. Henry VIII., Auctoritate Regia institutus. *Edited by* JOHN CALEY, Esq., and the Rev. JOSEPH HUNTER. Vols. 3 to 6, folio (1810, &c.), boards. *Price 25s.* each.

\*\*\* The Introduction is also published in 8vo., cloth. *Price 2s. 6d.*

ROTULI SCOTIÆ IN TURRI LONDINENSI ET IN DOMO CAPITULARI WESTMONASTERIENSI ASSERVATI. 19 Edward I.—Henry VIII. *Edited by* DAVID MACPHERSON, JOHN CALEY, and W. ILLINGWORTH, Esqrs., and the Rev. T. H. HORNE. 2 vols. folio (1814—1819), boards. *Price 42s.*

" FŒDERA, CONVENTIONES, LITTERÆ," &c. ; or, Rymer's Fœdera, A.D. 1066—1391. New Edition, Vol. 2, Part 2, and Vol. 3, Parts 1 and 2, folio (1821—1830). *Edited by* JOHN CALEY and FRED. HOLBROOKE, Esqrs. *Price 21s.* each Part.

DUCATUS LANCASTRIÆ CALENDARIUM INQUISITIONUM POST MORTEM, &c. Part 3, Calendar to the Pleadings, &c., Henry VII.—Ph. and Mary ; and Calendar to the Pleadings, 1—13 Elizabeth. Part 4, Calendar to Pleadings to end of Elizabeth. (1827—1834.) *Edited by* R. J. HARPER, JOHN CALEY, and WM. MINCHIN, Esqrs. Folio, boards, Part 3 (or Vol. 2), *price 31s. 6d.* ; and Part 4 (or Vol. 3), *price 21s.*

CALENDARS OF THE PROCEEDINGS IN CHANCERY, IN THE REIGN OF QUEEN ELIZABETH; to which are prefixed, Examples of earlier Proceedings in that Court from Richard II. to Elizabeth, from the Originals in the Tower. *Edited by* JOHN BAYLEY, Esq. Vols. 2 and 3 (1830—1832), folio, boards, *price 21s.* each.

PARLIAMENTARY WRITS AND WRITS OF MILITARY SUMMONS, together with the Records and Muniments relating to the Suit and Service due and performed to the King's High Court of Parliament and the Councils of the Realm. Edward I., II. *Edited by* Sir FRANCIS PALGRAVE. (1830—1834.) Folio, boards, Vol. 2, Division 1, Edward II., *price 21s.* ; Vol. 2, Division 2, *price 21s.*; Vol. 2, Division 3, *price 42s.*

ROTULI LITTERARUM CLAUSARUM IN TURRI LONDINENSI ASSERVATI. 2 vols. folio (1833—1844). The first volume, 1204—1224. The second volume, 1224—1227. *Edited by* THOMAS DUFFUS HARDY, Esq. *Price 81s.*, cloth ; or separately, Vol. 1, *price 63s.*; Vol. 2, *price 18s.*

PROCEEDINGS AND ORDINANCES OF THE PRIVY COUNCIL OF ENG-
LAND, 10 Richard II.—33 Henry VIII. *Edited by* Sir N. HARRIS
NICOLAS. 7 vols. royal 8vo. (1834—1837), cloth. *Price 98s.*; or
separately, 14*s.* each.

ROTULI LITTERARUM PATENTIUM IN TURRI LONDINENSI ASSERVATI,
A.D. 1201—1216. *Edited by* THOMAS DUFFUS HARDY, Esq.
1 vol. folio (1835), cloth. *Price 31s. 6d.*

*⁎* The Introduction is also published in 8vo., cloth. *Price 9s.*

ROTULI CURIÆ REGIS. Rolls and Records of the Court held before
the King's Justiciars or Justices. 6 Richard I.—1 John. *Edited
by* Sir FRANCIS PALGRAVE. 2 vols. royal 8vo. (1835), cloth.
*Price 28s.*

ROTULI NORMANNIÆ IN TURRI LONDINENSI ASSERVATI, A.D. 1200—
1205; also, 1417 to 1418. *Edited by* THOMAS DUFFUS HARDY,
Esq. 1 vol. royal 8vo. (1835), cloth. *Price 12s. 6d.*

ROTULI DE OBLATIS ET FINIBUS IN TURRI LONDINENSI ASSERVATI,
tempore Regis Johannis. *Edited by* THOMAS DUFFUS HARDY,
Esq. 1 vol. royal 8vo. (1835), cloth. *Price 18s.*

EXCERPTA E ROTULIS FINIUM IN TURRI LONDINENSI ASSERVATIS.
Henry III., 1216—1272. *Edited by* CHARLES ROBERTS, Esq.
2 vols. royal 8vo. (1835, 1836), cloth, *price 32s.*; or separately,
Vol. 1, *price 14s.*; Vol. 2, *price 18s.*

FINES, SIVE PEDES FINIUM : SIVE FINALES CONCORDIÆ IN CURIÂ
DOMINI REGIS. 7 Richard I.—16 John (1195—1214). *Edited by*
the Rev. JOSEPH HUNTER. In Counties. 2 vols. royal 8vo.
(1835—1844), cloth, *price 11s.*; or separately, Vol. 1, *price 8s. 6d.*;
Vol. 2, *price 2s. 6d.*

ANCIENT KALENDARS AND INVENTORIES OF THE TREASURY OF HIS
MAJESTY'S EXCHEQUER; together with Documents illustrating
the History of that Repository. *Edited by* Sir FRANCIS PAL-
GRAVE. 3 vols. royal 8vo. (1836), cloth. *Price 42s.*

DOCUMENTS AND RECORDS illustrating the History of Scotland, and the
Transactions between the Crowns of Scotland and England;
preserved in the Treasury of Her Majesty's Exchequer. *Edited
by* Sir FRANCIS PALGRAVE. 1 vol. royal 8vo. (1837), cloth.
*Price 18s.*

ROTULI CHARTARUM IN TURRI LONDINENSI ASSERVATI, A.D. 1199—
1216. *Edited by* THOMAS DUFFUS HARDY, Esq. 1 vol. folio
(1837), cloth. *Price 30s.*

REPORT OF THE PROCEEDINGS OF THE RECORD COMMISSIONERS,
1831 to 1837. 1 vol. folio, boards. *Price 8s.*

[B B 2]

REGISTRUM vulgariter nuncupatum "The Record of Caernarvon," e codice MS. Harleiano, 696, descriptum. *Edited by* Sir HENRY ELLIS. 1 vol. folio (1838), cloth. *Price 31s. 6d.*

ANCIENT LAWS AND INSTITUTES OF ENGLAND; comprising Laws enacted under the Anglo-Saxon Kings, from Æthelbirht to Cnut, with an English Translation of the Saxon; the Laws called Edward the Confessor's; the Laws of William the Conqueror, and those ascribed to Henry the First; also, Monumenta Ecclesiastica Anglicana, from the 7th to the 10th century; and the Ancient Latin Version of the Anglo-Saxon Laws; with a compendious Glossary, &c. *Edited by* BENJAMIN THORPE, Esq. 1 vol. folio (1840), cloth. *Price 40s.*

—— 2 vols. royal 8vo. cloth. *Price 30s.*

ANCIENT LAWS AND INSTITUTES OF WALES; comprising Laws supposed to be enacted by Howel the Good; modified by subsequent Regulations under the Native Princes, prior to the Conquest by Edward the First; and anomalous Laws, consisting principally of Institutions which, by the Statute of Ruddlan, were admitted to continue in force. With an English Translation of the Welsh Text. To which are added, a few Latin Transcripts, containing Digests of the Welsh Laws, principally of the Dimetian Code. With Indices and Glossary. *Edited by* ANEURIN OWEN, Esq. 1 vol. folio (1841), cloth. *Price 44s.*

—— 2 vols. royal 8vo. cloth. *Price 36s.*

ROTULI DE LIBERATE AC DE MISIS ET PRÆSTITIS, Regnante Johanne. *Edited by* THOMAS DUFFUS HARDY, Esq. 1 vol. royal 8vo. (1844), cloth. *Price 6s.*

THE GREAT ROLLS OF THE PIPE FOR THE SECOND, THIRD, AND FOURTH YEARS OF THE REIGN OF KING HENRY THE SECOND, 1155—1158. *Edited by* the Rev. JOSEPH HUNTER. 1 vol. royal 8vo. (1844), cloth. *Price 4s. 6d.*

THE GREAT ROLL OF THE PIPE FOR THE FIRST YEAR OF THE REIGN OF KING RICHARD THE FIRST, 1189—1190. *Edited by* the Rev. JOSEPH HUNTER. 1 vol. royal 8vo. (1844), cloth. *Price 6s.*

DOCUMENTS ILLUSTRATIVE OF ENGLISH HISTORY in the 13th and 14th centuries, selected from the Records in the Exchequer. *Edited by* HENRY COLE, Esq. 1 vol. fcp. folio (1844), cloth. *Price 45s. 6d.*

MODUS TENENDI PARLIAMENTUM. An Ancient Treatise on the Mode of holding the Parliament in England. *Edited by* THOMAS DUFFUS HARDY, Esq. 1 vol. 8vo. (1846), cloth. *Price 2s. 6d.*

MONUMENTA HISTORICA BRITANNICA, or, Materials for the History of Britain from the earliest period. Vol. 1, extending to the Norman Conquest. Prepared, and illustrated with Notes, by the late HENRY PETRIE, Esq., F.S.A., Keeper of the Records in the Tower of London, assisted by the Rev. JOHN SHARPE, Rector of Castle Eaton, Wilts. Finally completed for publication, and with an Introduction, by THOMAS DUFFUS HARDY, Esq., Assistant Keeper of Records. (Printed by command of Her Majesty.) Folio (1848). *Price 42s.*

REGISTRUM MAGNI SIGILLI REGUM SCOTORUM in Archivis Publicis asservatum. A.D. 1306—1424. *Edited by* THOMAS THOMSON, Esq. Folio (1814). *Price 15s.*

THE ACTS OF THE PARLIAMENTS OF SCOTLAND. 11 vols. folio (1814—1844). Vol. I. *Edited by* THOMAS THOMSON and COSMO INNES, Esqrs. *Price 42s.* Also, Vols. 4, 7, 8, 9, 10, 11 ; *price 10s. 6d. each.*

THE ACTS OF THE LORDS AUDITORS OF CAUSES AND COMPLAINTS. A.D. 1466—1494. *Edited by* THOMAS THOMSON, Esq. Folio (1839). *Price 10s. 6d.*

THE ACTS OF THE LORDS OF COUNCIL IN CIVIL CAUSES. A.D. 1478—1495. *Edited by* THOMAS THOMSON, Esq. Folio (1839). *Price 10s. 6d.*

ISSUE ROLL OF THOMAS DE BRANTINGHAM, Bishop of Exeter, Lord High Treasurer of England, containing Payments out of His Majesty's Revenue, 44 Edward III., 1370. *Edited by* FREDERICK DEVON, Esq. 1 vol. 4to. (1835), cloth. *Price 35s.*

—— Royal 8vo. cloth. *Price 25s.*

ISSUES OF THE EXCHEQUER, containing similar matter to the above; James I.; extracted from the Pell Records. *Edited by* FREDERICK DEVON, Esq. 1 vol. 4to. (1836), cloth. *Price 30s.*

—— Royal 8vo. cloth. *Price 21s.*

ISSUES OF THE EXCHEQUER, containing similar matter to the above ; Henry III.—Henry VI. ; extracted from the Pell Records. *Edited by* FREDERICK DEVON, Esq. 1 vol. 4to. (1837), cloth. *Price 40s.*

—— Royal 8vo. cloth. *Price 30s.*

NOTES OF MATERIALS FOR THE HISTORY OF PUBLIC DEPARTMENTS. By F. S. THOMAS, Esq. Demy folio (1846), cloth. *Price 10s.*

HANDBOOK TO THE PUBLIC RECORDS. By F. S. THOMAS, Esq. Royal 8vo. (1853), cloth. *Price 12s.*

STATE PAPERS DURING THE REIGN OF HENRY THE EIGHTH. 11 vols. 4to., cloth, (1830—1852), with Indices of Persons and Places. *Price 5l. 15s. 6d.* ; or separately, *price 10s. 6d.* each.

Vol. I.—Domestic Correspondence.
Vols. II. & III.—Correspondence relating to Ireland.
Vols. IV. & V.—Correspondence relating to Scotland.
Vols. VI. to XI.—Correspondence between England and Foreign Courts.

HISTORICAL NOTES RELATIVE TO THE HISTORY OF ENGLAND ; from the Accession of Henry VIII. to the Death of Queen Anne (1509 —1714). Designed as a Book of instant Reference for ascertaining the Dates of Events mentioned in History and Manuscripts. The Name of every Person and Event mentioned in History within the above period is placed in Alphabetical and Chronological Order, and the Authority whence taken is given in each case, whether from Printed History or from Manuscripts. By F. S. THOMAS, Esq., Secretary of the Public Record Office. 3 vols. 8vo. (1856), cloth. *Price 40s.*

# CALENDARS OF STATE PAPERS.

[IMPERIAL 8vo.   *Price* 15s. each Volume or Part.]

CALENDAR OF STATE PAPERS, DOMESTIC SERIES, OF THE REIGNS OF
EDWARD VI., MARY, and ELIZABETH, preserved in Her Majesty's
Public Record Office. *Edited by* ROBERT LEMON, Esq., F.S.A.
1856.
    Vol. I.—1547–1580.

CALENDAR OF STATE PAPERS, DOMESTIC SERIES, OF THE REIGN OF
JAMES I., preserved in Her Majesty's Public Record Office.
*Edited by* MARY ANNE EVERETT GREEN.  1857–1859.
    Vol. I.—1603–1610.
    Vol. II.—1611–1618.
    Vol. III.—1619–1623.
    Vol. IV.—1623–1625, with Addenda.

CALENDAR OF STATE PAPERS, DOMESTIC SERIES, OF THE REIGN OF
CHARLES I., preserved in Her Majesty's Public Record Office.
*Edited by* JOHN BRUCE, Esq., V.P.,S.A.  1858–1864.
    Vol. I.—1625–1626.
    Vol. II.—1627–1628.
    Vol. III.—1628–1629.
    Vol. IV.—1629–1631.
    Vol. V.—1631–1633.
    Vol. VI.—1633–1634.
    Vol. VII.—1634–1635.

CALENDAR OF STATE PAPERS, DOMESTIC SERIES, OF THE REIGN OF
CHARLES II., preserved in Her Majesty's Public Record Office.
*Edited by* MARY ANNE EVERETT GREEN.  1860–1863.
    Vol. I.—1660–1661.
    Vol. II.—1661–1662.
    Vol. III.—1663–1664.
    Vol. IV.—1664–1665.

CALENDAR OF STATE PAPERS relating to SCOTLAND, preserved in
Her Majesty's Public Record Office.  *Edited by* MARKHAM JOHN
THORPE, Esq., of St. Edmund Hall, Oxford.  1858.
    Vol. I., the Scottish Series, of the Reigns of Henry VIII.,
    Edward VI., Mary, and Elizabeth, 1509–1589.
    Vol. II., the Scottish Series, of the Reign of Elizabeth,
    1589–1603 ; an Appendix to the Scottish Series, 1543–
    1592 ; and the State Papers relating to Mary Queen of
    Scots during her Detention in England, 1568–1587.

8

CALENDAR OF STATE PAPERS relating to IRELAND, preserved in Her Majesty's Public Record Office. *Edited by* H. C. HAMILTON, Esq. 1860.

    Vol. I.—1509–1573.

CALENDAR OF STATE PAPERS, COLONIAL SERIES, preserved in Her Majesty's Public Record Office, and elsewhere. *Edited by* W. NOËL SAINSBURY, Esq. 1860–1862.

    Vol. I.—America and West Indies, 1574–1660.
    Vol. II.—East Indies, China, and Japan, 1513–1616.

CALENDAR OF LETTERS AND PAPERS, FOREIGN AND DOMESTIC, OF THE REIGN OF HENRY VIII., preserved in the Public Record Office, the British Museum, &c. *Edited by* J. S. BREWER, M.A., Professor of English Literature, King's College, London. 1862.

    Vol. I.—1509–1514.

CALENDAR OF STATE PAPERS, FOREIGN SERIES, OF THE REIGN OF EDWARD VI. *Edited by* W. B. TURNBULL, Esq., of Lincoln's Inn, Barrister-at-Law, and Correspondant du Comité Impérial des Travaux Historiques et des Sociétés Savantes de France. 1861.

CALENDAR OF STATE PAPERS, FOREIGN SERIES, OF THE REIGN OF MARY. *Edited by* W. B. TURNBULL, Esq., of Lincoln's Inn, Barrister-at-Law, and Correspondant du Comité Impérial des Travaux Historiques et des Sociétés Savantes de France. 1861.

CALENDAR OF STATE PAPERS, FOREIGN SERIES, OF THE REIGN OF ELIZABETH. *Edited by* the Rev. JOSEPH STEVENSON, M.A., of University College, Durham. 1863.

    Vol. I.—1558–1559.

CALENDAR OF LETTERS, DESPATCHES, AND STATE PAPERS relating to the Negotiations between England and Spain, preserved in the Archives at Simancas, and elsewhere. *Edited by* G. A. BERGENROTH. 1862.

    Vol. I.—Hen. VII.—1485–1509.

------

## In the Press.

CALENDAR OF STATE PAPERS RELATING TO IRELAND, preserved in Her Majesty's Public Record Office. *Edited by* H. C. HAMILTON, Esq. Vol. II.—1574–1585.

CALENDAR OF LETTERS AND PAPERS, FOREIGN AND DOMESTIC, OF THE REIGN OF HENRY VIII., preserved in Her Majesty's Public Record Office, the British Museum, &c. *Edited by* J. S. BREWER, M.A., Professor of English Literature, King's College, London. Vol. II.—1515–1518.

CALENDAR OF STATE PAPERS, DOMESTIC SERIES, OF THE REIGN OF CHARLES II., preserved in Her Majesty's Public Record Office. *Edited by* MARY ANNE EVERETT GREEN. Vol. V.—1665-1666.

CALENDAR OF STATE PAPERS, DOMESTIC SERIES, OF THE REIGN OF ELIZABETH (continued), preserved in Her Majesty's Public Record Office. *Edited by* ROBERT LEMON, Esq., F.S.A. 1580-1590.

CALENDAR OF STATE PAPERS relating to ENGLAND, preserved in the Archives of Venice, &c. *Edited by* RAWDON BROWN, Esq.

CALENDAR OF STATE PAPERS, FOREIGN SERIES, OF THE REIGN OF ELIZABETH. *Edited by* the Rev. JOSEPH STEVENSON, M.A., of University College, Durham. Vol. II.

CALENDAR OF STATE PAPERS, DOMESTIC SERIES, OF THE REIGN OF CHARLES I., preserved in Her Majesty's Public Record Office. *Edited by* JOHN BRUCE, Esq., F.S.A. Vol. VIII.

## *In Progress.*

CALENDAR OF LETTERS, DESPATCHES, AND STATE PAPERS relating to the Negotiations between England and Spain, preserved in the Archives at Simancas, and elsewhere. *Edited by* G. A. BERGENROTH. Vol. II. Henry VIII.

CALENDAR OF STATE PAPERS, COLONIAL SERIES, preserved in Her Majesty's Public Record Office, and elsewhere. *Edited by* W. NOËL SAINSBURY Esq. Vol. III. East Indies, China, and Japan.

# THE CHRONICLES AND MEMORIALS OF GREAT BRITAIN AND IRELAND DURING THE MIDDLE AGES.

[ROYAL 8vo.   *Price* 10s. each Volume or Part.]

1. THE CHRONICLE OF ENGLAND, by JOHN CAPGRAVE.   *Edited by* the Rev. F. C. HINGESTON, M.A., of Exeter College, Oxford.

2. CHRONICON MONASTERII DE ABINGDON.   Vols. I. and II.   *Edited by* the Rev. JOSEPH STEVENSON, M.A., of University College, Durham, and Vicar of Leighton Buzzard.

3. LIVES OF EDWARD THE CONFESSOR.   I.—La Estoire de Seint Aedward le Rei.   II.—Vita Beati Edvardi Regis et Confessoris.   III.—Vita Æduuardi Regis qui apud Westmonasterium requiescit.   *Edited by* HENRY RICHARDS LUARD, M.A., Fellow and Assistant Tutor of Trinity College, Cambridge.

4. MONUMENTA FRANCISCANA ; scilicet, I.—Thomas de Eccleston de Adventu Fratrum Minorum in Angliam.   II.—Adæ de Marisco Epistolæ.   III.—Registrum Fratrum Minorum Londoniæ.   *Edited by* J. S. BREWER, M.A., Professor of English Literature, King's College, London.

5. FASCICULI ZIZANIORUM MAGISTRI JOHANNIS WYCLIF CUM TRITICO.   Ascribed to THOMAS NETTER, of WALDEN, Provincial of the Carmelite Order in England, and Confessor to King Henry the Fifth.   *Edited by* the Rev. W. W. SHIRLEY, M.A., Tutor and late Fellow of Wadham College, Oxford.

6. THE BUIK OF THE CRONICLIS OF SCOTLAND ; or, A Metrical Version of the History of Hector Boece ; by WILLIAM STEWART.   Vols. I., II., and III.   *Edited by* W. B. TURNBULL, Esq., of Lincoln's Inn, Barrister-at-Law.

7. JOHANNIS CAPGRAVE LIBER DE ILLUSTRIBUS HENRICIS.   *Edited by* the Rev. F. C. HINGESTON, M.A., of Exeter College, Oxford.

8. HISTORIA MONASTERII S. AUGUSTINI CANTUARIENSIS, by THOMAS OF ELMHAM, formerly Monk and Treasurer of that Foundation.   *Edited by* C. HARDWICK, M.A., Fellow of St. Catharine's Hall, and Christian Advocate in the University of Cambridge.

9. EULOGIUM (HISTORIARUM SIVE TEMPORIS), Chronicon ab Orbe condito usque ad Annum Domini 1366; a Monacho quodam Malmesbiriensi exaratum. Vols. I., II., and III. *Edited by* F. S. HAYDON, Esq., B.A.

10. MEMORIALS OF HENRY THE SEVENTH: Bernardi Andreæ Tholosatis Vita Regis Henrici Septimi; necnon alia quædam ad eundem Regem spectantia. *Edited by* JAMES GAIRDNER, Esq.

11. MEMORIALS OF HENRY THE FIFTH. I.—Vita Henrici Quinti, Roberto Redmanno auctore. II.—Versus Rhythmici in laudem Regis Henrici Quinti. III.—Elmhami Liber Metricus de Henrico V. *Edited by* C. A. COLE, Esq.

12. MUNIMENTA GILDHALLÆ LONDONIENSIS; Liber Albus, Liber Custumarum, et Liber Horn, in archivis Gildhallæ asservati. Vol. I., Liber Albus. Vol. II. (in Two Parts), Liber Custumarum. Vol. III., Translation of the Anglo-Norman Passages in Liber Albus, Glossaries, Appendices, and Index. *Edited by* H. T. RILEY, Esq., M.A., Barrister-at-Law.

13. CHRONICA JOHANNIS DE OXENEDES. *Edited by* Sir H. ELLIS, K.H.

14. A COLLECTION OF POLITICAL POEMS AND SONGS RELATING TO ENGLISH HISTORY, FROM THE ACCESSION OF EDWARD III. TO THE REIGN OF HENRY VIII. Vols. I. and II. *Edited by* T. WRIGHT, Esq., M.A.

15. The "OPUS TERTIUM," "OPUS MINUS," &c., of ROGER BACON. *Edited by* J. S. BREWER, M.A., Professor of English Literature, King's College, London.

16. BARTHOLOMÆI DE COTTON, MONACHI NORWICENSIS, HISTORIA ANGLICANA (A.D. 449—1298). *Edited by* HENRY RICHARDS LUARD, M.A., Fellow and Assistant Tutor of Trinity College, Cambridge.

17. BRUT Y TYWYSOGION; or, The Chronicle of the Princes of Wales. *Edited by* the Rev. J. WILLIAMS AB ITHEL.

18. A COLLECTION OF ROYAL AND HISTORICAL LETTERS DURING THE REIGN OF HENRY IV. Vol. I. *Edited by* the Rev. F. C. HINGESTON, M.A., of Exeter College, Oxford.

19. THE REPRESSOR OF OVER MUCH BLAMING OF THE CLERGY. By REGINALD PECOCK, sometime Bishop of Chichester. Vols. I. and II. *Edited by* C. BABINGTON, B.D., Fellow of St. John's College, Cambridge.

20. ANNALES CAMBRIÆ. *Edited by* the Rev. J. WILLIAMS AB ITHEL

21. THE WORKS OF GIRALDUS CAMBRENSIS. Vols. I., II., and III. *Edited by* J. S. BREWER, M.A., Professor of English Literature, King's College, London.

22. LETTERS AND PAPERS ILLUSTRATIVE OF THE WARS OF THE ENGLISH IN FRANCE DURING THE REIGN OF HENRY THE SIXTH, KING OF ENGLAND. Vol. I., and Vol. II. (in Two Parts). *Edited by* the Rev. JOSEPH STEVENSON, M.A., of University College, Durham, and Vicar of Leighton Buzzard.

23. THE ANGLO-SAXON CHRONICLE, ACCORDING TO THE SEVERAL ORIGINAL AUTHORITIES. Vol. I., Original Texts. Vol. II., Translation. *Edited by* BENJAMIN THORPE, Esq., Member of the Royal Academy of Sciences at Munich, and of the Society of Netherlandish Literature at Leyden.

24. LETTERS AND PAPERS ILLUSTRATIVE OF THE REIGNS OF RICHARD III. AND HENRY VII. Vols. I. and II. *Edited by* JAMES GAIRDNER, Esq.

25. LETTERS OF BISHOP GROSSETESTE, illustrative of the Social Condition of his Time. *Edited by* HENRY RICHARDS LUARD, M.A., Fellow and Assistant Tutor of Trinity College, Cambridge.

26. DESCRIPTIVE CATALOGUE OF MANUSCRIPTS RELATING TO THE HISTORY OF GREAT BRITAIN AND IRELAND. Vol. I. (in Two Parts); Anterior to the Norman Invasion. *By* T. DUFFUS HARDY, Esq., Deputy Keeper of the Public Records.

27. ROYAL AND OTHER HISTORICAL LETTERS ILLUSTRATIVE OF THE REIGN OF HENRY III. From the Originals in the Public Record Office. Vol. I., 1216–1235. *Selected and edited by* the Rev. W. W. SHIRLEY, Tutor and late Fellow of Wadham College, Oxford.

28. THE SAINT ALBAN'S CHRONICLES :—THE ENGLISH HISTORY OF THOMAS WALSINGHAM, MONK OF SAINT ALBAN'S. Vol. I., 1272–1381. Vol. II., 1381–1422. *Edited by* HENRY THOMAS RILEY, Esq., M.A., Barrister-at-Law.

29. CHRONICON ABBATIÆ EVESHAMENSIS, AUCTORIBUS DOMINICO PRIORE EVESHAMIÆ ET THOMA DE MARLEBERGE ABBATE, A FUNDATIONE AD ANNUM 1213, UNA CUM CONTINUATIONE AD ANNUM 1418. *Edited by* the Rev. W. D. MACRAY, M.A., Bodleian Library, Oxford.

30. RICARDI DE CIRENCESTRIA SPECULUM HISTORIALE DE GESTIS REGUM ANGLIÆ. Vol. I., 447–871. *Edited by* JOHN E. B. MAYOR, M.A., Fellow and Assistant Tutor of St. John's College, Cambridge.

31. YEAR BOOKS OF THE REIGN OF EDWARD THE FIRST. Years 30–31, and 32–33. *Edited and translated by* ALFRED JOHN HORWOOD, Esq., of the Middle Temple, Barrister-at-Law.

32. NARRATIVES OF THE EXPULSION OF THE ENGLISH FROM NORMANDY, 1449-1450.—Robertus Blondelli de Reductione Normanniæ: Le Recouvrement de Normendie, par Berry, Herault du Roy: Conferences between the Ambassadors of France and England. *Edited, from MSS. in the Imperial Library at Paris, by* the Rev. JOSEPH STEVENSON, M.A., of University College, Durham.

33. HISTORIA ET CARTULARIUM MONASTERII S. PETRI GLOUCESTRIÆ. Vol. I. *Edited by* W. H. HART, Esq., F.S.A.; Membre correspondant de la Société des Antiquaires de Normandie.

34. ALEXANDRI NECKAM DE NATURIS RERUM LIBRI DUO; with NECKAM'S POEM, DE LAUDIBUS DIVINÆ SAPIENTIÆ. *Edited by* THOMAS WRIGHT, Esq., M.A.

35. LEECHDOMS, WORTCUNNING, AND STARCRAFT OF EARLY ENGLAND; being a collection of Documents illustrating the History of Science in this Country before the Norman Conquest. Vol. I. *Collected and edited by* the Rev. T. OSWALD COCKAYNE, M.A., of St. John's College, Cambridge.

36. ANNALES MONASTICI. Vol. I.:—Annales de Margan, 1066-1232; Annales de Theokesberia, 1066-1263; Annales de Burton, 1004-1263. *Edited by* HENRY RICHARDS LUARD, M.A., Fellow and Assistant Tutor of Trinity College, and Registrary of the University, Cambridge.

37. MAGNA VITA S. HUGONIS EPISCOPI LINCOLNIENSIS. From Manuscripts in the Bodleian Library, Oxford, and the Imperial Library, Paris. *Edited by* the Rev. JAMES F. DIMOCK, M.A., Rector of Barnburgh, Yorkshire.

38. CHRONICLES AND MEMORIALS OF THE REIGN OF RICHARD THE FIRST. Vol. I. ITINERARIUM PEREGRINORUM ET GESTA REGIS RICARDI. *Edited by* WILLIAM STUBBS, M.A., Vicar of Navestock, Essex, and Lambeth Librarian.

## In the Press.

LE LIVERE DE REIS DE BRITTANIE. *Edited by* J. GLOVER, M.A., Vicar of Brading, Isle of Wight.

RECUEIL DES CRONIQUES ET ANCHIENNES ISTORIES DE LA GRANT BRETAIGNE A PRESENT NOMME ENGLETERRE, par JEHAN DE WAURIN. *Edited by* WILLIAM HARDY, Esq., F.S.A.

THE WARS OF THE DANES IN IRELAND: written in the Irish language. *Edited by* the Rev. J. H. TODD, D.D., Librarian of the University of Dublin.

A COLLECTION OF SAGAS AND OTHER HISTORICAL DOCUMENTS relating to the Settlements and Descents of the Northmen on the British Isles. *Edited by* GEORGE W. DASENT, Esq., D.C.L. Oxon.

A COLLECTION OF ROYAL AND HISTORICAL LETTERS DURING THE REIGN OF HENRY IV. Vol. II. *Edited by* the Rev. F. C. HINGESTON, M.A., of Exeter College, Oxford.

POLYCHRONICON RANULPHI HIGDENI, with Trevisa's Translation. *Edited by* C. BABINGTON, B.D., Fellow of St. John's College, Cambridge.

OFFICIAL CORRESPONDENCE OF THOMAS BEKYNTON, SECRETARY TO HENRY VI., with other LETTERS and DOCUMENTS. *Edited by* the Rev. GEORGE WILLIAMS, B.D., Senior Fellow of King's College, Cambridge.

ROYAL AND OTHER HISTORICAL LETTERS ILLUSTRATIVE OF THE REIGN OF HENRY III. From the Originals in the Public Record Office. Vol. II. *Selected and edited by* the Rev. W. W. SHIRLEY, Regius Professor in Ecclesiastical History, and Canon of Christ Church, Oxford.

ORIGINAL DOCUMENTS ILLUSTRATIVE OF ACADEMICAL AND CLERICAL LIFE AND STUDIES AT OXFORD BETWEEN THE REIGNS OF HENRY III. AND HENRY VII. *Edited by* the Rev. H. ANSTEY, M.A.

ROLL OF THE PRIVY COUNCIL OF IRELAND, 16 RICHARD II. *Edited by* the Rev. JAMES GRAVES, Rector of Ennisnag, Ireland.

RICARDI DE CIRENCESTRIA SPECULUM HISTORIALE DE GESTIS REGUM ANGLIÆ. Vol. II., 872-1066. *Edited by* JOHN E. B. MAYOR, M.A., Fellow and Assistant Tutor of St. John's College, and Librarian of the University, Cambridge.

THE WORKS OF GIRALDUS CAMBRENSIS. Vol. IV. *Edited by* J. S. BREWER, M.A., Professor of English Literature, King's College, London.

HISTORIA ET CARTULARIUM MONASTERII S. PETRI GLOUCESTRIÆ. Vol. II. *Edited by* W. H. HART, Esq., F.S.A. ; Membre correspondant de la Société des Antiquaires de Normandie.

HISTORIA MINOR MATTHÆI PARIS. *Edited by* Sir FREDERICK MADDEN, K.H., Keeper of the Department of Manuscripts, British Museum.

ANNALES MONASTICI. Vol. II. *Edited by* HENRY RICHARDS LUARD, M.A., Fellow and Assistant Tutor of Trinity College, and Registrary of the University, Cambridge.

THE SAINT ALBAN'S CHRONICLES :—Vol. III., THE CHRONICLES OF RISHANGER, TROKELOWE, BLANEFORD, AND OTHERS. *Edited by* HENRY THOMAS RILEY, Esq., M.A., Barrister-at-Law.

CHRONICLES AND MEMORIALS OF THE REIGN OF RICHARD THE FIRST. Vol. II. *Edited by* WILLIAM STUBBS, M.A., Vicar of Navestock, Essex, and Lambeth Librarian.

DESCRIPTIVE CATALOGUE OF MANUSCRIPTS RELATING TO THE HISTORY OF GREAT BRITAIN AND IRELAND. Vol. II. *By* T. DUFFUS HARDY, Esq., Deputy Keeper of the Public Records.

## *In Progress.*

CHRONICA MONASTERII DE MELSA, AB ANNO 1150 USQUE AD ANNUM 1400. *Edited by* EDWARD AUGUSTUS BOND, Esq., Assistant Keeper of the Department of Manuscripts, and Egerton Librarian, British Museum.

LEECHDOMS, WORTCUNNING, AND STARCRAFT OF EARLY ENGLAND ; being a collection of Documents illustrating the History of Science in this Country before the Norman Conquest. Vol. II. *Collected and edited by* the Rev. T. OSWALD COCKAYNE, M.A., of St. John's College, Cambridge.

CHRONICON RADULPHI ABBATIS COGGESHALENSIS MAJUS ; and, CHRONICON TERRÆ SANCTÆ ET DE CAPTIS A SALADINO HIEROSOLYMIS. *Edited by* the Rev. JOSEPH STEVENSON, M.A., of University College, Durham.

DOCUMENTS RELATING TO ENGLAND AND SCOTLAND, FROM THE NORTHERN REGISTERS. *Edited by* the Rev. JAMES RAINE, M.A., of Durham University.

YEAR BOOKS OF THE REIGN OF EDWARD THE FIRST. 20th, 21st, and 22nd Years. *Edited and translated by* ALFRED JOHN HORWOOD, Esq., of the Middle Temple, Barrister-at-Law.

WILLELMI MALMESBIRIENSIS DE GESTIS PONTIFICUM ANGLORUM, LIBRI V. *Edited by* N. E. S. A. HAMILTON, Esq., of the Department of Manuscripts, British Museum.

*June* 1864.